The Spoken Word and
the Work of Interpretation

University of Pennsylvania Publications in *Conduct and Communication*
Erving Goffman and Dell Hymes, *General Editors*

Also by Dennis Tedlock:

Finding the Center: Narrative Poetry of the Zuni Indians (1972)

(with Barbara Tedlock) *Teachings from the American Earth: Indian Religion and Philosophy* (1975)

The Spoken Word and the Work of Interpretation

Dennis Tedlock

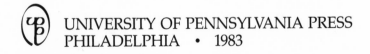

UNIVERSITY OF PENNSYLVANIA PRESS
PHILADELPHIA • 1983

Design by Adrianne Onderdonk Dudden

Photographs by the author

Copyright © 1983 by the University of Pennsylvania Press
All rights reserved

Library of Congess Cataloging in Publication Data

Tedlock, Dennis, 1939–
    The spoken word and the work of interpretation.

    Bibliography: p.
    Includes index.
    1. Zuñi Indians—Legends.   2. Quichés—Legends.
3. Story-telling.   4. Translating and interpreting.
5. Language and languages—Phonetic transcriptions.
6. Indians—Legends.   I. Title.
E99.Z9T43   1983   398.2'08997   82-40489
ISBN 0-8122-7880-1
ISBN 0-8122-1143-X (pbk.)

Printed in the United States of America

Contents

Illustrations

Acknowledgments

First, for sharing their stories and interpretations with me despite distances of language and community, I say *elahkwa* to Andrew Peynetsa, Joseph Peynetsa, and Walter Sanchez, and *maltiox* to Vicente de León Abac, Lucas Pacheco Benítez, and Andrés Xiloj Peruch. All of them know that there are times when the paths are dry and level, and times when they are muddy and cut clear across.

My work took the major turn from which much of this book follows at the end of the 1960s. To my wife-colleague, Barbara Tedlock, I say *elahkwa* and *maltiox*, both for sharing new paths in the field and for early and continuing support in seeking new ways of writing and speaking about those paths; she has meanwhile been telling her own stories about times and places and people in New Mexico and Guatemala.

Also quick to listen and grasp and comment at the turn were poets who have been influenced by anthropologists or linguists and who have had or will have their own influence in turn, including David Antin, George Quasha, Jerome Rothenberg, Gary Snyder, and Nathaniel Tarn. Others quick and early to respond were Theodora Kroeber and John Peck.

Special thanks go to Dell Hymes, who has provided encouragement and stimulating suggestions through more than a dozen years of correspondence and conversation, and who has not hesitated to risk providing the kind of help that can only be given by formulating counter-arguments. I have also profited from exchanges with many other scholars who work with the indigenous languages or verbal arts of the New World, including William Bright, Allan Burns, Regna Darnell, Larry Evers, Michael K. Foster, Ives Goddard, Tim Knab, Karl Kroeber, Howard Norman, Ronald Scollon, Suzanne B. K. Scollon, Joel Sherzer, and Michael Silverstein. Valued conversants who work with the verbal arts of other traditions have been Richard Bauman, Everett Fox, Elli Köngäs-Maranda, Harris Lenowitz, Katherine Loesch, William Mullen, Isidore Okpewho, Alessandro Portelli, Dan Rose, John Szwed, and Jeff Titon.

At the beginning it was an Oceanist, John L. Fischer, who made it possible for me to pursue my interest in the arts in an anthropological setting. Three of my anthropological interlocutors stand out for their concern with the philosophical foundations of the field: Stanley Diamond, Johannes Fabian, and Dorothy Lee. Still other conversants, with interests running well beyond both anthropology and the verbal arts, have been Gus Blaisdell, Paolo Fabbri, Peter MacNeilage, and Louis Marin.

For giving me a fuller sense of the balance between general knowledge and practical skills required of those who work in translation, I am indebted to a number of past and present colleagues in the University Professors Program at Boston University, especially William Arrowsmith, Rodolfo Cardona, Donald S. Carne-Ross, and Herbert Mason. For pointing me toward hermeneutics and providing me with the opportunity to question Paul Ricoeur and serve as a discussant for Hans-Georg Gadamer in the Boston University Institute for Philosophy and Religion, I thank Alan M. Olson.

Many of the chapters in this book were given their initial hearing time or reading space through welcome invitations, and for these opportunities I thank, in addition to others already mentioned, Michel Benamou, Robert M. Carmack, Bruno Gentili, Ronald J. Grele, Louise Lamphere, Alfonso Ortiz, Pino Paioni, William J. Samarin, and William V. Spanos.

My fieldwork in New Mexico has been supported, at various times, by grants or stipends from the National Institute of Mental Health, the Research Foundation of the City University of New York, the Center for Urban Ethnography of the University of Pennsylvania, and the Phillips Fund of the American Philosophical Society. Fieldwork in Guatemala has been supported by a fellowship from the National Endowment for the Humanities, while further work on Quiché texts has been made possible by a Translations Program grant from the same source and a sabbatical leave from Boston University. The publication of this book was aided by gifts from Boston University and Rollo G. Silver.

And then there are editors, whose work in bringing out books often rewards them with anonymity. Here special thanks go to John McGuigan, who has vigorously opened the way for this book since the time when it existed only in conversation. And for the exacting editorial efforts of Lee Ann Draud and Peggy Hoover and the designing eye of Adrianne Onderdonk Dudden, I say thanks yet again.

Time and money are spent in collecting remains in wood and stone, in pottery and tissue and bone, in laboriously collating isolated words, and in measuring ancient constructions. . . . But closer to very self, to thought and being, are the connected expressions of men in their own tongues.

Daniel G. Brinton, in *Aboriginal American Authors and their Productions* (1883)

Introduction

Here speaks the storyteller, telling by voice what was learned by ear. Here speaks a poet who did not learn language structure from one teacher and language meaning from another, nor plot structure from one and characterization from another, nor even an art of storytelling from one and an art of hermeneutics from another, but always heard all these things working together in the stories of other storytellers. And this poet, or mythopoet, not only narrates what characters do, but speaks when they speak, chants when they chant, and sings when they sing. A story is not a genre like other genres of verbal art, but is more like a complex ceremony in miniature, encompassing aphorisms, public announcements, speeches, prayers, songs, and even other narratives.

Across from the storyteller sits the mythographer, who inscribes a record of what the storyteller does by voice. But this mythographer is not scribbling furiously away in a notebook while the performer waits to see whether it will be necessary to go back or whether it will be possible to get on with the story. Instead, the initial version of the inscription is being made by a device that arranges invisible patterns of charges on a magnetic tape, charges that can later be transformed into a reasonable facsimile of the sounds that first produced them.

It is not only the voice of the storyteller that is set free by sound recording, but also the ear of the mythographer. Even as the story is being told, the ear already takes in a broader spectrum of sounds than the anxious ear that tried to hear how each word might be *spelled*. In fact, if the story is being told in a language that the mythographer has only recently begun to learn, the ear will mostly hear the *music* of the voice, the rises and falls of pitch and amplitude, the tone and timbre,

3

the interaction of sounds and silences. In short, the mythographer who postpones the use of pencil and notebook will hear precisely all the dimensions of the voice that the spelling ear tunes out.

And now, a second possibility. Here speaks the storyteller again, only the voice is the flat and halting one of schoolroom recitation. This time the poet starts from the spelling eye, piecing together the ancient and sometimes unfamiliar words of a story that was written down long ago, even centuries ago, but which contemporary storytellers have seldom had a chance to see. Suddenly he takes off his reading glasses and offers an interpretation, and now and again what he reads will even provoke him to tell a story, telling by voice what he learned by ear. And here again sits a mythographer, sometimes scribbling in the margins of the ancient text but also armed with a tape-recorder. This time the spelling ear comes first, listening for ways to improve the spelling and wording of the ancient text, but when the poet bursts into story the mythographer may find ways of hearing a fuller voice in the ancient text.

In either of these cases the tape, once made and removed to another time and place, has some of the properties of a written text. The patterns of charges on the tape may be likened to lines of ink on paper—though here disk recording provides a more vivid analogy, with a stylus that visibly marks a surface. But when the tape is read back, all those dimensions of the voice that the spelling ear tunes out are still there. And unless the mythographer has imitated studio technicians, producing a decontextualized voice that is in some ways the auditory equivalent of a carefully edited and printed text on a clean white page, the information on the tape is not limited to what that voice sounded like at the moment it left the lips. Even the performer's bodily movements are in evidence, affecting the sound of the voice as the head moves with respect to a microphone that was not tied around the neck. Also on the tape is evidence of the remarks or movements of an audience (including the mythographer), along with evidence as to whether the performance took place indoors or out, whether seasonal birds or insects were singing, and whether there was a violent wind or a thunderclap. Performance-oriented sociolinguists and folklorists call the mythographer away from a text-centered approach, urging that verbal art be studied in the contexts of its production, but if we come to think of everything that is fixed on a tape as our primary text, we need no longer feel torn between text and context.

Perhaps the most radical difference between a dictated text from a notebook and an audible text on a tape lies in the temporal dimension. Even though the audible text, like its predecessor, has been removed from the absolute chronological time of the original performance, the *internal* timing of the performance and the accompanying events is still there, not only in its sequences but also in the proportions of its durations. The halting hand of dictation starts up again at the same place it stopped, advancing according to the spatial needs of letters and words, but the tape keeps moving even when only the ambient sound of the room or the dooryard is there. Structuralists have said that myth is a device for the overcoming of time, but that would be a more accurate description of the dictated text of a myth than of an actual performance or an audible text.

Once the audible text is in hand, there is the question of how to make a *visible* record of its sounds. Such a record will not be necessary if the sole aim of the listener is to engage in an electronically aided apprenticeship, like that of a musician who learns new riffs not by reading them or having a teacher repeat them but by imitating tape-recorded sounds. But if the sounds from a tape are to be studied and compared at a distance from their original positions on actual tapes, some kind of visible notation will be required, sooner or later. In the case of a sound-effects technician, notation may be limited to grease-pencil marks on the tapes themselves, and ledgers indexing the footages where different classes of sounds may be found. But if the audible text is to be made available for close critical inspection and direct comparison with written literature, it must be brought to a standstill. Sounds on a tape can be repeated, slowed down, speeded up, or even reversed, but they disappear when the tape stops; the visible notation of sound, on the other hand, stays put. At the very same time, notation can make it possible for the reader to restore the temporal dimension—not only the ordering of the discrete or particulate aspects of sound in *serial* time, as in the case of alphabetic prose, but the flowing of long and short strings of sounds amid long and short silences in *measurable* time, which can be made visible through spacing. The ideal text would permit the reader to choose between the objectifying eye of stares and glances, which declares its independence from the temporality of sound, and the participating eye of what musicians call "sight-reading," in which the reader coordinates vision with the properly timed reenactment of sound.

But before we consent to a transcription of the audible text, it must be cautioned that no score can ever be so detailed and precise as to provide for the re-creation of the full sound of the tape. The audible text will remain the primary document, suggesting revisions of the dictated texts of the past and providing the basis for any number of future transcriptions or translations of its own contents. Periodically students of human speech have been excited by the potential of mechanical devices that make visible notations from audible sources, but these have their own limitations. During the 1920s, for example, there came the kymograph; with hoses attached to the very nose and mouth of the speaker, it scratched lines on smoked paper glued to a revolving brass drum. More recently, through the mediation of electrical signals, there have come scrolls bearing separate oscillographic readouts of amplitude and pitch. Such readouts, when inspected simultaneously with an audition of the tape from which they were made, can improve the reader-listener's sensitivity to pitch, loudness, and timing, but they cannot be sight-read. Just as a musician must parallel the staff notation of a song with a text of the words of the song, so the acoustical phonetician resorts to writing in words below the squiggles on a strip of graph paper. If the notation of the audible text of a storytelling event is to provide a *performable text*, it will have to follow a path between the conventions handed down in literate tradition and the purely hypothetical goal of total notation. Considered practically, notation should not be so complex as to slow the eye of the sight-reader below the proper pace for the reader's voice.

A mythographer could begin work on a performable text by blocking in the large shapes of the sounds and silences, but the force of tradition will probably guide the first pass of the hand down the narrow channel of the spelling and word-making ear, reducing all the complexities of the audible text to rows of alphabetic characters. In the case where the work starts from an ancient text, a prior spelling ear and hand have already made a pass, and the first new task will be to tune the ear finer, correcting the spelling and sometimes the wording, weighing the contemporary storyteller's readings against received scholarly opinion. For the time being, the storyteller's independent ventures into performance will seem like digressions, but they will provide the subject of a separate project that will itself begin with the spelling ear.

At the point where the spelling ear has exhausted its contribution to the hearing of the audible text, we come to a decision that will affect everything else we do, not only in making a visible text but in carrying out the further work of poetics and hermeneutics. If we are drawn down a familiar path, we may put the tape-recorder aside for a while and go on refining what we have written through a process of decipherment, looking for structures supposedly hidden there, but if we are haunted by echoes of the voice of the storyteller, we may go right back to the tape and listen all over again. We may determine the punctuation of our text by the deciphering eye, which will seek out patterns of syntax, but if we listen again we may discover that the "commas" and "periods" and "question marks" of the speaking voice, as signaled by pitch contours and stresses, may not obey the rules worked out by the deciphering eye. Linguists have observed that "good syntax" is more likely to be obtained in dictation than in continuous discourse, but that is not so if we give up the written sentences of our composition teacher for the "oratorical periods" of our speech teacher, allowing for *audible sentences*.

As with punctuation, so with the larger question of the general form the text should take on the page. If we follow the path of the deciphering eye, we may scan the alphabetic text already before us for repetitions of sound or sense that follow some quantifiable pattern, or if we find no scansion we may at least look for a systematic way to make the paragraph breaks called for by a prose presentation. But if we listen again we may discover that the stops and starts, the accelerations and retardations of the speaking voice, may not obey the rules worked out by the deciphering eye. As mythographers already know, "good scansion" is more likely to be obtained in dictation than in a continuous performance, but that is not so if we give up the scansion of our literature teacher for the "good timing" of our drama teacher, replacing readable measure with *audible measure*.

What we have done so far, if we have punctuated our visible text according to the rising and falling contours of oratorical periods and shaped its lines and stanzas according to the stops and starts of dramatic timing, is to begin to free ourselves from the inertia, from the established trajectory, of the whole dictation era, an era that stretches (in the West) all the way back to the making of the Homeric texts. We have begun to construct an *open text*—not a text whose notation closes in upon features that can be assigned certified membership in self-sufficient codes such as those of syntax and scansion, but a text that forces even the reading eye to consider whether the peculiarities of audible sentences and audible lines might be *good speaking* rather than *bad writing*. When an open text captures a particular configuration of contour and timing that occurs just once in just one audible text, the reader will have a chance to consider the possibility that such a configuration is not so much an error, a failure of performance to measure up to the standards of competence described by a theoretical poetics, as it is a brilliant stroke of *practical poetics* that enhances the audible impact of this one particular story.

If a story character quoted by a performer engages in formal oratory or prayer or even sings an aria, chances are that contouring, timing, and even syntax will move into a closer synchrony with one another, and the lines so produced may unfold their meaning in a parallelistic way. But even here oral delivery may not follow a pattern that could have been deciphered from a dictated prose text alone. A speech-maker, like a storyteller, is perfectly capable of making an important noun phrase, for example, *sound* like a complete sentence, while a person praying in private may make a perfect syntactical sentence *sound* like a mere phrase; in a like way, a singer may stretch a single monosyllabic word over several musical measures in one place, and rush through a long sentence in a single measure somewhere else. But if the study of an audible text does disclose passages with at least statistical patterns in the interrelationships between pitch and timing, on the one hand, and syntax and meaning, on the other, it may be possible to carry out a hypothetical reconstruction of the oral delivery of a dictated text from the past—given passages whose syntax and wording resemble those of passages from audible texts. But even then it will be difficult to predict the foregrounding of a particular meaning that is made possible by a sudden break in a pattern of pitch and timing, and it may be necessary to leave the straight narrative passages as prose, with their dramatic timing to be improvised by the reader. After all, even a musical sight-reader is sometimes confronted by a cadenza.

At a scale below that of whole words and phrases, the internal rhythms of lines in an audible text will vary every time there are major shifts in wording or syntax. The measuring out of long runs of lines with equal numbers of syllables, moras, or feet does not occur in audible texts from cultures whose verbal arts are not under the direct influence of literary traditions. In most languages, such fine-grained metrical schemes require an atomization of speech sounds that is precisely the forte of alphabetic and syllabic writing systems. As for the Homeric texts, no modern classicist holds them to be the unedited field notes of an ancient mythographer. The only *audible* epic texts with long metrical runs come from folk traditions within larger literate cultures. When we look for epics outside such cultures—a search that leads to non-Islamic Africa—metrical lines vanish in favor of a dramatic unfolding much like that of the spoken narratives we have been discussing, an unfolding in which the music provides a temporal constant against which the variability of narrative velocity stands out all the more.

Having come this far in opening up our visible text by way of the ear, already finding ourselves on a path where our lessons in grammar, composition, and Greek hexameter can no longer provide guidance, we need not fear to give our audible text still further hearings. There is, for example, the matter of amplitude. Our storyteller, making full use of a continuum of possibilities, ranges all the way from a whisper to a shout. The established images of good writing may suggest that this speaker has, in effect, used too many parentheses, underlines, exclamation points—and maybe even indulged in the use of CAPITALS! But once again, by sketching in at least the larger dimensions of the variability of the voice, the mythographer allows for the possibility that the speaker is once again following a practical poetics, foregrounding some words or lines or whole stanzas and backgrounding others in a way that helps give shape to the action of the story. The speaking storyteller is not a writer who fears to make use of the shift key, but an actor on a stage.

In the same move in which we open our visible text to the phenomena of practical poetics, we begin to extend our poetics into a region where linguistics—or a semiotics that models itself on linguistics—begins to lose its power to provide us with a paradigm. It is not just that the phenomena of contouring, timing, and amplitude have somehow been overlooked and present a new domain for decipherment, but that they have always resisted reduction to particulate units of the kind that can be ordered within a closed code. The pitch contours of an audible sentence mark it with a *degree* of incompleteness or finality; the range of possible lengths for an audible line or a silence occupies a *continuum*, and so does the range of possible loudness or softness within a line. Such phenomena have both obvious and subtle effects on the meaning of what the storyteller says, but the possible *shades* of meaning are infinite, whereas the deciphering eye allows no shadings. The eye of the mythographer can devise a system for the purpose of notating such phenomena, but this will be an improvised code for practical purposes rather than a code that aims for theoretical perfection. Some meanings will slip through its net, at one extreme, or its mesh may impose meaningless distinctions at the other, but in any case it is likely to remain a working hypothesis rather than becoming an established theory. Where linguists once saw alphabetic literacy as a code in need of economization, mythographers who seek to make performable scripts must see a poverty of expressive means.

Like an artist who sets out to work from life but discovers he has left his brush and paints at home and brought only his pens and india ink, we have so far sought graphic solutions to the problems of making a visible text. But when we listen once again and notice variability in the storyteller's tone of voice, we must either resort to the use of color or annotate the text with verbal descriptions in small capitals or parenthesized italics, such as are sometimes introduced into the script for a play. Sometimes even an oral performer may describe a character's voice rather than enacting it, using a phrase like "his voice became tense" instead of using a tense voice. But enough performers of the past have preferred enactment to description to leave the readers of conventional transcriptions with the impression that spoken narrative gives little attention to the emotional states of its characters. This impression—a mere appearance—will remain so long as the spelling ear continues to limit the writing of visible texts. There are linguists who recognize the problem of tone of voice, but they tend to separate it from the "cognitive" realm of language proper and exile it to the "affective" realm of the individual speaker's psyche, overlooking hidden affective implications of particular choices of wording or syntax, on the one hand, and the obvious fact that a performer may deliberately *simulate* an emotional tone, on the other.

Beyond tone of voice, we come to acoustical changes in the voice that accompany the bodily movements of the performer. Here we begin to leave the realm of the voice, but not that of the story. We might still draw a hard line between voice and gesture, but the fact that bodily movements can affect the sound of the voice is only the beginning of the problem with this distinction. A performer may say "she went southward" in one place, without any gesture, and say "she went over this way" at another point in the very same story, motioning southward with the hand and turning to look in that direction. Another case where voice and body movement are intertwined is that of the "aside," which may be an aside not only in the sense that the storyteller stops to make an interpretive remark *about* the action in the midst of narrating it, but in the literal sense that the storyteller turns to face a member of the audience while making that remark. The wording of such an aside may even break with the third-person ground of the narrative—in which "you" and "I" appear only within the dialogues among the characters—to touch base with the "you" and "I" of the dialogical ground occupied by audience and narrator.

In the matter of the aside we have a reminder, within the audible text itself, that the speaking storyteller is not merely addressing a hypothetical future audience, unlike the writer. The world evidenced by the audible text, considered in its entirety, includes not only the world projected by the story proper but the world of the performer and audience. The hearers may feel an aesthetic and historical alienation from the world of the story, much like the alienation experienced by the readers of a written text from a distant time or place, but the ongoing hermeneutical task of overcoming that alienation may sometimes be faced in the very midst of a performance, here and now and for these particular hearers. This is not only a matter of making the "separate" world of the story seem attractive or internally coherent and getting the hearers to project themselves into their private versions of that world, nor is it only a matter of achieving a "fusion of horizons" where the separate worlds of audience and story seem to have some distant areas of overlap. For the speaking storyteller, there is yet a third possibility, in which the world of the story, instead of being at the other end of a journey, enters the collective experience of the very room or dooryard where it is being told. There is a fusion of intimacies when the speaker calls attention to the fact that the stage set of a scene in the story was the same as the present set of its telling, or compares a character in the story with someone in the audience. Fusion moves to the cosmic level when the time of day or weather or season of the story is compared with what it is right now, and when a character moves east and the speaker motions eastward from the spot of telling about it, there is a momentary *fusion of centers*.

Even though we have not yet attended to any sounds made by people other than the storyteller, the making of an open text has already led us to the realization that the narrative monologue unfolds on the larger ground of dialogue, and that the hermeneutical task may be taken up even before the narrative stops. Now the text must be opened to the stirrings and assents and maybe even the comments and questions of the audience, still within the same temporal movement or notational space as the story itself. Once the visible text includes this dimension, our listening would seem to be close to completion. But now we come to the question of the maker of the tape. Even if the mythographer keeps absolutely silent throughout the time of recording—a feat the natives will not necessarily consider meritorious—there must sooner or later come the jagged sound of the charges a machine leaves on a tape when someone turns it off. This final zap serves to remind us that the mythographer was one of the parties to the events recorded and that the storyteller may have subtly shaped some passages with more than the native audience in mind. There is even the possibility that the "you" of some of the interpretive asides may have been none other than yours truly, the one who now sits here writing this, or that the performer was ultimately thinking of you who now sit somewhere reading this.

Here, then, writes the mythographer, telling by typewriter what was learned by ear, by transcription, and by oral recitation. The sight-reading of transcriptions does not wait for the finished product but takes place all along the way: just as the spelling ear and eye must test their choices by reading them back from eye to voice, so must the ear and eye that proceed to the notation of oratorical periods, dramatic timing, amplitude, tone of voice, asides, and responses. But even now there remains a distance between what the storyteller did on the occasion of the making of the audible text and the reenactment of that deed for the audience or readership of the mythographer, a distance that must be crossed by translation. Whether the work of translation is put off until there is a complete visible text in the language of the performer, or starts earlier in the listening process, it will be a different task from what it was in the days of dictation, a circumstance that is traceable to the same moment at which everything else changes. When the work of the deciphering eye, an eye that is perfectly content with what the spelling eye alone can present for its inspection, is held off in favor of continued listening, translation is itself transformed.

From the point of view of the linguist who seeks to crack the code of an unwritten language, translation from that language into his own will seem like a violation of the integrity of the discovered code, unless it takes the modest form of a series of labels or tags running alongside the words of the original language. Here the direction of movement is opposite to that of translation as practiced between two written traditions: whereas the professional translator brings what was said in another language across into the saying of his own, the professional linguist takes his own language partway across to the other, artificially creating a new variety of broken English. Not only that, but as Dell Hymes has pointed out, those who wish to keep what was said in the other language at a great distance, whether giving it the status of an early link in their own evolutionary past or filling out the spaces in a literary bestiary, will even take this broken English as a sign of authenticity.

By now we should be prepared to see that the paucity of viable translations of verbal art from spoken traditions is linked to the narrowness of established transcription practices in a single and strikingly asymmetrical economy of values. The deciphering eye, the same eye that so respects the integrity of the transcribed language as to find it untranslatable, nevertheless regards the ready-made apparatus of its own literacy—given some adjustments in the values assigned to the letters of the alphabet—as sufficient for the notation of whatever is meaningful in that other language. Keeping the transcriber's eye in service to the ear much longer than usual may not turn this economy upside down, but it does bring a practical confrontation with overlooked problems of opacity in the relationship between speech and writing, while simultaneously revealing some transparencies between languages—or at least languages as they are spoken. A finality of contour in the speaking of one language is translatable into a finality of contour in the speaking of another; a pause that leaves the hearer dangling in one language can be translated into a dangling pause in the other. As for amplitude, a sudden loudness does not serve as a means of emphasis in one language and a way of throwing a line away in another. Tones of voice may have conventional dimensions, but a breaking voice in one language will at least not be interpreted as a firm voice in another. Gestures, too, may have their conventionalities, but what is eastward for the storyteller is at least translatable into what is eastward for the mythographer.

What we have, then, is the possibility of a performable translation. There may be any number of differences between languages, cultures, genres, or individual artists in the economy of means employed in the enactment of a story, but the attempt to preserve the general proportions of this economy in translation is well worth the effort. The written and spoken arts of the English language may turn out to have more moments of analogy with the arts of remote storytellers than anyone would have expected, though these analogies may not lie in the areas of prose fiction or metered verse. The ideal translation will be one that retains substantial areas of plausibility as spoken English, never sounding broken where the original storyteller sounded perfectly smooth, while at the same time opening the ear to the possibility of new economies of means in English. Even in the passage between two literate traditions it is seldom the aim of literary translators to leave their own language intact, though the nearness of two such traditions may make for subtler tricks of the ear than those of the translating mythographer.

My own project in mythography begins from meetings with storytellers from two communities whose languages and cultures are indigenous to the New World. The most concrete practical purpose of the earliest meetings was the recording of what I once took to be the monologues of performers, but by the end of this book I come to consider storytelling as situated within a larger dialogue that reaches even beyond the immediate audience. In between are talks and essays addressed to various combinations of anthropologists, linguists, sociolinguists, folklorists, oral historians, ethnohistorians, philosophers of religion, literary critics, semioticians, dramatists, and poets over a period of a dozen years.

One line of my work in mythography began in 1964, just a little to the Pacific side of the Great Divide of the American continent and just a little south of the main road from New York to Los Angeles, at a town properly called Shiwin'a but more widely known as Zuni, in New Mexico. The other line began in 1975, a little to the Atlantic side of the Great Divide and a little north of the main road from Mexico City to Panama City, at a town properly called Chuua 4,ak but more widely known as Momostenango, in Guatemala. The language spoken at Zuni is an isolate (like Basque), spoken by about seven thousand people; the language spoken at Momostenango is Quiché, spoken by more than half a million people and belonging to the Mayan family, whose speakers total several millions. Both communities grow crops that are indigenous to the New World, both center everyday religious practice on the veneration of those who were once living, both have priests who visit sacred springs and peaks to pray for the living, both occupy a point at which a vertical axis passes through the center of a four-cornered world, and both think of distant places as occupying distant times. Both these towns began their relationships with Europeans by participating in armed resistance to Spanish expeditions that included Tlaxcalan Indian auxiliaries from Mexico; by comparison with neighboring Indian towns, both are traditionalist in religious matters and both are progressivist when it comes to technology.

In the matter of storytelling, the two towns could not be more different. Zuni stories are properly reserved for indoor winter evenings; sessions are often arranged in advance, and formal enough to place something of an invisible proscenium arch between performer and audience. A storyteller encountered in the middle of harnessing a horse down at his stables may turn out to be preoccupied with a silent review of the main features of a story he plans to tell a day or two later, but he will give only the barest outline on the spot. Tape-recording an actual performance presents few problems—especially not stage fright—but when the performance comes to an end and the conversation resumes, the machine must be shut off as abruptly as it was turned on. Among the Quiché, on the other hand, stories occur to people only when conversation or chance events bring them to mind. In the midst of a discussion of crocodiles and iguanas—remote beasts for the Quiché—someone says, "Well, there's a story about that," and proceeds to tell it then and there, regardless of season or time of day or whether one is indoors or out. This does not mean that storytelling is less of a performance at Momostenango than at Zuni, but that more of the Quiché art of performance consists in knowing how to seize the right moment, telling a story without leaving the thread of a conversation hopelessly far behind. Once again tape-recording is no problem, but in this case no one is bothered by having everything recorded, whether it is a story or not. As might already be guessed, Quiché conversation is itself more formal than Zuni conversation.

Storytellers can talk *about* stories, but their observations and speculations come from accumulated experience at hearing and telling stories, not from the recollection of a lesson plan. The future storyteller begins the learning process by hearing stories whole, all at once, not by being shown their component parts and then being taught rules for how to assemble them. For the mythographer, whose education has proceeded by parts, there is something overwhelming about the making of the first tape in the field: There it is, the story is all there, too much to deal with except by disassembling it. As a concession to the piecemeal way of learning things, I have followed this introduction with a guide to the main features of the notation I have worked out for open or performable texts, together with a guide to the pronunciation of Zuni and Quiché words. But then I go on to plunge you, the reader, directly into the script of a short Zuni story. I have given you three advantages the beginning mythographer does not have: The story is already off the tape, which means it is fully open to both the participating eye and the objectifying eye; the storyteller gives a brief introduction that sketches some of the story's cultural context; and except for a proper name or two, the whole thing is in English. The storyteller is myself, speaking in 1975 before an audience in Milwaukee, but as a rhapsode rather than a bard. This is a concert reading of one of my own performable translations rather than a performance that starts from memory alone, but in converting the tape-recording of this reading into a visible text, I have included my departures from the script.

The book also ends with a script, one that includes a Quiché Maya story, only this time the story is shown in the conversational matrix in which it originally occurred. The matrix is that particular kind of asymmetrical dialogue in which the ethnographer, seeking to isolate the pieces out of which things are supposed to be made, attempts to pursue a line of questioning to its conclusion while the native sharpens his own skill at keeping topics open to the full extent of their richness. In between this final script and the opening one are others that also come directly from tapes: a long Zuni tale told in a popular Zuni style by Walter Sanchez (Chapter 2), a Zuni tale that was invented by Andrew Peynetsa (Chapter 14), and a Quiché story from a conversation with Andrés Xiloj (Chapter 10). Elsewhere, a short Zuni prayer from a text dictated and published half a century ago is partially restored to the forms of oral recitation (Chapter 6), and the same is done for the opening section of the Popol Vuh, a sacred Quiché text first transposed into alphabetic writing during the 1550s (Chapter 4). The most direct confrontation between the performing voice and an old written text comes when Andrés Xiloj reads the Popol Vuh story of the defeat of an alligator by a crab (Chapter 15), uncovering ribaldry that had eluded a century of scholarship and finding it no presumption to introduce a story of his own. The most direct confrontation between what I have learned from storytellers and the norms of academic writing comes when I cast one of my own talks about performance in the form of a script (Chapter 3). Unlike the opening script of the book, which merely provides a setting for a story, this one tries to get the upper hand over stories by quoting small bits from lots of them.

Following the opening script are four chapters that stay close to the processes of transcription and translation. In Chapter 1, I outline a century of oral narrative translation in North America and go into detail for Zuni in particular, proposing a general method for the making of performable scripts. Chapter 2 pushes beyond the limits set in the first, especially in translating proper names, archaisms, and onomatopoeia; by Chapter 3, the kinds of verbal art considered are greatly widened, going beyond Zuni tales into song texts, sacred history, recent history, and narratives of personal experience. At the end of Part One, in Chapter 4, I survey the role of writing in the indigenous cultures of North and Middle America (both before and after the European invasion) and go into greater detail for the Maya. Then, with the Popol Vuh as my case study, I propose that even some of the older post-European texts might be opened to improved translation and interpretation through a process I call "ethnopaleography," which involves taking a text back to the descendants of those who produced it in order to draw analogies with contemporary spoken arts and obtain commentaries from contemporary readers.

The poetics explored in Part Two is of course an oral poetics, and as such it diverges from an old line of thought (passing from Aristotle down to Jakobson) that closely allies the art of poetry with the alphabetic (or phonological) dimension of language and separates it from the art of performance, thus pulling poetry hard within the domain of the reader and away from the audience. In an oral poetics, actual performance is not the imperfect realization of a playwright's lofty intentions by lowly actors, nor is it an incomplete obedience to the rules set forth in an imaginary mental handbook of the poetic art. Instead, if I may paraphrase Richard Bauman, performance is *constitutive* of verbal art, and each performance has the potential for making changes, large or small, in the constitution of future verbal art. The comprehensive description of a poetic art, in which the critic plays the part of Logos with respect to the fleshly actions of humankind, works best (as it did for Aristotle) as an autopsy performed over the surviving corpus of a literate tradition that has come near the end of its productive life. But when the tradition is a living and oral one, poetics must remain phenomenological, exploring what has been manifested in past performances, remaining open to what may happen in future ones, and remembering that whatever durable corpus may accumulate through the efforts of mythographers is a small and nonrandom sample.

The aspects of oral poetics explored here include a whole range of Zuni techniques for achieving verisimilitude in storytelling (Chapter 5); a Zuni technique for changing normal stress and pitch patterns in order to mark what is being said (in everything from conversation to ritual chants) as carrying importance and completeness (Chapter 6); and Zuni control of the pace and quality of narrative action through the relative durations of sounds and silences, the placement of silences with respect to intonational contours, and the stretching out of vowel sounds in verbs (Chapter 7). At the end of Part Two, in Chapter 8, I take up a more traditional aspect of poetics—that of scansion—and focus on Mayan texts written down in the past, but the evidence of contemporary performance is brought in to elucidate the patterns exhibited by those texts. Further, I interpret variations of pattern not as breakdowns in the realization of an abstract poetic art but as delicate maneuvers in a shifting balance between form and meaning.

Like the poetics of the second section, the hermeneutics of the next cannot be carried over intact from its origins in written tradition. In the first two chapters of Part Three, both of which start from audible texts (Zuni in Chapter 9 and Quiché in Chapter 10), the modification begins with the fact that when a storyteller speaks to a present audience, the narrative and hermeneutical tasks may be undertaken by the same person and at the same time. The Zuni story of the Beginning (unlike Zuni tales) does exist in an authoritative liturgical version that is recited verbatim, but that simply has the effect of displacing interpretation to the telling of unofficial versions, which are (in effect) hermeneutical acts in their entirety. The case of the Quiché narrative that occurs in conversation is a fully hermeneutical matter in a different sense: Here the "text" upon which the storyteller expounds is given by the conversational topic, or by an event that just happened to the conversants. The difference between these Zuni and Quiché examples and the hermeneutical discourse in a written tradition is that however exegetical the oral performance may be, there is still the obligation to tell the *story*.

The remaining two chapters in the hermeneutical section, Chapters 11 and 12, take up a more familiar problem, that of the exegesis of a written text (here the Popol Vuh), but I carefully follow the interpretive guideposts set up by whoever authored it or dictated it to a scribe. At the most general level, the four hermeneutical chapters taken together diverge from the founding line of Western hermeneutics—the biblical line—at the fundamental level of ontogeny. Even though the Zunis preserve verbatim an oral "Book" of the Beginning, and even though the Quiché author of the Popol Vuh appeals to the authority of a visible Book, neither Zuni nor Quiché begins the world from nothing, and neither traces it to the Intention of a single Author, that monologue artist who is so obviously alphabetically literate: "I am the Alpha and the Omega." Instead, Zuni and Quiché gods need spoken dialogue just as much as humans do.

With dialogue we come to Part Four, which begins (in Chapter 13) with the revelation that even the Zuni tale, a genre that constructs a more elaborate stage for itself than the Quiché conversational story, may have performers who come right out into the audience and confront its members individually. This level of interaction is more likely to happen when the tape-recorder (and the abstract future audience it implies) is absent, thus leaving the mythographer without a text— unless (as in this case) a recording of the "same" story was made on a separate occasion, a recording that will now seem rather dull. But the unrecorded version does not constitute a more authentic performance than what took place in the recording session—if "authentic" means unaffected by an observer—since the tapeless mythographer is quite likely to be among those singled out for confrontation by the liberated storyteller. Next (in Chapter 14) we take an even longer step away from minimizing the role of the observer when a Zuni performer boldly invents a new story for the purpose of having the mythographer record it. Then comes a three-way dialogue (Chapter 15) in which a Quiché, reading a Quiché text brought to him by the fieldworker, answers an ancient story given in that text by presenting the fieldworker with a contemporary story.

If the mythographer interprets fieldwork as an uphill battle to make an "objective" record of storytelling, then the three tapes discussed in Chapters 13 to 15 are hardly likely candidates for an anthology purporting to reveal the stories nonliterate natives tell while no outsider is listening. The first is unlively by comparison with the unrecorded version of the same story, the second documents a violation of tradition, and the third was made by a native who had just taken off his reading glasses. In all three cases, the dialogical ground on which storytelling takes place opens wide enough to reveal the mythographer. If we recognize this ground not as a new object for an old kind of study but as the very ground that makes mythography (and ethnography in general) even possible, then such cases move out of the periphery and toward the center of interest. The reporting of ethnographic field experience is no longer a choice between a third-person account in which the natives talk (if at all) only to each other and a first-person confessional account in which the observer talks mainly to himself, but a problem in how to present an encounter in which two participants construct a textual world between them.

The move away from what I call the "analogical" tradition and toward a dialogical anthropology will keep us in motion, seeking not a higher vantage point but a better knowledge of roads; it will not only affect our ideas of how fieldwork might be done, but also change our notion about who might be counted among our predecessors—predecessors who will now include people from the other side of the conversation. But these are matters I will leave for Chapter 16.

At the point of finishing this introduction, I cannot resist one further remark about the difference between listening to a speaker and reading what someone has written. Introductions may come first in a book, but they are in fact written last. This one is ready for the post office, which will have its own version of what today is, but for the distant Quiché it is a day for feeding stones, especially the kinds of stones that are sometimes heard to whistle. Closer at hand—just twenty miles northwest of here, in fact—there is singing and feasting going on at Cochiti, and we'll soon be on our way over there. May the occasion of your reading be a pleasant one, as pleasant as the promise of this day.

July 14, 1982
Cerrillos, New Mexico

Guide to Reading Aloud

"The cold is dangerous
the snow is deep
and you shouldn't go out at a
    time like this.
•
It isn't your place," so he told his
    granddaughter.

In passages set in poetic lines, pause at least half a second each time a new line begins at the left margin, and at least two seconds for a dot separating lines. Do not pause within lines; indented words are continuations of long lines.

NOW THEN, LOOK OUTSIDE
    and see how far in the night
    it is.

Use a loud voice for words in capitals.

The fire was going out, (*softly*)
    the light was dim.

Soft passages, dramatic tones of voice (sharp, kind, etc.), and gestures are marked with parenthesized italics.

some$_{one}$ is ^{cha}$_{sing}$ meeeeee$_{e}$$_{e}$$_{e}$

He went o———n.

Chant split lines, with an interval of about three half-tones between them. Draw out repeated letters (and hold vowels followed by long dashes) as long as it would take to say the words occupying an equal amount of space. Spilling letters indicate a glissando.

CAUTION: Do not attempt mechanical accuracy. In narrative passages, slow down to the pace of someone telling a story without any script.

Pronouncing Zuni Words

a, e, i, o, u	Vowels should be given their Continental values.
aa, ee, ii, oo, uu	Double vowels should be held longer than single ones, like the long vowels in Greek.
ch, h, k, l, m, n, p, s, sh, t, w, y	These consonants should be pronounced as in English, except that *p* and *t* are unaspirated.
lh	This sounds like English *h* and *l* pronounced simultaneously, something like the *Ll* in Welsh "Lloyd."
ts	This is like the *ts* in English "bats."
', ch', k', kw', ky', ts'	The glottal stop is like the *tt* in the Scottish pronunciation of "bottle." When it follows the other consonants indicated, it is pronounced simultaneously with them.
cch, hh, kk, ll, llh, mm, nn, pp, ss, ssh, tt, tts, ww, yy, "	Double consonants are held a bit longer than single ones, like the double consonants in Italian.
'	Stress is always on the first syllable, except in words marked with accents.

Pronouncing Quiché Words

a, e, i, o, u	Vowels should be given their Continental values.

aa, ee, ii, oo, uu	Double vowels indicate a vowel followed by a glottal stop.
b	This is glottalized *p*.
c (before a, o, u), qu (before i, e), ch, m, n, p, r, t, y	These consonants should be pronounced as in Spanish.
h	This should be pronounced like Spanish *j* or German *x*.
k	This is a uvular stop, pronounced with the tongue farther back in the mouth than for *c* (*qu*), which is velar.
l	This is like Zuni *lh* (see above).
x	This is like English *sh*.
z	This is like English *s*.
tt	This is a glottalized *t*.
tz	This is like Zuni *ts* (see above).
4, 3	These are, respectively, a glottalized *c* (*qu*) and *k*.
4h	This is a glottalized *ch*.
4,	This is a glottalized *tz*.
	Stress is always on the final syllable of a word.

Prologue: When the White Mask Is Worn

Now
I'll
tell you one of those Zuni stories.
(*opening a book*) My apologies for
relying on the
SCRIPT
this is the story of the Shumeekuli.
Shumeekuli
is something like a kachina, one of these
beings who wears a mask whenever you see him—
when they're among themselves they don't wear masks; when they
     come to visit people they do.

First published in *Alcheringa*, n.s. 2, no. 1 (1976): 130–32, as part of a transcript of a tape-recording of a longer talk given at the First International Ethnopoetics Symposium, held at the University of Wisconsin at Milwaukee in March 1975. The book referred to is Dennis Tedlock, *Finding the Center*, where the story retold here was first published (pp. 217–22). Behind that version is a tape-recording of a 1965 performance in the Zuni language by Andrew Peynetsa, available in the library of the American Philosophical Society in Philadelphia.

Kachinas live over THERE (*indicates west*)
but the Shumeekuli live over here, to the east (*indicates east*).
It's a FLAT (*hand as if pressing on a flat vertical surface*)
kind of mask
they come in SIX COLORS
they come in
yellow (*indicates north*)
and in blue (*indicates west*)
and in red (*indicates south*)
and in white (*indicates east*)
and in multicolored (*motions upward*) and in black (*motions
    downward*).
And this is a story mostly about the Shumeekuli who
has to do with
the east
the white one.
•

I've chosen this particular story because
this is one that can be told at any time of year, it's getting a little late
    to tell stories, and they really shouldn't be told in the day like
    this either.
This is a story, though, that can be told at any time of day or night
and whether there are snakes around or not.
The thing about that—
that's another good point too—
a book
you can take down off the shelf any time you please, twenty-four
    hours a day
twelve months a year.
Or any year.
In an oral culture
there are some kinds of words you allow yourself to hear only
    maybe
at certain seasons.
Or at certain times of day
maybe even only once a year
and other things that you hear only every fourth year, and other
    things that you hear only
every
EIGHTH year.
And that's part of the whole secret of making a story really FIT
HERE

NOW
in THIS PLACE.
It's got to fit the calendar, too.

•

Well then
there were villagers at Hawikku
there were villagers at GYPSUM PLACE
there were villagers at WIND PLACE
there were villagers
all around
and the priest
there at Gypsum Place
spoke of having a Yaaya, a Yaaya dance.
When the word went out, people from a————ll the villages started
      gathering.
The date had been set and
they lived on
for four nights
they practiced the Yaaya.
The Yaaya practice went on, and
they were gathering
for four nights they kept gathering
o————n it went, until
the day came
and the HELIX SOCIETY
went into session, and on the eve of the ceremony their
      SHUMEEKULI dancers came in.
The Shumeekuli came.

•

And
the next day
was to be the day
for dancing the Yaaya.
Then it was the morning of the dance.
On the morning of the dance
the villagers gathered
and then
they were going to
get up to dance.
O————n they went until at noon they stopped to eat, and when they
      had eaten they got up again
they got up in the afternoon

and when they had done about
two sets
there were four rings of dancers.
Then the HELIX SOCIETY brought in their
SHUMEEKULI.
And when these were brought in, the Horned Ones were also
     brought in.
They kept on dancing this way UNTIL THEIR
White Shumeekuli came, he was brought in when
there were four rings of dancers
and a————ll the villagers had gathered
there was a BIG CROWD, a big crowd and
the dance kept on
their White Shumeekuli
kept going around the tree, he danced around it, and for some
     reason
(*softly*) he went crazy.
•

The people HELD ON TIGHT, but somehow he broke through their
     rings and RAN AWAY.
•

He ran and ran
and they ran after him.
They ran after him, but
they couldn't catch him and still they kept after him shouting as
     they went
he was far ahead, the White Shumeekuli was fa————r ahead of them.
They kept on going until
they came near Shuminnkya.
Someone was herding out there.
He was herding, his sheep were spread out (*sweeping gesture toward
     the east*) when
they came along there shouting.
(*chanting*) "THE————RE GOES OUR WHITE ^SHU———^ MEEKULI
     RUNNING A ^WA———Y^
     WHOEVER IS ^OUT^ THERE PLEASE ^HELP^ US
CATCH HIM FOR US!"
That's what they were shouting as they kept after him.
(*in a low voice*) "Ah yes, there's a Yaaya dance today, something
     must've happened."

That's what the herder was thinking about.
They were coming closer.
After a time their Shumeekuli
(*looking westward*) came into view.
He was still running.
The herder stood
under a tree (*indicates an imaginary tree in front of him*)
where he was going to pass (*indicates a path from the west past the tree*)
and waited for him there (*stands beside the tree facing west*).
Then
going straight on
the Shumeekuli headed for the place (*indicates the path again*)
where the herder was standing.
Sure enough, just as he
came up past the TREE
the herder CAUGHT him (*grabbing with both arms*) for them.
(*facing the audience again*) There he caught him.
The White Shumeekuli
who had run away from the Yaaya dance.
The others came to get him
and took him back.
They brought him back, and when they
tried to unmask him
the mask
was stuck
to his face.
Some of his
flesh peeled off (*pulls at his face*).
He was changing over.
•

Then
the one who had come
as the White Shumeekuli
lived only four days
before he died.
They lived o———n until, at ZUNI
when the Middle Place had become known
the date was again set for the Yaaya
and when the date had been set they gathered for four nights.
They gathered for practice, that's the way
they lived

and when the day of the Yaaya arrived
the villagers came together on the morning of the dance.
Again the YAAYA
dance began
and again the Shumeekuli dancers were brought in
they were brought in and they danced properly, but then there came
    one who costumed himself as the
(*slowly*) White Shumeekuli, and he went around
until it happened AGAIN.
He went crazy.
He struggled then, but
this time they held onto him.
It happens when
ever somebody impersonates that one
because of the FLESH that got inside that MASK in FORMER TIMES
when someone comes into the Yaaya dance as the White
    Shumeekuli
(*with precision*) something will inevitably happen to his mind.
This is what
happened and because this happened
the White Shumeekuli came to be feared.
That's all.

and Translation

4

On the Translation of Style
in Oral Narrative

Those who have sought to transform the spoken arts of the American Indian into printed texts have attempted to cross linguistic, poetic, and cultural gulfs much larger than those faced by translators who merely move from one Indo-European written tradition to another, but they have had very little to say about translation as such. Franz Boas simply advocated a "faithful rendering of the native tales,"[1] which for him and most of his followers meant what professional translators would call a "crib" or a "trot"—not a true translation into literate English, but rather a running guide to the original text, written in an English that was decidedly awkward and foreign. If "faithful renderings" were faithful to anything, they were faithful to a linguistic position that places so much importance on the differences among languages as to cast suspicion on the very possibility of translation. But it must be understood that Boas and his students were reacting

First published in the *Journal of American Folklore* 84 (1971): 114–33. The five introductory paragraphs are new, and so is the epilogue.

1. Franz Boas, *Race, Language, and Culture*, p. 451.

31

against collectors and "retellers" who avoided direct contact with the original languages, instead working from the English of performers or interpreters for whom English was a second language. In such work the poetic qualities lost in the process of transmission were restored through the collector's own inventiveness rather than through an appreciation of native poetics. Here was another form of non-translation, what translators call a "version."

Herbert Spinden, commenting in 1933 on past translators of American Indian verbal art, observed that "as a rule the professional linguists are prosaic: it seems that they pay attention merely to [grammatical] structures and to the denotation of words, neglecting the connotation. It is the old story of botanists not seeing the beauty of flowers."[2] He sets his own sights neither on the "crib" nor the "version" but on translation itself, proposing "the double standard of fidelity to the original source and artistic quality in the rendering."[3] He engaged in the practice of what Dell Hymes would later call "anthropological philology," analyzing previously published native texts in order to retranslate them in a way that would better reflect their original poetic dimensions.[4]

In 1965 Dell Hymes went a step further than Spinden in criticizing the Boasian cribs, not only finding them unlovely but also questioning their claim to authenticity, declaring that "it is a mark of naïveté, not objectivity, to identify pristineness with the ethnological translations."[5] He states the problem of the relationship between linguistics and translation dialectically, writing that "the study of language is too important to be left solely to linguistics . . . , the texts too valuable to be interpreted by any who ignore linguistics."[6] His own work focuses on the problem of carrying the formal dimension of native poetics over into English, a dimension that often went unnoticed by earlier linguists and ethnologists whose notion of structure left out everything between the level of grammar and that of the plot.

Among all those Americanists who have had something to say about translation, Knud Rasmussen and Washington Matthews appear to be alone in placing their focus squarely on the question of audience. Matthews, in the introduction to one of his Navajo collections, wrote in 1897 that "the tales were told in fluent Navajo, easy of

2. Herbert Spinden, *Songs of the Tewa, Preceded by an Essay on American Indian Poetry*, p. 68.
3. Ibid., p. 64.
4. Ibid., esp. pp. 16, 22, 65–68.
5. Dell Hymes, "Some North Pacific Coast Poems: A Problem in Anthropological Philology," p. 334.
6. Ibid., p. 337.

comprehension, and of such literary perfection as to hold the hearer's attention. They should be translated into English of a similar character."[7] Rasmussen later espoused a similar theory of translation in his Eskimo work, writing that his "endeavor has been to *put life and substance into the legends so that in English they read almost as they are apprehended in Eskimo by one who understands that language as his native tongue*" (his italics).[8] But it was Matthews who had the frankness to take stock of a further translation problem that defied solution for those who collected texts through handwritten dictation, noting that a Navajo story "was often embellished with pantomime and vocal modulations which expressed more than mere words, and which the writer is unable to represent."[9] Here was a problem whose solution awaited the use of recording devices.

In the present essay I trace the history of translation for a single widely published narrative tradition, that of the Zuni Indians of New Mexico, beginning a century ago and coming down to the time of my own work with a tape-recorder. In the process I hope to show what has gone wrong in the past and what might be done differently in the future.

The Zuni narratives collected by Frank Hamilton Cushing in the 1880s have always attracted more attention than any others: "The Beginning of Newness" has been anthologized by Margot Astrov and Stith Thompson, "The Poor Turkey Girl" by Thompson and John Greenway, and "The Cock and the Mouse" by Greenway and Alan Dundes.[10] But the apparent attractiveness of Cushing's work is anything but a measure of its reliability as a representation of Zuni literature. "The Beginning of Newness," together with the rest of Cush-

---

7. Washington Matthews, *Navaho Legends*, p. 53.
8. Knud Rasmussen, *Iglulik and Caribou Eskimo Texts*, p. 7.
9. Matthews, *Navaho Legends*, pp. 53–54.
10. Cushing's translations may be found in Frank Hamilton Cushing, "Zuni Fetiches," pp. 13–19, 21–24; "Outlines of Zuni Creation Myths"; *Zuni Folk Tales*; and *Zuni Breadstuff*, pp. 20–54, 58–124, 270–88, 395–515. Two additional Cushing interpretations were recorded by men who visited him in the field: John G. Bourke, "Diary" (unpublished manuscript in the library of the U.S. Military Academy at West Point, 1881), pp. 2565–85; and H. F. C. ten Kate, "A Zuni Folk-Tale." "The Beginning of Newness," from "Outlines of Zuni Creation Myths" (pp. 379–81), is reprinted in Margot Astrov, *The Winged Serpent* (pp. 240–42) and in Stith Thompson, *Tales of the North American Indians* (pp. 17–19). "The Poor Turkey Girl," from Cushing's *Zuni Folk Tales* (pp. 54–64), is reprinted in Thompson, *Tales* (pp. 225–31), and in John Greenway, *Literature Among the Primitives* (pp. 228–34). "The Cock and the Mouse," from *Zuni Folk Tales* (pp. 411–22), is reprinted in Greenway (pp. 151–58) and in Alan Dundes, *The Study of Folklore* (pp. 269–76).

ing's "Outlines of Zuni Creation Myths," has long been a problem for students of Zuni culture. Cushing himself says that these "outlines" are just that and not direct translations,[11] but it is his additions to the narratives rather than any deletions which have caused the trouble, for, as Ruth Bunzel has written, the work "contains endless poetic and metaphysical glossing of the basic elements, most of which explanatory matter probably originated in Cushing's own mind."[12] The "metaphysical glossing" referred to includes strong overtones of monotheism (also found in Matilda Coxe Stevenson's work) which reflect the theoretical preoccupations of nineteenth-century anthropology rather than Zuni belief.

"The Poor Turkey Girl" and "The Cock and the Mouse" are cited by the anthologists as classic examples of the American Indian adaptation of European tales. Cushing relates the history of "The Cock and the Mouse" as follows: He had told an Italian version of it to some Zunis he had brought to New England; about a year later, back at Zuni, he heard one of these same men tell (in Zuni) a considerably adapted and expanded version which was later published.[13] Exciting though the Zuni version may be, it is not clear what the original Italian version used by Cushing was like, for, as Dundes has pointed out, the Zuni version contains some distinctly European motifs which are lacking in the Italian version printed beside it in Cushing's book.[14] There are further problems: Cushing necessarily told the story to his Zuni audience in the Zuni language (the three men were monolinguals), and some of the "Zuni" alterations could well have originated with Cushing in the process of the telling. Moreover, as will be seen in detail shortly, Cushing was given to elaborations when rendering Zuni tales in English, and there is no reason to believe he restrained himself in the present case.

Whatever the special problems with "The Beginning of Newness" and "The Cock and the Mouse," the opinion has been widely held that the quality of Cushing's translations is quite good. The novelist Mary Austin is extravagant with her praise, writing that Cushing "is the only American who notably brought to bear on [primitive lore] adequate literary understanding," and that Cushing's is "the best-sustained translation of aboriginal American literature," and, still further, that Cushing made no effort to "popularize" his stories.[15] Mar-

11. Cushing, "Outlines of Zuni Creation Myths," p. 375.
12. Ruth L. Bunzel, "Zuni Origin Myths," p. 547.
13. Cushing, *Zuni Folk Tales*, p. 411.
14. Dundes, *Study of Folklore*, p. 274.
15. Cushing, *Zuni Folk Tales* (1931 ed.), pp. xix–xx, xxvi.

got Astrov, in the introduction to her anthology, lists Cushing as one of those ethnologists who has best met "the two requirements" of the translator: "linguistic fidelity to the original" (short of strictly literal translation) and the communication of the "cultural matrix" of the original.[16] But Dell Hymes has shown how far Astrov has gone wrong in judging the quality of song translations,[17] and in a similar spirit I hope to show here that narrative translations, too, are not always what they seem.

Among the more curious things in Cushing's major collection, *Zuni Folk Tales*, are the oaths used by the characters. Austin cites these as one of the things she admires most and gives "By the delight of death!" as an example;[18] other oaths include "Souls of my ancestors!" "Demons and corpses!" "By the bones of the dead!" "Oh, ye gods!" and "Beloved Powers!"[19] But the Zunis have no such oaths; they never make profane use of words denoting death, souls, ancestors, corpses, "Powers," and gods. They do use a good number of interjections in tales, such as *tísshomahhá* (dread), *hiyáhha* (fright, female speaking), and *ya"ana* (disgust, male speaking), but there is not a single one of these interjections which has any denotation other than the emotion it is supposed to express. In this case, then, Cushing's translations do not represent "linguistic fidelity to the original," and, further, they misrepresent the "cultural matrix" of the tales.

Perhaps the most serious difficulty with Cushing's *Zuni Folk Tales* is that he embroiders the tales with devices, lines, and even whole passages which are clearly of his own invention and not mere distortions. Similes are totally lacking in all other translations (and in texts as well), but they abound in Cushing's tales. For example, a young man attacked by a swarm of mosquitoes was "crazed and restless as a spider on hot ashes,"[20] and a person outdoors at night saw a "light that was red and grew brighter like the light of a camp fire's red embers when fanned by the wind of the night-time."[21] These passages may have literary merit in English, but they do not even have literary existence in Zuni.

Another kind of embroidery, not so serious as some of the others, is Cushing's insertion of explanatory material for the benefit of his readers. For example, he begins one tale with a lengthy expla-

16. Astrov, *The Winged Serpent*, p. 5.
17. Hymes, "Some North Pacific Coast Poems."
18. Cushing, *Zuni Folk Tales* (1931 ed.), p. xxviii.
19. Ibid. (either ed.), pp. 134, 182–83.
20. Ibid., p. 6.
21. Ibid., p. 24.

nation of the geographical location and appearance of its setting,[22] whereas a Zuni narrator would take his audience's knowledge of local geography for granted. In another example, Cushing describes how a suitor ate very little when given a meal at a girl's house (which a Zuni narrator would do) but then adds, "You know it is not well or polite to eat much when you go to see a strange girl,"[23] again a case in which a Zuni narrator would take his audience's knowledge for granted. Of course it is possible that some of this explanatory material was inserted by Zuni narrators for Cushing's own benefit, but whatever its origin it does misrepresent normal Zuni practice.

The most distressing of all Cushing's inventions are his moralistic passages. As I have shown in detail elsewhere, the didactic content of Zuni tales is usually either implicit or addressed by one tale character to another, and it is never addressed by the narrator directly to his audience.[24] But Cushing begins one tale this way: "Listen, ye young ones and youths, and from what I say draw inference. For behold! the youth of our nation in these recent generations have become less sturdy than of old; else what I relate had not happened."[25] In some other cases, he points out the moral in the third person, but his tone is still excessively moralistic, as in this example from the end of an Orpheus tale: "But if one should live as long as possible, one should never, in any manner whatsoever, remembering this youth's experience, become enamored of Death."[26]

It should now be sufficiently clear that Cushing frequently violates the linguistic and cultural requirements which Astrov sets for translators, and that a good deal of what Austin calls "color . . . so delightfully rendered" (including the oaths)[27] looks more like Victorian quaintness on close examination.

The work of Matilda Coxe Stevenson, a contemporary of Cushing, avoids his stylistic embroideries, but her major compendium of narratives in *The Zuni Indians* is not a translation of actual Zuni performances but rather a descriptive summary in her own words.[28] Much of the apparent order in these materials is her own. She ignores the possibility of alternate versions and attempts to place each story in a chronological sequence which reflects her own Western preoccupation with history more than actual Zuni practice. Elsewhere in

22. Ibid., p. 203.
23. Ibid., p. 3.
24. Dennis Tedlock, *The Ethnography of Tale-Telling at Zuni*, chap. 3.
25. Cushing, *Zuni Folk Tales*, p. 185.
26. Ibid., p. 53.
27. Ibid. (1931 ed.), p. xxviii.
28. Matilda Coxe Stevenson, "The Zuni Indians," pp. 23–61.

the same volume, however, she does present one narrative which (though abbreviated) appears to be a direct translation.[29]

Beginning in the second decade of the present century, a veritable army of Boasian fieldworkers descended upon Zuni. The first members of this army to publish translations of Zuni narratives were Franz Boas himself, Elsie Clews Parsons, and Edward L. Handy;[30] hard on their heels came Ruth L. Bunzel and Ruth Benedict.[31] Only Parsons and Bunzel published native-language texts, and only Bunzel published texts in any quantity.[32]

Members of the Boasian school, at Zuni and elsewhere, typically valued translations that were "direct" or "close" or "literal," published with as few changes as possible from the sort of English used by interpreters or bilingual narrators. Thus Parsons could write, in introducing a collection with which she was particularly pleased, that the tales "interpreted by L—— are as close to the original Zuni, I think, as it is possible to get in English narrative,"[33] and when she showed these translations to A. L. Kroeber, who had trained her interpreter, he said, "In reading them, I can hear L—— speaking Zuni."[34] One can indeed "hear L—— speaking Zuni," especially when awkward choices of English words are preserved or when English words are organized according to Zuni grammar, as in these passages: "The straps the man carried wood with, in the other room he would hang up," "This way you were going to do to me," and, incredibly, "Then one of his legs he threw up."[35]

The literalism in most other translations of Zuni narratives, including those of Boas and Benedict, does not reach the absurd extremes of Parsons. Benedict followed the usual practice of her contemporaries in asking her informants to give "literal" translations, but it was her stated intention to smooth out "their inadequate English" in her published versions.[36] She did indeed eliminate obvious grammatical errors, but stylistic inadequacies remain, including a choppi-

29. Ibid., pp. 135–37.

30. Franz Boas, "Tales of Spanish Provenience from Zuni." Elsie Clews Parsons and Franz Boas, "Spanish Tales from Laguna and Zuni, New Mexico." Elsie Clews Parsons, "Notes on Zuni," pp. 302–27; "Pueblo-Indian Folk-Tales, Probably of Spanish Provenience"; "The Origin Myth of Zuni"; "The Scalp Ceremonial of Zuni," pp. 28–34; "Zuni Tales." Edward L. Handy, "Zuni Tales."

31. Ruth L. Bunzel, "Zuni Origin Myths," "Zuni Katcinas" (narratives are scattered throughout this work), *Zuni Texts*. Ruth Benedict, *Zuni Mythology*.

32. Parsons, "Zuni Tales" (texts are given for only two of these narratives); Bunzel, *Zuni Texts* and "Zuni Origin Myths."

33. Parsons, "Zuni Tales," p. 2.

34. Ibid., p. 2 (quoted by Parsons).

35. Ibid., pp. 6, 30.

36. Benedict, *Zuni Mythology*, vol. 1, p. xxxviii.

ness and lack of grammatical complexity common to much of the work of this period. Zuni narrators, like many others, frequently keep a story in motion by combining strings of clauses into long sentences and by joining these sentences with parallelism. But one would never know this from reading Benedict's translation:

> Her eyes were almost shut. She was skin and bones. She was too weak to sit up and she scratched herself all the time. He jumped up. He ran to the house of Pekwin's son. His wife was just as old. She had gray hair and was bent double. The two young men were angry. They would not talk to their wives. They drove them away. The two old women went off leaning on their canes. They were too weak to travel. There was no rain. The people were hungry.[37]

Such a disaster probably results not only from informant English but also from the stops and starts of the dictation process and from a tendency to treat parallelisms as not worth preserving in print. But whatever their sources, Benedict's distortions are not purely the result of dictation. Bunzel's translations, which were based on dictated Zuni rather than dictated English, have a very different character:

> They laid the deer down side by side. They laid them down side by side and they made the boy sit down beside them. After they had made him sit down they gave the deer smoke. After they had given them smoke they sprinkled prayer meal on them. After they had sprinkled prayer meal on them the people came in.[38]

Probably as a result of dictation, the parallelism here (A, AB, BC, CD, DE) is more mechanical than the parallelism in my own tape-recorded Zuni narratives, and the sentence length (as elsewhere in Bunzel's work) fails to reach the extremes possible in uninterrupted narration. Despite these flaws, the text translations of Bunzel display the qualities of oral performance better than any of the other Zuni work of this period.

Aside from their frequent lack of parallelism, the narratives of the Boasian school tend to be condensations of what a performer would tell in a normal, spontaneous situation. A. L. Kroeber, Dorothy Demetracapoulou and Cora DuBois, and Gladys Reichard, all of

---

37. Ibid., p. 219.
38. Bunzel, *Zuni Texts*, p. 109.

whom recognized this problem in their own collections of American Indian narratives, place most of the blame on the tediousness of dictation and the consequent absence of a responsive native audience.[39] Substantiating their view is the fact that the narratives in my own Zuni collection, related in all instances to at least a small native audience and taken down by tape-recorder, average nearly twice the length of the narratives in Benedict's collection.[40]

After the 1930s, collection of American Indian narratives went into a rapid decline. Texts and translations (other than Zuni ones) continued to appear sporadically, but many of these later collections, such as Melville Jacobs's *Clackamas Chinook Texts*,[41] were delayed reports of fieldwork done during the main period of Boasian activity rather than reports of anything new. In the Zuni case, the thirty years which separated the appearance of Benedict's *Zuni Mythology* (in 1935) from the beginning of my own fieldwork saw the publication of only one minor collection of fresh narratives.[42] Generally instead of fresh materials there appeared analytical treatments of old ones that reflect the two main currents in modern narrative theory: Bert Kaplan sees Zuni myths as possible projections of "the repressed unconscious processes of the id,"[43] while Claude Lévi-Strauss finds Zuni myths (among others) exhibiting a logical structure which he believes to be a substratum in all human thought.[44]

While advances may have been made in the analysis of oral narrative content since the 1930s, the art of translation has seen no substantial gains since the turn of the century. The tape-recorder should improve this situation, but its full possibilities have yet to be exploited. It has been a practical and accurate field instrument for only a short time, and the theoretical interests of many of its users (or poten-

39. Alfred L. Kroeber, "A Mohave Historical Epic," p. 133. Dorothy Demetracapoulou and Cora DuBois, "A Study of Wintu Mythology," p. 400. Gladys A. Reichard, *An Analysis of Coeur d'Alene Indian Myths*, p. 5.

40. Dennis Tedlock, *Finding the Center: Narrative Poetry of the Zuni Indians;* see also "The Girl and the Protector" in Chapter 2, below, the longest Zuni narrative I have yet published.

41. Melville Jacobs, *Clackamas Chinook Texts*.

42. Anna Risser, "Seven Zuni Folk Tales." After my main period of fieldwork at Zuni (November 1964 through January 1966), the Duke Indian Oral History Project of the University of Utah made a collection of Zuni narratives. At one time the University of New Mexico Press announced the publication of two volumes based on this project, to be edited by C. Gregory Crampton, but in 1972 they published instead, under the authorship of The Zuni People, *The Zunis: Self-Portrayals*. See Dennis Tedlock, Review of *The Zunis: Self-Portrayals*.

43. Bert Kaplan, "Psychological Themes in Zuni Mythology and Zuni TAT's."

44. Claude Lévi-Strauss, "The Structural Study of Myth."

tial users) are centered on "content," which they presume enjoys a certain independence from the fine points of "style" and translation. John L. Fischer, for example, says that in sociopsychological analysis the primary concern "is with the semantics of folktale; with the message or 'tale picture' which can be transmitted by the codes of various languages, or by various equivalent constructions in a single language." [45] Lévi-Strauss holds a similar view, though his particular analytical interests differ from those of Fischer: "The mythical value of the myth remains preserved, even through the worst translation. . . . Its substance does not lie in its style, its original music, or its syntax, but in the *story* which it tells." [46]

Even when a scholar does show interest in the stylistic aspects of narrative traditions, there is no guarantee that he will give much thought to translation. Melville Jacobs, for example, though he promises that his analysis of style or form in Clackamas Chinook narratives "will greatly enhance enjoyment" of that literature, offers translations which are typically Boasian in being "almost literal." [47] Despite the literal translation, the reader does not experience directly the "terseness" which is supposedly one of the principal characteristics of Clackamas style, for Jacobs has made hundreds of "explanatory" parenthetical insertions to rescue him from that terseness.

In some cases the neglect of translation is doubtless related to a belief that style, or at least the better part of it, is simply untranslatable. Franz Boas and A. L. Kroeber, for example, held that style (or "literary form") was so bound up with the peculiarities of particular languages that it was unlikely to survive translation. [48] If their view of style is combined with the view that content survives even bad translation, then there is no room at all for an art of translation. It may be that no one scholar has ever held both these views simultaneously in their pure form, but many scholars of the past four generations might as well have done so.

Some collectors of American Indian narratives have taken issue with the narrow linguistic view of style. Demetracapoulou and DuBois even go so far as to say that in the Wintu case, given an interpreter or narrator who is fluent in English, a translation involves no distortion at all. [49] Jacobs finds in the Clackamas case that all but a very

45. John L. Fischer, "The Sociopsychological Analysis of Folktales," p. 237.
46. Lévi-Strauss, "The Structural Study of Myth," p. 430.
47. Melville Jacobs, *The Content and Style of an Oral Literature*, pp. 3, 6.
48. Boas, *Race, Language, and Culture*, p. 452. Kroeber, "A Mohave Historical Epic," p. 133.
49. Demetracapoulou and DuBois, "A Study of Wintu Mythology," p. 386.

few features of narrative form are independent of the particularities of Clackamas linguistics,[50] the implication again being that translation problems should not pose any great difficulty. The Zuni narrative tradition displays more stylistic manipulation in phonology, lexicology, and syntax than Jacobs indicates for the Clackamas, but once more a large part of style lies outside of what is traditionally thought of as linguistics, and I would add that even the linguistic features of Zuni style do not create insurmountable translation problems.

On the phonological level, Zuni narrative style involves only two common distortions of normal patterns, and both of these also occur in everyday speech, although they are more frequent in narrative. One of the distortions involves a combination of stress shift and vowel lengthening: A tale character may start off an ordinary greeting with something like *hom nana*, "My grandfather," with stress on the first syllable of *nana* (as is normal), but if the occasion calls for exceptional formality or seriousness, he will shift the stress and lengthen the final vowel as follows: *hom naná—*. It might be hard to get a similar effect by shifting the stress on "grandfather" in translation, but a syntactic shift to "Grandfather of mine" succeeds, I think, in reproducing the original effect of formality.

The other major phonological distortion in Zuni narrative involves a combination of intonation change and vowel lengthening: "Thus they lived on" would ordinarily be intoned as follows, with the lowest pitch at the end:

$$2 \quad\quad 3 \quad\quad 1$$
lesnolh aateya'kya

But the length of time involved may be emphasized by shifting the highest pitch to the final syllable and drawing out the final vowel for as much as two or three seconds:

$$2 \quad\quad 1 \quad\quad 3$$
lesnolh aateya'kya———

The same operation may be performed on a verb like *akya*, "he went," to indicate a long distance (but not necessarily a long time). Such forms might be translated as "Thus they lived on and on and on," and "He went and went and went," but in Zuni this sort of repetition usually indicates repeated action rather than drawn-out action (or state of being), as in lines like, "And all the people who had come killed the deer, killed the deer, killed the deer." To translate drawn-out Zuni

---

50. Jacobs, *The Content and Style of an Oral Literature*, pp. 7–8.

verbs as repeated ones would mean collapsing two stylistic devices into one. A more direct translation seems a better solution: "Thus they lived on———," and "He went on———" (in which the *o*'s should be held). This rendition may seem strange on the printed page, but comparable lengthening does occur in spoken English, as in "It's been such a lo—ng time."

There are no grammatical differences between everyday speech and formal narrative in Zuni, except for a greater tendency to construct long sentences in the latter. The following, in strict syntactic terms, is a single sentence (each line break indicates only a slight pause):

> *Towayalan ahayuut aach ky'akwap,*
> *he'shoktan aatoshle*
> *aachi*
> *ky'akwap,*
> *itiwan'an lhuwal'ap,*
> *pinnaawan lhuwal'ap, ky'ak'iima lhuwal'ap,*
> *lesnolh lhuwalaa ullapnap, taknan kwayilep, taknan kwayilena kwa' ky'ak 'aawina'ma.*[51]

There is no translation problem here. Given as a single English sentence, this runs as follows:

> At Corn Mountain the two Ahayuuta had their home,
> at He'shokta the Aatoshle
> the two of them
> had their home,
> at the Middle Place there were villagers,
> at Winds' Place there were villagers, at Ky'ak'iima there were villagers,
> there were villagers all around going out to gather wood, and when
>   they went out to gather wood they did not come home.

This is somewhat cumbersome by the normal standards of written English prose, but such length would not be extraordinary for an oral narrator in English (unless he were reading from a written text) or for a large number of English poets.

Most of the remaining "linguistic" manipulation in Zuni style involves the choice of lexical items or formulaic phrases which would be rare or absent in completely neutral everyday speech. As Stanley Newman has shown, Zuni vocabulary runs along a continuum from

51. From "The Ahayuuta and the Aatoshle," narrated by Andrew Peynetsa. Unpublished tape and manuscript in my possession.

items labeled as slang (*penaky'amme*) to items labeled as sacred (*te-wusu*), with various shadings and a large unnamed neutral category in between.[52] Anything clearly recognized as slang is systematically excluded from formal narratives, but at least one slightly substandard term is used: *okyattsik'i*, which Zunis translate as "old lady." A hideous old ogress named *aatoshle*, for example, may be referred to irreverently as *aatoshle okyattsik'i*; translating this simply as "Old Lady Aatoshle" preserves the original effect quite well.

Except for esoteric origin stories, Zuni narratives do not include many words or phrases that are clearly sacred, but they do include a fair number of items, mostly archaisms, which fall between the neutral and the truly sacred. Among these items are the formulas used in greeting exchanges. The usual contemporary greeting in Zuni is *kes-shé*, which has the effect of "Hi," and the reply is the same or *tosh iya*, "So you've come." But a tale character, on entering a household other than his own, may say, *Hom aatacchu, hom chawe, ko'na'to tewanan aateyaye?* and someone will reply, *K'ettsanisshe, ho'naawan cha'le, tosh iya, s'iimu.* A straightforward translation of this exchange preserves its stilted quality and even a touch of its archaic connotation: "My fathers, my children, how have you been passing the days?" "Happily, our child, so you've come, sit down."

The archaic interjections used by characters in serious tales are difficult to translate. As was mentioned earlier, these are not oaths, but simply give direct expression to emotions. English interjections having only covert religious reference or lacking such reference, such as "Wow!" "My goodness!" and "Dear me!" sound ludicrous in the mouth of a heavy tale character, and those which are archaic in addition sound even worse, "Gadzooks!" "Zounds!" and "I'll be switched!" for example. Probably most of the Zuni interjections in serious contexts should be left untranslated; even at that, most of them would require little explanatory notation, for contexts usually make their meanings fairly clear. When a young man who has just been turned into an eagle because his wife failed to demonstrate her love begins his lament with *hanáhha!* or when a father who has just been told that his son plans to exchange bodies with a bloody dead man replies with *tísshomahhá!* the reader is not likely to go far astray in judging the feeling tone of these interjections; at least he will not be likely to think them equivalent to "Gosh!" or "Good grief!"

Not all archaisms are serious—some are used to embellish humorous tales. It is difficult to place these on Newman's slang-sacred

52. Stanley Newman, "Vocabulary Levels: Zuni Sacred and Slang Usage."

continuum. The fact that they are old should make the terms highly valued, but, in fact, they are employed to make a character seem foolishly old-fashioned rather than serious or sacred. They are probably not of slang origin, but hearing these archaic phrases mouthed by foolish characters is somewhat like hearing someone use out-of-date slang. This makes them easier to translate than serious archaisms. A fool named Pelt Kid, who has just gotten married but knows nothing about sex, suddenly remembers his grandmother's instructions and says, in his hoarse voice, *A'ana ha'la! Hom to' kwili yalaa teshunholh hakky'akkya, ha'holh shiwaya kwayip yam shuminnkya kwatoky'anaknanna.*[53] The beginning interjection, *a'ana ha'la!* is an archaism rarely heard even in tales, and an archaic term is used for "penis" (*shuminne*, sandhied and run together with another word in the quotation). The following translation, which takes these archaisms into account, conveys Pelt Kid's ridiculousness well enough: "Golly whizz! You told me to look for two hills, and if it's steamy there I should put my peeny in."

The onomatopoeic words in Zuni narratives may be considered a part of linguistic style, since they are used more frequently in narratives than in everyday speech, though unlike archaisms they are neutral where the slang-sacred continuum is concerned. Context usually makes the reference of onomatopoeic words obvious enough that it is unnecessary to attempt to translate them, as in this passage (again, each line break represents a slight pause):

An suwe kululunan pololo
(low, hoarse voice) tuu————n teyatip,
an papa wilo"anan pololo, wilo"ati
(low, hoarse voice) too————w teyatikya.
Sekwat lo'lii pottikya.
Laky'antolh lhiton iya.
Lhiton ikya, ikyas
isshakwakwa hish ky'aptom el'ikya.[54]

His younger brother rolled the thunder
(*low, hoarse voice*) *tuu*————n it began,
his elder brother rolled the lightning, lightning struck
(*low, hoarse voice*) *too*————w it began.
Now the clouds filled up.
Here comes the rain.

53. From "Pelt Kid and his Grandmother," narrated by Walter Sanchez; full translation in Dennis Tedlock, *Finding the Center*, pp. 191–213.
54. From "The Ahayuuta and the Aatoshle."

The rain came, it came
isshakwakwa the water really did come down.

One might render *isshakwakwa* as "it splattered" and the thunder sounds as "boom" or "rumble," but no clarity would be gained and the reader would not have his experience of onomatopoeia enriched by the Zuni words.

While it may be that past translations of Zuni narratives have suffered somewhat from neglect of the "linguistic" features of style discussed above, they have suffered much more from neglect of "oral" or "paralinguistic" features such as voice quality (tone of voice), loudness, and pausing. Boas wrote long ago that "the form of modern prose is largely determined by the fact that it is read, not spoken, while primitive prose is based on the art of oral delivery and is therefore more closely related to modern oratory than to the printed literary style."[55] He might have added, had he not so easily labeled oral narrative as "prose," that it is also related to that portion of modern poetry in which attention is given to "the art of oral delivery." But Boas and his followers, in translating oral narratives, have treated them as if they were equivalent to written prose short stories, except in cases where the originals were sung or chanted. Jacobs has called for a "dramatistic" approach to oral narratives and has made extensive use of dramatic terminology,[56] but his translations follow the familiar short-story pattern, except for occasional notations of voice quality.

The presence of the tape-recorder has so far failed to wean post-Boasians from the short-story approach. Systematic schemes for the notation of paralinguistic features have been proposed recently,[57] but such notation is not yet in wide use; and no one seems to have given much thought to preserving these features in translations. Yet such features are, at least in the Zuni case, highly "translatable," and it is possible to represent them without making the result look as formidable as a symphonic score. The necessary literary conventions have

55. Boas, *Race, Language, and Culture*, p. 491; from an article originally published in 1925.

56. Jacobs, *The Content and Style of an Oral Literature*, p. 7. Jacobs was anticipated in his dramatistic view of oral narrative by Jeremiah Curtin, who preceded each of his Modoc tales with a list of dramatis personae (*Myths of the Modocs*), and by Herbert Spinden, who presented a section of a Tewa myth in the format of a dramatic script (*Songs of the Tewa*, pp. 89–93, 120n.).

57. George L. Trager, "Paralanguage." Robert E. Pittenger et al., *The First Five Minutes*, pp. 194–206.

been there all along, but they are to be found in drama and poetry rather than in prose. Pausing, as in two of the narrative passages already presented, can be represented by line breaks as in written poetry; unusual loudness can be represented by exclamation points, doubled to represent extreme loudness; and unusual softness, together with unusual voice qualities and various other features, can be noted in parentheses at the left-hand margin, as is commonly done in plays. The straightforwardness of these procedures places minimal barriers in the path of a potential reader.

The control of volume in Zuni narrative can be illustrated by a pastiche of twenty of the loudest (in capital letters) and softest lines from a story of more than five hundred lines; these twenty lines reveal the skeleton of the story, complete with opening and closing formulas and the moments of greatest emotion:

SO' NAHCHI.
The little baby came out.
"Where is the little baby crying?" they said.
He was nursed, the little boy was nursed by the deer.
"I will go to Kachina Village, for he is without clothing, naked."
When she got back to her children they were all sleeping.
"HE SAW A HERD OF DEER.
BUT A LITTLE BOY WAS AMONG THEM."
"PERHAPS WE WILL CATCH HIM."
THEN HIS DEER MOTHER TOLD HIM EVERYTHING.
"THAT IS WHAT SHE DID TO YOU, SHE JUST DROPPED YOU."
The boy became
very unhappy.
AND ALL THE PEOPLE WHO HAD COME KILLED THE DEER,
    KILLED THE DEER, KILLED THE DEER.
And his uncle, dismounting,
caught him.
"THAT IS WHAT YOU DID AND YOU ARE MY REAL MOTHER."
He put the quiver on and went out.
There he died.
THIS WAS LIVED LONG AGO. LEE——SEMKONIKYA.[58]

The extremes of loudness and softness overlap in function in that they both draw special attention to a line. The softness of "He was

---

58. This and all further Zuni narrative quotations are from "The Boy and the Deer," narrated by Andrew Peynetsa; a full translation may be found in Tedlock, *Finding the Center*, pp. 1–32.

nursed, the little boy was nursed by the deer" seems more appropriate than a loud rendition, and the line about the killing of the deer seems properly loud, but some other lines could have been rendered either way, "But a little boy was among them," for example.

The manipulation of voice quality in Zuni narration has a diversity I have only begun to explore; only a few examples can be given here. One of the narrators represented in my collection delivers the opening lines of his tales, including formulas and the names of the major characters and the places where they live, with a formality which approaches that of a chant: His stresses are heavier, his enunciation more careful, and his pitch control greater (but not as great as in singing) than they would be in his normal narrating voice. As he moves into the first events of the story, this formality slowly dissolves, over the space of eight or ten lines, until his voice is normal. The only other fully predictable manipulation of voice quality on the part of the same narrator involves the quotation of story characters. The words of the Ahayuuta (twin boys, the war gods), for example, are usually delivered in a high, raspy voice, and most female characters, except where their speeches are long, are given a tense, tight (but not high) voice. Since a male native speaker of English might prefer to render female voices in narratives by raising his pitch, one might "translate" the Zuni "tight" voice into an English "high" one. Neither of these practices is a more objective rendition of the female voice than the other; both represent a selective imitation of the common properties of female speech.[59]

There are many less conventionalized (and less common) uses of voice quality in Zuni narratives, two examples of which will suffice here. When a character is trying to pull some tough blades loose from a yucca plant, the narrator may render "He pulled" with the strain of someone who is trying to speak while holding his breath during great exertion. When a passage involves intense emotion, the narrator may combine the softness mentioned earlier with a break in his voice, as if he felt like weeping. The use of this voice technique is exemplified in the following passage in which a man is killing three deer who are the foster mother and siblings of his nephew:

The third uncle
(*softly, voice breaking*) dropped his elder sister

---

59. Tightness, or "squeeze," is more common among women than among men, according to Pittenger et al., *The First Five Minutes*, pp. 202–3.

his elder brother
his mother.

Loudness and voice quality are obviously worth noting, but it seems to me that pausing is foremost among the paralinguistic devices that give shape to Zuni narrative and distinguish it from written prose, and the same could probably be said of many other oral narrative traditions. Igor Stravinsky has said, "I dislike the organ's *legato sostenuto*, . . . the monster never breathes,"[60] and he could have said the same thing of written prose. The spoken word is never delivered in the gray masses of boxed-in words we call prose; indeed, according to Frieda Goldman-Eisler, as much as half the time spent in delivering spontaneous discourse is devoted to silence, and "pausing is as much a part of the act of speaking as the vocal utterance of words itself."[61] But of all the past anthropological collectors of so-called prose narratives, only one, Paul Radin, seems to have shown any real sensitivity to pausing. For several passages from Winnebago texts, he marks pauses of three different lengths; he also breaks these passages into lines. Here his intention is unclear: Each line break coincides with a pause, but there are also pauses within lines.[62] Unfortunately he preserves neither pause marks nor line breaks in his translations.

In dealing with the pauses in Zuni narratives, I have found it best to divide them into two types: "ordinary" pauses, represented by line breaks, and "long" pauses, represented by double spaces between lines (here marked by a dot •). I initially spotted pauses only by ear, running through the tape of a half-hour narrative several times. An oscillograph of the same tape later revealed that my "ordinary" pauses ran from four-tenths of a second to two seconds, with the average at three-fourths of a second. The longer pauses ran from two to three seconds. Some other listener might come up with slightly different boundaries for ordinary and long pauses than I did, or might want to make more than two distinctions; but any listener, given a reasonably good ear, could probably make fairly consistent notations without the aid of an oscillograph.

Intonation poses no great problems where Zuni pausing is concerned. Except for the special intonational device used to lengthen time or space (discussed earlier) and a few other, rarer deviations,

60. Igor Stravinsky, album notes to *Symphony of Psalms.*
61. Frieda Goldman-Eisler, "Discussion and Further Comments," pp. 118–19.
62. Paul Radin, *The Culture of the Winnebago: As Described by Themselves,* pp. 42–44, 61–62, 103, 106–8. I infer from Radin's remarks on p. 42 that these pauses were reconstructed rather than recorded in the field.

Zuni narrative patterns can be covered by a general rule rather than marked for each line: The boundary between one intonation contour and the next is strongly marked where a change of phrase or sentence corresponds with a pause or where a quote begins, and less strongly marked where a change of phrase or sentence occurs within a line or where a pause occurs within a phrase. This pattern seems close enough to the normal tendencies of an English speaker so as to create no translation problems. As far as the internal details of the contours are concerned, the typical Zuni contour does not happen to be very different from that of a declarative sentence in English.

The following passage, with silences and intonation contours as indicated above, will serve to illustrate most of the properties of pausing in Zuni narrative ("they" in the first line refers to a herd of deer):

> *Yam telhasshi k'uushina yalhtookwin aawanuwa aayemakkya. Aayemakna*
> *   lesnolh chimkwat iskon aateya tom sunnhap tutunaa paniye.*
> *Aateya'kya————koholh lhana*
> •
> *ist*
> *an lhuwal'an*   5
> *an kyakholh*
> *imat lhatakky'an aakya. Lhatakky'an 'aana*
> *imat paniinas'ist*
> *uhsi lak'ist*
> *wi'ky'al'anholh lesna paniina uhsist lak*   10
> •
> *k'uushin yalhtan uhsi tewuuli yalhtookwin holh'imat ky'alhkonholh yemakna.*

> They went back up to their old home on the Prairie Dog Hills. Having
>   gone up they were living there and coming down only to drink in
>   the evening.
> They lived on————for some time
> •
> until
> from the village   5
> his uncle
> went out hunting. Going out hunting
> he came along
> down around
> Worm Spring and from there he went on toward   10
> •
> the Prairie Dog Hills and came up near the edge of a valley there.

The problems encountered in preserving the original pauses in English are minimal. Occasionally Zuni word order makes the transposition of lines or parts of lines desirable, but this can usually be done without serious distortion of the effect of the original: In the above passage no transposition seemed advantageous, except that "down" in line 9 of the translation is a partial rendition of *paniinas* in line 8 of the text, but elsewhere in the same story a literal rendition would produce lines like "Her clothes / she bundled," and "His kinswoman / he beat," which call for transposition.

Where the length of lines is concerned, it would be difficult and foolish to slavishly follow the exact Zuni syllable counts in translation, but it is possible to at least approximate the original contrasts in line length. The importance of such an approximation may be seen from the fact that the length of lines—or, to look at it in another way, the frequency of pauses—is the major source of apparent variations in the rate at which human speech is delivered. Passages with short lines (many pauses) will seem slow, while those with long lines (few pauses) will seem fast.[63] In the above passage, the narrator rapidly tells of the deer herd's residence on the Prairie Dog Hills (lines 1–2), then slows down, with suspenseful effect, as the man goes out hunting (lines 4–9), and finally speeds up again with the excitement of the man's arrival at the Prairie Dog Hills (line 11). Preserving such patterns in narrative pace obviously precludes the insertion of any but the smallest bits of "explanatory" material by the translator: Where the Zuni word *lapappowanne* means "a headdress of macaw tail-feathers worn upright at the back of the head," for example, he will have to settle for something like "macaw headdress" in his translation and leave the rest to a note or a picture, though Cushing might have done otherwise. And where it is frequently unclear which characters are responsible for quotations, as in Clackamas (but not Zuni) narratives, the translator may find it best to place the names of the speakers outside the main left-hand margin, as in a play.

One of the most striking things about the lines in Zuni narrative is that they are not always dependent on the major features of syntax. In the above excerpt some of the pauses do correspond with changes of phrase or sentence, but five of them (the pauses following lines 4, 5, 6, 9, 10) leave the hearer hanging, syntactically speaking, thus adding to the suspense already noted for this passage.[64] The longer

63. Goldman-Eisler, "Discussion and Further Comments," p. 120; she adds that the rate of syllable articulation (between pauses), by contrast with the rate of pausing, is almost constant. Nevertheless, a deliberate slowing of articulation can be used to confer prominence on selected words; see Tedlock, *Finding the Center*, pp. 199, 200, 208, for examples.

64. One-third of the lines produced by Andrew Peynetsa involves this kind of phrase-splitting, which is twice the proportion of splitting (or "necessary enjambment") reported for Yugoslav epics by Albert Lord (*The Singer of Tales*, p. 54).

pauses in Zuni stories often correspond to sentence boundaries, but in the present excerpt they occur between two phrases of the same sentence (after line 3) and in the midst of a phrase (after line 10). The first of these pauses is a sort of paragraph marker between the affairs of the herd and the hunting expedition of the man; its location within a sentence keeps the listener on the string in much the same way that the placement of a chapter division within an episode (instead of between episodes) keeps the reader of a novel on the string. With the second of these pauses the narrator keeps the listener dangling for a moment and then suddenly lets him know, in the first words of the next line, that the hunter has arrived at the Prairie Dog Hills, where the herd is.

The treatment of oral narrative as dramatic poetry has a number of analytical advantages. Some of the features of oral narrative which have been branded "primitive," on the basis of comparisons with written prose fiction, can now be understood as "poetic" instead. It has been said, for example, that while most of our own prose narrative is highly "realistic," primitive narrative is full of fantasy: A stone moves about like an animal, an animal speaks like a man, a man jumps through a hoop and becomes a coyote. Yet when we encounter gross and unexplained distortions of reality in Yeats, for example, we are apt to call them not "primitive" but "dreamlike" or "mystical" and to regard them as highly poetic.

It is also said that "primitive" narrative, again unlike written prose fiction, seldom describes emotional states. This is true enough, but the comparison with prose misses the point: What oral narrative usually does with emotions is evoke them rather than describe them directly, which is precisely what we have been taught to expect in poetry. In the Zuni case, such descriptions of emotions as do exist are very simple, "The boy became / very unhappy," for example, but evocations are myriad and sometimes quite subtle, as in this passage:

> He went out, having been given the quiver, and wandered around.
> He was not thinking of killing deer, he just wandered around.
> In the evening he came home empty-handed.

According to both the narrator and a member of his audience, these lines clearly indicate (to the Zuni, at least) that the person referred to is depressed, and they regarded this person's death three days later as a sort of suicide, though it was described in the story as an accident.

Another distinguishing feature of "primitive" narrative, according to Boas and many others, is repetition, ranging from the level of words or phrases to that of whole episodes.[65] At least one of the kinds of repetition in Zuni narrative is indeed rare in our own prose (and poetry as well), and that is the linking of two sentences or major clauses by the conversion of the final element of one into the initial element of the next, as in these lines (from the last passage quoted in the previous section): "His uncle / went out hunting. Going out hunting / he came along. . . ." But the same device is common in epic poetry, as in this Yugoslav example: "And may God too make us merry, / Make us merry and give us entertainment!"[66] Unless we want to call epic poetry "primitive," this particular kind of repetition must be properly understood as "oral" and not "primitive," and the same thing goes for the repeated use of stock formulas in both epic poetry (epithets, for example) and Zuni narrative (greeting exchanges, for example).

When it comes to the repetition of whole passages, "primitive" narrative may be compared to epic poetry and also to refrains in songs (from both literate and nonliterate cultures) and in written poetry. Refrains are often varied from one rendition to the next, and the same is true (although in a less structured way) for the repeated passages in Yugoslav epic, as shown by Albert Lord,[67] and in Zuni narrative. In the following Zuni passage, a boy's foster mother is quoting to him what he must say when he addresses his real mother, who abandoned him as a baby:

> My Sun Father
> made you pregnant.
> When you were about to deliver
> it was to Nearing Waters
> that you went down to wash. You washed at the bank.

But when the boy actually confronts this real mother later in the same story, this is what the narrator has him say:

> My Sun Father
> made you pregnant.
> When he made you pregnant you
> sat in there and your belly began to grow large.
> Your belly grew large
> you

65. Boas, *Race, Language, and Culture*, pp. 491–93.
66. Lord, *Singer of Tales*, p. 32.
67. Ibid., p. 82.

you were about to deliver, you had pains in your belly, you were about
    to give birth to me, you had pains in your belly
you gathered your clothes
and you went down to the bank to wash.

The remaining kinds of repetition in Zuni narrative are of the sort
we approvingly call "parallelism" when we find them in our own poetry. A line like "And all the people who had come killed the deer,
killed the deer, killed the deer!" cannot honestly be called primitive
unless we call Shakespeare primitive when he has Hamlet say, "You
cannot, sir, take from me anything that I will more willingly part
withal: except my life, except my life, except my life." And not all the
parallelism in Zuni narrative involves simple repetition:

> *Tewuuli kolh nahhayaye. Nahhayap*
> *lalholh aksik ts'an aksh allu'aye, kwan lheyaa k'ohanna.*
> *Muusilili lheya'kwip an lapappowaye.*
> *Lapappow lesnish aawanelap, ten aktsik'i*
> *ottsi*
> *ho"i akshappa.*

In the valley was the herd of deer. In the herd of deer
there was a little boy going around among them, dressed in white.
He had bells on and was wearing a macaw headdress.
He was wearing a macaw headdress and was handsome, surely it
    was a boy
a male
a person among them.

What all this means, simply stated, is that (remarkably enough) there
was a human being among the deer, but the narrator chooses to explore the fact in half a dozen different ways.

    Repetitions and other poetic features of oral narrative have im-
plications even for those who focus on content analysis and choose to
ignore "style." The implications for psychological analysis, which is
normally based on the content of prose translations, may be illustrated by the following passage, in which a boy has just exposed the
woman who secretly abandoned him as a baby (parentheses indicate
softer portions):

At that moment his mother
embraced him (embraced him).
His uncle got angry (his uncle got angry).
He beat

his kinswoman
(he beat his kinswoman).

This passage might have appeared in a conventional prose rendition as "At that moment his mother embraced him. His uncle got angry. He beat his kinswoman," thus having lost the nuances and greater intensity given it by the repetition, the changes of loudness, and the frequent pauses.

The complications of poetic style have especially strong implications for those who seek to measure the social and psychological content of narrative by means of word counts. "Killed the deer," repeated three times in a line quoted above, might well have been reduced to a single occurrence in the translations of the past. Moreover, it seems crude to give the same weight to a word like "killed" when it is shouted and when it is rendered flatly. And the indirect expression of emotion, as in the case of the depression and suicide mentioned earlier, would escape a word counter entirely.

Lévi-Strauss and other structuralists operating on an abstract level assume that any translation will do for their purposes, but poetic subtleties have a potential for radically altering surface meanings, irony being an obvious example. The more concrete structural analysis proposed by William Hendricks, on the other hand, does take the "linguistic" aspect of poetics into account, since each basic element in his system consists of a single semantic "function" that may be served by several lower-level "linguistic" (phonological, morphological, or syntactic) elements.[68] But even Hendricks overlooks "paralinguistic" matters, though it is precisely at the level of semantic function that the arbitrary wall between "linguistics" and "paralinguistics" collapses. In Zuni narrative, for example, the semantic function of marking the start of a quotation may be served by such "linguistic" devices as a sharp intonation change or the words "The deer spoke to her son," but it may also be served by such "paralinguistic" devices as a pause or a change in voice quality.

The treatment of oral narrative as dramatic poetry, then, clearly promises many analytical rewards. It should also be obvious that there are immediate aesthetic rewards. The apparent flatness of many past translations is not a reflection but a distortion of the originals, caused by the dictation process, the notion that content and form are independent, a pervasive deafness to oral qualities, and a fixed notion of the boundary between poetry and prose. Present conditions,

---

68. William O. Hendricks, "On the Notion 'Beyond the Sentence,'" pp. 32–35.

which combine new recording techniques with a growing sensitivity to verbal art as performed "event" rather than as fixed "object" on the page, promise the removal of previous difficulties. "Event" orientation, together with an intensified appreciation of fantasy, has already led modern poets to recognize a kinship between their own work and the oral art of tribal peoples. As Jerome Rothenberg points out in *Technicians of the Sacred*, both "modern" and tribal poets are concerned with oral performance, both escape the confines of Aristotelian rationalism, both transcend the conventional genre boundaries of written literature, and both sometimes make use of stripped-down forms that require maximal interpolation by audiences.[69] This last point recalls the Clackamas "terseness" discussed by Jacobs, and I am reminded of the Zuni who asked me, "When I tell these stories do you picture it, or do you just write it down?"

The effort presented here is intended more as an experiment than as the final word on the poetic features of oral narrative and their presentation on the printed page. I hope it will encourage others to make further experiments.

Epilogue

The argument that American Indian spoken narratives are better understood (and translated) as dramatic poetry than as an oral equivalent of written prose fiction may be summarized as follows: The content tends toward the fantastic rather than the prosaic, the emotions of the characters are evoked rather than described, there are patterns of repetition or parallelism ranging from the level of words to that of whole episodes, the narrator's voice shifts constantly in amplitude and tone, and the flow of that voice is paced by pauses that segment its sounds into what I have chosen to call lines. Of all these realities of oral narrative performance, the plainest and grossest is the sheer alternation of sound and silence; the resultant lines often show an independence from intonation, from syntax, and even from boundaries of plot structure. I understand the fundamental sound-shape of spoken narrative in much the same way that Robert W. Corrigan understood drama when he wrote that "the playwright—and also the translator—cannot really be concerned with 'good prose' or with

---

69. Jerome Rothenberg, *Technicians of the Sacred*, pp. xxii–xxiii.

'good verse' in the usual sense of those terms. The structure is action; not what is said or how it is said but *when*."[70] It is above all the *when*, or what dramatists call "timing," that is missing in printed prose.

Since I first proposed my scheme for the transcription and translation of spoken narrative,[71] it has been extended, with welcome variations and refinements, far beyond its original Zuni context. To mention only those experiments that have already been published, pause-determined lines in texts and/or translations have been used by Ronald and Suzanne B. K. Scollon for several northern Athabaskan languages, by Dick Dauenhauer and others for Tlingit, by Barre Toelken and Tacheeni Scott for Navajo, by Kathleen Sands for Papago, and by Tim Knab for Nahuatl.[72] Entire books showing not only pauses but other dramatic features now include, in addition to my own *Finding the Center*, Allan Burns's *An Epoch of Miracles*, on the Yucatec Maya, and—passing beyond the American Indian sphere—Peter Seitel's *See So That We May See*, on the Haya of Tanzania.[73] There have also been applications to English-language folk narratives and sermons, both Afro- and Anglo-American, by Peter Gold, by Daniel Crowley, and by Jeff Titon and Ken George.[74]

Meanwhile, Dell Hymes has shifted his continuing work in anthropological philology from the written texts of songs to those of spoken narratives. He breaks the published prose of dictated texts into lines, verses, and stanzas on the basis of what he calls "measured verse" (as opposed to metrical verse in the sense of syllable or mora or stress counts), finding tendencies to numerical regularities in narratives of Chinookan, Sahaptin, Takelma, and Tonkawa provenience; he has searched for similar patterns in the Zuni story of "Coyote and

70. Robert W. Corrigan, "Translating for Actors," pp. 135–36.
71. The scheme was first described and demonstrated in Tedlock, "Finding the Middle of the Earth," published in 1970.
72. The Athabaskan narratives in question may be found in Ronald Scollon and Suzanne B. K. Scollon, *Linguistic Convergence*, pp. 45–51 (Chipewyan); Chief Henry of Huslia, *The Stories That Chief Henry Told* (Central Koyukon); and Gaither Paul, *Stories for My Grandchildren* (Tanacross). The Tlingit work of Dauenhauer and others appears in Robert Zuboff, *Táax'aa: Mosquito* and *Kudatan Kahídee: The Salmon Box*, and in Susie James, *Sít' Kaa Káx Kana.aá: Glacier Bay History*. For Kathleen Sands's Papago work, see Ted Rios, "The Egg." Barre Toelken and Tacheeni Scott do a Navajo tale in "Poetic Retranslation and the 'Pretty Languages' of Yellowman." Tim Knab's work from Nahuatl tapes is in "Three Tales from the Sierra de Puebla."
73. Allan Burns, *An Epoch of Miracles: Oral Literature of the Yucatec Maya*. Peter Seitel, *See So That We May See: Performances and Interpretations of Traditional Tales from Tanzania*.
74. Peter Gold, "From 'Easter Sunrise Sermon.'" Daniel Crowley, "The Singing Pepper Tree." Jeff Titon, "Son House: Two Narratives." Jeff Titon and Ken George, "Dressed in the Armor of God" and "Testimonies."

Junco," reorganizing a text I had published in a pause-divided for-mat.[75] His most impressive contribution is to show how initial par-ticles with meanings such as "now" and "then" are widely used to mark off units of the size he reckons as verses and stanzas, but his attempts to break the verses into lines are far less convincing. The lines in question are based on "certain features of syntax," not always the same ones, but "each predication in a text is likely to be a line."[76] The problem is that when the object of the analyst is to divide verses internally so that their lines will add up to a pattern number, and when there is no metrical scheme (in the strict sense), line-making is wide open to gerrymandering, however clear the larger units—verses and stanzas—may sometimes be.

William Bright, in transcribing and translating a tape-recorded Karok narrative, has attempted to combine Hymes's measured verse analysis with my own attention to pausing, but he reduces pause to the status of a general and open-ended rule to the effect that most Karok lines are "without audible pause" at the end, that lines with verbs of saying may be "with or without" such a pause, that verses do have a pause at the end, and—here is the problem—that "acciden-tal hesitations of speech obscure the pause phenomena that define verses and lines."[77] Since his published presentation of this narrative follows a line, verse, and stanza scheme constructed after the manner of Hymes and omits the notation of pauses as such, we cannot judge Bright's formulation of this rule of occurrence. Most important, we cannot decide for ourselves whether the "accidental" pauses he refers to might in fact come at dramatic moments in the action or mark the quoted speech of excited characters. These troublesome pauses might obscure what Corrigan called "good verse," but for all we know they might conform to his dictum that in drama, "the structure is action."

What is at stake in the tension between action and verse may be illustrated by comparing just three short passages from Hymes's ver-

75. Dell Hymes, "Particle, Pause and Pattern in American Indian Narrative Verse." I first published the text and translation of "Coyote and Junco" in *Finding the Center* (both editions), pp. 75–85; a thoroughly revised version was given in 1978 in Tedlock, "Coyote and Junco." Hymes consulted only the older version. For more on "measured verse," see his *"In Vain I Tried to Tell You,"* chaps. 3–6.
76. Hymes, "Particle, Pause and Pattern," p. 7.
77. William Bright, "A Karok Myth in 'Measured Verse': The Translation of a Per-formance," pp. 118–19. More recently the problem of the relationships among pause, intonation, syntax, and measure has been taken up by Anthony C. Woodbury for Yup'ik Eskimo, by M. Dale Kinkaid for Chehalis, by Joel Sherzer for Kuna, by Ellen Basso for Kalapalo, and by Sally McLendon for Eastern Pomo. As of this writing, their work is still in progress or in press.

sion of "Coyote and Junco" with the lines that were actually delivered by Andrew Peynetsa when he first told the story. First some Zuni lines as arranged and punctuated by Hymes in accordance with considerations of syntax and verse:

> *Taas an tenne.*
>> *Tenan yanikwatinan.*
>
> *Taas aakya;*
>> *lak teshoktaawan holhi.*[78]

Here, then, are two "verses," each beginning with *taas*, "again," and each consisting of two "lines." The first of these two verses ends what Hymes reckons as a stanza consisting of four verses; the second verse begins a new stanza of four verses. Here is the translation, as arranged by Hymes; his only change from the original wording is to make the translation of *taas* consistent, changing its second occurrence from "and" to "again":

> Again she sang for him.
>> He learned the song.
>
> Again he went on;
>> he went through a field there.

And now here are the performer's own lines as originally published, divided by pause and punctuated according to intonation:

> *Taas an tenne.*
> *Tenan yanikwatinan taas aakya.*
> *Lak teshoktaawan holhi.*

We can now see to what extent Hymes has allowed considerations of syntax and verse to overrule those of pause and intonation. In the course of dividing the second of the original lines not only between two verses but between two different stanzas (as noted above), he has legislated a sentence end (marked by a period) in the midst of what was originally a single smooth intonational contour. Further, in constructing the second of his verses, he has reduced the punctuation following its first line from a period to a semicolon and has inserted a period at the end of its second line, where the original contour was

---

78. All the passages quoted here are from Hymes, "Particle, Pause and Pattern," and Tedlock, *Finding the Center.*

left incomplete before a pause. The net result is that he has made the reading eye interpret the final line of the quoted passage as belonging to what precedes it rather than to what follows it, which is not the way the performer had delivered that line to the ears of his audience.

The original translation was presented as follows, except for one change: Conceding to Hymes that *taas* might be translated the same way for both of its occurrences, I have changed the initial "again" of the passage to "and," matching the "and" in the second line:

> And she sang for him.
> He learned the song and went on.
> He went through a field there

These translated lines, like the Zuni ones, follow the action rather than the demands of versification. By this point in the story, Coyote is in a hurry to get back to his children; between learning the song from Junco and then going on (both in the second line), he does not wait for the quadruple boundary between separate sentences, lines, verses, and stanzas that Hymes has constructed for him. The third line, "He went through a field there," belongs to what follows it because the field is where the next surprise awaits Coyote, the next line being, "and broke through a gopher hole." The gopher hole waits to cave in under Coyote—and the audience—just beyond the suspense of a pause that interrupts the intonation of the sentence that began with "He went through a field there"; it does not politely await the stately change of sentence and verse that Hymes interposes.

If the lines as actually delivered follow the action, so they also follow characterization. Junco, who would prefer to mind her own business, speaks in a rather tight voice;[79] she is put off by Coyote's aggressive questioning. Here is part of an exchange between them, spoken by Andrew Peynetsa as two lines separated by a pause lasting a full two seconds (and here indicated by a double space with a dot):

> *"Kwap to kyawashey'a?" le'. "Ma'*
> •
> *teshuk'o taap k'ushuts'i" le'holh anikwap. "Hayi.*

The translation runs this way:

> "What are you winnowing?" he said. "Well
> •
> pigweed and tumbleweed," that's what she told him. "Indeed.

79. Tedlock, "Coyote and Junco," p. 171.

Note that although Junco starts her response to Coyote's question right away, she hesitates, quite markedly, before producing the answer. This is now his second direct question, and for her it is already one too many. Once she produces the answer, Coyote begins his own turn right away, just as she did, but where she started off with a vague *ma'*, "well," he starts off with a definite *hayi*, "indeed," and it will only take him a short pause (not like hers) to think of yet another question. Hymes rearranges these lines in a stanza of two verses with two lines each (and puts Coyote's "indeed" in his next stanza, not given here):

> "What are you winnowing?"
> he said.
> "Well, pigweed and tumbleweed,"
> that's what she told him.

Gone is the immediacy of Zuni conversational turn-taking, and gone is Junco's tense and lengthy hesitation between her "well" and her reluctant answer to Coyote's unwanted question.

Eventually Coyote's aggressive demands become too much for Junco, and her reluctance hardens into refusal. When he keeps forgetting the song she gives him and asks her to teach him a fourth time, she remains silent. He then threatens to bite her if she hasn't sung the song by the time he counts to four. After the count reaches two come the following words, delivered with three completed intonational contours (indicated by periods) but not a single pause:

> *Kwa' tena'ma. "HAA"I. ALHNAT ho' penuwa," le'.*

> She didn't sing. "THREE. I'll count ONCE MORE," he said.

Hymes interposes a change of line, verse, and stanza after "She didn't sing" and presents the rest of the original line as a verse of three separate lines:

> "Three.
> "I'll count once more,"
> he said.

The removal of the original capital letters (indicating loudness) may have been a typographical error; in any case the rough-and-ready shapes of action have once again given way to the geometry of versification. When "she didn't sing," Coyote didn't wait for a line, verse, and stanza break to get back to his countdown, and in the same breath in which he said "THREE" he went right on to remind Junco that there was only one number to go. Coyote is an impatient fellow at best, but by this time he's ready to kill.

What happens, in the passage from the dramatic art of storytelling to the literary art of verse-measuring, is a transformation of the constantly changing sounds and silences of action into regularized typographical patterns that can be comprehended at a single glance by a symmetry-seeking eye. David Antin points to the role of the eye when he questions whether meter plays an important role in the sound of English blank verse, arguing that the printed lines of such verse are best understood not as a "sound structure" but as "a visual framing effect" that "places whatever language is within the frame in a context of 'literature.'"[80] In seeking exhibition space in the galleries of literature, Hymes specifically addresses the jury that requires lines of poetry to show measurement when he argues that his analysis of American Indian narratives "makes it possible, indeed essential, to regard such texts as works of literary art."[81] But I take the word "poetry" to cover much more than "verse," if by verse is meant discourse that scans by meter or by measure; in so doing, I must appeal to juries that are both more arcane and more modern than this one.

In Chaucer's time, poetry included all forms of verbal art; no one defined it as being coterminous with metrical verse until Wordsworth, who confessed that he did so "against my own judgment" (quoted in the *Oxford English Dictionary*). Among modern poets, Charles Olson refused even to surrender the term "verse" to metrical discourse, calling for a "projective verse" or "OPEN verse" that would "catch up and put into itself certain laws and possibilities of the breath," even where "this brings us up against syntax." In projective verse, the poet may "indicate how he would want any reader . . . to voice his work," and "FORM IS NEVER MORE THAN AN EXTENSION OF CONTENT" (Olson's capitals).[82] Olson looked forward to a day when poets would return to subjects of epic and dramatic proportions. His, I think, is a poetics that fits the task of listening to the drama of spoken narratives and translating their poetry into scripts that will play.

80. David Antin, "Notes for an Ultimate Prosody," pp. 176–78.
81. Hymes, "*In Vain I Tried to Tell You*," p. 332.
82. Charles Olson, *Selected Writings*, pp. 15–26.

The Girl and the Protector:
A Zuni Story

Introduction

The moment has arrived to put into practice the idea that a translation of an oral narrative should be presented as a performable script. But if I were to follow the normal practice of anthropologists, linguists, and folklorists, I would now send you, dear reader, to an appendix or else to a separate volume—a memoir, a monograph, or the annual report of some institution. That kind of separation may be appropriate when stories are treated as raw products, as ores to be mined for motifs, archetypes, social charters, or mythemes, rather than as events that might be reexperienced through re-presentation in a new language. But when literal trots are left behind and the task of translation is taken seriously, we need no longer be content with those farther reaches of books and libraries where all those masses of words not meant to be read are kept.

First published in *Alcheringa*, n.s. 1, no. 1 (1975): 110–50. The translations of the opening and closing lines of the story have been revised, and so has the discussion of them; in the story, capital letters have replaced boldface as an expression of a loud voice.

So it is that I have already chosen to give you a glimpse of a translated oral performance right up front in the prologue of this book, and now I propose to set aside enough time—here translated into space—for a more fully developed narrative, a Zuni *telapnanne*, or "tale," rendered in a popular style. The particular tale in question fills an important gap in the collection I offered in *Finding the Center*. There, the only two long tales—and by long I mean tales lasting more than three-quarters of an hour—have their roots in the esoterica of Zuni medicine societies and rain priesthoods, whereas the present tale, although the very gods eventually play roles in it, takes the stuff of everyday life as its starting point. It was Andrew Peynetsa, a longtime medicine society member and specialist in society liturgy, who told the longer tales of *Finding the Center*; our present narrator is Walter Sanchez, whose religious life was that of a layman and whose esoteric interests lay in the areas of old-time craftsmanship, hunting procedures, popular sayings, and domestic rituals—areas about which he knew more than Andrew. Walter's storytelling work is represented only by a couple of short tales in *Finding the Center*, but here, in "The Girl and the Protector," we will see (or hear) him in the full exercise of his skills.

Walter runs to novelistic length in his detailed descriptions of the making of snow boots and the hunting of rabbits. Joseph Peynetsa, in the course of collaborating with me in the first stage of the translation, commented, "He's telling it as if he were actually there," which is the highest compliment one can pay a Zuni narrator (see Chapter 5 for more on verisimilitude). Andrew Peynetsa, on the other hand, preferred complexity or novelty of plot to Walter's elaborate scene-painting, and when he told his own version of the present story it came out less than one-third as long.

Walter told "The Girl and the Protector" on the evening of January 22, 1965, with Andrew and myself present (along with the impersonal ear of a tape-recorder). It runs an hour and five minutes, which makes it longer than any of the seven tales and three segments of sacred history presented in *Finding the Center*. More is the wonder, then, that this was the first time Walter had ever told this particular story! He had learned it two days before, from an old man who has a large cornfield near Yellow House, where the humans in the story live. Of course it was not totally different from all the tales Walter already knew, whether on the large scale of its plot segments or the small scale of its phrasing, but these structural features should be seen more as practical aids in the task of keeping a story moving than as providing its very substance, at least where Walter's particular style

This was the first time Walter had ever told this particular story: Walter Sanchez with his wife and a grandson, in a farming hamlet near Zuni.

is concerned. That he was competent enough neither to drop into a Homeric nod nor to leave any loose ends caused no comment; what was worthy of notice was that he was "telling it as if he were actually there."

The story certainly has its formulaic phrases in the opening, the formal greetings, the prayer, and the closing, but when Walter brings to life the sounds and sights of the episodes in which the boots are made, the rabbits are hunted, an ogress approaches in the dark, the fire in a cave dies down, a girl's lover reveals his identity, and the little Protector plays a joke on his grandmother, his speech is no more formulaic than that of any person with an ability to relate a vivid personal experience. At these moments it is the *images* of the story that take the lead, not the forms of its language (see the discussion of the formal and material imaginations in Chapter 8).

The most unusual event in the present performance comes when the heroine's grandfather is about to teach her a prayer. Walter turns to Andrew at this point, thinking Andrew might provide an appropriate prayer and thus temporarily take over the role of the grandfather. Andrew shakes his head briefly in refusal, and Walter, before continuing with the story, replies by saying, "Your word is short." Ordinarily a narrator would make no such request as Walter's, but Walter knew Andrew to be a master orator.

The translation goes beyond the limits set in *Finding the Center* in a number of ways. There I left opening and closing formulas of the kind that are used here untranslated, but now I have some idea as to what these lines may have meant before long use transformed them into their present shapes, rounded and diminished like river pebbles. The opening line, *so'nahchi*, may once have been something like *s ho'na ahhachi*, "Now we are taking it up," with the *-ch-* indicating repetitive action. It is as if the story had been left lying somewhere and were being picked up again, piece by piece. In the second part of the opening, *sonti inoote*, only the first word is a mystery, the second one meaning "long ago"; the full line may once have been something like *s onati inoote*, "Now it begins to be made long ago." What we are about to hear, then, is a reenactment of how the story came into being, how it came to be lying where it lies. Walter, despite his general tendency to go on at great length, usually left out the second part of the opening, as he did here, but his next lines follow standard form in giving the name of one of the places where the characters in the story lived—the place where the story was left lying, so to speak. The closing line, *lee semkonikya*, may have been shortened from *lessi semme konikya*, "Enough, the word was short," in which *se-* is an archaic stem appearing in modern Zuni only in the term *selhasshi,* "old word," which refers to talk that has been handed down, including narratives of the kind presented here.

The audience response to narratives of the present genre is *eeso,* given periodically throughout a performance, but Andrew, with the tape-recorder on, could not be persuaded to give more than the one such response which is obligatory, immediately following the opening formula. Like that formula, the word *eeso* is heard only when stories are told, which leaves it without an easy English equivalent. The problem is only partly soluble through etymology: *e* is the commonest Zuni way of saying "yes," and *eeso* might be an archaic form of it, but English "aye" will not do as a translation of *eeso* because it is presently laden with parliamentary connotations that are inappropriate to a storytelling context. On the other hand, abandoning the search for an English expression of assent in favor of a full glossing of the general "sense" of *eeso* would result in a cumbersome phrase such as "Yes, I hear that a story of the genre that begins with *so'nahchi* is being told." What is needed is something that sounds less casual than "yes" alone but that remains a reasonably simple phrase of assent, something without a noun or a verb in it. Here I have settled on "Yes, indeed," but the reader may think of other solutions.

I have resorted to etymology and to "sense," as balanced by the need to avoid lengthy glosses, in unlocking what would otherwise be untranslatable proper names. The ogress in the story is part of a husband-and-wife team called *aatoshle aachi,* "The Two Aatoshle." Although *aatoshle* is at present taken to be their name rather than a descriptive term, it appears to be the plural of *toshle,* which is an archaic kinship term probably meaning "maternal grandmother's brother." Thus the term for the ogre and ogress together could be translated "The Two Granduncles." Only the ogress is mentioned in the story, where the name *aatoshle* (still in the plural) is modified by *okyattsik'i,* "old lady," to distinguish her from her husband, after whom she seems to have been named. Dropping the plural, I have here called her "Old Lady Granduncle," which, I think, is appropriately chilling in its effect.

In translating *ahayuuta,* the name of the hero and his brother and grandmother, I have resorted to "sense" rather than etymology. In the anthropological literature the two brothers (and their cognates in other traditions) are usually called "the twin war gods," but this places undue emphasis on one aspect of their character. In addition to being warriors, they are at other times hunters, athletes, and gamblers; above all, they are the guardians of the Zuni people, constantly on the lookout for enemies of all kinds, human or otherwise. I have therefore called them "The Protectors."

Zuni exclamations are difficult to translate into English because none of them is obscene or blasphemous or in any other way makes use of words that normally belong elsewhere. I have restricted myself to the limited supply of innocent English exclamations, even though "Oh no!" does not have the elaborateness or gravity of the Zuni *tísshomahhá*. Zuni onomatopoeia, on the other hand, is easy to translate, since English is as rich in this quality as any other language. In *Finding the Center*, I left Zuni onomatopoeia untranslated wherever I preferred its sound to that of the English alternative, but I have since come to the view that an onomatopoeic word helps give a story immediacy, an immediacy that would be lessened by the sudden intrusion of a foreign word in the translation. Therefore *hasshán*, the sound a person makes when swallowing a huge mouthful at one gulp, here becomes "glom," and *ch'ilhi*, the sound of shells being shaken together, becomes "chinking," to give but two examples.

The Zuni use of kin terms is sometimes troublesome for the English-speaking audience, but this is one area in which I refuse to come to the rescue by reducing the world of kinship to the narrow scope we now give it in English. The girl in the story lives alone with a very old man; whether she is an orphan who was adopted by him or he is her blood kin, he is her grandfather in his actions and she calls him grandfather. At the same time he is the only elder male she can depend on, and it is quite natural that she should also call him father. For his part, he calls her both granddaughter and daughter, sometimes in the same sentence. When the little Protector enters the scene, he respectfully calls the old man by the same terms the girl uses. When the girl enters the household of a priest, she greets everyone present by respectfully calling them fathers and mothers. Zunis use kin terms to describe the whole world of interpersonal relationships, and they always let the actual quality of a relationship take precedence over the genealogical facts.

The Zuni narrator sometimes changes from the past to the present tense where an English-speaker might use the imperfect; previously I rendered such passages in the imperfect tense on the grounds that the present would be too obtrusive in English narrative. That may be so on the page, but I now realize that it is not so in speaking aloud. In English we know the present-tense narrative best from play-by-play sportscasts and the like. The Zuni narrator uses the present in his own striving after immediacy; he is, as it were, giving an eyewitness account of the events he sees before his eyes. There are two such passages here, and I have kept them in the present tense.

For a guide to the oral delivery of the script of the story, see pp. 20–21, above.

And now a word of warning. The written medium gives us unlimited access to words that are really appropriate or effective only for certain times of the day or year. A Zuni story like this one should be told late at night; if you tell it during the day you will hasten the coming of the darkness. If you tell it after the snakes have come out in the spring and before they go underground in the fall, take care to omit the first and last lines and to hold a flower in one hand while you speak. Otherwise the story may attract the attention of the snakes.

The Girl and the Protector

NOW WE TAKE IT UP.
(*audience*) Ye———s, indeed.

•

THERE WERE VILLAGERS AT YELLOW HOUSE.
There were villagers at Yellow House
and in a hollow at the foot of the hills
around there
a girl and
her grandfather were living together
at about this time of the WINTER.
At this time of winter
there was a lot of snow.
There at Yellow House, every day, the young men
went out during the day
to pull the rabbits out, they went out, went out hunting and in the
      evening
they always brought back long strings of rabbits.
They brought them back, but that girl
lived with her grandfather and her grandfather was very old.
Because of this
he couldn't go out to kill rabbits.
This girl
this girl was very hungry for rabbit meat.
She thought of going hunting herself

and she asked her grandfather about it
one night
she said, "Grandfather
TOMORROW
I would like to go out hunting rabbits.
Every day at dusk
the people who live up there
bring home strings of rabbits.
I've been thinking about going hunting tomorrow.
I like the taste of rabbit so much
so I've been thinking about it," she told her grandfather.
It was because her grandfather was so old.
"Oh, no! daughter
this can't be, you're a girl.
The cold is dangerous
the snow is deep
and you shouldn't go out at a time like this.
•

IT ISN'T YOUR PLACE," so he told his
daughter, his granddaughter.
"Even so, I want to go.
I, tomorrow, that day
I will go out hunting rabbits."
That's what she told her grandfather.
"Oh, no! daughter
what about the things you'd need to wear in the cold?
We don't
have them.
•

Well, my daughter, you must think whether
there's anything warm to wear in this cold weather.
HOW WILL WE GET IT?" he said to his daughter. "But wait, I'm
going in the next room," then she went in the next room and
got a pelt there
and brought it out. When she brought it out:
"You'll have to make snow boots for me with this," so she said. Her
    poor grandfather was very OLD.
She handed it to her grandfather and he was feeling it.
"Well then
tonight, I'll
make you

good snow boots, they'll be warm."
That's what her grandfather told her. When her grandfather had told
    her: "Now then
you must spray this and then wait

•

until the water soaks in
then come here
in front of me and put out your foot, because
I have no sight, and if I didn't know what your foot was like
they wouldn't turn out right, I need your foot size to make your
    snow boots," so he told his daughter.
She quickly went where the water was kept, took some in her
    mouth, and sprayed the pelt.
When she'd sprayed it all over, she folded it up.
She folded it up, and when the water had soaked in, a little later
she told her grandfather, "Well, I've
done what you told me, I've already done it.
I think it's all damp now," she said. "Well then, bring it right here."
She brought the pelt to her grandfather
and handed it to him.
Feeling the pelt, he said, "Perhaps this will do," and he kept the
    pelt.
Her grandfather pulled out a short stool and spoke to her:
"Now, daughter, come over
and place your foot here
so we can mark the pelt around it, measure your foot, and this very
    night
they'll be finished," so he told his
daughter.

•

She pulled out a stool for her grandfather and her
grandfather sat down on the stool. He sat there and his
granddaughter stood before him and
put her right foot out
on the other stool
and her grandfather asked her, "Which one
am I measuring first?"
"This is my
right foot you're about to measure," and when he'd measured two
    finger widths away from her foot
enough of the big pelt was left over.
"This sole

is good enough
now let's try the other one," he told his daughter. She set out her
     other foot for him.
"Is this the left one?" he said. "Yes, this is the left one."
She set out her left foot and he marked the
pelt all around it. When it was marked: "Well then
do we have any cordage?
I need that to sew them up," so he told his granddaughter.
"What kind?" "Well, the narrow yucca blades
and they should be about this long (*indicates about two feet*).
Give me that kind, I'll
use them because they're rough and strong.
I'll use them to sew for you," so he told her. "Well, there are some of
     those around
there were some left over
when I last made tamales." "Well then, get them."
So she went in the other room
and a moment later she brought them out and showed them to him,
     and
her grandfather was VERY OLD
so he felt them. They were long.
"Well THIS, this is the kind I was telling you about," and then
he took one out of the bundle and stripped it until he had only the
     center fiber.
It was a long one.
"Well, I'll use this for sewing," so he told his
daughter.
He sewed on until, when he was almost finished, his
cord ran out. When it ran out:
"How much more do you need? Did it run out?" "All I need is an
     arm's length to finish it."
She got more yucca. "Well, it'll probably take one more fiber to
     finish it.
Why don't you strip it for me the way I did the other one, so I can
     finish?
About this long (*indicates about eighteen inches*)," so her grandfather
     told her, and his
granddaughter started to
strip it.
She finished. When she had finished
he started up again where he'd left off.
He finished it. When he'd finished: "Now then

try it on, perhaps it'll be all right," he said.
His
daughter tried on the snow boot.
(*tight*) "Well
well, it's a little too large," she told him.
"It's fine for it to be a little too large
because you'll have to use strips of fur
to wrap your feet in before you put it on.
You have to put them on tight," so he told her.
That's what he told his granddaughter.
"There's some cord left over, well
it can be used too.
If you stripped about three more of these
then I could use them
to finish the other boot.
I could finish it this very night," so he told his
granddaughter.
She took them
and stripped the edges of the blades until the center fiber was left.
"What did you do next, grandfather?" she said.
"Give it to me, I'll have to do that part myself."
So she gave one to her grandfather
and when he twisted the fiber of the narrow yucca
it was almost like a ligament, a deer's ligament.
It came out long.
Her grandfather pulled it tight, then he said, "Well, it's quite long.
But we'll need another one," he said, and his
granddaughter got to work again and she
started to strip it
the yucca
and she gave it to her
father.
When this was done: "Maybe this will do for finishing the other
    one.
You'll have to put the first one on so it won't get hard," so he told
    his
daughter. "Very well then."
And she put on the one that was already finished.
"And when you
dress yourself tomorrow, you must make your clothes snug.
Because there's a lot of snow, not just a little," so he told his
daughter. Then

he started on the other one and kept on, kept on sewing
and when he was almost finished
his yucca cord ran out. "Well, my
sewing cord is gone.
Another like the last one I made should finish it, about an arm's
    length.
NOW THEN, LOOK OUTSIDE and see how far in the night it is."
That's what he told his granddaughter, then his granddaughter
    looked outside. "Well now
Stars-in-a-Row
has almost gone down." "Ah, then
I'll be able to finish this."
That's what he told his daughter. (*excited*) The girl came back inside
    and she was ALL EXCITED
because she never got to eat rabbit, and the young men
came back every evening with them, long strings of them.
That's why she'd made up her mind to go hunt rabbits.
That's why
snow boots were being made for her.
"There's only a short way to go, so
I'll be able to finish before Stars-in-a-Row goes down, I should be
    able to finish."
"Well, here it is," and she gave
the stripped yucca to her grandfather so he could twist it.
He felt it and said, "This should finish it."
He felt for the place where he'd left off and started up again until he
    was done.
He had some cord left over when he finished.
Then he
tied it off and he was finished.
The boots were finished.
"So
daughter, they're finished.
Now then, try this one on, because
you must think about keeping warm, these will be warm and your
feet won't get cold."
That's what he told her, then his
daughter, the girl, granddaughter, went in the other room again and
    she
found some rabbit skins
old ones
that he had there

and she took them out and sprayed them, then
she wrapped her feet with them, one side then the other side.
She tried the snow boots on again
and they just fit her.
"So
they fit you well
but you'd better spray them and fold them up
and put them away.
Well, we should go to bed
but first you need to make yourself some provisions for tomorrow
you need to make lots of
provisions, and
I'll be waiting for you here
so you must think about me, you
must think," so he told his granddaughter.
"Very well, I'll go do that, there's still time."
She went in the other room and got out
a small dish
of corn flour

•

then she made some tortillas, and
she kept on making them till she had a tall stack, then her dough
    was gone.
"Well, perhaps this will do."
That's what she told her grandfather. "Well, it'll do, since I'm
never very hungry
so
if I can't eat
I'll wait for you, and if you're lucky enough
to make a kill and get back in time, then we
can eat together, for when you eat by yourself the food doesn't taste
    good," her grandfather told her.
"Yes, that's the way it is." "Now you can make
your preparations
get everything ready.
Back there where
my
cornmeal pouch is, inside it you'll find
a fire drill.
That's something
we'll have to get ready tonight," so he told his daughter.

"Where is it?" she said. "It's right THERE
just as you go in, my
cornmeal pouch, the things inside.
It's the fire drill, get that thing I use to start a fire, get that.
So then tomorrow, if you
don't get back by evening
you can start a fire, I'll show you how," so he told his daughter.
So she went in and there
by the antlers was his cornmeal pouch
hanging there.
(*softly*) "Perhaps this is it," she said.
She took it down
and brought it to him. "Is this it?"
"Yes, THIS is it, this is my
cornmeal pouch. Now look inside that small pocket and see if all
my fire-making things
are there. Perhaps they're still there, well then hand them to me."
So his poor daughter

•

opened it
and took out
the fire drill and the platform the sparks fall from.
She took them out
then: "Is EVERYTHING THERE?"
her grandfather said, his sight wasn't good, he was so old.
When he'd taken them: "THESE are the ones.
When evening comes
when the sun is going down, think of your home
and if it's too far away you must think about the cold
and if you can't make it back
you must think of shelter for the night, even before
sunset you must think about this. First, you
have to find a sheltered place and you
make a clearing there.
If you don't want to carry this pouch
you can leave it there.
Get some bark
find some mountain mahogany and
peel the bark and have it ready.
Before the sun goes down
you'll gather some wood and have it ready.

Before the sun goes down, even if it's about to set
you must turn this fire drill toward the sun
so it will blossom.
Then you'll pass a good night," so he told his
granddaughter. "Yes, may it be so."
That's what she said. Then her grandfather instructed her:
"There is the FAST KIND:
their tracks will not be numerous, well, their
tracks will be far apart, but the other kind, the cottontail rabbits
will make tracks closer, closer together.
Where the surface of the snow is clear
the tracks of the fast kind will be farther apart.
Their tracks won't show whether
they've gone into a hole.
But the kind you're going after tomorrow is the cottontail.
When you find his tracks in clear snow
they're the tracks that are closer together.
Those are the tracks you must follow, and if you're lucky
the tracks will lead into a hollow in a tree
or a crevice in the rocks.
If they go inside—
well that's what I'll
prepare you for."
So he had a STICK, it was
the length of both arms. He asked her to get it.
"You put this in the hole, and if he's TOO FAR IN
you won't be able to touch him with it, but
if you're LUCKY he'll only be a SHORT WAY INSIDE
and you'll put your arm in. This is the way
rabbits are hunted in winter," so he told his daughter.
•

"Very well, I'll
keep all this in mind as I go around."
That's what she told him.
"But it is not
by strength alone
that you can go against these Raw People
so I will give you
the cornmeal pouch."
•

THAT'S WHAT HER GRANDFATHER TOLD HER, he spoke
to his daughter: "TOMORROW

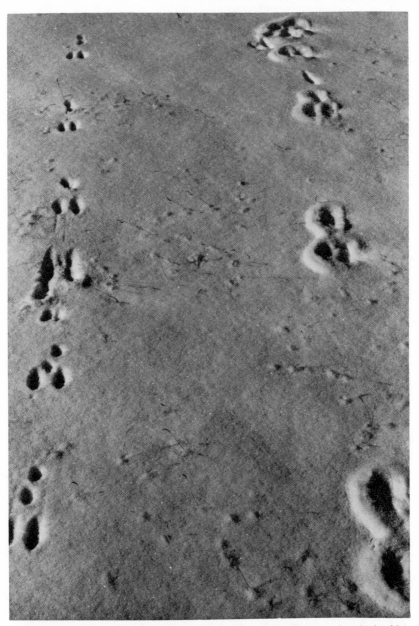

There is the fast kind, but the other kind will make tracks closer together: Jackrabbit tracks (*right*) and cottontail tracks (*left*) in clear snow.

when you leave your home here
you'll go along, and as you go you
must watch for your Sun Father.
When he is up this far (*thrusts out an arm a little above the horizontal*),
    then, beside a tree or a bush
   •

you
must ask for Daylight.
Well, it doesn't matter how far he has gone, how far the Sun has
    gone
it could even be just as he reaches the place where he goes in.
But when you ENTER upon the ROADS of the RAW PEOPLE
THEN, WITH THESE WORDS, YOU
WILL OFFER THEM PRAYER-MEAL," so he told his daughter.
That's what he told her, he spoke it, spoke it (*turning to a man in the
    audience as if expecting him to speak*)
(*the man shakes his head, refusing to take the part of the girl's grandfather*)
(*to the man*) Your word is short.
When he had finished: "You must give thanks in this way
my daughter, you must do this.
Now let's go to bed."
(*softly*) They
went to sleep, they slept o———n until the next morning.
The next day, early in the morning, they got up and his
daughter
got herself ready
for she was very anxious.
When she'd built up the fire
she went in the next room
and there
   •

she got a little bowl
of water
and she
(*softly*) put it by the fire
and made some meal cakes.
When they'd eaten well:
"Daughter, you must be sure
to remember
that the cold is dangerous, and if you can't get home
by tonight
then, while our Sun Father is still up

you must think, as you go along, about where you will shelter for
     the night.
Over there
•

in the village there are young men, and these young men, around
     sunset
that's when
they bring back their strings
of rabbits
and for this reason
you have decided to do the same. I won't say no to you, for you are
     at the beginning of your life.
If you have to stay overnight
you must think of your happy return.
But now you must go fix all your provisions
you must get ready:
if you're going to spend the night
you
must think of making yourself ready," so he told his
granddaughter. "You told me that last night.
Well, I think probably I
have all I need to last me, I'm ready," she said, and
she'd made tortillas
and these
(*softly*) were in a tall stack.
She wrapped some up.
When she'd wrapped them:
"My grandfather, my father, I'm going now, may you
have a happy day."
That's what she told her father. "My daughter, may it be the same
     with you
may you be happy," so he told his daughter.
She went out. When she went out she stood on the roof, and over
     there (*points north*)
was Yellow House, where the young men lived, and
it was to the south of Yellow House
in a hollow below there
that the girl lived with her very old grandfather.
Every evening those young men
brought in strings
of rabbits
and for this reason the girl

had made up her mind
and so her snow boots had been made, and now, the next day
she got herself ready and went out.
She went
southward
she went on, she went on until
(*softly*) she found a cottontail's tracks, and when she found the
    cottontail's tracks
they went on and on until they entered a yucca thicket.
When she came to the yucca thicket: "Oh yes, my father, this is
    what you told me about."
And then
it seems
she put her hand inside her dress
she
took out her cornmeal
and
spoke the way her grandfather father had told her:
she asked that this would bring her Daylight
that the day would not be wasted, that she
would enter upon the Roads of the Raw People, that they would
    enter her house
holding their Waters, forever bringing in their Roads as they lived.
And when the poor girl had said THIS
she sprinkled the cornmeal. Having sprinkled the cornmeal she
    went on her way.
When she found some more tracks
a jackrabbit ran out, STOPPED for an instant, and then made a long
    jump.
(*softly*) "This is the fast kind you told me about.
Then it's just as well that you be on your way."
And she went on a short distance until
she came to a thicket, and there
she saw the tracks of a cottontail:
his marks were going along there.
"This must be the one."
Then the girl FOLLOWED him, FOLLOWED him until she came to
    some ledges.
When she found where he'd gone inside, she looked all around
and there weren't any tracks
there weren't any tracks coming back out.

"Well, this is what you told me about."
She took her stick and
stuck it in. When it was in: "You must be just a short way in." There
was rustling.
(*softly*) "Well, this must be what you meant," she said
and the girl put her hand in. She put her hand in—
she almost had him, but he huddled himself together.
And again she lay down, and she stretched her arm until she caught
his feet.
She pulled him out, but she didn't know how to kill a cottontail, this
was something her
grandfather hadn't explained. She pinched the cottontail's nose until
finally she managed to KILL him.

•

When she'd killed him she laid him on the ground.
She put her stick back in
and there was another one
and she worked the stick.
"This is what you told me to do."

•

She lay down on her side
put her hand in
until her hand stopped
and again she pulled one out.
When she'd pulled out this one, she had two cottontails.
"Well
at least I've killed two.
I didn't think I could do it
in such a short time." The girl
was SO HAPPY, she kept thinking she might see more of them, this
was her thinking.
Carrying the two, she went
eastward.
She went down until she saw more tracks going along
and these tracks
were distinct in the clean snow.
They went northward to where
he had jumped
and when she got there the jump was too long.
"Well
this isn't the right kind, this is the fast kind you told me about."

Well then the girl went back to where she'd first seen these tracks.
When the girl got there, some new tracks went on and on this way
     (*points south*)
the tracks headed this way, southward, they
were headed this way.
"This is what you told me about."
     •
Well she
WENT ON AND ON until she came to some ledges, and there
(*softly*) his tracks went inside, they went inside.
They went in underneath.
"Well, maybe you're inside."
And
THEN just as her
father had told her to do
she PUT HER STICK IN and there was rustling.
The girl then
put her hand in
and again she TOOK ONE OUT, and again, just as she had done it
     the first time
she pinched his nose and BURIED HIM
in the snow
and when she finally managed to kill him she put him down. There
     were now
three cottontails.
When there were three cottontails
she PUT HER STICK IN AGAIN, AND AGAIN there was rustling.
And then she
broke away some dirt from the edge of the hole and put her hand in
and now he was not far in
and again she pulled one out.
This was now her fourth cottontail
this was the count.
When this was the count it was dusk. "Well
this is what you told me to do."
And she started across there
and came to Line of Pines
and on to Cliff House, the girl crossed a ravine.
Having crossed she came
to the rocks, to a small cave there.
When she entered it there was a small dry clearing.

(*softly*) "I think this is a good place.
This is what you told me about."
And then
she gathered wood. Having gathered wood
the girl brought it inside.
The bark of the mountain mahogany was very loose.
She peeled some off and
brought it inside.
She put that on the ground.
Oh, her grandfather had told her this:
"Before you start a fire
you must present the fire drill to the sun so
you'll have a better chance of getting it lit," so her grandfather told
    her. "Oh yes
that's what you told me."
When she remembered this
the sun was still up (*points west, a little above the horizon*).
Having done it
she took her fire drill back inside
and was trying to get a piece of bark started.
For the third time she tried, and about the fourth time she had the
    edge of it glowing.
She took it outside
instead of blowing on it, since
there was a light breeze and sssssso came the flame.
She went back inside
and soon the fire was going, the fire was really going.
·
Now she took off her snow boots and laid them aside
then she
opened up her provisions.
(*softly*) It was very dark by the time she started eating, she ate until
    she had enough.
"Well
(*almost yawning*) I'm sleepy, I'll lie down," that's what
she's thinking.
Now she warms herself, and she takes some of the wood she
    gathered and puts it on the fire
the fire blazes up.
(*softly*) Now
there's a voice.

Now there's a voice
and she hears it.
"Perhaps
you are
someone from the village who's lost the way
and you're calling out.
Well, I'll answer you, and
perhaps I could depend on you for the night."
That's how the poor girl felt.
She quickly put on her snow boots, then
she went out in the clearing to the edge of the firelight.
(*as if from a distance, and very high*)
hoooooooooooohaaaaaaaaaaaaaaaaaaaaaaaaa
a
a
a
a
a
y it said.
(*calling out*) "Come over here, I'm spending the night here," the girl
said.

•

And then
there was another call then:
hoooooooooooooooooooohaaaaaaaaaaaaaaaaaaaaaaaaaaa
a
a
a
a
y it said.
(*calling out*) "Come over here, I'm spending the night here," the girl
said again.

•

The girl went inside and PUT MORE WOOD ON, the fire was really
blazing, then it came CLOSER.
It came closer
calling
hoooooooooooooooooooooooohaaaaaaaaaaaaaaaaaaa
a
a
a
a
y it said.

The girl heard it very clearly now.
(*gasping*) "Eeee! this is why you
warned me.
Why did I answer?
So this is why you told me
that I shouldn't have a fire late at night.
Well, I asked for it," she said, and the girl

was SCARED, and at the spot where she'd eaten she had the four
     rabbits
her four rabbits there on the ground.
•

She could hear her coming now: it was the Old Lady Granduncle.
She had a crook
and the little shells tied to it were chinking as she came.
•

After a time she came to the edge of the light.
She had bulging eyes and was carrying a basket.
(*softly*) She was speaking in a strong voice as she came.
•

THEN SHE CAME UP
to the fire.
•

"Why is it
that a girl like you spends the night away like this?
TONIGHT
I shall have
MEAT
I shall eat salt."
THAT'S what
the Old Lady Granduncle said, speaking in a strong voice.
The poor girl was frightened and didn't say a thing.
Then
she got back in where she'd been before, and
there was just enough room for the girl to get in
•

and when she got in as far as she could
the fire was going out, (*softly*) the light was dim.
The Old Lady Granduncle
could see her rabbits now.
"WHAT are those tasty TIDBITS there?" "Well my RABBITS."
"COME ON, THROW ONE OUT TO ME," she told her.
"I had a hard time killing them
•

so why should I
throw one out to you?"
"If you don't throw one out to me right now
then I'm going to eat you," she told her.
The poor girl now
got so frightened

that she threw the smallest rabbit out to her.
Holding it like this (*dangles an imaginary rabbit above the mouth*),
  GLOM!
she swallowed it.
She looked in again:
"WHAT tasty tidbits are THOSE?" "Well my rabbits again."
POOR THING, SHE HAD ONLY FOUR RABBITS TO GIVE HER.
•

NOW, here she was giving her the THIRD ONE
and over there at CORN MOUNTAIN
the Twin Protectors lived with their grandmother.
This GRANDMOTHER of theirs was about to go to bed, and then
she stepped outside, and far away, near
Cliff House, all this was going on, and the girl was in a cave.
Now
she was going outside to pee when she heard the girl crying
and the chinking sound there, the strong voice there.
•

The Grandmother Protector got excited and BAM! she went inside.
"Grandsons
someone is crying somewhere.
And there's a chinking sound, and somebody's speaking in a strong
  voice.
'Tonight
I shall
eat you.
That's the way somebody's talking," she said. "Aha!
at Yellow House village
just below there to the south
is a girl
who lives with her grandfather, and this
grandfather
is very
weak, very old.
The young men bring in rabbits every evening, and so
she decided to do the same.
SHE WENT OUT HUNTING.
It must be HER."
THAT'S WHAT THE LITTLE PROTECTOR SAID, and he got
  himself ready, he
put it on, put on his quiver.
His elder brother said, "Well now, go ahead
by yourself, younger brother.

With luck you can take care of it before the night is over.
But you'll have to HURRY," he told his younger brother.
"Well then, that's the way it will be."
And
as soon as he got outside he started to run.

•

He runs along below Blackweed Row, and then
as he runs along, the girl cries out again:
"Grandfather
come
come help me
I'm about to die.
She says she'll eat me.
Grandfather come help me." (*rasping*) The Old Lady answers in a
     strong voice:
(*sharply*) "How could your grandfather come, your grandfather is old
     and he can't see.
How
could he come and help you?"
So says the Old Lady.
The poor girl is crying.

•

THE LITTLE PROTECTOR RUNS, and he circles around to the
     south of them
going along
until he sees them there
and then
he sits down on top of a cliff.
As he sits down, the poor girl speaks
again: "Grandfather
come and help me.
For some reason she wants to eat me."
That's what she keeps saying, and the Old Lady gets mad again:
(*sharply*) "You've got an old grandfather who can't see.
How could anybody
help you?"
So says the Old Lady Granduncle.
"THEN I will HELP YOU," the little Protector says now.
He's sitting on top of a cliff and the Old Lady glances around.

•

AND NOW, NOW she runs against the cave entrance and hits it, a
     rock gives way
she's about to get inside.

She chips the rocks away, and again the girl
speaks:
(*weakly*) "Grandfather
come and help me.
For some reason I'm going to die tonight.
Come on now, grandfather, help me," she said.
Again the little Protector spoke:
"I'LL HELP YOU
I've come to help you," he told her.
The Old Lady stopped and looked up, she looked up.

•

When she looked up she said:
"Well then, TONIGHT
you've come to help her.
Well then, tonight
if you are going to help her
then we shall have a CONTEST tonight," she said.
(*modestly*) "Well, go ahead and test me, if
you are strong
then go ahead and hook me and pull me down
then perhaps you
can eat both of us, tonight you might eat."
That's what
the little Protector told the Old Lady Granduncle.
He was up there on a narrow ledge
sitting up there, the little Protector was sitting there.
Then she hooked him with her crook
she pulled down on it
she pulled, but because he was a being of the Raw kind
he was stuck on tight.
(*with strain*) She PULLED and she pulled, and she failed.
"Oh! I'm tired," she said.

•

"If you're really going to eat us, come on, COME ON AND TRY
     THE OTHER ARM.
Perhaps you can pull me down by the other arm," so
he told her, the Protector told the Old Lady.
He stretched out his arm. When he stretched out his arm
she hooked him by the right hand.
The Old Lady Granduncle (*with strain*) pulled
she pulled
and she failed.

"Aha——
•

well now, it must be that this girl is the lucky one tonight, now that I
    have entered upon
entered upon your Roads.
(*sharply*) I had thought that
you would know everything," he told her, "but no.
I'm not holding on very tight here, but you couldn't pull me down."
•

Then the Old Lady Granduncle told the little Protector: "YES, in
    truth
you must be stronger than I
for I
couldn't pull you down, I failed"
she said.
"You FAILED
and tonight
I shall
kill you.
You made
threats against me.
Tonight
I shall certainly
kill you."
That's what he said, then the little Protector slid down.
HE SLID DOWN and stepped forward
(*softly*) while the Old Lady Granduncle stood at the edge of the
    light.
He placed an arrow and shot her. When he placed an arrow and
    shot her
she fell down.
When she'd fallen he went to the girl.
(*kindly*) "Alas! my child
my mother
all this
cold is very dangerous
•

but I have entered upon your Road.
Well, tonight
you were lucky that I entered upon your Road.
You have nothing to fear now:
you can go back inside again

for the night.
I'll keep watch over you."
That's what the little Protector told the girl
he told her.
The girl's
rabbits had been eaten.

•

"WHAT IS IT
that she took from you to eat?" he said. "Well, I had four rabbits:
she ate them," she told him.
He went to where the Old Lady was lying.
He turned her so her head was toward the east.
(*softly*) She was lying on her back, and he took his stone knife and
    sliced her belly open.
When he sliced her belly open
THERE WERE THE POOR GIRL'S SNOW BOOTS.
    (*audience laughs*)
HE TOOK THESE OUT
but left the rabbits in.
"Let THOSE be HERS.
You shouldn't
cry about it, but put your things on again, you
can have a good sleep while I stand guard for you here.
You won't have anything to fear.
The one who tried to eat you is finished
so there's nothing to fear, may you
have a good rest."
That's what he told the girl.
The poor girl
put on her snow boots and put some wood on the fire to make it
    bright.
She lay down but she COULDN'T GO TO SLEEP.
She STILL HADN'T SLEPT (*turns west and lowers the arm below the
    horizon*) when Stars-in-a-Row went down.
She didn't go to sleep and the little Protector
knew it.
"Alas! daughter, mother, you haven't gone to sleep," he said. "No."
"YOU'RE AFRAID OF ME, BUT I WON'T DO ANYTHING TO
    YOU.
The one who tried to kill you is dead.
I've saved you.
What is there

to be afraid of? I've
rescued you.
You'll last the night."
That's what he told the girl. "Dear me! is it true?"
"It's REALLY TRUE: because of my thoughts
nothing will happen.
There
is the one you were afraid of, and now she lies dead, you have
    nothing to be afraid of."
Then the poor girl lay down and finally went to sleep.
The Protector watched the girl as she
slept through the night. The night passed, then
just before dawn
the little Protector
fixed the fire and had it going. Because it had taken her a long time
    to fall asleep
she slept on and on until finally she woke up, the girl woke up.
"Are you awake now?" "Yes, I'm awake now."
"Then you can
eat your
meal," he told her. The poor girl
had saved some meal cakes.
She ate these, she ate well.
"Have you had enough?" "Yes, I've had enough."
(*kindly*) "Let's go now.
Your father
is very sad, because
the weather is cold and there's a lot of snow.
It isn't a girl's place to be out like this
but you've been out overnight
you've passed the night
and got some sleep
(*sharply*) but your father hasn't slept the whole night."
That's what the little Protector told the
girl he'd saved, that's what he told her. "Is that true?"
They went a little way, and BECAUSE HE WAS A BEING OF THE
    RAW KIND
he pulled out some rabbits for her, pulled them out. They went on,
    went on
until they had two strings of rabbits.
"Well now, if we
carry them this way

they'll be too heavy.
Wait now, let me fix them the way I think they should be."
The TWO OF THEM WENT ON AND ON until
they came near the village. Before they got there
they came to some dead wood.
When they got there
(*softly*) he cut the wood, he cut it and laid out two sticks, these two
he laid out side by side
and then across these two
he laid the rabbits, facing in alternate directions
and in this way HE MADE A LADDER OF RABBITS.
It was done
and it was good, and because he was a Wonder Worker, he
made it so it wasn't heavy.
"Now then, try it on
to see if it's all right, or if it's heavy, because we still have some way
    to go."
That's what he told the girl. The girl did this (*bending forward*),
    standing up, while the
little Protector put it on her, and now he was speaking in a very
    hoarse voice.
        (*audience laughs*)
When she'd first met him, he spoke in a normal voice, but now he
    was being SILLY.
He put four ladders of these rabbits
on the girl's back
and because he was a Wonder Worker he made it so they weren't at
    all heavy for the girl.
"Well, we'll let this be enough
and now we can go on over there," he said.
They watched the Sun until he was JUST ABOUT
to go in, and they arrived at the girl's
house JUST as he was going in, and they all went in.
When they went in
they entered upon the Road of their grandfather.
"Daughter, have you come now?" (*with relief*) "Yes, we've come."
    "Thanks be.
So you've come, it's good that you've come back. Ever since you left
I haven't eaten.
And, "All Raw PEOPLE, holding your Waters, holding your Seeds
enter here into my house upon your Pollenways':

that's what I've been saying
and now you've COME BACK." "Yes, we've COME," she said.
•

The little Protector came in and said, "My grandfather, my father,
      how have you
been passing the days?" "Happily, so you've come now."
"Yes, we've come."
And THERE THE TWO OF THEM
entered upon the Road
of their father, their grandfatherly father.
Then
they untied their rabbits
and spread them out.
When they'd spread them out
the girl went in the next room. Going in the next room
she brought out ears of corn and put one alongside the breast of
      each rabbit. When she'd done this:
"Have you done it?" he said.
"Daughter, have you done it?" he said. "Well, I've
done it," she said.
"Now then, come over here and help me stand up," he said, and
(*softly*) the girl went to help her grandfather stand up.
When he came to where they'd spread them out:
•

"Well, where's our
prayer meal?" he said. "Well, I've got it here."
Then
she handed it to her grandfather. (*softly*) He held it
and while the little Protector sat there
on the wood pile, her grandfather spoke a prayer:
(*almost monotone, but with a higher pitch on stressed syllables*)
•

NOW in truth, ON yesterday's day, when our Sun Father by whom
      we LIVE
FROM his holy place
CAME out standing
ENtered upon our Roads, MY child here
HOLding holy meal
SENT this with prayer upon the Pollenway; RAW People:
HOLding your Waters
HOLding your Seeds

YOU are first upon the Pollenway; OUR child
STANding last behind you
SENT there the Pollenway.
OUR father
THERE at the place where he sets has a small space to go
OUR children, RAW People, HOLding your Waters, HOLding your
    Seeds
BRING in your Pollenways, FLESH by which we live, FLESH of
    white corn, HOLY meal, strong meal
WE give these into your hand; FORever
HERE into our houses, HOLding your Waters, HOLding your Seeds
YOU will live the entering Pollenway; BY your flesh, (*normal voice*)
    by your EVER presence we shall live."
That's what her father said.
He sprinkled the meal on the rabbits, and the little Protector said,
    "Just SO, in truth, that is the way
you shall live," THAT'S HOW HE RESPONDED
TO HER FATHER, STANDING THERE.
IN THIS WAY HE COMPLETED IT. Having completed it
he sprinkled them too. Having sprinkled them:
"Well
let's eat, I haven't eaten since yesterday, since you left," so
the grandfather told his daughter, and his
daughter went in and

    •

got out the flour and boiled some water. Having boiled some water
she made meal cakes. Having made meal cakes
she served dinner and they ate. While they were eating the little
    Protector said, "Ah
this is what I really wanted," he said, in his
very HOARSE VOICE.
He was speaking in a hoarse voice, and they ate until they were full.
The little Protector said to her, to his
well, to his wife:
"Don't you have relatives?" he said.
"Yes indeed, we
have relatives."
"Then go and tell the Priest of the Bow
to come.
Ask him to come
here
and I will speak to him.

Well, summon him," so the little Protector
told the girl.
"Very well, I'll GO."
And it was in a hollow that they
had their house.
She went out and WENT UP to the village, to the house of the Priest
     of the Bow. There was a noise.
(*softly*) "Oh, somebody's coming," they said. "Yes, yes," they said.
A moment later she entered. When she entered
she stood by the ladder: "My fathers my
mothers, how have you
been?" "Happy."
When they got a look at her
it was the girl who lived with her old grandfather.
"Our child, you've
come. There must be a word of some importance
there must be something to say, for you wouldn't enter upon our
     Roads for no reason
you wouldn't enter here," the Priest of the Bow told the girl.
"Yes, in truth, you
must make it known to all your children
that tonight they will come
•
they will come to my house, where we have something
that will make all of you happy." (*with pleasure*) "Very well indeed,"
     he said.
As the girl left she said, "My fathers, may you have a good night,"¹
     so the girl said
and she left. The Priest of the Bow went out
and shouted the announcement, then everyone gathered where the
     girl and the old man were.
They gathered at their place, where the rabbits were being skinned
     for them.
They skinned them until everybody in the village got some: because
     of
the thoughts of the little Protector
all the villagers got some. When they got theirs there were some left
     over
for the girl and her grandfather. With some left over, the people
     dispersed. When they'd dispersed
•
his

wife said, "Well, let's
go in the next room, that's where I sleep," she said.
"You two go in the next room and, well, I'll
sleep in here, you
get some rest," so their
father said, then she fixed a bed and their father lay down.
(*softly*) The two of them went in the other room. When they went in
he sat down. He sat there until
his wife finished making the bed, then the little Protector said, "I'm
    so thirsty.

   •

I'm so thirsty, get me
some water to drink, I'm so thirsty."
So then the girl
went back to get him some water, and he TOOK HIS FOREHEAD
    IN HIS HAND
and there, he
pulled off his homely self, he pulled it off and SAT DOWN ON IT.
He was sitting on it when the girl
came back with his water. He was facing her
and she didn't give him his water. "Come on, give me my
water," he said.
(*tight*) "WHERE'S THE ONE WHO CAME HOME WITH ME?" she
    said to him.
(*tight*) "Who's the one who came home with you?" he said. "The
    one who came home with me, you aren't
him." "Yes indeed, that's me," so the Protector said.
"That's ME," he said.
"He wasn't LIKE YOU. He was UGLY," she said.
    (*audience laughs*)
(*laughing*) That's what she told him.
   •

Again the girl asked him.
"Yes, that's me," he said, for the second time.
"That's me.
This person who
came home with you:
do you really love him?" he said. "Yes, certainly:
because of his thoughts my life was saved.
Last night
there
where I was spending the night

the Old Lady was about to eat me, and because of his thoughts
I was saved.
I really do love him," she said.
"I'M the one who saved you, I'm the ONE," so he told her, for the
    third time
the third.
"No, he wasn't like you, he was
well, he was ugly."
That's what the girl told him, and she REFUSED HIM THE WATER,
    she wouldn't give it to him.
"Do you REALLY love him?" he said. "Yes, certainly
I love him. Because of his thoughts I regained the Daylight."
That's what she told him.
He raised up a little and showed her his costume.
"HERE he is, I only impersonate him.
And we are not just one.
My elder brother is with our grandmother.
Last night
when my grandmother went out to pee
the Old Lady Granduncle was there
running up against the rocks of your cave, and because of the noise
our grandmother came in and told us about it.
My elder brother sent me
and I went there.
THIS is the one," he said, and HE PULLED OUT HIS COSTUME
    AND TOSSED IT OVER TO HER.
HE TOSSED IT TO HER and when the girl saw it: "Oh! so it was
    you—
so this is the way you are."
THERE SHE GAVE HIM THE WATER AND HE DRANK IT, AND
    THERE THE LITTLE PROTECTOR GOT MARRIED.
He got married, and when
he'd stayed two nights, after he'd stayed his first two nights
he thought about going out hunting, on the third day he went
    hunting, and on that day he told his
father and his
wife:
"I'm
going out hunting.
Well now
the sun has only gone a short way.
I'll go hunting

over this way."
That's what
he told his
grandfatherly father.
His wife said, "I'll fix you some provisions." "Oh
I'm going right now:
the sun is already up.
I'll be back in a short while," he told his wife.
The little Protector put on his quiver
and started on his way up.
He went on up, and some time later he killed a deer.
He killed a deer, gutted it, and before the sun
went down, he carried the deer home.
He was carrying the deer on his back when he came, and the
    villagers
noticed him.
"That
girl who lives alone with her
old grandfather must've married someone.
He brought home a deer
he brought a deer and went inside," so they were saying.
And the little Protector took his deer inside.
His wife, when she heard a noise, his wife said:
"Perhaps that's you." Her grandfather
had told her this:
"Daughter
granddaughter
I THINK
he's not
one of the people who live at Yellow House, he's not
not one of them.
He must be some
Wonder Worker, because he saved you out there, and the way he
    speaks:
perhaps he's not a being of the Daylight kind.
But
but let's wait awhile
and IF HE'S THAT OTHER KIND OF BEING he'll surely bring
(*smiling*) SOMEONE OF HIS OWN KIND WITH HIM," SO HE
    TOLD THE GIRL.
Her father was the first to guess it, he guessed it.
SURE ENOUGH, before

the sun had set
(*softly*) the little Protector brought a deer, there was a noise.
"Daughter, go out.
You must
take the holy meal and bring their Pollenway in, you must bring
    them in."
That's what he told his daughter. His
daughter then
took some cornmeal and went up.
"So you've come now." "Yes we've come now," he said.
(*softly*) She brought in their Pollenway.
The little Protector came in with his deer.
It was a very large deer with very large antlers.
Yet he was so small: how could he have carried it?
He brought it inside on his back.
When he got down inside:
"My father, how have you been?" "Happy, so you've come, be
    seated," he was told.
His wife
helped take the deer off his back and lay it out with the head toward
    the east.
    •

"You must do the same thing you did the first time, you must lay an
    ear of corn alongside his breast
and we shall ask for Daylight."
That's what her
father told her.
The poor girl did this
(*softly*) and they sprinkled the deer and asked for Daylight.
They ate.
When they had eaten
when they had eaten well:
"Now let's
skin him."
The little Protector then
    •

took out his stone knife and cut it, (*softly*) slit-slit-slot
slit-slit-slot, he skinned it
until he was finished.
Meanwhile
the Priest of the Bow was notified again.
He called the priests to a meeting

the Priests of the Daylight were notified, and they were the ones
    who
did the BUTCHERING.
When the BUTCHERING was done
they hung the
    •

meat on yucca fiber ropes that were
strung across.
Some of it was given to them and they
took it home
and for four days the little Protector was bringing in the deer this
    way.
They lived ON this way
until
the little Protector had been there eight nights
and on a night like this one he told his father:
"TOMORROW, on that day
I shall
enter upon the Roads of my grandmother and my elder brother
for I am a being of another kind."
That's what he told his
grandfather, he told the girl's grandfather.
    •

"Very well, on tomorrow's day
you must
enter upon the Road of your grandmother.
I had guessed
that you were not a being of the Daylight kind.
The Daylight beings
live around here
and the Raw beings cannot enter upon their Roads
to live in the SAME PLACE with them.
You are THAT OTHER KIND OF BEING
and it is because of your thoughts
that we now have so many provisions
to live by," he told him.
(*gently*) "Tomorrow
I shall
enter upon the Roads of my grandmother, my elder brother."
That's what he told his father, who
told the girl, "Daughter." "What is it?" "Get my bundle of feathers."

She got her grandfather's bundle of feathers
and he cut some sticks.
.

He cut eight sticks
(*softly*) and feathered them. When he'd made them, finished them
they passed the night. The night passed
and on the next day
just as the sun came up
and they had eaten
the little Protector spoke:
"Well, I'm going now.
I shall
enter upon the Roads of my grandmother
and my elder brother.
I shall
enter upon their Roads," he said. His
wife said, "I'LL GO ALONG WITH YOU," so she said. "Indeed?
If you went along it wouldn't turn out well
for I am another kind of being.
The way I
was a husband to you:
THAT'S what
you must think about, you must find someone who will provide for
        you as I did:
you must keep that in mind.
Because of my thoughts
you now have
the flesh
of the Raw People.
This will be ever present because of my thoughts
as you live."
THAT'S WHAT HE TOLD THE GIRL. When he'd told her, the girl
        asked him
FOUR TIMES
and still he refused. (*sadly*) "Well then
well then, go by yourself."
That's what she said. Then her
father, grandfather
told her: "Daughter
don't think of following him, don't speak of it, for he
is truly

He cut eight sticks and feathered them: Andrew Peynetsa feathering willow sticks for his family's monthly offerings.

of a different kind," he said.

Then he told them his name:

"I AM THE PROTECTOR," he told them.

His wife asked him, "WHAT IS THE PROTECTOR?" she said.

"Well, I am the Protector

and my other name is MA'ASEWI," he said.

And her father spoke: "Daughter, because of him there is a———ll
    the EARTH.

YOU MUSTN'T ASK ANY QUESTIONS. It is good

•

that he should return

to his own land," so he told her. He took the sticks he'd cut

the bundle of offering sticks, and

gave it

to his child, the Protector.

By his word he gave it.

Her grandfather spoke a prayer to the Protector

(*softly*) while the Protector stood there and answered. The prayer
    said that

there would be Waters on the earth forever, that ALL OVER

the wide earth

the Raw People would enter the house upon the Pollenway forever

that by means of their flesh, their skins, by their

EVER presence we would live: these were the words he spoke,
    while

the little Protector answered, "Just so, in truth."

When he had finished his words

the Protector stepped forward:

"My father

my child, may you live happily," he said. "By all means may it be the
    same with you, may you be happy."

WHEN THIS WAS DONE THE PROTECTOR LEFT.

WHEN THE PROTECTOR LEFT he went toward the place where
    he'd killed the Old Lady, he went that way.

ON HE WENT until he came to the place where he'd saved the girl.
    There

the Protector

skinned that—

the Protector skinned the Old Lady Granduncle

then he sewed her skin up like a sack with yucca. He got some
    yucca fiber and sewed until it was done and

when it was sewn he made it stand up.

When he'd made it stand up: "Ah, this should work." And there
he put it on his back. Having put it on his back
he climbed up Corn Mountain, up past
the Place Where Rainbows Are Kept, with this thing on his back.
    When he reached the top he made this
Old Lady stand up, (*softly*) he tried it there
he tried it
and it was working. When it was working
HE STARTED OFF, and when he'd gone a way the Protector began
    to call out (*as if from a distance, very high*):
"Grandmaaaaaaaaaaaaaaaaaaaaaaaaa $_{\text{come}}$ help $_{\text{me,}}$ some $_{\text{one}}$

    is ^{cha} $_{\text{sing}}$ meeeeeeeeeeeeeeeeeeeeeeeee ^{e} $_{\text{e.}}$"

His grandmother was making porridge.
AFTER A MOMENT HE CALLED AGAIN and his grandmother
    heard him.

•

When she looked outside he called again:
"Grandma $_{\text{come}}$ help $_{\text{me,}}$ some $_{\text{one}}$ is ^{cha} $_{\text{sing}}$ meeeeeeeeeeeeee ^{e} $_{\text{e,}}$" he

    said.
"Dearie me! grandson, you big fool," she said.
Then she
TOOK HER STIRRING STICKS, and she painted the left side of her
    face with ashes and the other side with soot
and then his grandmother ran outside. He was getting closer
and he'd tied up that
dead Old Lady
so it LOOKED LIKE SHE WAS RUNNING AFTER HIM.
He was fooling his grandmother.
His grandmother came down and (*rasping*) killed her, killed her.
"Come on, DON'T KILL THE POOR THING, SHE'S BEEN DEAD A
    LONG TIME," he said. "DEARIE ME! GRANDSON, YOU BIG
    FOOL."
THAT'S WHAT SHE SAID, AND THEY WENT ON UP.
They went on up to the house and passed the night. They passed
    the night
o———n they went by, four of them, a third, and on the fourth, on
    that night
their grandmother spoke to them:
(*seriously*) "If we continue to live together here, it won't turn out well
    for US.

Tomorrow, on that day, we
shall go
to the separate places which will be our shrines.
You, the ELDER BROTHER
will go to Hanging Wool.
You, the younger brother, will go to Twin
Mountains
and I WILL GO over there to the Middle Place
to the north side of it.
There, at the solstice
the Yellow One plants his feathers."
So it was that their grandmother told them where they would live
     forever.
"So it will be that whenever someone from the Middle Place wants
     to bear a child
I will not be far away and she can enter upon my Road
there.
That will be my shrine," so she told
her two grandsons.
They PASSED THE NIGHT
and on the following day
just as
the sun came up
they went to their separate shrines. This was lived long ago.
     Enou————gh, the word is short.
(*narrator and audience rise and stretch their arms above their heads as the*
    word "enough" is spoken)

NOTES TO THE STORY

Yellow House is a ruin about eight miles east of Zuni, New Mexico; it was abandoned at least five centuries ago.

Stars-in-a-Row is Orion's belt, which sets in the west after midnight in midwinter.

The fire drill is a pointed stick rotated rapidly between the hands, held vertically while the pointed end is inserted in a conical socket on a small plank. The socket is near enough to the edge of the plank's upper surface to have a break in its wall; thus the socket is open not only from the top but from the side. The sparks, actually red-hot specks of wood, fall from the side of the plank while the drill is rotated.

Raw People are all the living beings who do not depend on cooked food, including, in this story, the rabbits, the Sun Father, the Old Lady Granduncle, the Protectors, and the deer. Human beings, on the other hand, are Cooked or Ripe People; their life is the Daylight given them by the Sun Father.

Prayer meal or holy meal is a mixture of cornmeal with crushed turquoise, coral, and shell. The Waters of the Raw People consist of all forms of precipitation and of their own bodily fluids; they bring fecundity. Their Seeds are their powers of fecundity. Their Pollenways are the courses of their lives, marked out by pollen which is again their fecundity.

The hoarse voice of the little Protector is adolescent and flirtatious. In the homely state in which he normally appears, he is dirty and has messy hair full of lice.

The Priest of the Bow is a warrior and the town crier. The Priests of the Daylight are forbidden to kill anything and spend much of their time on religious retreats.

Offering sticks are feathered sticks given as personal sacrifices to Raw People; the maker brings the sticks to life with his own breath while he prays over them, and the recipient takes the life from the sticks when he takes the words of the prayer.

The Middle Place is the village of Zuni itself; Hanging Wool is southeast of there and Twin Mountains is northwest. The Yellow One is a warrior kachina whose impersonator sacrifices feathered sticks at the shrine where the Grandmother Protector, a patron of childbirth, now dwells.

---3---

Learning to Listen: Oral History
as Poetry

Introduction

Beyond the question of how to score oral performances lies the further question of how to talk *about* such performances. Might it not be that such talk, when published, should *itself* escape the prose format, arguing its case not only in its words and sentences but also in its graphic design? David Antin and myself, at a time when he had begun publishing the talks that were later gathered in *Talking at the Boundaries* and I had begun publishing scripts of Zuni stories, made a pact that we would never again allow our own words—even our critical discourse—to be published in a prose format. Neither of us kept the pact for much more than a year—it would have left me, at least, with very few places to publish—but it did prompt me to a couple of experiments, one of which is excerpted in the prologue and the other of which follows below. Ever since then, even when using a prose format, I have raised editorial eyebrows with the strategic use of italics

First published in *Envelopes of Sound: Six Practitioners Discuss the Method, Theory, and Practice of Oral History and Oral Testimony*, ed. Ronald J. Grele (Chicago: Precedent, 1975), pp. 106–25. © 1975 by Precedent Pub., Inc. Reprinted by permission.

and exclamation points (more than handbooks would allow), predications that do not make sentences (but are nonetheless followed by periods), the first and second persons, contractions, and occasional notations of tone of voice or gesture.

Shortly after I had made my pact with Antin, Ronald J. Grele asked me to join a session on oral history he was organizing for the 1973 meetings of the Organization of American Historians. I decided to compose my remarks on a tape-recorder, allowing myself the luxury of going back a line or two to refresh my memory or to rephrase something, but otherwise moving only forward. What I had in front of me as I did this were slips of paper bearing the scripts of selected examples of Zuni oral delivery, arranged in the order in which I planned to quote them; my commentary, on the other hand, was developed entirely orally. When the talk was completed I transcribed it in the format used below. Next I read it aloud, being careful not to rush my delivery beyond that of the orally composed passages, and timed it. I then eliminated some lines (rather than speeding up my delivery) so that the talk would exactly fit the time allotted to me. In this procedure I departed from the common practice of media tape editors, who frequently destroy the proper timing of speech by shortening the silences without making proportionate cuts in the words; in effect, they make people sound as though they were rushing through a classroom recitation (or reading from a prompter) rather than talking on their feet to a live person who might care what they say.

On seeing the size of my script, the person chosen to chair Grele's session immediately warned me not to go beyond my allotted time. In fact I had even made allowances for a few asides—"and the IDEAS of history just spoken of by Mr. Grele [pronounced *grayly*]" being one of them—and, by Mr. Grele's watch, I finished in twenty seconds under the scheduled time. The hardest thing to learn when reading from a script is to hold back the tempo.

When Dell Hymes read this talk he wondered whether my decision to present both the quoted Zuni passages and my own remarks in the same format might indicate an ethnocentric assumption that the Zunis and myself "are the same when it comes to basic form," and whether my format might not be so much a "discovery" (a word I have never applied to it) as a "Western homogenizer." I responded that "if basic form means that when one speaks one must pause and will sometimes speak louder and sometimes softer, then yes, the Zunis and I are the same." If there are differences between Zunis and, say, Anglo-Americans in matters of speech, there will be a greater variety of evidence for those differences in performable scripts than in run-on prose. There *is* a problem with ethnic boundaries in the talk, but not the one Dell supposes: I have learned a great deal about how to speak in public from Andrew Peynetsa, the Zuni who is most quoted there. There might be something Zuni about my English.

And now, dear reader, try to transport yourself to a meeting room in the Palmer House in Chicago and imagine yourself speaking to a crowd of historians, nearly all of them closely cropped and necktied.

The Talk

POETRY is oral HISTORY
and oral HISTORY
is POETRY.
•

FIRST of all, historical information
and the IDEAS of history just spoken of by Mr. Grele[1]
are found not only in
the relatively casual
conversational narratives of the interview situation
but also in forms of oral discourse which are traditionally classified
as POETRY—
songs and chants, for example.
SECOND
conversational narratives THEMSELVES
traditionally classified as PROSE
turn out, when listened to CLOSELY
to have poetical qualities of their OWN.
•

Here are two texts from the Zuni Indians of New Mexico
which demonstrate the FIRST point.
On the surface both of these examples
would appear to contain nothing of historical value.
The first example is the text of a song first performed by
masked kachina dancers just this past summer.
It goes like this:
•

"Rejoice! holy bundles, sacred bundles, because of your wise
    thoughts
there in the east your Moon Mother spoke, gave her word

---

1. In a paper given in the same session with this talk, Ronald J. Grele pointed out that oral historical documents reveal not only historical data but also historical ideology. See his *Envelopes of Sound*, pp. 137–39.

when we went over there with the dragonfly, entered upon her
    road.
Rejoice! you will be granted many blessings, flowing silt,"
the two stars are saying this to all the sacred bundles here.[2]
   •

At one level this text is typical of Zuni rain songs.
The songs mention silt
because in desert country one of the main signs of
good recent rains is the presence of
fresh silt deposits all over the landscape.
The sacred bundles mentioned are the very powerful fetishes in the
    keeping of Zuni priests.
On another level the song is an ALLEGORY:
the sacred bundles
are HOUSTON CONTROL
the dragonfly is a ROCKETSHIP
the silt is the alluvial deposits recently hypothesized for the moon's
    surface
and the two stars, who were reporting the silt to the sacred bundles
are the ASTRONAUTS.
   •

At another level the song is saying that the Zunis have ALWAYS had
    a way to the Moon Mother
through the
sacred bundles and the priestly prayers that go with them
and that the idea of
traveling to the moon is not
really something entirely NEW to them.
It's simply that the Zuni priests are capable of making SPIRITUAL
    journeys to the moon
rather than MECHANICAL ones.
The song is an attempt by them to come to terms
with an historical event
and at the same time reassert
tradition.
I would suggest that oral historians working in the larger American
    society might find similarly important clues
to the meaning events have for people
in contemporary song texts.
   •

2. Translated from a recording made in the field by Dennis and Barbara Tedlock,
1972, XXII.

Now this next example comes from the Zuni story of
the creation.
It belongs to a genre that
we, looking on from the outside
would unquestionably label as myth
partly simply because the events described in it seem implausible
     to us.
Some of the lines, as you will hear
are in chant form.
The Zuni priests have just asked the Ahayuuta
the twin war gods
to look for the middle of the earth:
"Very well indeed.
I'm GOING," the twins said.
They came this way until they CAME TO ZUNI.
When they came here to the present village, they summoned the
     water-strider.
WHEN THEY SUM_{MONED HIM}

he entered upon their roads.
There they spoke to him: "NOW
this very day
we have summoned you here.

•

You
must bend over here.
YOU MUST STRETCH OUT YOUR ARMS AND LEGS.
BY THE POSI_{TION}

_{OF} YOUR HEART
The Middle Place will then become known."
That's what they said. "Indeed.
Is this your reason for summoning me?"
"Yes, this is why we have summoned you.
Now then, stretch yourself OUT.
By the position of your heart
_{IT} WILL BE KNOWN
WHERE THE MIDDLE PLACE IS," that's what
the Ahayuuta told him.
"Very well."
Bending over toward the east
he stretched out, (*softly*) stretched out all his legs.

When they were ALL OUT FLAT
    WHEN THE AR_{MS}

LE_{GS}
stretched
A——LL _AROUND TO THE O_{CEANS}
his heart
rested

at the ^{site} named the ^{MID}DLE PLACE.
•

They stood there:
"Very well, here is the middle
here is the middle of the EARTH."[3]
•

The water-strider is that insect (*hold out hand with fingers spread but bent downward*) that floats on the surface of ponds.
On the face of it this passage would seem to be describing a
water-strider SO gigantic
that its legs
can span an entire continent.
This is far into the realm of what we ourselves would call imaginary or mythic
but it is in fact a description of an actual experience.
Whenever the Zuni priests have something important to divine
they go into retreat to seek a vision.
In this case they are guided in that vision by the Ahayuuta
and one of them impersonates a water-strider by stretching out his arms (*stretch arms out horizontally to the sides*)
in the four directions, two at a time.
When the priest does this he IS the water-strider and his arms DO reach all the way to the oceans:
that is his experience.[4]
It is simply that the narrator does not specify which events are visionary ones.
•

Now the point that texts like this
rain song
and this section of a creation story

3. Dennis Tedlock, *Finding the Center*, pp. 278–80. A translation.
4. See Ruth L. Bunzel's version of this same episode in her "Zuni Origin Myths," pp. 601–2; for a discussion of Zuni divination, see Dennis Tedlock, "Zuni Religion and World View," p. 506.

can refer to historical events
or ideas of history is not new to
Professor Vansina and other oral historians
who have worked in nonliterate societies.[5]
But what I would suggest HERE is that
oral historians working in literate societies should also pay attention
to such texts.
People do not reveal their ideas of history only when they are
conversing with an interviewer.
It's hard to imagine an oral history of the youth of the sixties, for
example
without some reference to their songs
and to the wild stories that went around then.

•

Clearly
highly metaphorical or poetical speech events
can be
a source of history.
This brings me to my other major point which is that the
relatively casual
conversational narratives
which are the more ORDINARY business of the oral historian
are THEMSELVES highly poetical
and cannot be properly understood from prose transcripts.
The MEANING of SPOKEN narrative
is not only carried by the sheer words as transcribed by alphabetic
writing
but by the placement of SILENCES
by TONES of VOICE
by whispers and SHOUTS.
In ancient Greece
written narratives
were still composed with oral delivery in mind.
Herodotus
for example
gave public recitations of his Histories
among other places at the Olympic Games.[6]
Right up through the Middle Ages written narratives
still retained their oral form, they were full of repetitions
formulaic phrases, the things that characterize oral performance.[7]

5. Jan Vansina, *Oral Tradition: A Study in Historical Methodology*, pp. 143–54.
6. Ruth Crosby, "Oral Delivery in the Middle Ages," p. 88.
7. Ibid., pp. 102–8.

The punctuation and spacing that were used then came
much closer to representing actual
features of oral delivery than does the punctuation we use today[8]
and the manuscripts were accompanied by a tradition
of oral performance
carried on by professionals
who knew how to make the words SOUND right.
And not only professional performers but
other literate individuals
always read aloud
even in private.
The only recorded exception in all the time before the Renaissance
was St. Ambrose.
His ability to read silently greatly disturbed St. Augustine
who had never seen anyone one else do it[9]
but even St. Ambrose probably moved his lips, at least.

•

It was not until the Renaissance that there began to develop the
    kind of prose narrative we know today[10]
the kind that is
read silently and has lost many of its oral features.
Today's prose is no longer in the care of professional performers
    who know
how to turn it back into the oral
nor is it accompanied by performance notations
and so it is an EXTREMELY poor medium for the transcription of
    tape-recorded discourse
EVEN the most ordinary conversation.

•

We must question whether HUNDREDS of REELS of oral history
    TAPE
ought to be converted into THOUSANDS of PAGES of PROSE
    typescript
after which the tapes are all too often ERASED.
To use a VISUAL analogy, such a procedure is as absurd
as preferring to
make pencil sketches from photographs of historical events
and then destroy the photographs.

8. Robert D. Stevick, "Scribal Notation of Prosodic Features in *The Parker Chronicle*, Anno 894 [893]."
   9. I would like to thank Sizzo de Rachewiltz for pointing this out to me. Augustine reports this incident in his *Confessions*, Book VI.
   10. Charles Sears Baldwin, *Renaissance Literary Theory and Practice*, p. 14.

Nobody, whether in a
literate society or not SPEAKS in PROSE
unless he is
unless perhaps he is
reading aloud
from WRITTEN prose
and in the flattest possible voice.
The WORST thing about written prose is that there is no SILENCE
    in it.

•

•

Even in an extended well-rehearsed discourse
the speaker of any language may spend forty to fifty percent of his
    time being silent.[11]
The punctuation we use today is not an accurate guide to these
    silences
though it is true that
people reading aloud usually stop at each period.
But in oral discourse a person may go right on from one sentence to
    another without pausing, or else he may pause in a place
where there would ordinarily be no punctuation in writing.
Here is an example of pausing from a Zuni narrative:

•

"You'll get to the dance in plenty of time," that's what
her children told her. "Then that's the way it will be," she said, and
    she left. It was getting SO hot.[12]

•

In the second of those two lines there were two complete sentences
and a part of a third sentence, all delivered without a pause.
In this next passage there are eight different pauses
and no fewer than five of them occur where there would be no
punctuation
in a written version:

•

They brought him back, and when they
tried to unmask him
the mask
was stuck

11. For a discussion of pausing, see Frieda Goldman-Eisler, "Continuity of Speech Utterance: Its Determinants and Its Significance," and "The Distribution of Pause Durations in Speech." For the psychological meaning of pauses and other delivery features, see G. F. Mahl, "Exploring Emotional States by Content Analysis," and R. E. Pittenger et al., *The First Five Minutes*.

12. Tedlock, *Finding the Center*, p. 71. A translation.

to his face.
He was changing over.
•

When they unmasked the young man, some of his
flesh peeled off.[13]
•

Sometimes pauses
reveal great hesitation and doubt on the part of the speaker
as in this passage:
•

Well
there were about
(*softly*) a hundred and
hundred annnnn
(*normal*) hundred and six Zunis
signed up for it.[14]
•

But frequent pauses like these
don't always indicate hesitation, sometimes
pauses
are used
•

to create suspense
or to set off a series of elements that are in parallel construction
as in this next passage.
This passage
also illustrates the use of tone of voice.
The speaker is telling of a time when
B.I.A. officers
had to capture Zuni children in order to get them in school:
•

And I didn't see the POLICEMAN that came around.
Finally he came up behind me—
(*low and gravelly*) he caught me and dragged me down to the school.
•

Then in the NOONTIME
I came home
as a BLUEbird:
had a blue shirt on
corduroy pants on

13. Ibid., p. 220. A translation.
14. Dennis and Barbara Tedlock, field tapes, 1971, A.

corduroy cap on:
a new boy.[15]
•

Besides pausing prose also fails to convey the way in which
    speakers may range all the way from a whisper
up to a shout.
We have italics and exclamation points of course
but we have been taught and taught and taught that any but the
    most sparing use of such devices
is unbecoming to written composition.
And we have no device at all that is suitable for
marking an especially quiet voice.
Here is a passage in which a speaker alternates between a normal
    speaking voice and a near whisper:
•

(*softly*) His wife
was fixing her lover's hair.
(*louder*) He found out.
(*softly again*) He found out.
(*louder*) The young man got angry.[16]
•

Notice that the speaker repeats "He found out" twice
in terms of alphabetic writing that is
but when we restore the changes in amplitude we discover
that in fact he does not say the same thing twice in the same WAY.
•

In this next passage
the speaker alternates between
a normal voice and something approaching a shout.
In the realm of tone of voice
he makes use in a couple of places of a sharpening or
tensing of the voice
and in one line he uses
a gentle or kind tone, although as you will hear in context this turns
    out to be ironic.
He is talking about the head of the Zuni tribal government:
•

Look, HOW MANY TRIPS HAS THE GOVERNOR MADE TO
    WASHINGTON?

He's got a GOOD
                NAME

15. Ibid.
16. Tedlock, *Finding the Center*, p. 36. A translation.

(*sharply*) on ACCOUNT OF
these B.I.A. guys like John Gray
and John Taylor
(*kindly*) he's got a good RECORD, he's made a good EFFORT
in WASHINGTON
but what about his people?
HIS PEOPLE DON'T KNOW ANYTHING.
WHEN HE SITS IN HIS OFFICE LIKE WE ARE IN HERE
we don't know what's going on over there
right on the other side of the creek in the (*sharply*) Zuni village.[17]
•

In this next example a speaker makes use of stress
hard stress on individual words rather than making entire lines
    loud.
He also makes use in a couple of lines here of a staccato delivery
where the stresses on words are evenly spaced
to give a constant beat:
•

That was the HARDEST job because
up there in Kansas
the weather is too HOT
even around
nine o'clock, ten, twelve o'clock
bo———y that's hot.
(*staccato*) The héat cómes úp to yóur FACE
and the héat cómes ón yóur BACK—
(*throaty*) gosh!
And you're pressing on
on the hot ground with your BARE HAND
your KNEES—
(*fading*) we almost gave up on it.[18]
•

Now in this next case, patterns of amplitude, including a marked
    falling off of the voice in many lines
combine
with pausing
with tone of voice
and a general softness of articulation
to give the entire episode a strong
sustained emotional flavor.
The passage concerns a time

17. Field tapes, 1971, C.
18. Ibid., A.

in the 1880s when
the U.S. Army was sent to Zuni to prevent the execution of a man
    accused of witchcraft.
They brought cannons with them and camped
on the opposite side of the river from the village
facing it.
It was the winter solstice, a time when the
medicine societies were in retreat to say prayers and meditate:
•

(*with a sad tone throughout*)
Because a person's life was being threatened
•

the soldiers came.
The villagers were not happy, (*falling off*) because the village might
    be destroyed.
The medicine societies were in retreat.
Their food was brought to them, but "Yes, I'll eat," (*softly*) that's not
    what the society members were thinking
(*falling off*) because the village might be destroyed.
They were not happy.
This is the way it w a s

with the societies in retreat.
Now in OUR society
the one who was our
father
was a small boy.
When the food was brought (*falling off*) no one ate.
(*gently, with a boy's voice*) "Let me eat—
I'll eat so I'll be good and full when I die."
That's what
(*falling off*) the one who was our
father said.
A small boy doesn't understand
so that's the way he talked
(*louder*) while he sat there eating.[19]
•

So far we've been talking about words and the way words are
    delivered
but the sounds in an oral performance include some
which are not

19. Dennis Tedlock, field tapes, 1965, 8. A translation.

verbal
as in this next passage
which speaks of a long famine:
•

After four years
•

(*sighing*) there was really
nothing.[20]
•

Now this next passage needs a cigarette—
(*while taking and lighting a cigarette*) a good performer can use a
    cigarette in a way that effectively punctuates his pauses
and can add to the suspense and mystery of a passage.
This is a story about a Zuni named Pelhna, the strongest Zuni who
    ever lived, who was famed for (*puffing on cigarette*)
robbing and killing white men.
Here a Mexican is going to Gallup
to sell his cows (*puffing*)
and Pelhna is thinking about ambushing him on his way back:
•

They drove the cows to Gallup
they passed through Zuni.
They went to that shortcut
where
Whitewater is, you know. (*a double puff*)
•

Well he saw them driving the cows through there so (*double puff*)
•

he decided he wanted to CHECK on them
so
two days after the
cows passed
he went NORTH (*double puff*)
•

on that ROAD
where he could meet that Mexican again. Probably when he sold his
    cows, why he might come around THIS way.
Well
before Old Man Pelhna got to Whitewater he decided not to go too
    far
that's outside the reservation so (*double puff*)
•

20. Tedlock, *Finding the Center*, p. 38. A translation.

he came back.
And he waited right where this (*single puff*)
Vanderwagen's ranch is right now
and that's the closest and narrowest SPOT there.[21]
•
The cigarette is something like an instrumental accompaniment in
    that episode.
Here is another example of instrumentation:
•
HE'S NOT LOOKING OUTSIDE.
HE TELLS THE PEOPLE TO GO AHEAD AND WORK IT OUT but
    (*rapping table at each accent*) hé's ríght insíde hís óffice.[22]
•
And then of course some of the motions made by a speaker are
    direct illustrations of what he is saying.
Here are a couple of passages in which gesture is in fact ESSENTIAL
    to the understanding of the
exact meaning.
First:
•
They brought a bowl
about so (*indicates a one-foot diameter with hands*), not a big bowl, and
    put the flour in there.[23]
•
And here is the other example:
•
(*softly*) He hid and
peeped (*louder*) over
the little hill:
one guy's cooking and two guys are talking to each other you know.

FIRST HE AIMED IT	(*closes left eye and holds up both*
and decided	*forefingers, some distance apart, out*
how he could	*in front of the right eye, at arm's*
kill	*length, shifting them back and forth until,*
two	*on the word "two," both fingers are in a*
one shot.	*line with the right eye*)[24]

•
Sometimes

---

21. Field tapes, 1965, 5.
22. Field tapes, 1971, C.
23. Dennis Tedlock, "When the Old Timers Went Deer Hunting," p. 81.
24. Field tapes, 1965, 5.

a narrator makes use of the immediate circumstances in which he's
    performing:
    •

I know one man named Kaskala, he used to live down below
where that Chauncey's wall is (*points out the window, down to the*
    bottom of the hill, to the southwest, in Upper Nutria, New Mexico).
Well back of it there used to be houses around there.[25]
    •

There was a use of place. A narrator may also make use of the
    immediate time, time of day or time of year:
    •

And we got to Zuni about this time I think.
Oxen go slow, you know.[26]
    •

Here the transcript must be annotated
to show that the narration took place
around the time it was getting dark.
    •

In its main features the system of notation
I've used here
in the passages recited here is a very simple one.
I use a line change as in poetry for a short pause
a double space, that is a strophe break
for longer pauses
capitals
for words or lines that are loud
and parenthesized italics, as in a play
for softness and a good many other features
such as voice qualities and gestures.
This system of notation catches I think at least the main
outlines of specifically oral features
and displays them graphically
and at a glance, without resort to
a complicated inventory of technical symbols
such as is used by researchers in paralinguistics.[27]
Professor Vansina has rightly said
that one cannot properly understand a text
without understanding its form,[28] and I submit that the oral features

---

25. Tedlock, "When the Old Timers Went Deer Hunting," p. 79.
26. Field tapes, 1971, C.
27. See Pittenger et al., *The First Five Minutes*, and George L. Trager, "Para-language."
28. Vansina, *Oral Tradition*, p. 65.

I've been talking about are part and parcel of that form.
Once the importance of these features is accepted
then
it is clear
that tape-recordings are infinitely preferable
to texts taken down in dictation.
Dictation hopelessly distorts delivery
especially in the case of a narrative that does not have fixed
    wording.
The transcription of tapes
should
if at all possible be done by the interviewer
and it should be done while the interview is
still fresh in his mind
so that he can provide such details as might not be clear from the
    tape alone
such as gestures.
Far from being a mere clerical task
the act of transcription is ITSELF of analytical value
when it is pursued with attention to oral qualities.
There is no better way to find out just exactly what it is that you've
    got on that tape.
The finished transcription shows at a glance
the structure
of the narrative
and its delivery
and even provides a much quicker guide to its content
than densely packed prose.
No visual transcription can of course be complete
so it is still absolutely essential that the original tape be saved.
The transcript provides a ready index to the tape in case there is
    need to refer back to it.

•

If anthropologists, folklorists, linguists, and oral historians
are interested in the full meaning
of the spoken word
then they must stop treating oral narratives
as if they were reading prose
when in fact they are listening to dramatic poetry.

Translating Ancient Words:
From Paleography to the Tape-Recorder

As a mythographer who has learned to regard oral narrative as a performing art rather than a direct analog of literary narrative, I have aimed my work in transcription and translation at the production of a performable and breathable script or score, rather than milling out scanned verse or justified prose. This work started with tape-recordings of live performances of Zuni narratives, coming full circle with the scoring of tape-recordings of my own oral performance (in English) of the scores of the Zuni performances, as embedded in my talks before live audiences on the subject of oral narrative and related verbal arts. But there is another place or moment from which to begin the work of producing scores, and that is a conventional prose text based on a performance that took place generations or even centuries ago. This is the kind of work I have undertaken among the Quiché Maya of Guatemala, introducing contemporary Quiché speakers to an alphabetically written text from which most of them have been sepa-

The text of this chapter appears here for the first time. My completed translation of the Popol Vuh will be published by Simon and Schuster.

124

rated for more than four centuries, while at the same time listening to the stories and speeches they speak today. It has been a work of restoration, an attempt to hear the voices of the dead, but with the help of their living descendants.

Within their own social and cultural worlds, native North Americans of the post-Columbian era have seldom made much use of phonetic writing without the direct and continuing intervention of European missionaries and scientists. Some of the exceptions remind one of Lévi-Strauss's decidedly materialist view of the beginning of writing, as when the Giktsan keep notes on the gifts brought to a potlatch,[1] or when the Zuni hosts of the Sha'lako ceremony write a list of the major gifts they receive on paper plates nailed to the wall of their storeroom. But there is an ideological side to the picture: Wovoka transmitted the Ghost Dance doctrine by handwritten letters, George Sword wrote a comprehensive work on Oglala religion, and the Cherokee syllabary invented by Sequoyah was extensively used for the notation of prayers and charms.[2] Here and there, as among the Eskimo and Cree, writing systems introduced by missionaries have partially escaped their original purposes, but most native-language literacy projects, down to the present day, remain closely entangled with the proselytic purposes of Europeans, whether their missions be religious or—as in the case of the Rough Rock Demonstration School among the Navajo—avowedly secular.

In Mesoamerica the story has been a different one. There the advent of writing and of books did not await the arrival of Europeans, and it is now abundantly clear that Mayan writing, like Egyptian and Chinese, included (but was not limited to) a phonetic dimension.[3] All over Mesoamerica, Spanish missionaries introduced native-language literacy projects utilizing the roman alphabet, starting immediately after the conquest, but it was especially among the Mayan peoples, in both the lowlands of Yucatán and the highlands of Guatemala, that alphabetic writing was converted to the purposes of native priests and politicians whose purposes were independent of those of the Roman church. There was not a little justice in this, given the thousands of hieroglyphic books that had been burned by the early missionaries.

1. John W. Adams, *The Gitksan Potlatch*, pp. 75–76. For a Nambikwara adoption of writing for economic purposes, see Claude Lévi-Strauss, *Tristes Tropiques*, p. 289.
2. James Mooney, *The Ghost-Dance Religion*, pp. 22–23; "Sacred Formulas of the Cherokees." Raymond DeMallie called my attention to George Sword's work, which was written in the nineteenth century but is not yet in general circulation, except in mimeographs and photocopies that are much in demand on Sioux reservations.
3. David Humiston Kelley, *Deciphering the Maya Script*, chap. 9.

Only three full books in Mayan hieroglyphic writing are known today; they are made all the more exciting as clues to pre-Columbian culture because they appear to be copies of books that antedate the conquest by centuries.[4] There has been considerable progress in the reading of their mathematical and lexical contents, and the romance of hieroglyphic "decipherment," whether it affects these books or the inscriptions on funerary vessels or commemorative stone monuments, will continue to exert a powerful hold on the imaginations of Mayanists and their followers. But for Europeans and Euroamericans, there is an economy in the interpretability of native American texts, taking effect above the level of numbers and syllables and lexical items, that dictates a persistence of obscurity in proportion to the aboriginal "purity" of the text (even where the aboriginal "code" is deciphered), and an increase in clarity in proportion as an aboriginal author (whatever his code) addresses a text to an audience whose cultural horizon already includes Europeans. This clarity reaches its maximum when the text is produced in the context of an active dialogue with a European, so that it is interspersed with or accompanied by interpretive remarks or discussions addressed to that European. But for those who long for pure otherness, the situation is analogous to that described by Lévi-Strauss for the traveler.[5] The "earlier" one arrives in a distant world—early with respect to the Western presence—the less one will be able to describe it with any insight; the "later" one arrives, the more one will be overcome with nostalgia, itself a handicap in the description of the present world one has entered.

In the case of Mayan texts, the economy of interpretability is such that sixteenth-century alphabetic writings in Mayan languages will always remain richer sources for the description of Mayan worlds, even if they are worlds on whose horizons Europeans have already appeared, than the surviving hieroglyphic books, which speak of a world that was already receding into the past of the world whose inhabitants recopied these books one last time before the conquest. The alphabetic documents themselves vary in interpretability, but for reasons other than gross differences in temporal remoteness. Some, like the Chilam Balam or "Jaguar Priest" books of Yucatán and the Ahilabal 3ih or "Count of the Days" manuscripts from the Quiché of Guatemala, seem to be closely based on hieroglyphic originals;[6] these docu-

4. See J. Eric S. Thompson, *A Commentary on the Dresden Codex* (pp. 3–14), for a full discussion of Mayan hieroglyphic books.

5. Lévi-Strauss, *Tristes Tropiques*, p. 45.

6. For a Yucatecan book, see, e.g., Ralph L. Roys, *The Chilam Balam of Chumayel.* The unpublished Ahilabal 3ih manuscripts are Quiché divinatory calendars from the

ments are terse and highly esoteric, with many passages that are almost incomprehensible without an extensive effort at interpretation that goes far beyond an ability to gloss the sheer words—even where the subject matter is the affairs of the postconquest world. Other documents, like the annals and the land and tribute titles of Guatemala, are relatively verbose and self-explanatory;[7] these books may be, in effect, transcriptions of what priests or scribes or court historians might have said before an audience, rather than direct transliterations of the hieroglyphic texts that served as the sources or authorities for their pronouncements.

The longest and richest of the surviving Guatemalan works is the Popol Vuh, or "Council Book," put into alphabetic form between 1554 and 1558 by a survivor of the ruling house of the Quiché kingdom, which fell to Hapsburg Spain in 1524.[8] The writer does not identify himself, but we at least know his patronym: Cauec. Like the major books of a number of other ancient civilizations, in both the Old and New Worlds, the Popol Vuh is an anthology. It begins with the beginning of the world and the deeds of the gods, then moves on through the migrations of the Quiché people and the formation of their kingdom, ending with dynastic roll calls whose final names (extending into the beginning of the Spanish period) help date the manuscript.

Despite the fact that the Popol Vuh is (in general) more transparent in its meanings than the Chilam Balam books, it is far from being adequately understood and cannot even be said to be completely glossed at the word-by-word level. It remained hidden from the Spanish for a century and a half before the Dominican friar Francisco Ximénez discovered it and made a copy and the first translation.[9] Although Ximénez drew upon a firsthand knowledge of Quiché language and culture, he was hampered not only by the temporal gap between his day and that of the manuscript but also by his position as a declared enemy of indigenous—or what he called "Satanic"—religious practices,[10] a stance that cut him off from those

---

eighteenth century; the originals are lost, but there are facsimiles in the Berendt collection of the main library at the University of Pennsylvania.

7. The most famous examples are *The Annals of the Cakchiquels*, translated by Adrián Recinos and Delia Goetz, and *Title of the Lords of Totonicapán*, translated by Dionisio José Chonay and Delia Goetz (published under one cover).

8. For a discussion of the dating of the Popol Vuh text, see Adrián Recinos, Delia Goetz, and Sylvanus G. Morley, trans., *Popol Vuh*, p. 23.

9. This manuscript is in the Newberry Library in Chicago and is the only surviving manuscript version of the text. The Guatemalan Ministry of Education has published a highly legible and generously proportioned facsimile (Francisco Ximénez, *Popol Vuh*).

10. Ximénez makes his views known in his prologue to the Newberry manu-

Quichés who might have been of greatest help in translating difficult passages.

Today there are half a million speakers of Quiché in Guatemala, and as one moves away from the center of the old Quiché kingdom, where the European impact has been the greatest—even today, there is an army base near the ruins of the ancient capital—one finds communities in which indigenous priests burn incense at mountain shrines and are barred from the Eucharist, and in which Roman priests make the same denunciations of Satanism that Ximénez made nearly three centuries ago. Even time is reckoned differently here: Alongside those events regulated by the familiar Gregorian calendar are others scheduled according to the interlocking 260- and 365-day cycles of the ancient Mayan calendar, with new solar years beginning on the same days that began them during the Classic period, more than a millennium ago.[11] It was in one of these communities, during the summer of 1975 and the whole of 1976, that I undertook a project in what might be called "ethnopaleography," seeking to clarify the language and culture of the Popol Vuh and even to reconstruct its sounds as they might have been heard in full oral delivery.

Broadly speaking, paleography is the study of ancient texts, and not just the transcription of those texts; I understand it to be a branch of philology, which is concerned with texts in general.[12] By *ethno-paleography*, I mean something analogous to ethnoarchaeology, in which ethnographic research is undertaken with the purpose of elucidating the archaeological record. I do not mean that more familiar undertaking in which paleographers (or archaeologists) consult published ethnographic sources after the fact. Ordinary ethnography in Mesoamerica often has its ethnopaleographic moments, as when Quiché consultants are asked, "Does the name Zipacna mean anything to you?" or "Do you know any stories in which someone claims to be a maker of mountains?" or "Does the name Hunahpu have any translation?" In these moments, the ethnographer uses the knowledge of an ancient text as an eliciting device, but the focus is on ethnography and lexicography rather than ethnopaleography. In systematic ethnopaleographic research, complete sentences and larger stretches of ancient texts (and not just single words or items of content) would be directly presented to consultants for interpretation.

---

script; see Chapter 11, below, for a further discussion of his interpretation of the Popol Vuh.

11. See Barbara Tedlock, *Time and the Highland Maya* (chaps. 4 and 5), for the fullest discussion of these matters.

12. For a general discussion of philology in its Americanist applications, see Ives Goddard, "Philological Approaches to the Study of North American Indian Languages."

This might be done by reading passages aloud, but the ideal consultant would be one who could read the document itself. When it comes to reconstructing oral performance, the ethnographer is likely to have to depart from the consultant's direct reading of the text, resorting to the examination of tape-recordings of contemporary performances that are analogous to ancient ones. These might well be stories or speeches that came to the mind of the consultant during the work with the document. The potential benefits of the ethnopaleographic process, taken as a whole, range from the phonetic and lexical levels on up to those of performance (oral interpretation) and hermeneutics (interpretation of meaning).

In some ways, ethnopaleography as I conceive it resembles the "anthropological philology" proposed and practiced by Dell Hymes, particularly in that moment where we see him working over Chinookan texts collected by early ethnographers with contemporary speakers of Chinookan.[13] But work in ethnopaleography attempts, in two different directions, to bridge a larger gap than the one explored by Hymes: at the far edge, such work starts from a text that is centuries rather than generations old, while at the near edge, it enlists the tape-recorder into its efforts to hear a voice in the solid and silent prose of that text.

A word of caution seems necessary here: An attempt to *hear* an old prose text is not the same as an attempt to break it into metrical or parallelistic verse, though considerations of verse may enter. The most extensive versification project to date has been that of Franz Rosenzweig and Martin Buber, who produced a German translation of the Hebrew Testament that takes into account the parallelism embedded in the Hebrew text.[14] Dell Hymes is the most recent Americanist to rework texts along the lines of parallel verse, comparing his own efforts with those of a sculptor working in stone.[15] The trouble with such projects is that they do not answer the question of how such verses might be delivered orally, even with regard to the simple issue of the alternation of sound and silence. An oral performance of "sculpted" texts with the pauses determined by parallel versification would be based on nothing firmer than the schoolroom habit of pausing between each line of a printed poem. That is why I have brought tape-recordings of contemporary Quiché oral performances into my

---

13. Dell Hymes, *"In Vain I Tried to Tell You,"* chaps. 1 and 3.
14. The publication of their work began in 1934 with *Die Fuenf Beucher der Weisung*, translated by Martin Buber and Franz Rosenzweig, and eventually encompassed the entire Hebrew Testament.
15. Hymes, *"In Vain I Tried to Tell You,"* p. 341.

consideration of an ancient Quiché text, even though its prose is far stonier, at least in terms of the total elapsed time since it was laid down, than that of the North American texts considered by Hymes. One result of my procedure, as can be seen even from a brief inspection of the Popol Vuh excerpt given at the end of this essay, is that the score bears little resemblance to printed verse that is measured out according to its horizontal stress or syllable counts, or according to its vertical line counts. Rather, it resembles the "projective verse" proposed and practiced by Charles Olson, a verse whose "measure," if that is the word for it, is the breath.[16]

A number of modern translators of the Popol Vuh have drawn upon a firsthand knowledge of Quiché language and culture, beginning with Brasseur and including Schultze Jena, Recinos, Villacorta, and Edmonson.[17] None of these translators gives an indication that he favored Quiché consultants with the hearing or reading of whole connected passages from the Popol Vuh text, but my own ethnopaleographic approach to that text was nevertheless preceded by other projects with a partially similar intent. The first of these was undertaken by none other than the ubiquitous J. P. Harrington. He is mainly known for his field research in North American languages, but in 1922 he worked through Brasseur's version of the Popol Vuh text with Cipriano Alvarado, a Quiché-speaker who had been brought to Charlottesville, Virginia, by William Gates. So great was Harrington's fixation on purely phonetic matters (characteristic with him) that his manuscript record of this project, though it includes a complete phonetic reinterpretation of the Popol Vuh (transcribed from Alvarado's word-by-word enunciations), offers only a few scattered English glosses (less than one per page!) that seem heavily dependent on Brasseur's French translation.[18] The only running translation in evidence, included as an appendix in Harrington's unpublished Quiché grammar, covers the opening section of the Popul Vuh.[19]

16. Charles Olson, *Selected Writings*, pp. 15–26.
17. Charles Etienne Brasseur de Bourbourg, *Popol Vuh: Le livre sacré et les mythes de l'antiquité américaine*. Leonhard S. Schultze Jena, *Popol Vuh: Das heilige Buch der Quiché-Indianer von Guatemala*. Adrián Recinos, *Popol Vuh: Las antiguas historias del Quiché*. José Antonio Villacorta Calderón, *Popol Vuh*. Munro S. Edmonson, *The Book of Counsel: The Popol Vuh of the Quiché Maya of Guatemala*.
18. Harrington's Quiché papers are in the National Anthropological Archives at the Smithsonian Institution; a copy (in his own hand) of his phoneticized Popol Vuh text may also be found in the special collections of the library at Brigham Young University.
19. The manuscript of Harrington's *Quiché Grammar* is in the National Anthropological Archives at the Smithsonian; it was prepared (in 1948) for publication as a Bulletin of the Bureau of American Ethnology but was shelved.

A project not unlike Harrington's was later undertaken by Dora M. de Burgess, a missionary at the Instituto Bíblico Quiché near Quezaltenango, who worked with a Quiché-speaking Protestant convert, Patricio Xec, to produce a modernized text and a new Spanish translation for the entire Popol Vuh.[20] The published results illustrate the two main pitfalls of ethnopaleographic research: the underestimation of linguistic and cultural change, leading to commonsense solutions based on current usage; and the problem of the depth of knowledge of traditional culture (and the language in which that knowledge is expressed) on the part of the native consultant. With respect to the work of Burgess and Xec, the first problem has been pointed out by Robert M. Carmack, who takes them to task for not paying more attention to ethnohistorical sources.[21] The second problem has been pointed out by Barbara Tedlock, who notes that Xec's distance from Quiché traditions leads to a translation of *zaqui coxol* (more accurately *zaki 4oxol*, to correct the Popol Vuh manuscript but retain its orthography) as "culebra coral."[22] Thus an anthropomorphic and primarily beneficent Quiché deity—one who is still impersonated in dances and still encountered in dreams and in dark forests or caves—is transformed into a poisonous reptile and a Christian symbol of evil.

More recently Adrián Chávez, a Quiché speaker from Quezaltenango, has published a version of the Popol Vuh arranged in four columns: a close paleographic reading of the manuscript; a rereading in what proves to be a mixture of modern Quiché with the original Quiché, using a modern orthography; a literal Spanish translation; and, finally, a "free" Spanish translation, leaving the manuscript's prose format intact.[23] In moving across these columns, Chávez has acted, in effect, as his own ethnopaleographer, but his work, like that of Burgess and Xec, has ethnohistorical flaws. Like many other translators, he reinterprets the first consonant of the manuscript's *4ucumatz* as *3*, shifting it from a glottalized velar to a glottalized uvular position, but instead of attending to the abundant ethnohistorical reasons for regarding this name as a compound of *3u3*, "quetzal," and *cumatz*, "serpent," he instead reads the first syllable as *3uu*, "cover," translating the name as a whole as *"ocultador de serpiente."*[24] In so doing, he severs one of the Popol Vuh pantheon's most obvious ties to the larger culture of pre-Columbian Mesoamerica. Again and again he

20. Dora M. de Burgess and Patricio Xec, *Popol Wuj.*
21. Robert M. Carmack, *Quichean Civilization*, p. 26n.
22. Barbara Tedlock, "El c'oxol: Un símbolo de la resistencia quiché a la conquista espiritual."
23. Adrián I. Chávez, *Pop Wuj.*
24. Ibid., pp. 1–1a.

softens or even removes the totemistic elements found in the proper names of the Popol Vuh; in the example just given, the god *3ucumatz* does not partake of serpent qualities but is rather an "obscurer" of serpents. In the case of the name *uucub caquix*, generally interpreted on the basis of colonial dictionaries as *uukub cakix*, "Seven Macaw," totemism gives way to the Bible when Chávez reads *uukub ka4ix*, "Nuestras Siete Vergüenzas,"[25] in effect turning the story of the defeat of Seven Macaw into a medieval morality play.

It was Carmack, in criticizing Edmonson's Popol Vuh as badly wanting "from an ethnological perspective," who first suggested in print that "what we need to do now is to talk with traditional Quiché priest-shamans (*chuchkajaw*) using the *PV* in order to gain more insight into the esoteric and up until now unseen cultural meanings of the ancient text."[26] This is precisely what I ended up doing in my own fieldwork, undertaken in a town that has had a reputation as a center for traditional Quiché religion ever since Pedro de Alvarado's Indian auxiliaries named it "Town of the Altars." But it was also my desire to find a Quiché-speaker, shaman or not, who could read the Popol Vuh text himself, although Edmonson had categorically stated that "with the exception of students of the Instituto Biblico Quiché, the modern Indians cannot read the Popol Vuh in Quiché."[27] Indeed, the first person to whom I showed the Popol Vuh text, an official of the town government who was of a highly secular bent and highly literate in Spanish, proved unable to "read" it, though not in the sense Edmonson had in mind. He accounted for the text's divergence from the Quiché language as he knew it spatially rather than temporally, declaring that it was written not in the Quiché language but in Cakchiquel!

Present on the occasion of this dismissal was a second man who held his counsel for the moment, Andrés Xiloj. He, too, had served in the town government (in a higher post), but he was less fluent in the ways of alphabetic writing and more fluent in matters of Quiché culture and ritual language. He was, in fact, the head priest-shaman for his patrilineage, a *chuchkahau* (to stay with Popol Vuh orthography) or "motherfather" with a knowledge of Quiché calendrics, divination, and dream interpretation. Diviners are semioticians by profession; they start from signs (*etal*), in this case signs that take forms other than those of spoken words, and try to arrive at a "reading," as we would say, or *ubixic*, "its-being-said" or "an announcement," as is said in Quiché. As the Popol Vuh makes clear, reading in the sense of liter-

25. Ibid., pp. 12–12a.
26. Carmack, review of *The Book of Counsel* by Munro S. Edmonson, p. 507.
27. Edmonson, *The Book of Counsel*, p. xv.

Quiché diviners like to have at least one book: Andrés Xiloj (*at right*) with two other diviners, outside the home of an incense-seller on the sacred mountain of Nima Sabal. Both of his companions are specialists at providing a chanted accompaniment at rites devoted to the earth deity; the book shown here is a Breviarum Romanum.

acy and "reading" in the sense of divination were closely linked among the Prehispanic Quiché. The reader of the "original book" (*nabe uuhil*) and "ancient writing" (*oher tzibam*)—that is to say, the lost hieroglyphic version of the Popol Vuh—is called *ilol*, "seer"; the book itself is referred to as an *ilbal*, "way of seeing" (see lines 20–27 in the passage translated below), and what was "seen" there was the past and the future.[28] In keeping with the Quiché link between literacy and divination, I have chosen to translate *ilol* as "reader"; this English word itself contains such a link, all the way from its Teutonic beginnings down to its contemporary range of use.

Present-day Quiché diviners do not make use of the Popol Vuh (whether alphabetic or hieroglyphic), but they do like to have at least

28. See "Word, Name, Epithet, Sign, and Book in Quiché Epistemology," Chapter 12 in this book, for more on this topic.

one book of a divinatory character in their possession. Most often this will be a current popular almanac (printed in Guatemala City), noting such things as saints' days but also showing the signs of the zodiac and making comments about the weather. The owners of such almanacs may jot down the Quiché names for some of the days (from the 260-day divinatory cycle) in the appropriate spaces; these will be days of important ceremonial obligations (such as 8 Queh) or else the days on which unusual dreams occurred, the purpose being to compare later dreams with similar content or occurring on days of the same name. Less often a diviner will possess a copy of *Oráculo novísimo o sea el libro de los destinos* (printed in Mexico City), an occult text whose title page claims it was copied from an Egyptian book owned by Napoleon. This work contains hundreds of prognostications, chosen through chance operations in which the Quiché diviner may or may not follow the printed instructions. The results are read out of the book in Spanish, but when their relevance to the problem at hand is not apparent, they may be interpreted in the same way as the results of traditional divination, through metaphor and sound play rather than literally.[29]

By this time it should be apparent why a Quiché diviner, given sufficient literacy, might be more than willing to take on the task of reading the Popol Vuh. When don Andrés, the diviner in question here, was given a chance to look at the Quiché text without the interference of his earlier companion, he produced a pair of spectacles and began reading aloud, word by word. He required only a few orthographic instructions; on the syntactic front, it was necessary to point out, for example, that *xch-* (a composite prefix no longer used in Quiché) is something like the future tense in Spanish. I offered glosses of archaic words when it was apparent he was not going to come up with anything from his own Quiché vocabulary; in time, of course, he readily recognized the more frequent archaic forms.

In describing don Andrés's readings of the Popol Vuh, it is hard to draw sharp lines between his contributions at the phonetic and lexical levels from those at a broader interpretive level. The Popol Vuh is full of lexical ambiguities even where it does not depart from modern usage, since *c-* (or *qu-*), which should have been used only for the unvoiced velar stop, is frequently pressed into service for the glottalized velar stop (properly *4*), the unvoiced uvular stop (properly *k*), and the

29. See Barbara Tedlock, "Sound Texture and Metaphor in Quiché Maya Ritual Language."

glottalized uvular stop (3). Since the Quiché language is replete with monosyllabic stems, this means that one word in the Popol Vuh text, when considered as an isolated lexical problem, may have as many as four different readings, all equally plausible if one's sole purpose were to establish a grammatically correct text.

Solving lexical ambiguities requires interpretive moves that may carry the reader to the neighboring words, to a broader recollection of what the passage has been about so far, and to a knowledge of language and culture that lies outside the text at hand. When don Andrés encountered *ucutunizaxic, ucalahobizaxic* (line 7 in the passage translated below), he read it not as *u3utunizaxic, u4alahobizaxic*, which would have meant something like, "its pulverization, its organization into a stack," but easily decided on *u4utunizaxic, u3alahobizaxic*, which means, "its demonstration, its clarification." Right on their faces the two words demand some kind of parallel interpretation, since they are identically affixed with *u-*, "its," and *-izaxic*, "being caused or made." But it wasn't simply that don Andrés decided that the meanings "demonstration" and "clarification" were in better parallel than pulverizing (the stem *3utun-* is used primarily in connection with chili powder) and stacking (*4ala-* is used primarily with firewood). Rather, he knew from the larger context of what he had already read that what was being talked about was neither chili nor firewood, but *oher tzih*, the "ancient word" announced in the opening line of the text. In Quiché usage one may demonstrate or clarify the ancient word, but one does not powder it or stack it.

In the above reading, as it happens, don Andrés merely confirmed a reading that is already generally agreed upon, having been arrived at through a process involving a critical comparison of Ximénez's original Spanish translation with colonial and modern dictionary entries, measured in turn against the sense of immediate context and of broader Quiché usage possessed by various later translators, with or without any contribution from a direct knowledge of spoken Quiché. What I wish to concentrate on here are those instances in which don Andrés consulted or cited a knowledge of Quiché practice that goes beyond what I could have already gleaned from the consultation of documents. I will start as close as possible to the lexical level, at which the movement from text to interpretation starts from one or a few words, and work toward movements that take place on a larger scale.

The passage at hand here fairly bristles with divine names and epithets, most of them absent from the vocabulary of modern Quiché narrative, liturgy, or theological discussion. But even here, at least when the names or epithets are relatively transparent in their etymologies, the ethnopaleographic approach has its rewards. The epithets *4,akol* (*tzacol* in the text) and *bitol* (line 9 and elsewhere) do not occur in the contemporary lexicon in just these forms; *4,ak-* and *bit-* were familiar to don Andrés, but he had never heard them with an *-ol* suffix. Yet he easily grasped the agentive sense given by this suffix; he remarked that *4,akal* would be better form in modern Quiché, but could not attest to a modern agentivized form parallel to *bitol*. Of *4,ak-* he commented, "This is to make or construct, like a building, a wall," whether of adobe brick or stone; *ah4,ak*, with an occupational prefix, denotes a mason. In interpreting *bit-* he said, "This *bitic* is to form, as when we were small and played with mud; we made forms, *kabitic* [we form it]." In the context of the passage, he saw *4,akol* as the deity who would amass the clay from which the earth would be made, and *bitol* as the one who would make shapes from it, like a person modeling a pot or a figurine. Just as *3utun-* and *4ala-* (discussed earlier) carry their chili and firewood with them, so *4,ak-* and *bit-* carry their clay, only this time the associations make a parallel fit, a fit that is confirmed in the text when these two deities do indeed take part in the formation of the earth. Knowing of the firm material associations of both words, an association that is underlined when they occur together, gives us fair warning that we are not dealing with creation *ex nihilo*, as it occurs in Western theology. The English translations I have chosen are "maker" (for *4,akol*), which in its common usage implies construction from preexistent materials (and can even be traced back to a Germanic root referring to mud-wall construction), and "modeler" (for *bitol*), which is even closer to its Quiché counterpart than "maker."

In the same list of names and epithets as *tzacol* (*4,akol*) and *bitol* are found *hunahpu uuch* and *hunahpu utiu* (line 10), in which *uuch* (better *uu4h*) and *utiu* are transparently "possum" and "coyote," respectively, but in which don Andrés perceived *hunahpu* as a proper name, one of the twenty day names belonging to the Prehispanic 260-day divinatory calendar. It can be etymologized as consisting of *hun*, "one," and *ah-*, the occupational prefix, with *pu* derived from *pub*, a classical Quiché term for "blowgun." But *hun* is so thoroughly embedded in the word that when the day name is combined with numbers to designate specific dates, whether in classical or modern Quiché, those dates include *hun hunahpu*, "One Hunahpu." Further, the Popol Vuh designates blowguns not with *pub* but with *ub*—and so, as it happens, does the contemporary Quiché speaker. In the face of these difficulties, Edmonson simply sets aside the problem of *hun* and translates *hunahpu* as "Hunter."[30] But my argument would be that the translation of proper names should stop at what is relatively transparent; to find a blowgun in *pu* and thus hunter in *ahpu* crosses a line that is not crossed in the translation of *tzacol* and *bitol*. I doubt that a Quiché speaker notices hunter in Hunahpu any more than an English speaker notices Thor in Thursday. When meanings are given to the Mayan day names by modern Quichés (and ancient Yucatecans), this is done not by etymologization but through sound-play.[31] Therefore I render *hunahpu uuch, hunahpu utiu* as "Hunahpu Possum, Hunahpu Coyote."

Further down the list come *ah raxa la3* and *ah raxa tzel*, "those of the blue-green plate" and "those of the blue-green bowl" (line 10). Don Andrés recognized *la3* (it should have been written *lak*) as "plate," but he did not know *tzel*, which, I then told him, is classical Quiché for "bowl." He immediately commented, "Then this must be the *ah awas, ah warabalha*"—that is, "master of the shrine" and "master of the foundation," titles referring to the head priest-shaman of a contemporary patrilineage (and titles which don Andrés himself holds for life). But in contemporary prayers, the *ah awas* talks about *lak* and *tasa* (*tasa* being Spanish for "cup") instead of *lak* and *tzel*. He can also be called *ah4hahbal lak, ah4hahbal tasa*, meaning "washer of the plate, washer of the cup," referring to the fact that he alone can reopen and clean the pottery-covered shrines of a lineage whose head has died, preparatory to the training and initiation of a successor.[32] There is further support for don Andrés's interpretation in the fact that the Popol Vuh passage under discussion directly links the keepers of the blue-green plate and bowl to the deities known as Xpiyacoc and Xmucane (line 12), who (like modern lineage priests) are diviners and whose grandchildren are the first characters in the Popol Vuh to venerate their deceased patrilineal predecessors.

Don Andrés had never heard the names given in the text as Xpiyacoc and Xmucane. Once it was clear to him from a passage beyond the present one that these two characters were diviners, he did venture etymologies, but only on request. The first of these names, he

---

30. Edmonson, *The Book of Counsel*, p. 4. In the case of the Zuni story of "The Girl and the Protector" (Chapter 2, above), I went even further than Edmonson in seeking translations for proper names, but in the present case I have drawn the lines differently.
31. Barbara Tedlock, "Sound Texture and Metaphor."
32. Barbara Tedlock, *Time and the Highland Maya*, chap. 3.

suggested, might contain the verb *yequic* (*yaquic* in neighboring dialects), used when a diviner asks of a patient, *la cayequic*, "Can he/she be lifted up [put in order]?" But that leaves *xpi-* unaccounted for, and *-oc* (which should be *-ok*) is an intransitive ending. For part of the second name he suggested *moquic*, "to be hired," since the services of diviners are for hire, but that too leaves much unexplained. The names are clearly quite opaque for a Quiché-speaker, and even Edmonson, who perhaps attempts more glosses of names than any previous translator of the Popol Vuh, leaves them as they are.

The case is quite different with *iyom* and *mamom* (line 12). *Iy* and *mam* are respectively a woman's and a man's term for "grandchild," but the forms *iyom* and *mamom* do not appear in colonial dictionaries. Edmonson, apparently assuming that *-om* is something like the *-om* suffix that puts transitive verbs in the perfect, translates "Woman with Grandchildren" and "Man with Grandchildren."[33] Given that both the Popol Vuh and modern Quiché have perfectly clear terms for grandparents (*atit* and *mam*), the use of *iyom* and *mamom* (which have the appearance of circumlocutions) should alert us to look for a figurative or ceremonial meaning—even before we have any help from ethnopaleography. As it happens, don Andrés found these two words familiar enough: *Iyom* is the common term for "midwife," and in a bride-asking ceremony, the prospective groom's marriage-broker is addressed as *mamom*. Midwifery and the brokerage of marriage are two of the major specialized subfields open to Quiché diviners, so it came as no surprise to don Andrés to find Xpiyacoc and Xmucane spoken of in these terms.

One other divine name, occurring much later in this passage, was elucidated by don Andrés, though he had never before heard the name as such. That is *huracan* (line 81), which may be read literally as a contraction of *hun rakan*, "one his leg"; Edmonson translates "One Leg."[34] Don Andrés allowed for the possibility of such a reading, but he pointed out that *akan*, "leg," is used in counting animate things (much as we might use "head" in counting cattle in English); thus *huracan* might not mean that the deity in question has "one leg," but rather that he is "one of a kind." This would make *huracan* equivalent to *hunab ku*, the "solitary god" of the Chilam Balam books of Yucatán, whose name sets him apart from the "thirteen gods" who are also mentioned in those books.[35] That the writer of the Popol Vuh was

33. Edmonson, *The Book of Counsel*, p. 5.
34. Ibid., p. 11.
35. J. Eric S. Thompson, *Maya History and Religion*, pp. 203–5.

struck by Huracan's apparent singularity (rather than by any such thing as one-leggedness) is indicated by the pains he takes to point out, immediately after the first mention of the name, that Huracan (whatever the name might indicate) actually designates three different deities (lines 82–85).

On a wider beam than don Andrés's ability to shed light on localized lexical problems such as names was his sense of the internal threads of a whole passage and their relationship to Quiché experience and ideology. In the passage on the quartering of the world (lines 29–30), it was a long time before he settled on glossing *cahtzuc* as "four sides" (a reading that fits the entry for *cahzuc* in the Basseta dictionary), since this compound is no longer used in contemporary descriptions of the world. But even with this missing link, he readily recognized *cahxucut*, a form much used in contemporary prayers, as "four corners"; *etaxic* as "measurement"; *ucah cheexic* as a fourfold driving in of stakes; *umeh camaxic* as *umeh 4aamaxic*, referring to measurement with a "folded cord" or *meh 4aam* (equal to half a cord, a unit of land measurement still in use); and *uyuc camaxic* as *uyuk 4aamaxic*, referring to measurement with a "stretched cord" or *yuk 4aam* (a full cord). He then stopped to point out that the Popol Vuh is here describing the beginning of the world as if a rectangular milpa were being measured out with cords, with a stake driven at each corner. He knew of no contemporary narrative offering such a metaphor, but he found it very attractive, and I might add that his interpretation fits the other agricultural metaphors with which the Popol Vuh abounds.[36]

Just beyond the measuring is a passage describing the primordial state, before the establishment of the earth; here a series of words with reduplicated stems (*tzinin-, chamam-, lolin-*) has generally been interpreted as referring to silence (lines 37, 54). But don Andrés read these words as onomatopoeic for very soft sounds; *lolin-*, for example, is commonly used for the hum of nocturnal insects. The point of the passage is that there are steady, repetitive, meaningless sounds of the kind that prevail when there are no human voices or animal cries; there may be a hush (note the onomatopoeic quality of this English word), but there is not an utter silence—any more than there is any

---

36. Edmonson (*The Book of Counsel*, p. 8) translates this passage as having to do with creations, humiliations, knowledge, and punishments where I have siding, cornering, measuring, and staking; he thus removes it from its immediate Quiché context and interprets it as referring to the fourfold creation and destruction of the world, a theme well developed among the Aztec but only incompletely represented among the Quiché. The Popol Vuh describes only one Aztec-style cataclysm, or at best two.

other unqualified absolute in this Quiché description of the primordial world.

When the gods introduce the earth into the primordial world of sky and sea, they bring about its *uinaquiric* (line 102). This word has been repeatedly read as "being created" or "creation." Don Andrés himself acknowledged *creación* as a standard Spanish translation, but he much preferred "beginning to be separated (or differentiated)." The Quiché word contains the inchoative suffix, *-ir*; in general, it applies to situations in which something arises and grows from what was already there, as when scum forms and grows on a pool; it does not imply creation from nothing. Knowing this helps make sense of the following lines (106–7), which compare the scene of the earth's first appearance to a cloud's or a mist's *uinaquiric* and *pupuheic*, thus setting up an apparent contradiction between *uinaquiric*, if that is taken to mean "creation," and *pupuheic*, which can be read as "fragmentation." Don Andrés saw no problem here, pointing out that "It's just the way it is right now. There are clouds, then the clouds part, piece by piece, and now the sky is clear." Perhaps the mountains were there in the primordial world all along and were revealed, little by little, as the clouds parted. But don Andrés complicated this interpretation by saying, "Haven't you seen that when the water passes—a strong rain—and then it clears, a vapor comes out from among the trees? The clouds come out from among the mountains, among the trees." This lends a cyclical movement to the picture: the clouds come from the mountains, then conceal the mountains, then part to reveal the mountains, and so on.

But it is also possible to see the formation of the clouds (where there were none before) and the parting of those clouds as a simile for the formation and differentiation of the mountains themselves rather than as something happening in the atmosphere *around* the mountains. Such a simile would give the mountains themselves, and not their mere appearance as confused by clouds and mists, a certain insubstantiality. Don Andrés swung toward such an interpretation when he read that it was the *naual*, the "genius" or "spirit familiar" of the gods, that had been at work here (line 110); he concluded that "these mountains are for no other reason than representing that there *are* hills or volcanoes"—that is to say, he took the mountains of the text to be mere signs (*etal*) rather than substantial. But just as when the clouds and mists are taken to be covering real mountains rather than to be similes for mountains, there turns out to be something hard hidden behind the insubstantiality. When he read, further on, that the gods Heart of Sky and Heart of Earth were the first to "discover" or "realize" that the sky and earth were hidden (lines 128–29), don Andrés took this realization to be an act of *self*-discovery on their part, comparing them to the present-day *u4ux puuak* or "Heart of Metal (or silver or money)," which reveals itself to the fortunate. As he explained, "When one has luck, one picks up some kind of rock [an iron concretion], but in the form of a little animal; this is the Heart of Metal. When the moment comes, suddenly it appears." The finder takes such an object home and keeps it out of sight, and "this is where one prays, this is where the fortune, the money, abounds. Here in the Popol Vuh, the Heart of Sky and the Heart of Earth appeared, and this is where the earth was propagated." His interpretation is lent support by a much later passage in which the names "Heart of Sky" and "Heart of Earth" are addressed to stone idols whose owners keep them from view. The earthiness of these Quiché idols is clear enough; their connection to the sky may be explained by the fact that their contemporary counterparts are said to have been formed when the sun's first appearance petrified the earliest animals (in the case of concretions) or else when lightning struck the ground (in the case of ancient stone artifacts).

It remains to discuss those moments when the three-way encounter between don Andrés, the Popol Vuh text, and myself sent him into a lengthy aside in the form of a story. Such an aside might be occasioned by anything from our completion of the reading of one of the Popol Vuh's own narrative episodes to the discussion of a single word. In the passage under discussion here, the only narrative aside was occasioned by the word *tziiz* (ziz today), referring to the coati (line 10). Don Andrés pointed out that this word can also refer to any mammal with its testicles inside the body and suggested that since it is here paired with *ac*, "peccary," it might refer to a male peccary, leaving *ac* as the female—after all, in Quiché a female and male are usually listed with the female first, just as *ac* precedes *tziiz*. But at this point he put peccaries aside and thought of a story about the coati. It was about a woman who puts a coati's urine into her husband's coffee as an aphrodisiac; the urine proves to be so powerful that her husband, who until then had been innocent of sex, loves her to death. I have not given the full story here, since its contents have little to do with the text at hand, but it must be said that the narratives don Andrés offered at other points in our reading were often in close parallel with the Popol Vuh. The point is that in the present case, as elsewhere, he fully adopted the mode of oral delivery appropriate to

Quiché narratives, a mode which proved to have its applications to the Popol Vuh text.[37]

In a passage much beyond the section given here, when don Andrés encountered a prayer, he stopped to quote from the wording of contemporary prayers but did not adopt the mode of delivery used in actual praying, a mode which could only be studied through tapes made on separate occasions. This was because among the Quiché it is perfectly appropriate to introduce a tale into conversation—broadly speaking, tales occur only in such a context—whereas a prayer is appropriate within conversation only if the clock has reached 6:00 or 12:00 (A.M. or P.M.), at which time the conversants may greet one another (as if meeting all over again) and then say a brief prayer. Ethnopaleographic problems of this sort will obviously vary greatly from one field site to another.

The points of formal similarity between the Popol Vuh and modern Quiché discourse, considered purely from a textual point of view without yet raising the problem of scoring for oral delivery, begin with the question of length. It is true that the Popol Vuh (especially in the sections following the present one) has narrative passages of tremendous length, but when the stories of its hero twins are broken down into units that could perfectly well stand as autonomous stories, they are no longer than the present-day tales already mentioned above. Taken as a group of interconnected stories, they resemble the Trickster cycles of North America more than they resemble the lengthier (by several times) and more thickly descriptive and tightly plotted tales that may be found in the Plains, the Pueblos (including Zuni), and in some places on the Northwest Coast.[38]

Another general feature of Quiché narrative, whether ancient or modern, is that it does not necessarily unfold everything in chronological order. In North America, a narrator may go back by quoting a character's retelling of something that already happened, or go forward by quoting instructions or predictions, but among the Quiché the third-person narrative itself may progress unevenly,[39] and the narrator may even give away the outcome of a story well before it actually takes place. In the Popol Vuh, the account of the beginning of the world starts with the measurement of the sky and earth (lines 39–55), then goes back to a state in which the earth does not yet exist (lines

37. Contemporary Quiché narratives may be found in Chapters 10 and 13, below, and in the Epilogue.

38. For Trickster cycles, see Paul Radin, *The Trickster*. For Plains prolixity, see, e.g., George A. Dorsey, *The Pawnee: Mythology*; for the Northwest, see some of the longer stories in Franz Boas, "Tsimshian Mythology."

39. See Chapter 10, below, for an example.

56–94), then describes the gods as planning the earth (including its measurements) and humankind (lines 95–115), then goes back and re-tells this same episode as a dialogue among the gods (lines 116–31), then describes the enactment of the plan but leaves humankind as a loose end that will not be taken up again in the remainder of this section (lines 132–48), then goes back and describes the enactment once again (lines 149–58), and ends by recalling the planning process once more (lines 159–64). The fact that the human thread remains may link this section to others that follow, but it hardly makes for a tightly woven plot. It is just this sort of thread that links present-day Quiché tales to the conversations that surround them.[40] With tape-recorded discourse, as with the text of the Popol Vuh, it is impossible to cut out what one would like to be a patch of autonomous narrative without leaving frayed edges, but these are edges that leave one wondering about context rather than dangling in suspense.

At the level of words and phrases the most obvious formal feature of Quiché texts is parallelism, especially in the form of couplets that are semantic, syntactic, or both. Edmonson has rightly pointed out that Quichés often produce couplets in everyday discourse, but his statement that the Popol Vuh "is entirely composed in . . . couplets" is an accurate description only of his own printed version, wherein every last word of the text is forced into pairs of lines.[41] It would be more accurate to say, of both ancient and modern Quiché discourse, that couplets, rather frequently varied with triplets,[42] may be encountered throughout the spectrum of formality, but they are most frequent and have their longest unbroken runs in formal oratory and prayer. The more one leaves speech-making in favor of narrative (except where narrative borrows or quotes from the speech repertory), the less frequent syntactic and even purely semantic parallelism become, while the decisions involved in working out the scansion become more and more arbitrary. Even in highly formal passages there are likely to be single phrases, at the beginning or end or at internal points of transition, that do not stand in parallel with any other phrase (as in lines 36 and 39).

Questions of oral delivery begin with the alternation of sound and silence; between two silences is an unbroken sequence of sounds I call the line. Syntax and scansion may be read out of an alphabetical text, but lines (as I define them) must be reconstructed on the basis of recorded oral performances whose syntax and scansion are analogous

40. See Chapter 10 and the Epilogue, below.
41. Edmonson, *The Book of Counsel*, p. xii.
42. See Chapter 8, below.

to that text, and even then one can speak only of probabilities. Lines may follow major boundaries in syntax or scansion according to a few simple rules where the intention is that every performance should be the same with respect not only to content but also to wording, as in chants or songs, but wherever a speaking voice is used and the wording is flexible, as in Zuni and Quiché spoken narrative, the question of line is much more complicated. What follows is a probabilistic description of Quiché lines given in terms of their relationship to syntax and parallelism.

In Quiché, quotative words or phrases (in which speakers identify what is about to be said or has just been said as a name, a figure of speech, or a direct quotation from someone else) and performative words or phrases (in which speakers refer to what they themselves are about to say or have just said, in effect putting quote marks around their own words) stand as independent lines when they precede the line or lines they refer to (as in line 36). When they follow, they are run on with the last of the lines referred to (as in line 10), unless they identify the source of those lines (as in line 14), specifying the speaker, the language, the occasion, or perhaps offering an etymology. When quotatives and performatives contain parallelism (line 11), which they usually do not, their internal line divisions follow the same rules (given below) that apply to other cases of parallelism.

A demonstrative or conjunctive word or phrase that introduces a new clause, provided that it consists of three or more syllables and is not repeated in a parallelistic construction, is likely to form an independent line (line 63); otherwise it may be run on with what follows it.

When two successive clauses are parallel neither in meaning nor in syntax, they will fall into two separate lines (as with lines 40–41), and the same will also be true if they are parallel in meaning but not in syntax (lines 108–9). The more parallel two successive words or phrases are in their internal syntax and in their larger syntactic context, the more likely they are to be delivered within a single line, even if they could each stand as an independent clause (as could the clauses in line 93). In the situation of maximal syntactic parallelism, prepositions, modifiers, and affixes remain the same while only a single noun or verb stem changes (line 11). With the introduction of a further variation in the wording or affixation, so long as this merely subtracts something (line 17) and/or adds or replaces no more than a single syllable (line 28), the parallel words or phrases may still be run on as a single line. Beyond this level of variation a line division becomes increasingly likely (lines 25–26), but what has already been said about the running on of quotatives, performatives, demonstratives, and conjunctives applies even beyond this level.

When two (and sometimes three) phrases sufficiently parallel to be joined in a single line provide verbs for a single specified subject (no example here), contain verbs with a single specified object (line 3), provide subjects or objects for a single verb (lines, 27, 74) or prepositional phrase (lines 33, 69), or possess or are possessed by a single noun (lines 4, 79), then this single subject, object, verb, prepositional phrase, possession, or possessor is likely to be run on with the parallel phrases to which it is linked. But when two separate sets of *internally* parallel phrases are linked in any of these same ways, as when two parallel *verbs* have two parallel *subjects* (lines 94–96), a line break will appear between the two sets.

Generally, parallel words or phrases joined in a single line will not run beyond two or three parallel units (line 7). The exception is lists of nouns or noun phrases such as are frequently invoked in oratory and prayer (line 10). Here, so long as quotatives, performatives, demonstratives, and conjunctives do not intervene in the ways already described, the speaker may go on without interruption indefinitely, the ultimate limitation being an exhaustion of the capacity of the memory or the lungs. The nouns in these lists tend to form pairs (line 32) or threesomes (the first three nouns in line 42) when considered semantically, but the mode of delivery takes little notice of this, except perhaps to mark the first member (or two) of each such unit with a rise in intonation and the second (or third) with a fall. When a parallel pair consists solely of two nouns (without prepositions, modifiers, or affixes) of one or two syllables each (line 35), even the marking of the word boundary may well disappear, leaving a single stress on the final syllable of the second word.

There are other kinds of running on and dividing up than those described here, caused by undue haste or else virtuoso efforts at speed, on the one hand, and by awkward hesitation or else efforts to create suspense, on the other. These I have not attempted to reconstruct, but I will remark that contemporary Quiché narrators, in keeping with their tendency to give away the outcome of events before they even happen, make very little effort to keep their hearers dangling the way Zuni narrators do. I might also point out that Quiché narrative lines, relative to Zuni ones, are rather short in the first place. When it comes to prayer, in which both languages make heavy use of parallelism, both styles of delivery involve very long lines, though in the Zuni case these are broken up into short pieces for prayers that are loudly declaimed in public.

The passage given below occupies the first folio and a half of the Popol Vuh manuscript (running from 1r.1 to 2v.1).[43] In the Quiché text, I introduce lines based on oral delivery rather than on the original columns of prose, but in matters of punctuation and orthography I follow the manuscript exactly except for writing the *tresillo* (the numeral three in mirror image) as 3 and for discarding the *u / v* distinction (*u* and *v* are allographs, and either of them can indicate a vowel or a consonant). In following the manuscript as closely as I do, I cast my lot with Schultze Jena rather than with those who have sought to fully phoneticize (Harrington) or phonemicize (Burgess and Xec, Edmonson) the text. Such efforts at transformation may be likened to overzealous attempts to restore ruins. The changes produced are often trivial, at one extreme, and misleading, at the other. No great victory for clarity is won when all occurrences of *cate cut*, a common phrase that is perfectly clear to the reader even though a more consistent writer might have rendered it as *4ate 4ut* (thus indicating glottalization), are transformed by Burgess and Xec into *c'ate c'ut* (according to their own system for indicating a glottalized velar stop). Edmonson, in handling this same phrase, even succeeds in introducing a problem that did not exist in the text, writing *kate q'ut*, which (in his orthography) leaves the *cate* of the manuscript uncorrected and overcorrects *cut* to a glottalized uvular stop rather than a velar one. At least the writer of the Popol Vuh has both these words beginning with the *same* consonant, which indeed they do. And when Edmonson changes *ilbal*, "means of seeing," to *ilobal*,[44] he is not so much correcting the text as moving it from the dialect in which it was written, a highly "clipped" Quiché that may still be heard in the central Quiché area today, and placing it in a more westerly area. Edmonson, at least, footnotes many of his important departures from the original text, whereas the changes made by Burgess and Xec are inescapable.

Ideally, all reporting of paleographic research (ethnopaleographic or otherwise) should leave it perfectly clear what a document actually says, without the reader's having to go back to the document itself. But as Ives Goddard has pointed out, "The practices of Americanists must be said to fall far short of the standards adhered to by editors of textual materials in Old World languages. There seems to be little sympathy for the idea that published texts should follow as closely as

43. This manuscript reference may be read as follows: folio 1 (recto), line 1, to folio 2 (verso), line 1. Classicists use a uniform system in referring to their texts, and it is high time Mesoamericanists did the same.
44. Edmonson, *The Book of Counsel*, p. 7.

possible the primary record, with emendations kept carefully apart."[45] With the Old World standard in mind, I have chosen to put rereadings or corrections in my commentaries (already offered) rather than inserting them in the text itself and explaining them away after the fact.

The stanza breaks are based on the notion that when phrases of a performative, demonstrative, or conjunctive nature stand as independent lines and begin new sentences, they have the effect of marking the beginning of new paragraphs. The same also applies to introductory quotatives (especially where the preceding line consists of or contains a concluding quotative), but not when they fit directly into the stream of ongoing narrative action. In performance these stanza breaks may be marked by a longer pause than ordinary line breaks, but it should be cautioned that this longer pause will sometimes *follow* rather than precede the first line of the new stanza. After all, it is much easier for a narrator to say *are cut*, "and here" (line 6) than to follow up on the promise made by such a phrase.

The reader may note that my English translations of Quiché demonstrative, conjunctive, and prepositional words and phrases— those little bits that fill up the interstices of languages—are not followed out with mechanical consistency. That is to say, if I translate *quehe cut* as "and so" in one place, I will not necessarily do so in every other place. The reason is that such words do not have one-to-one correspondences across languages, but rather divide up their functional territories differently; there is no use in using "and so" in an English context where no one would ever choose those particular words, unless one's aim is to do what classicists call a "trot" rather than attempting a translation.

Here, then, is the opening of the Popol Vuh. The reader should leave a fully audible pause—that is, a pause of at least half a second— before beginning any new line at the extreme left-hand margin, but should speak continuously everywhere else. Indented lines are simply spillovers from previous lines and do not call for pauses. Stanza breaks call for a pause of up to two seconds, which may fall at the break itself or one line later. Words given entirely in capitals follow the manuscript, but this particular writing convention, unlike the evening up of columns of prose, does have its counterpart in oral delivery: In Quiché, as in Zuni, lines that introduce major sequences (such as entire stories) are likely to be markedly louder than most of those that follow.

45. Goddard, "Philological Approaches," p. 87.

ARE UXE OHER Tzih
uaral Quiche ubi.
Uaral xchicatzibah ui xchicatiquiba ui oher tzih,
uticaribal, uxenabal puch ronohel xban,
pa tinamit quiche, ramac quiche uinac;   5

are cut
xchicacam ui ucutunizaxic, ucalahobizaxic, utzihoxic puch
euaxibal zaquiribal
rumal tzacol bitol alom, 4aholom quibi
hunahpu uuch, hunahpu utiu, zaqui nim ac tziiz, tepeu,   10
    4ucumatz u4ux cho, u4ux palo, ah
        raxa la3, ah raxa tzel chu4haxic,
rach bixic, rach tzihoxic
rii iyom, mamom xpiyacoc, xmucane ubi,
matzanel chuquenel camul yiom, camul mamom
chu4haxic pa quiche tzih.
ta xquitzihoh ronohel   15
ru4 xquiban chic
chi zaquil 4olem, zaquil tzih
uae xchicatzibah chupan chic u4habal Dios
pa christianoil chic
xchiquelezah rumal mahabi chic ilbal re   20
popo uuh.
ilbal zac petenac chaca palo.
utzihoxic camuhibal
ilbal zac 4azlem chu4haxic.
4o nabe uuhil,   25
oher tzibam puch
xa eual uuach ilol re, bizol re,
nim upeoxic, utzihoxic puch,
ta chiquiztzuk ronohel cah uleu,
ucah tzucuxic, ucah xucutaxic retaxic, ucah cheexic,   30
    umeh camaxic, uyuc camaxic upa cah, upa uleu
        cah tzuc, cah xucut chu4haxic
rumal ri tzacol bitol uchuch, ucahau
4azlem uinaquirem, abanel, 4uxlanel, alay rech,
    4uxlaay rech zaquil amaquil, zaquil al, zaquil
        4ahol,
ahbiz, ahnaoh chirech ronohel
ato 4ol ui
cha uleu cho palo   35

THIS IS THE BEGINNING OF THE ANCIENT Word,
here in this place called Quiché.
Here we shall inscribe, we shall implant the ancient word,
the potential and source for everything done
in the town of Quiché, in the nation of Quiché people.
•

And here
we shall take up the demonstration, revelation, and account
of how things were put in shadow, brought to light
by the maker, modeler named Bearer, Begetter,
Hunahpu Possum, Hunahpu Coyote, Great White Peccary, Coati,
    Tepeu, Plumed Serpent, heart of the lake, heart of the sea,
        those of the green plate, those of the blue bowl, so to speak,
named together, invoked together
with the midwife, marriage broker named Xpiyacoc, Xmucane,
advocate, refuge, twice a midwife, twice a marriage broker,
as is said in the words of Quiché,
when they accounted for everything—
and did it, too—
as enlightened beings, in enlightened words.
We shall write this now amid the preaching of God,
in Christendom now.
We shall bring it out because there is no longer a way to see it,
the Council Book,
the way to see the light from across the sea,
the account of our darkness,
the way to see the dawn of life, so to speak.
There is the original book
and ancient writing,
but the reader, interpreter has a hidden identity.
Great is his rendition and account
of the marking of all the sky/earth,
the fourfold siding, fourfold cornering, measuring, fourfold staking,
    halving the cord, stretching the cord, in the sky, on the earth,
        the four sides, the four corners, so to speak,
by the maker, modeler, the mother, father,
of life, humankind, those who breathe, those who have heart, born,
    conceived in light, in kinship, born in the light, begotten in
        the light,
the caretaker, knower of everything,
whatever there is:
sky/earth, lake/sea.
•

ARE UTZIHOXIC UAE
ca catzininoc, ca cachamamoc catzinonic ca cazilanic, ca calolinic,
catolona puch upa cah.

Uae cate	
nabe tzih nabe uchan.	40
mahabio3 hun uinac, hun chicop	
tziquin, car, tap, che abah, hul, ziuan, quim, quichelah;	
xa utuquel cah 4olic.	
maui calah uuach uleu;	
xa utuquel remanic palo upa cah ronohel,	45
mahabi naquila camolobic,	
cacotzobic, hunta cazilobic	
camal caban tah, cacotz caban tah pa cah.	
xma 4o ui naquila 4olic,	
xa calic;	50
xa remanic ha, xa lianic palo,	
xa utuquel remanic,	
xma 4o ui naquila lo 4olic;	
xa cachamanic catzininic	
chi que3um, chi a3ab	55
xa utuquel ri tzacol, bitol, tepeu, 4ucumatz e alom,	
* e 4aholom 4o pa ha*	
zac tetoh	
e 4o ui e mucutal	
pa cuc, pa raxon	
are ubinaam ui	60
ri 4ucumatz	
e nimac etamanel, e nimac ahnaoh chiqui 4oheic;	
quehe cut	
xax 4o ui.	
ri cah 4o nai puch	65
u4ux cah	
are ubi ri cabauil chu4haxic.	
Ta xpe cut utzih	
uaral xul cu4 ri tepeu 4ucumatz	
uaral chi quecumal chi a3abal	70
x4hau ru4 ri tepeu 4ucumatz,	
xe4ha cut,	
ta xenaohinic, ta xebizonic, xerico quib,	

THIS IS THE ACCOUNT:
it still ripples, still murmurs, ripples, still whispers, still hums,
and it is empty under the sky.
•

There follow
the first words, the first eloquence.
Still there is not one person, one animal,
bird, fish, crab, tree, rock, hollow, canyon, meadow, forest.
Only the sky alone is there:
the face of the earth is not clear.
Only the sea alone is pooled under all the sky:
there is nothing whatever gathered together.
It is at rest, each thing is motionless,
it is kept solitary, kept at rest under the sky.
Whatever might be is not yet there:
all is scattered.
Only the pooled water, only the level sea,
only it alone is pooled,
whatever might perhaps be is not yet there,
only murmurs, whispers
in the blackness, in the night,
all alone, the maker, modeler, Tepeu, Plumed Serpent, Bearers,
        Begetters are in the water,
a glittering light:
they are there, enclosed
in quetzal feathers, in blue-green.
Thus the name:
the Plumed Serpent.
They are great knowers, great thinkers in their very being.
•

And so
they are alone there
and there is also the sky,
Heart of Sky.
This is the name of the idol, so to speak.
•

So then came his word,
he came here to the Tepeu, Plumed Serpent,
here in the blackness, in the night,
he spoke with the Tepeu, Plumed Serpent,
so they talked,
then they thought, then they wondered, they agreed with each
        other,

xquicuch quitzih, quinaoh,
ta xcalah ta xqui4uxlaah quib xeui zac   75
ta xcalah puch uinac,
ta xquinaohih utzuquic uuinaquiric
che, caam,
utzuquic puch 4azlem uinaquirem
chi que3umal, chi a3abal,   80
rumal ri u4ux cah huracan ubi,
caculha huracan nabe,
uiab cut chipa caculha,
rox chic raxa caculha
chi e cu oxib rii u4ux cah   85
ta xeul cu4 ri tepeu 4ucumatz
ta xnaohixic zac 4azlem,
hapacha ta chauaxoc ta zaquiro puch,
apachinac tzucul cool
tachuxoc   90
quixnohin tah.
are ri ha
chel tah chihama tah,
chi uinaquir ua uleu ulaquel ta cu rib chata cut,
ta chauaxoc ta zaquiroc,   95
cah uleu,

ma ta cut
uquihilabal ucalaibal
rii catzac cabit
ta uinaquiroc uinac tzac uinac bit xe4ha cut   100
ta xuinaquir cu ri uleu cumal;
xa quitzih x4ohe ui uuinaquiric
chi uinaquir uleu,
uleuh xecha
libah chi xuinaquiric;   105
quehe ri xa tzutz xa mayui
uuinaquiric chic upupuheic
ta xtape pa ha ri huiub
huzuc nimac huyub xuxic
xa quinaual xa quipuz xbanatah ui   110

unaohixic huyub tacah,
huzuc rach uuinaquiric uquizizil, upachahil uuach.

they joined their words, their thoughts,
then it was clear, then they reached accord in the light,
and then humanity was clear,
then they conceived the growth, the differentiation
of trees/bushes
and the nourishing of life, of humankind,
in the blackness, in the night,
by the Heart of Sky, named Only One,
Thunderbolt Only One first,
second, Lastborn Thunderbolt,
and third, Sudden Thunderbolt,
so there were three of them, as Heart of Sky,
when they came to the Tepeu, Plumed Serpent.
Then the dawn of life was conceived:
"How should the sowing and dawning be?
Who is to be the provider, nurturer?"
"Let it be this way:
think ahead.
There is this water:
it should recede, should empty out
for the separation of this, the earth's own surface and platform.
Then let it be sown, then let it dawn:
the sky/earth.
•

But then
for the celebration, the proclamation
of our work, our design,
let there arise the human work, the human design," they said.
Then the earth was separated by them,
it was simply their word that brought it forth:
for the separation of the earth,
"Earth," they said.
Suddenly it came forth,
it was just like a cloud, like a mist
now arising, unfolding,
when the mountains came from beneath the water,
the great mountains came into being all at once.
By their genius alone, by their cutting edge alone, they carried it
    out:
the craftsmanship of the mountain/plain,
which all at once was grown over with groves of cypress, groves of
    pine.
•

quehe cut
xquicot ui ri 4ucumatz,
utz mixatulic 115
at u4ux cah, at huracan,
at pu chipi caculha, raxa caculha,
xchutzinic catzac cabit xe4ha cut.

nabe cut
xuinaquir uleuh 120
huyub tacah,
xchobochox ube ha
xbiniheic colehe racan xoltac huyub,
xa chobol chic xe4ohe ui ha,
ta xcutuniheic nimac huyub. 125

quehe cut
uuinaquiric uleu
ri ta xuinaquiric cumal ri u4ux cah u4ux uleu
queuchaxic rii cut e nabe xquinohih
xcolo ui ri cah, 130
xcolo nai puch uleuh chupan ha.

quehe cut
unohixic ri ta xquinohih ta xquibizoh
rutzinic ubanatahic cumal.

At this
the Plumed Serpent was pleased:
"It's good that you've come,
Heart of Sky, Only One,
and Lastborn Thunderbolt, Sudden Thunderbolt,
our work, our design will turn out well," they said.

•

So first
the earth was separated,
the mountain/plain,
the channels of water were divided,
their branches wound among the mountain ranges,
now all the waters were divided there,
when the great mountains appeared.

•

So this
was the separation of the earth,
when it was brought forth by the Heart of Sky, Heart of Earth,
as those who first conceived it are called.
The sky was put in place there
and the earth was also put in place, amid the waters.

•

So this
was its conception when they thought, when they wondered
about how they would arrange and complete it.

PART TWO

Poetics

The Poetics of Verisimilitude

It is my purpose here to take a look at features of narrative style and structure which have to do with the ways in which narratives reflect or distort the world of everyday experience. I will center the discussion on Zuni fictional narratives and draw comparisons with our own and other narratives or narrative-like phenomena, including everything from horror films to scientific proofs. The result will, I hope, add to the already abundant reasons for considering oral narratives to be something other than just primitive ancestors of written prose fiction and for viewing the minds which produced those narratives as very much like our own but applying themselves, as Lévi-Strauss would have it, to different subject matter.[1]

Excluding less formal accounts of recent history and personal experience, Zuni narratives fall into two categories: Either they are a part of the *chimiky'ana'kowa* (origin story) which can be told at any

Reprinted by permission of the University of New Mexico Press from *New Perspectives on the Pueblos*, ed. Alfonso Ortiz, a School of American Research Advanced Seminar Series book © 1972 by the School of American Research. Considerable revisions have been made here.

1. Claude Lévi-Strauss, *Structural Anthropology*, p. 227.

time of day or in any season, or they are *telapnaawe* (tales) which are told only at night and during winter.[2] Both kinds of narrative are set in the *inoote* (long ago) before the introduction of objects and institutions recognized as belonging to the period of European contact,[3] but the *chimiky'ana'kowa*, which accounts for most of the major features of Zuni social organization, belongs to a period when the world was "soft," while the *telapnaawe* are set in a world which had already hardened, though it was still not quite like the present world. The *chimiky'ana'kowa* is regarded as literally true, even by some Zunis with Christian leanings, but *telapnaawe* are regarded as fiction:

> One day as we were driving into Zuni from the east, Andrew Peynetsa began recalling a *telapnanne* he had previously told me. He pointed out the cave where Haynawi (a monster) had trapped a little girl in the story; several miles beyond, at Corn Mountain, he pointed out the place where the Ahayuuta twins (protector gods) had been living when they heard the girl's cry for help.[4] He noted the distance between the two places and said, "Nobody would believe they could hear her. That's just a story."

Joseph Peynetsa expressed a similar view of *telapnaawe*: "When you are a kid you believe them, but then you grow up and realize they couldn't have happened," and Walter Sanchez when he was unable to think of any real parallel for the events in one of his own narratives, gave as his excuse the fact that the narrative in question was a *telapnanne*.

When a narrative is a *telapnanne* it is clearly identified as such by the formulaic frame which encloses it:

OPENING
1. The narrator says (loudly), *SO'NAHCHI*, which may once have meant, "Now we are taking it up"; this word does not occur in Zuni speech except as a framing or keying device in tale-telling.[5] The narrator then pauses while his audience replies

2. Some narratives are hard to classify according to this dichotomy; see Dennis Tedlock, *The Ethnography of Tale-Telling at Zuni*, pp. 214–15.

3. Some obvious European content is present in tales recognized by Zunis as having been borrowed from Mexicans, but these are only a small part of the repertoire. Otherwise the only European presence in tales is that of the horse.

4. Narrative H-8. Tape and transcript in the author's possession. Abstracts of all the unpublished narratives cited here may be found in Tedlock, *The Ethnography of Tale-Telling at Zuni*, pp. 279–97.

5. For a general discussion of "keying" or "framing" in performance, see Richard

with *eeso*, "yes, indeed," which is also a word peculiar to tale-telling.

2. The narrator says, *SONTI INO———TE*, in which the first word (occurring only in tale-telling frames) may once have meant, "Now it begins to be made," and the second word is transparently "long ago." Now there is a second pause while the audience again says *eeso*.

3. The narrator, using a standardized syntactic framework, lists the major characters and the places where they live, for example:

   THERE WERE VILLAGERS AT HE'SHOKTA
   and
   up on the Prairie Dog Hills
   the deer
   had their home.[6]

Note that the loudness of the first two framing lines carries over into the first of these new lines but is then dropped in favor of a normal speaking level. Next the narrator will proceed with the events of the story itself.

CLOSING

3. The narrator may move away from the events of the story with an etiological statement, such as, "That's why the Hopis knew how to WORK WONDERS,"[7] or even with a whole series of such statements.

2. The narrator says, *Le'n inoote teyatikya*, "This was lived (or happened) long ago," while the audience begins to stir.

1. The narrator says, *LEE——— SEMKONIKYA*, in which the first word means "enough" and the second (occurring only in tale-telling frames) may once have meant, "the word was short." The audience rises and stretches while this final phrase is spoken.

The mirror-image structure of the opening and closing frames is immediately apparent. Each of the opening steps (1, 2, 3) moves the audience closer to the story itself, and each of the closing steps (3, 2, 1) moves the audience back out of the story. The first two (1, 2) and last two (2, 1) steps apply to any *telapnanne*, while the innermost steps (3)

Bauman, *Verbal Art as Performance*, pp. 15–24; his point of departure is Erving Goffman's *Frame Analysis: An Essay on the Organization of Experience.*

6. Dennis Tedlock, *Finding the Center*, p. 3.

7. Ibid., p. 62.

differentiate particular stories. The purely formulaic words come first and last, while the standardized but transparently meaningful words or phrases are closer to the story itself, at either end. There is a slight asymmetry here; it is as if the transparent words were carried closer to the end of the story and pulled farther from its beginning by the forward motion of the story events. It should be added that narrators move faster at the end than at the beginning, pausing less often and sometimes abbreviating the closing by giving only its latter two steps, delivered without a pause between them.

The *telapnanne* frame provides a series of clues to the relationship between the events described in the story and everyday experiences of the kind that might be narrated in conversation. The outermost words at either end disconnect the story from conversation abruptly and decisively; it is not just that these words occur exclusively in tale-telling, but that they lack transparent referential meaning. They follow the normal rules of Zuni phonology, but their effect is, as it were, abstract rather than representational, only vaguely suggesting the glosses offered above. A similar abstractness enters the opening and/ or closing frames of Seneca, Wintu, Karok, Klikitat, and probably many other North American tale-telling traditions.[8] Just as these frames stand apart from plain speech, so the events they enclose stand apart from narratives of everyday experience.

The Zuni narrator relinquishes all claims to a personal knowledge of tale events by removing them to an indefinitely distant past, as marked in the middle parts of both the opening and closing. The story floats free in that past, with its edges located with respect to the experienced present only through place names at the beginning and a last-minute etiological leap at the end. The *chimiky'ana'kowa* narrative, on the other hand, begins precisely four countable worlds before the present one, with the first human experience of light, extends (in Andrew Peynetsa's view) as far forward as the American military intervention in Zuni witchcraft prosecutions in the late 1800s, and is anchored with etiological claims throughout its entire length.

The third part of the *telapnanne* opening is something like the Chinookan tale titles discussed by Dell Hymes, which give information about the internal structure of a story.[9] In the case of the Zuni opening, the third part gives some of the broadest terms of a particular story's dialectic or argument, providing clues to several different

8. Dennis Tedlock, "Verbal Art."
9. Dell Hymes, "*In Vain I Tried to Tell You*," pp. 272–73, 283.

layers of meaning at once. In the example quoted above we are told, in effect, that

villagers: He'shokta::deer:Prairie Dog Hills

and as Zunis we will know not only that this arrangement places the villagers to the east and the deer to the west, but also that west is the direction in which human beings travel after death in order to become kachinas (at a place farther west than the Prairie Dog Hills) and that when kachinas die they become deer. The place names anchor the story in "real" space, but at the very same time they put villagers in a place that has been abandoned for centuries and deer in a place that is no longer good for hunting—and as if all of this were not haunting enough, the names align the story in a symbolic space that calls for encounters between those who were living long ago and those who were, even then, already dead.[10]

Highly formal framing or keying procedures like this Zuni one have long been treated by collectors as if they were a peculiar artifact of oral transmission whose importance vanishes when the enclosed stories are committed to print; as in the case of Ruth Benedict's *Zuni Mythology*, frames are often abbreviated or even eliminated altogether, with the etiological part being the most likely to survive. But we ourselves are no strangers to framing devices, not even in written tradition. A book begins with a cover, and this is followed by some or all of the following features: flyleaves (corresponding, perhaps, to the pauses of the Zuni narrator), title page (with the title, in former times, often taken from the opening line of the text proper), foreword (by someone other than the author, a sort of audience-member), preface (by the author himself), table of contents, chapter heading, and finally the work itself. At the end of the book we may find the date on which the author finished it and his place of residence at that time, followed by "the end" or "finis," and of course a back cover. One might argue about the details, but the general structure of this book frame is the same as the Zuni tale frame in that it moves into and out of the actual narration by stages. It is also worth noting that title pages, section headings, and sentences beginning chapters are set in large type or completely in capitals, which parallels the Zuni narrator's practice of rendering his opening three steps in a loud and chantlike voice which

10. For more on Zuni eschatology, see Dennis Tedlock, "An American Indian View of Death." For an exploration of the symbolic importance of the geographical arrangements in Tsimshian stories, see Claude Lévi-Strauss, "The Story of Asdiwal."

does not drop into a normal narrating voice until after he has delivered a few lines of the actual story.

There is some indication that the need for framing may be proportional to the extent to which the enclosed narrative departs from what the audience accepts as reality. In the Zuni case no particular frames are prescribed for the *chimiky'ana'kowa* or for other "true" narratives; and like the Zuni, the Ashanti, Yoruba, Kimbundu, Marshallese, Trobrianders, and probably many others have fixed opening (and in some cases closing) formulas for their fictional narratives, but not for narratives regarded as true.[11] A similar case cannot be made out for our own books, but there are suggestive parallels where performance is concerned: Live drama requires more of a frame than a professional lecture, and horror films on television, inasmuch as they are often introduced by emcees who try to be funny, seem to require more of a frame than ordinary films.

The correlation between frames and the departure from the "real" suggests that the confinement of Zuni tales to winter nights may simply be a part of the tale frame, since "true" Zuni narratives are not so confined. The Fulani, Yoruba, Marshallese, and Trobrianders also restrict fictional narratives, but not "true" ones, to the night.[12] We ourselves confine most drama (whether stage, screen, or television), except for highly realistic soap operas, to the night, and we tend to confine horror (both on screen and television) to the late night; moreover, except for summer repeats on television we confine drama largely to the winter. Newscasts and public lectures, by contrast, occur day or night and at any time of year.

Though it is true that the Zunis generally regard their *telapnaawe* as fiction, they do recognize certain kinds of "truth" in them, often citing etiological claims in the closings such as these:

> The sun sometimes has a halo now, and deer are now capable of witchcraft and must therefore be hunted with special precautions.[13] Asked whether this tale were true, Andrew Peynetsa said, "Almost. That's why the sun is that way"; asked on another occasion whether this narrative were a *telapnanne*, he said, "Yes, it's a *telapnanne*, and after the *telapnanne* was acted the deer became all wicked." Joseph Peynetsa, asked whether this tale really happened, said, "No. I say no, but I don't know why the hunters do this. Somewhere, somebody must have found out. Somehow,

11. William Bascom, "The Forms of Folklore: Prose Narratives," pp. 6, 9.
12. Ibid., p. 6.
13. Narrative H-2.

maybe an accident. Maybe it wasn't like this, but later something must have happened to make people think the deer were witches. Anyway, all the hunters know this."

There are some marks on a rock at a place now called "Turkey Tracks."[14] Asked whether this tale really happened, Walter Sanchez said (in Zuni), "Where the turkeys made the tracks—it's true in that part." Asked the same question, Joseph Peynetsa said, "No, but there's a place called this. I don't know how it came about; maybe somebody told the story and they named it. I don't know."

The Hopis and not the Zunis know how to weave the kinds of clothing worn by kachinas.[15] Asked whether this tale really happened, Joseph said, "Well, it might have happened. Maybe that's why the Hopis know how to make the kachina clothes, or somehow they must know."

Ducks now waddle rather than walking straight.[16] Asked whether this tale were true, Andrew said, "Yes, that's true. Ducks really walk that way."

Explanatory elements, then, since they refer to real conditions, lend an air of reality to the stories that lead to them. This is paralogism, a literary device described by Aristotle: "Whenever, if A is or happens, a consequent, B, is or happens, men's notion is that, if the B is, the A also is. . . . Just because we know the truth of the consequent, we are in our own minds led on to the erroneous inference of the truth of the antecedent."[17] Faulty logic it may be, but Aristotle approved of it as a verisimilitudinal device.

At present, our own use of this sort of paralogism is to be found mainly in historical and scientific narratives. Of course our own creators of "that's-why" narratives have more varieties of information at their disposal than did the societies which created oral narratives (as pointed out by Lévi-Strauss), and the dialectical process which gives internal coherence to narratives was not applied programmatically in the latter case. But it cannot be denied that the reality of World War II

14. "The Girl Who Took Care of the Turkeys," in Tedlock, *Finding the Center*, pp. 65–72.
15. H-7.
16. I-19.
17. Aristotle, *Rhetoric and Poetics*, p. 259. The quotation is from 1460a in the *Poetics*.

reflects back upon an account of its origins; that biological evolution is made more believable by the immediately observable existence of fossils, of apes, and of Darwin's point; and that atomic physics, for all its problems, is lent considerable credence by Hiroshima and Nagasaki.

A good deal of the truth which Zunis see in their fictional narratives derives not from the final etiological elements but from the efforts of the narrator to create the appearance of reality within the body of the story itself. The ability to create this appearance is the most important measure of the individual narrator's skill, ranking above such considerations as accuracy of memory or size of repertoire. Discussing differences in skill, Joseph said, "Some are good storytellers, not because they may know the story, but because of their voices and gestures, and they make it exciting. Some tell it like they were actually part of it, had witnessed it." Asked what makes a good story, the husband of Andrew's eldest daughter, rather than citing favorite characters or plots, said, "When you hear a good story there's more action to it. There are more interesting words to attract people to it, so people can see it right before their eyes. If you are really true to a story you make it like it's right in front of you." Andrew, who was present when this statement was made, agreed with it and added, "You're right with that story, like you were in it. Some guys, the way they tell it, it seems like they were really in it. I ask them after it, 'Were you really in it?' . . . [A good storyteller], the way he talks, he explains just how it was, and he makes motions too. It seems like he was really in it. Like it's not a story, but he just got that word [from a person who was involved]."

The primary vehicle for a Zuni tale is, of course, the verbal description of its events, but in seeking to create the appearance of reality a narrator has recourse to a number of devices which stretch the limits of verbal description or transcend them, including gesture (mentioned above by both Joseph and Andrew), quotation, onomatopoeia, and the linking of the story to the actual context of its narration. A few gestures seem to be standard usages in tale-telling: A sweeping motion of a partially outstretched arm and hand may indicate the horizontal or vertical motion of a tale actor; a completely outstretched arm and hand, accompanied by the words, "It was at this time," may indicate the height of the sun at a particular point in the story; the forefingers or palms may be held a certain distance apart to indicate the size of an object; and so forth. Andrew, by his own admission, does not exceed these ordinary gestures in his own performances, and neither does Walter. But the kind of kinetic activity that helps make a narrator seem "like he was really in it" may go far beyond standard devices. Andrew described to me how a certain well-known narrator (now deceased), in telling the tale of Greasy Kid (*Ishana Ts'ana*) and Snow Man (*Suniyashiwani*),[18] "went through the motions": Where Greasy Kid puts feathers under his arms and moves his arms rapidly in an effort to generate enough heat to melt Snow Man, this narrator actually moved his arms, vigorously; where a girl at a well takes a bowl off her head to give Snow Man a drink, this man acted as if he were taking a pot off his own head and setting it down; and so on through the story. Another narrator of wide reputation mentioned by Andrew used to get up from his place and walk around to show how a story character walked. In all of these kinetic activities Zuni narrative is comparable to our own theater, and specifically to the monologue.

A Zuni narrator may devote as much as half of a tale performance to the quotation of tale characters rather than to straight descriptions of actions and scenes. Even when he does not change his voice quality for these quotations they contribute to the appearance of reality through their immediacy: Greetings, interjections, and the use of the first and second person are found only in quotations and differentiate them sharply from the rest of the narrative. Special voice qualities heighten this immediacy: Andrew, for example, usually gives the Ahayuuta the high, raspy voice they are reputed to have, and he often gives female characters a tense, tight voice, especially when they scold or want something. Once again the modern parallel is in the theater: Written fiction sometimes contains a fair amount of quotation, but the best a writer can do for voice quality is something like, "He spoke in a hoarse voice" or "she said, insistently."

In keeping with the fact that tales take place "long ago," the Zuni narrator keeps all modernisms out of his quotations and inserts archaisms. Nearly all of the greetings and interjections used are archaic: Where a present-day Zuni would say *kesshé* (Hi), the tale character says something like *Hom tacchu, hom cha'le, ko'na'to tewanan teyaye?* (My father, my child, how have you been passing the days?). And where today's Zuni might express surprise and horror with *Tii———*, *tosh lesnuky'a?* (*Tii———*, what are you doing?), the tale character may say *Tisshomahhá!* (untranslatable). Our own writers make similar use of archaisms in trying to recreate the past, as when they have characters in a Western say "Guff!" (male speaking) or "Land's sake!" (female speaking); and of course literature written in the distant past brings its own archaisms with it. The writers of science fiction, on the

18. H-1.

other hand, may try to invent the inverse of an archaism, what might be called a futurism, as when their characters say, "By Mars, I'll get this one!" or "Crazy planetoid!"

Onomatopoeia is, as it were, the quotation of nonverbal sounds. In my experience, at least, the Zuni narrator does not attempt such "quotation" through the use of nonverbal sound effects; rather, he relies on the large fund of onomatopoeic words provided by the Zuni lexicon.[19] Such words cover a great variety of situations: *taláa* or *tawáa* is a person descending a ladder at great speed; *tenén* is a body falling to the ground; *ts'ok'ok'o* is liquid coming in spurts from a container with a constricted opening, as from a severed head; and *ch'uuk'i* is a liquid plop or pop, as when an eye pops out of its socket. In English the use of onomatopoeia is more typical of poetry than of prose, as in the "flirt and flutter" and "rapping, tapping" of Poe's "The Raven." In theater the function of such words is taken over by mechanical devices or simply the acting out of the sound-producing events.

Gesture, quotation, and onomatopoeia, considered in isolation, do have an appearance of reality, but they are often embedded in what are otherwise fantastic scenes; they sharpen these scenes by lending some of their reality. When size is indicated by gesture it may be the size of a notched stick with which a deranged boy measures the vaginas of his suitors;[20] a quotation may come out of the mouth of the Aatoshle ogress as she threatens to eat up a little girl;[21] and when *isshakwakwa* reproduces a hard rain it may be a rain caused by the Ahayuuta as they roll stolen thunder and lightning stones on the floor of their house.[22]

With all the devices discussed so far, whatever the realism imparted, the tale picture stays more or less within its frame, but there are a number of devices by which the narrator can cause the picture to come jumping right out of its frame and into the lives of his hearers. One of the more common of these devices simply involves the insertion of a phrase such as "It was about this time of year" or "It was a night like this." Another involves the laying out of the story action as if it were centering on the narrator's own house: Andrew, for example, frequently represents the protagonist's house as being in a relatively high place, just as his own house is, so that the protagonist

---

19. On the other hand, the use of vocal but nonverbal (nonphonetic) imitations of animal sounds is reported for the Cherokee and the Wind River Shoshone (see Tedlock, "Verbal Art").

20. "The Female Ahayuuta," discussed in Chapter 13, below.

21. "The Girl and the Protector," presented in full in Chapter 2, above.

22. H-9.

"goes down" to neighboring houses or other locations and "goes up" when he returns. Narrators may not be fully conscious of this particular form of realism, but Joseph readily recognized it in the tales of Andrew and Walter and repeatedly called it to my attention.

The most startling breaking of the tale frame comes when the narrator, in the course of his performance, makes reference or obvious allusion to individuals present in his audience or to their actions. I have little idea of how extensive this sort of thing may be, since I have witnessed only a few tale-telling sessions which got under way spontaneously and which were, at the same time, free of the somewhat inhibiting effects of my tape-recorder, but I can say that in such sessions that I did witness, members of the audience were *always* dragged into the story.[23]

The remaining links between the Zuni tale and Zuni reality depend more on what the narrator says in his role as narrator than on what he does as actor and special-effects man. Among these links are the psychological bases of the behavior of the tale characters, a matter of special interest here since it has often been observed that oral narratives take little trouble to explain such things as motivation, unlike much of our own written prose fiction. Dostoevski, for example, goes to great lengths to explain what led Raskolnikov to commit murder, while a Zuni narrator may explain a person's murderous tendencies by doing little more than calling that person a witch. But the Zuni tales do have modern parallels: Bergman and Fellini, for example, who assume a certain knowledge of Freudian psychology on the part of film viewers, present the full-blown psychotic women of *Through a Glass Darkly* and *Juliet of the Spirits* without ever really explaining how they came to be that way. If we take this cue and abandon the comparison with modern fiction (especially the older, more realistic part of it), the proper question to ask about Zuni tales is not Why are motivations and the like not fully explained? but Does the native audience understand these things? All indications are that Zuni audience members, through the application of the same ethnopsychology which they use in everyday life, understand a great deal. The following cases show their understanding of motivation in particular:

A girl whose only relative is a disabled grandfather sees men bringing in rabbits and decides to try hunting rabbits herself.[24] Joseph said, "I think she did it because her grandfather was old,

23. See Chapter 13, below.
24. "The Girl and the Protector."

and she thought it was easy. Like my wife always likes to go fishing with me; she puts her line in but the fish never get on her hook. She thinks it's easy, but it's not." He said that a real-life girl might wish to go hunting, like the girl in the story, but would not actually go.

A young man who is the son of a priest or whose grandfather is a priest and whose father is the Sun is approached by a series of young women who want to marry him.[25] Joseph found the girls' initiative intelligible in the context of the stories, since in real life many girls would want to marry a person of high status, but he also said that in real life a girl would never be the one to propose marriage.

A man's wife constantly tells him, "I really do love you"; he decides to test her to find out whether she really does love him.[26] Andrew found the man's irritation perfectly plausible, and Joseph said, "He might have gotten irritated all right, for her saying that all the time. It got on his nerve." Asked whether a real husband would get so annoyed, Joseph said, "Yes, I guess because after a while you might doubt it: 'How do I know what she is saying is true?' It's like Elizabeth Taylor and Richard Burton. The Hollywood people predict that will last five years."

A man follows his deceased wife to Kachina Village (where the dead live); he is unable to join her there and goes home, where he becomes ill and dies.[27] Joseph, asked for a real parallel, said, "I don't think anyone has ever followed a dead person, but I always hear people say, 'When her husband or his wife died, then he got sick because his spouse passed away.'"

A boy who was abandoned as a baby and raised by deer is reunited with his human relatives; for three days he wanders around with a bow without any intention of hunting; on the fourth day, attempting to gather some yucca blades, he stabs himself to death with them, apparently by accident.[28] The narrator (Andrew) never said anything about the boy's emotional state, but Joseph explained the boy's wandering by saying, "He

25. H-6 and H-2.
26. H-6.
27. I-3.
28. "The Boy and the Deer," in Tedlock, *Finding the Center*, pp. 1–32.

was lonesome," and Andrew himself said, "All that time he was with his deer folks, and all that time after his capture he had it on his mind. He never did grow up with his real family, but with those deer, and probably he didn't like it in the house." Of the boy's death Joseph said, "It was almost like he committed suicide," and Andrew said, "Probably he had it in his mind to kill himself, that's the way I felt when I was telling it."

In this last case, two Zunis immediately see a motive in the boy's death even though it is treated in the story as if it were an accident. We might make the same analysis, but perhaps not so readily, and we would have to make appeal to the concept of the subconscious.

The ethnopsychology of these next cases involves fixed personality traits rather than immediate motivational circumstances:

The Ahayuuta twins play tricks on the Aatoshle ogre and ogress, on the Uwanammi (rain-makers), and finally on their own grandmother (*hotta*, mother's mother).[29] Joseph indicated that a penchant for joking is common among boys and gave this example: "At ———— there were two brothers who stayed there a lot of the time. One day they killed a rat. They brought it home to their *hotta*; they said it was a rabbit and asked her to fix it. She couldn't see too well; she put it in the oven and they were just laughing. Some people call them the Ahayuuta; they were raised by their old *hotta* and *nana* (grandfather) and didn't have parents." Joseph also cited a practical joke which he himself performed as a boy: "One time we were home toward the close of school and there was a big dance. My older brother came home, my younger brother came home, but my youngest brother didn't come home. We didn't have enough beds, so my mother had to make a bed for my youngest brother on the floor. We put a dust pan under the pillow and a board under the bedding. When he lay down, we laughed."

A young woman stays in a room on the fourth story down weaving baskets and never goes out;[30] a young man stays inside all the time weaving blankets and never goes out to help his father in the fields.[31] Joseph said that the term for this sort of person is *ayyulhasshina*, "a very quiet person, doesn't speak"; this term is

29. H-9.
30. H-2 and "The Boy and the Deer."
31. H-6.

never used in the tales, but it is used for real-life people with re-clusive tendencies. Asked for a real-life parallel to the constant weaving in the tales, Joseph immediately cited silversmithing.

A young man is so devoted to the care of his pet eagle that he refuses to go courting or to attend a social dance.[32] Joseph, think-ing of this tale, remarked, "Even today there are people who've got about twenty cats; they don't want to give them to anybody, they want to treat them as friends," and he cited a newspaper story about such a person. Asked whether any Zunis are this way about pets, he said, "Maybe there are with other domestic animals, like a horse or a sheep. I know my cousin, when he was left an orphan as a little child, he used to herd sheep, and when he got about my girl's size [six years] he used to play with the lambs and talk to them. . . . Oh, and another one, ————'s elder sister's daughter, she's kind of a queer girl, she's got dogs and cats and she talks to them, brings them into the house and puts their clothes on them. I think she's a little bit out of her head."

Witches try to kill a successful hunter and, failing that, kill his wife;[33] witches try to kill the best deer-hunter in the village, who is the son of a priest.[34] Joseph, asked what might happen that would resemble the former tale, said, "If you are well-to-do, or if you've got a good-paying job or a lot of sheep, then the witches will get jealous and try to kill you or your relatives." Asked about the latter tale, he said, "Well, maybe we don't have good hunters, as of long ago, but a witch can always witch you, if you are wealthy or belong to a family who has more, or if your father is a high priest, some sort of leader in the village."

Benedict treated witch attacks in tales as "compensatory daydreams" rather than as reflections of reality,[35] but so far as the Zunis them-selves are concerned the witch personality in tales is intelligible in terms of the witch personality in real life. The witches in Zuni tales should not seem strange to us, either, when we consider the extraor-dinary prominence which our own mass media (both fictional and "non-fictional") give to such stereotyped and menacing figures as Eastern European spies, Sicilian gangsters, New Left students, and the carriers of the highly contagious psychedelic syndrome.

32. H-15.
33. I-3.
34. H-16.
35. Ruth Benedict, *Zuni Mythology*, vol. 1, pp. xix–xx.

However real the motives and personality traits in Zuni tales may be in themselves, they, like gesture, quotation, and frame-breaking, are the servants of fantasy. In every one of the cases cited the real motive or trait is the taking-off point for behavior that would be extreme or nonexistent in real life: The girl who wishes she could go hunting actually goes ahead and does it, the man who doubts his wife's sincerity devises a test in which she must join him in suicide to prove her love, the girls who wish to marry an illustrious young man go and propose to him, the despondent boy lets a fatal "accident" happen to him, the reclusive young woman leaves her house only to get rid of her unwanted child, the young man with the eagle so prefers its company to that of humans that he wants to go away from the village with it, and the Ahayuuta play their jokes even on powerful persons. The ethnopsychological bases of these actions reverse the paralogic of the tale-ending explanatory element: In the case of the ending, the true consequent lends verisimilitude to the fictional antecedent, while in the case of the motive and the personality trait, the true antecedent lends verisimilitude to the fictional consequent.

One of the most important devices a Zuni narrator has for giving the appearance of reality to a tale comes into play between the motive and the final consequent, and that is the description of the technology and ritual employed by the characters:

> A girl's grandfather makes her a pair of snow boots (*upchaawe*) so she can go out in the snow, and she goes rabbit hunting; both the making of the boots and the hunting are described at great length.[36] Joseph, while translating the passage about the boots, remarked, "Walter always has to go into every little detail, like he was actually there," and while translating the passage about the hunting, he said, "He's telling it like he really lived it." Andrew, who was present when Walter narrated this tale, cited it as the sort of thing that would be popular with audiences because "it is almost true" and explained that he was thinking mainly of the rabbit hunting.

Benedict recognized such details as a major feature of Zuni tale-telling and noted that narrators could use (and display) personal firsthand knowledge in making these descriptions.[37] Here is an example of firsthand knowledge from my own collection:

36. "The Girl and the Protector."
37. Benedict, *Zuni Mythology*, vol. 1, pp. xxx–xxxii.

He's telling it like he really lived it: Walter Sanchez on his favorite mount, about to drive his herd of horses to a creek.

A young man has a pet eagle; eagle behavior and eagle-keeping are described in detail.[38] When I pointed out to Joseph that Andrew once kept eagles, he said, "I think a lot of this storytelling is taken from [the narrator's] own environment," and he added that if this were not the case, "the story would be short."

Like all the other verisimilitudinal devices in Zuni tales, descriptions of technology and ritual, even when so real as to be based on personal experience, are embedded in fantasy: The rabbit-hunting girl uses real techniques and wears real snow boots, but in fact girls do not go hunting, and what is more, this girl's expedition leads her into an encounter with the Aatoshle ogress; the young man with the eagle cares for it in the real way at first but later goes off and marries it. But context is not the only thing which removes descriptions of the real from the everyday world of the audience; narrators never devote these detailed descriptions to activities familiar to just anyone (such as the public portions of the Sha'lako ceremony) but instead to activi-

38. H-15.

ties which are known only by certain individuals or groups, or which are rare or have now passed out of existence. Deer hunting, for example, is pursued only by adult men, and by no means all of them; thus, for women, children, and some men, a detailed description of the ritual aspects of deer hunting would be quite informative and a bit exotic.[39] Of course one would not expect tales to contain such highly esoteric and valuable information about a ritual as belongs properly to only a few religious officeholders. To be proper material for tales, then, a real activity must be neither excessively ordinary nor excessively sacred, and deer-hunting ritual represents just such a compromise.

Tale descriptions of activities which are now rare or nonexistent cover such matters as rabbit hunting by means of the extraction of the rabbits from their burrows and eagle-keeping, already mentioned, together with stick racing (including preliminary physical training and ritual), the Yaaya (a social dance), and various crafts (including textile weaving).[40] Such technological and ritual archaism is in keeping with the long-ago setting of the tales; it is not simply that the tales have stood still while the rest of Zuni culture has changed. Some sort of archaism, though it may have increased recently, must always have existed in the tales: It is easy to imagine, for example, that the tales of Pueblo III peoples might have had characters living in pit houses just as present-day Zuni tale characters have aboveground houses but with roof entrances.

The kind of archaism so far discussed serves the ends of fantasy and realism simultaneously: The ritual and technology in question are removed from real life and yet do not stretch the limits of the imagination. But there are also cases in which the long ago is used as a license for introducing events which go much further beyond the everyday world than a defunct sport or social dance:

> An abandoned child is nursed and raised by a deer.[41] Andrew commented, "Up to date, if someone threw this one away, he couldn't get the milk, couldn't get the deer."

Some of the events which, like the adoption of children by animals, used to be possible (but no longer are) are described with as much detail as activities which lapsed within living memory, including the

39. H-2, H-40.
40. Rabbit hunting is described in "The Girl and the Protector" and H-8, eagle keeping in H-15, stick racing in H-7 and I-16, the Yaaya dance in H-6 and H-15, and textile weaving in H-6.
41. "The Boy and the Deer."

turning of a witchwoman into a deer through the use of deer earwax, the means by which a living person may temporarily assume the form of the bloody corpse of another person, and the means of reconstructing and reviving a person who has been decapitated and has lost some blood.[42]

Zuni tale characters (especially human ones) almost never perform their more fantastic actions without going through some sort of technical or ritual procedure; even the turtle, one of the most sacred and savant of beings, may have to make at least a small bow in this direction:

> A turtle discovers an abandoned child and carries him home on his back.[43] Andrew commented, "One thing that's surprising about that story: How could a turtle carry a baby? Well, it was tied with yuccas. That's one thing that's surprising, but anyway, he carried the baby to his old lady."

We might object that the turtle, even if he could conceive of tying something with yucca, would not be able to do so with his claws, but the idea of the yucca does make this episode seem at least a trifle more plausible. The more fantastic portion of our own fiction constantly makes use of a technical logic which is only partially plausible: James Bond may fly his way out of a pickle by strapping a jet-pack on his back, but how did he come up with a jet-pack at that particular moment?

The modern parallels to the Zuni use of technical and ritual knowledge go far beyond the minor technical tricks just mentioned. The unordinary activities in Zuni tales range from those which are no longer possible down to those only recently lost or known only by a few; this spectrum has a direct parallel in horror films set in the past, and again it is repeated in inverted form in science fiction set in the future, which commonly ranges from that which is not yet possible down to that which is not yet in general use or is only in the experimental stage. It may be objected that some of the Zuni tale activities, unlike those in science fiction, involve a supernatural connection between cause and effect (as in the case of the restoration of a head to its body), but the mere fact that science fiction carries the science label does not make it science in fact: Spaceships, for example, are constantly described as flying faster than the speed of light, which in a way is more fantastic than anything in a Zuni tale. Just as a Zuni tale-

---

42. H-2, H-11, and "The Women and the Man" (Tedlock, *Finding the Center*, pp. 85–132), respectively.
43. H-2.

teller makes no distinction between what we would divide into technology and magic, so the writer of science fiction makes no distinction between plausible technology and impossible technology.

When science fiction and horror are set in the present, they often rely on a variation of the time-distancing scheme: The monster or the invaders are living fossils from the distant past (and were frozen in the Arctic ice, perhaps), or they are somehow transported from the future; or else the protagonist himself travels in time. If time is not stretched, then the trouble must come from a distant and a little-known place, such as Transylvania, an unmapped Pacific atoll, the interior of the earth, or some other planet; or it must come from a distant "place" in the mind, as when the whole story or part of it is represented as a dream or as the fantasy of a drug-user or psychotic; or the scale may be shifted, as when the protagonists of *Fantastic Voyage* travel through the human body in a microscopic submarine. Fantasy, then, looks in one way or another for a distant place to happen.

I hope it is clear by now that one need not look to modern children's fairy tales, or to modern dreams, or to the concept of a "prelogical mentality" (which still survives, implicitly, in psychoanalytic attempts to treat tales as collective dreams) to understand the fantastic features of oral narratives. The Zunis place their fantasy in the past while we often place it in the future, but that is more a question of where our respective interests lie than of our mental structures. The end results of the fantasy process are much the same, whatever the setting, ranging from extreme actions of human beings (such as murder and suicide) to Kafkaesque transformations and unnatural monsters. Both the Zunis and ourselves maintain a constant tension between the fantasy and the real world: The Zunis shore up their fantasy with all the devices their particular traditions and experiences provide, drawing upon gesture, quotation, onomatopoeia, ethnopsychology, technology, and ritual, together with tale-ending paralogic.[44] If our sound effects are better or if The Thing, who drinks human blood in a film, seems more real than Haynawi, who collects human hearts in a tale, this difference is largely a matter of the technology available to the artists working in the respective media. And both the Zunis and ourselves, whenever we bring these strange and dangerous worlds into being, feel the need to throw up some sort of frame around them.

44. Paul Ricoeur, who sees the distancing of fiction as "a distantiation of the real from itself," might argue that realism is not so much a means for shoring up fantasy as it is the means by which fantasy opens up new possibilities in real life (*Hermeneutics and the Human Sciences*, p. 142).

On Praying, Exclaiming, and Saying Hello in Zuni

In Zuni there are two ways of radically removing speech (*penanne*) or song (*tenanne*) from the plane of everyday vocalization. The speaker or singer may either *ana k'eyato'u*, "raise it right up," or else *yam ik'eenannakkya peye'a*, "utter it with his/her heart." In the case of singing, "raising up" affects the last two parts of a five-part song of the Kachina (masked dance) Society. The first three parts all have the same tonic, but the tonic of the fourth part may be raised higher and that of the final part still higher.[1] When a song is sung "with the heart," on the other hand, it is silent in its entirety, though the lips may move.[2] In the case of raised-up speaking, strong stress and high

---

This chapter had its beginnings in a paper delivered at the 1972 Georgetown Round Table in Linguistics; a revised version of that paper appeared in *Language in Religious Practice*, ed. William J. Samarin (Rowley, Mass.: Newbury House, 1976), pp. 72–83. The present text is further revised (and expanded) in both its arguments and its examples, principally in order to take account of fresh hearings of raised-up sacred words at Zuni (words that cannot be tape-recorded) and of recent writings by Michael Silverstein.

1. For a thorough discussion of Zuni kachina song structure and performance at Zuni, see Barbara Tedlock, "Songs of the Zuni Kachina Society."

2. Silent singing is also reported for the Hopi (Alexander M. Stephen, *The Hopi Journals*, pp. 80–81).

pitch are given to syllables that would otherwise be weak and low, whereas speaking with the heart makes no sound; either way, the resultant sound pattern is directly opposed to the normal pattern, in the one case by inversion (a term I have borrowed from music) and in the other by negation. Our primary concern here will be with raised-up speaking.

The phonemic inventory of Zuni, as described by Stanley Newman, includes two stresses (strong and weak) and three pitch levels.[3] In the case of the stresses, the first syllable of a word of two or more syllables takes the strong stress (´), as in *pénanne*, "word." Sometimes a clause-initial monosyllabic word also takes the strong stress, as in *hóp to áane*, "Where are you going?" In words of four or more syllables there is sometimes a secondary (and subphonemic) stress (`) on the penult or antepenult, as in *tómtonànne*, "log drum." All other syllables take the weak stress (unmarked here).

In the case of pitches, the sentence or independent clause begins with a middle pitch (2), sometimes sags to a low pitch (1), and then, on the final word, if it is polysyllabic (which it usually is), rises to a high pitch (3) on the first syllable and drops steeply to a low pitch (1) on the last:

<pre>
2   1 3   1
láak'i ápi yam hótta án'ik'oshàkya
today Ivy her maternal-grandmother played-with
</pre>

Today Ivy played with her grandmother.

A shorter sentence or clause may simply begin on (2) and drop to (1) at the end:

<pre>
2   1
ápi íya
Ivy is-coming
</pre>

Ivy is coming.

Sometimes the deemphasis entailed in the combination of weak stress and low pitch on the final syllable is carried a step further: The vowel may lose its voicing and the final consonant (if any) may become inaudible.

If we were to stop our discussion of Zuni stress and pitch right here, we would still be well within the bounds of traditional gram-

---

3. Stanley Newman, *Zuni Grammar*, pp. 13–15. Willard Walker reduces the stress inventory to a single item, omitting "weak" stress ("Toward the Sound Pattern of Zuni," p. 247).

mar. Whether we chose to assign stress and pitch to the phonemic or segmental level, as Newman does, or to a prosodic or suprasegmental level, as others might do, we would have kept the discussion within the boundaries where sound patterns comfortably match up with the hierarchical structures according to which words, clauses, and sentences are constructed. But if we are to discuss the inversion of stress and pitch in speech that is "raised up," tracing out the full range of its occurrences and arriving at a general statement, we must exceed ordinary linguistic boundaries in several different ways. At the outset it is necessary to introduce what I like to call "lines," which cut across patterns of stress and pitch. Each line is an uninterrupted sequence of sounds, falling between two silences.[4] The line is not to be confused with the "breath group": Many silences in extended discourse, Zuni or otherwise, are not accompanied by the taking of breath—indeed, they may be accompanied by a closing of the glottis. Nor is the line to be confused with the "utterance," unless we can free ourselves from the linguistic notion that the utterance must necessarily mesh directly with syntactical units. The line I am speaking of is the line as actually delivered.

In the case of Zuni *télapnaawe*, or "tales," lines often end in the middle of a clause, sometimes even on a modifier whose noun or verb is delayed until the next line. In the following example the two lines are separated by a pause of a little less than a second:

> ²   ¹   ³   ¹ ²
> *hánatte tom'aan téna'u níishapak hom*
> quick you sing-it mourning-doves my
> ¹ ³   ¹
> *ténan ókky'anàpkya*
> song caused-to-forget

> Quick, sing it, mourning doves made me
> forget my song.[5]

Conversely, a new clause or sentence may begin in the middle of a line:

> ² ¹ ³   ¹ ²   ¹   ² ¹ ³   ¹
> *kóp to' léye'a lé' ánikwap má' ho kyáwashè'a*
> what you doing that he-said-to-her well I am-winnowing

> "What are you doing?" He said that to her. "Well, I'm winnowing."

---

4. For a more extensive discussion of lines, see Chapter 1, above.
5. This example and the next are from Dennis Tedlock, *Finding the Center*, pp. 76–83.

In either situation the regular patterns of stress and pitch are usually undisturbed, as in the examples given. The effect of such lines, when they occur frequently in extended discourse, is analogous to that of syncopation in music: There are silences where notes might have been expected, or notes where silences might have been expected. In tale-telling, as in music, syncopation builds tension. It also occurs, if less frequently, in Zuni conversation, as in our own.

Zuni *téwusu pénaawe*, or "sacred words," usually prayers, sound very different from tales or conversation, even to a person who does not know the language. When prayers are intended to be heard and understood not only by an audience of *ky'ápin áaho"i*, "raw people" (nonhuman beings), but also by one of *ték'ohànnan áaho"i*, "daylight people" (humans), stress, pitch, and line all come into concert in the mode of delivery known as "raising it right up." Each line is treated as if it were a clause (whether it is one or not), except that the sag to (1) after the initial (2) is now carried all the way to the penult of the final word, and the (3), instead of occurring on the first syllable of the final word, now occurs on the last. That same last syllable, instead of taking a weak stress or even being unvoiced, now takes the heaviest stress of the entire line, with a consequent lengthening of the vowel. What would normally be the strong stresses elsewhere in the line are reduced to the level of the secondary stresses, and what would normally be secondary stresses are reduced to weak stresses. The changes constitute an inversion in that what would have been lowest becomes highest, what would have been highest becomes lowest, and what might have been the weakest syllable in the entire line now becomes the strongest.[6] Lines no longer separate modifier from noun or verb, and there are no longer shifts from one clause to another within lines, but lines may still end within a clause, and there are few if any lines that could stand by themselves as grammatically complete sentences. The following prayer to the Sun Father (adapted from Ruth L. Bunzel's "Zuni Ritual Poetry") illustrates this raised-up delivery of sacred words:

2   1 3
lùkkya yàtonnée
this day

---

6. This strengthening of the final vowel led Ruth L. Bunzel to suppose that there were special word endings for prayers: "Words ending with consonants—for example, the participles in *-nan* and *-ap*—take special forms . . . *-nana* and *-apa* when occurring finally" ("Zuni Ritual Poetry," p. 620n.). But these are not "special forms"; it is just that their final vowels, which are commonly unvoiced in rapid everyday speech, came to her attention only in raised-up delivery.

2   1   3
hòm yàtokkya tacchúu
my daylight-instrument father

2   1   3
yàm tèlhasshinakwíi
your terrestrial-old-one-at

2   1   3
tò yèelana kwàyiky'appáa
you standing come-out

2   1   3
yàm ky'àkwi yàana te'onáa
my/your water-at become-whole that-which-is

2   1   3
hàlawtinannée
cornmeal (esoteric term)

2   1   3
lìilha tom ho' lhèya'uppáa
here to-you I hand

2   1   3
yàm ona yàanakyáa
your/my road become-whole-instrument

2   1   3
yàm lhàsshiyakyáa
your become-old-instrument

2   1   3
yàm ky'ashimáa
your moisture (occurring in nature)

2   1   3
yàm tòoshonannée
your seed (for native domestic plants)

2   1   3
yàm ùtenannée
your wealth (connotes display)

2   1   3
yàm sàwanikyáa
your become-powerful-instrument

2   1   3
yàm tsèmakwin tsummée
your thoughts-at strength

2   1 3   1
témlha hom to' ánikchiyànna
all me you would/will-bless-with[7]

This very day!
My Sun Father!

7. Bunzel, "Zuni Ritual Poetry," p. 635; translation mine. I have glossed *yam* as "my/your" and "your/my" in the fifth and eighth lines of the interlinear translation because its references are not resolved until the seventh and last lines, respectively.

At your shrine!
You stand out!
Water by which we live!
Maize meal!
I hand it here to you!
Your long road!
Your old age!
Your moisture!
Your seed corn!
Your wealth!
Your courage!
Your strength of will!
May you bless me with everything.

Each of the first fourteen lines of this prayer is emphatically complete, as far as stress and pitch are concerned, and the last line has the completeness of a clause in ordinary speech, but the fifteen lines together, considered grammatically, constitute one single sentence. The verbs in the fourth and seventh lines are subordinated (by their *-ppa* suffix) to the final verb, which alone completes the sentence.

A prayer delivered before an audience that includes humans may be answered with periodic affirmations, as when a man or woman praying before the altar of a medicine society is answered by a man who sits behind the altar. Like the prayer itself, the response may be raised up, taking the form *èleetée*, "Just so!" or *hacchíi*, "For certain!"

There are times when a person delivering a prayer does not "raise it up." This is especially likely to happen when there are people present other than the intended audience. A prayer is valuable and potent in inverse proportion to the number of people who know it,[8] and there is always a chance that an eavesdropper might steal it from its owner. This is the problem of a man who wishes a kachina dance to continue for another day. He must go to the dance leader, right out in the plaza, and must cast his request in the form of a prayer, but this prayer is intended for the dance leader, not for the general public. In addition to lowering his voice, he may go on at much greater length without pausing, running together two, three, and even four phrases that might otherwise have been delivered as clearly separate lines. Each of these phrases will still be marked, but now the initial secondary stress (`) will become a primary stress (´), and the initial pitch (2) will be the highest pitch attained; all other stresses will be strongly suppressed, and the terminal pitch (3) will be leveled all the way to

8. Bunzel, "Introduction to Zuni Ceremonialism," pp. 493–94.

(1).[9] For example, the second and third lines of the above prayer might turn out as follows:

$$\overset{2}{y\acute{a}m}\ \overset{1\ 2}{telhasshinakwi\ t\acute{o}}\ yeelana\ \overset{1}{kwayiky'appa}$$

When this mode of delivery is sustained, the elimination of many pauses and the flattening of pitch give it the effect of a rapid paternoster.

As a rule, the person who prays in solitude, as a man does when he goes to his cornfield at sunrise, will use the flat and rapid delivery just described. But if, despite all this man's previous prayers and sacrifices, the raw people have failed to bring the expected summer rains to his field, he may use the raised-up delivery and even give the strong stresses a little more punch than usual. As one Zuni put it, "Sometimes you have to really tell them. The old man says, 'If they don't bring rain you might as well scold them.'" Bunzel's statement that Zuni prayer "is never the spontaneous outpouring of the overburdened soul," but "more nearly a repetition of magical formulae"[10] holds true only for the *wording*, not for the *delivery*.

Some prayers are so valuable to their owners that they are "said with the heart," without any interpretable sound.[11] This is the case, for example, with the prayers of dance leaders during the winter night performances of the Kachina Society. A prayer of this kind would be spoken aloud on only two occasions during the lifetime of a religious officeholder, the first when he learned it and the second when he trained his successor. Even a person praying in solitude will not risk the oral delivery of such a prayer; as one man put it, "You'll never know who might come around within a minute or two." In "saying it with the heart" we have a "speech event," if that is the word, of which no transcription can be made.

There are a few prayers which, even though valuable and potent, are fully intended to be heard by the public. These prayers are protected from being too widely known by their great length and by the fact that they are delivered only once a year (and in some cases only once in four years). Such is the case with the *péna táshana*, or "Long Talk," performed by the impersonator of the Long Horn kachina at

---

9. See the prayer in "The Girl and the Protector" (in Chapter 2, above) for a translation of an extended example of this kind of delivery.

10. Bunzel, "Zuni Ritual Poetry," p. 615.

11. Stephen reports that the most powerful Hopi prayers are soundless except for a faint breathing that is too soft even to constitute an intelligible whisper (*The Hopi Journals*, p. 58).

the Sha'lako ceremony in December,[12] a prayer intended to benefit the entire community for the entire coming year. The delivery is an extreme form of raising it up. The line-initial (2) is maintained evenly, without any sag to (1), all the way up to the last syllable of the line, which is then delivered with a (3–1) glide lasting two seconds or so. Enunciation is exceptionally clear, with all long vowels and geminate consonants held longer than in a normal speaking voice. At the end of each line there is a deafening silence of two full seconds or more, and then, at the same moment the performer pronounces the first syllable of the next line, he shakes his rattle (a bunch of deer shoulder blades held in the hand) and stomps his right foot. This brings us to the borderland between speech and song: The pitch control approaches that of the singing voice, though the "melody" is simple; the rattle provides a beat, if an unevenly spaced one; and the stomp of the foot suggests kachina dancing.[13]

Some *téwusu pénaawe*, or "sacred words," are not prayers—that is, their audience is solely human except in the sense that raw people might be listening in. Again the pattern of delivery depends on the audience. When the impersonator of the Kyaklo kachina gives a six-hour narration of the *chímiky'anà'kowa*, or "Beginning," before Kachina Society members, or when the Bow Priest announces a communal rabbit hunt to the whole village, they raise it up. But when the head of a household has a formal exchange with a medicine man whose services he is contracting, and when their words are not intended for others who may be in the room, the delivery tends toward the flat and rapid one described earlier.

Although series of lines with stress and pitch inversion are most frequently found in ritual settings, such passages do occur in speech events that are only peripherally sacred. Episodes of the "Beginning," for example, may be told in a hearthside setting, with some passages retaining a raised-up delivery despite the secular occasion. Moreover, *télapnaawe*, or "tales," which are not in and of themselves sacred at all, may contain quotations of raised-up sacred words. In either kind of narrative, the lines in question usually involve formal exchanges (including greetings) between two parties, at least one of whom is either a raw person or a priest. In the following example a priest, after an exchange of greetings, asks a roomful of people why they called him to their house:

12. Bunzel, "Zuni Ritual Poetry," pp. 710–56.
13. Long Horn's talk roughly fits George List's description of "chant"; on List's map of the field of pitch variables connecting speech and song, chant lies closer to song than to speech ("The Boundaries of Speech and Song").

<pre>
2   1 2   1 3
</pre>
iitekkunakkya pìshle shìwani síi
he questioned-them north priest now

<pre>
2   1   3
</pre>
hom àatacchúu
my fathers

<pre>
2   1 3
</pre>
hom chawée
my children

<pre>
2   1 3   1
</pre>
kwá'chi kó' le on ákkya
what thing which because-of

<pre>
2   1   3
</pre>
hom to' ànteshemaawée
me you summon[14]

He questioned them, the North Priest did: "Now!
My fathers!
My children!
For what reason
did you summon me?!"

At this point, or after another line or two, the quoted priest will pass
to a less formal mode of delivery (note that he already did abandon
raised-up speech in the next-to-last line above, but then resumed it).
Then one of his hosts will reply with *ee ìinamilhtée*, "Yes, in truth!"
and perhaps a few more lines with stress and pitch inversion, again
passing to a less formal mode before he finishes.

On rare occasions the hearthside narrator may raise up his words
elsewhere than in quotations, as in this passage from the "Beginning"
in which the twin protector gods first learn that evil has come into the
world:

<pre>
2   1   3   1
</pre>
áachi lakw úkkwayikya tékkwin técchip
two there coming-out-instrument place come-to

<pre>
2   1 3
</pre>
pòwayalayée
is-sitting-on-the-ground

<pre>
2   1 3
</pre>
àmpe'sáy
sorcerer

<pre>
2   1 3
</pre>
ho' ànchi'mowáy
person unclean

14. See Tedlock, *Finding the Center*, p. 237, for the larger context of this passage.

2   1 3
ho' àttannii
person dangerous
2 1   3
hàlhikwii
witch[15]

When the two come to the Place of Emergence:
There he sits!
A sorcerer!
Someone unclean!
Someone dangerous!
A witch!

The third and fourth lines of this example illustrate a phonological feature of raised-up speech that sometimes appears when emphasis on the final stress reaches its greatest peaks: The final vowel may be diphthongized (with the addition of -*y*) rather than lengthened.

The use of a whole series of raised-up lines was formerly limited to the kinds of religious and quasi-religious contexts just described. Public announcements have always been raised up (with a long terminal glide like the one in Long Horn's "Long Talk"), but formerly they were delivered by the Bow Priest, who was unlikely to have any messages of a wholly secular nature. Today, however, public announcements are made by a civil official who brings news of an election or a fair, sometimes raising it up even though using a public-address system that would permit a more relaxed delivery.

If we were to stop our examples of stress and pitch inversion right here, we might still keep this phenomenon apart from the problem of writing a phonological chapter in a Zuni grammar, assigning inversion to "poetics" (which deals with verbal art) rather than "linguistics" (which deals with ordinary speech), or else leaving it to "sociolinguistics," that extension of linguistics in which social contexts other than that of the formal linguistic interview enter into the description of what people might do when they speak. One thing we are already precluded from doing is assigning inversion to "discourse analysis"—to the extension of the hierarchy of linguistic entities "beyond the sentence"—since inversion can occur repeatedly within a single sentence. But instead of stopping here we must now take account of the fact that inversion occurs outside of religious contexts or formal public announcements. In these further cases it is limited to a

15. See *Finding the Center*, pp. 258–59, for the larger context of this passage.

single line, never extending to a whole series of lines. The simplest examples consist of a single onomatopoeic word or an interjection.

In the case of onomatopoeia, which occurs in both formal and informal narratives, the sound imitated in a raised-up style is sudden, brief, and unrepeated: *hasshán* is the sound of a large object, such as a rabbit, being swallowed at one gulp; *kolán* is the sound of a person entering a house precipitously; *lhapáa* is the sound of a turkey starting into flight. These words are never pronounced in any other way, even when they occur medially instead of occupying a line of their own. A word imitating a continuous or repeated sound, on the other hand, never takes stress inversion: The sound of insects on a hot summer day, for example, is *ts'ílili*.

An interjection frequently used in tales is *tisshomahhá*, which expresses horror combined with a pleading attitude; a man might say it when he learns that his son is planning to exchange bodies with a man who died of an axe wound to the head, for example. Other interjections, almost always delivered as a single line with stress inversion, are frequently heard in everyday life. A woman may express sudden pain or anger with *atúu*; a man may express his desire to avoid a task with *ya"aanáa*. Neither these nor any other Zuni interjections have any denotative meaning, unless they could be said to denote the emotions they express; they lack the religious reference carried by so many English interjections. Whereas English opens up the boundary between the sacred and the secular by lexical means, the Zuni interjections open that boundary (if they open it at all) by means of sound, in the sense that they bear a general sonic resemblance to a single line of prayer.

Beyond onomatopoeia and interjections, the use of stress and pitch inversion in secular contexts extends to greetings, interrogations, descriptive exclamations of surprise, imperative statements, and sudden announcements of news. The most common greeting, *kesshé* or *kesshéy*, "Hello!" is always delivered with final stress—except, perhaps, when it is elicited as a vocabulary item in a formal interview. Interrogatives, which otherwise carry first-syllable stress, may be given a sense of urgency and importance with stress inversion: *kwa'píi*, "What?!" *hoppíi*, "Where?!" *chùwapíi*, "Who?!" A woman, in trying to get her diversely occupied family to the dinner table, always says *itonaawéy*, "Eat!" (plural subject), and if she has to repeat herself she increases the final stress and widens her pitch intervals. A girl who sees a carful of visitors coming may run into the house and address everyone there with *chòlin aawiyáa*, "Jo Ann [and others] are coming!"

Exclamations of amazement commonly consist of *hish* or *sish*, "very," followed by a word that describes the thing or event remarked upon. Learning that a woman had paid sixty cents apiece for some cabbage seedlings, I said to her:

```
2   3 1
hish téhya
```
Very expensive.

She replied, as if correcting me or perhaps going me one better:

```
2   1 3
hish tehyáy
```
How expensive!

Raised-up delivery in everyday life most frequently appears in the remarks addressed by adults to children. The most common single item is *lesmáa*, "Don't." During a tape-recorded interview, an older man was told by a child that a playmate had been throwing rocks at the screen door; he dealt with the matter as follows:

```
 2 1 3
chùwapíi
```
Who?!

```
       2 1
(answer) ápi
```
Ivy.

```
2   1   3
àpi lesmáa
```
Ivy, don't!

Here are other lines this same man addressed to Ivy (three years old) when she interrupted interviews:

```
2       1 3
lèsma paniyúu
```
this-no get-down

Don't, get down!

```
2                     1   3
lèsma lèsma lèsma lèsma lèsmáa
```
this-no this-no this-no this-no this-no

Don't, don't, don't, don't, DON'T!

```
2   1   3
hòppi tammée
```
where father-diminutive

Where's daddy?! (i.e., go away and find him)

     2   1 3
hòtta les àn'ik'oshée
maternal-grandmother this-one play-with-hortatory

Go on and play with Grandmother!

   2   1 3
sìsh to' pèye'a tèlokky'anáa
very you talk be-quiet

You talk too much, be quiet!

In most such scolding, the meaning is carried not only by the words and the raised-up delivery, but by a tight and sharp voice quality as well.

It remains to abstract the common features of all these examples of lines with stress and pitch inversion, ranging from prayer to reprimand. A Zuni man, asked to comment on a tape-recorded narrative passage in which a quoted priest uses such lines, told me, "He's saying it in a way that is not ordinary. He's trying to stress, to bring out an important idea. It shows authority, and to have a complete thought at the same time, not just trailing off." In one way or another, these remarks can be applied to all the examples.

First of all, stress and pitch inversion attracts more attention than ordinary delivery and implies that what is being said is "important"; the speech event in question "is not ordinary" and will take precedent over any other speech event that may already be in progress. Even a small child can get the attention of an entire household, cutting right through the preoccupations of its members with a raised-up delivery. In the case of ritual exchanges with a priest, inversion marks the beginning of a speech, but once importance and attention have been established it is possible for the speaker to relax his delivery. In the case of the public prayer of Long Horn, on the other hand, extremely formal delivery is sustained for several hours, with a sudden relaxation in the very last line. In effect, Long Horn's every line demands the same kind of attention that a small child demands for only one line. The affirmations with which a raised-up prayer may be answered are a subtler case: The affirming person is not trying to get attention or be important, but to carry his assent beyond the lexical level ("just so" or "for certain") by *echoing* the stress and pitch inversion of the prayer, thus making a sonic assent. The use of onomatopoeic words by a narrator is also an echoing: It is not so much that he is trying to get attention (he already has that), but that he is imitating the attention-getting quality of sudden (and important) noises.

Second, stress and pitch inversion "shows authority." This is clear enough in the case of sacred words; in fact, sacred words carry authority in and of themselves, but a raised-up delivery shows that the speaker has the proper authority to use them. The exercise of authority is also clear in the case of raised-up orders and reprimands. In other cases it is present only in the sense that the speaker has a *temporary* right to demand attention in such a powerful fashion. In all contexts that are not even peripherally sacred, even including those calling for orders and reprimands, this right is limited to the delivery of a single line, after which ordinary speech is used. The sole exception to this is the public announcement delivered by a civil official.

Third, lines with stress and pitch inversion are clear and complete. They do not "trail off" into a low pitch, a weak stress, and even a loss of voicing, but rather stand in direct opposition to the most obvious weaknesses of everyday speech. This befits their importance and authority.

In the case of "saying it with the heart," importance and authority ride entirely on the lexical potency (as opposed to sonic potency) of the prayer and on the legitimacy of sacred office. These properties are sufficient to attract the attention of the raw people, who are able to "listen" to hearts.

It should be mentioned, before closing, that phenomena similar to raised-up speech in Zuni probably occur in all the other languages of the Pueblo Indians, though not necessarily with such extreme alteration of normal stress patterns. I have heard heavy line-final stress, accompanied by high pitch and sometimes by a downward glide, in announcements made to spectators at Jemez and Hopi dances,[16] and Alfonso Ortíz tells me that Tewa announcements are delivered in this manner. Going beyond the Southwest, Michael Foster reports a mode of delivery for Iroquois Longhouse speeches that is different from Zuni raised-up speech in its exact phonological dimensions, but the same in the sense that each phrase is delivered as if it were an emphatically complete sentence.[17]

The place occupied by the inversion of stress and pitch in the full spectrum of Zuni speech suggests that the kinds of concerns opened up by poetics and sociolinguistics do not necessarily lie outside or beyond or even on the boundary of proper linguistics, but may open up a breach that penetrates to the very core of linguistics. Inversion plays

16. See C. F. Voegelin and Robert C. Euler, "Introduction to Hopi Chants," and Robert A. Black, "The Hopi Grievance Chants."
17. Michael K. Foster, *From the Earth to Beyond the Sky*, pp. 192–93.

no part in Newman's description of Zuni phonology, though in his dictionary he does take note of a single instance of final stress (the entry for *atúu* but not the entries for other interjections).[18] Yet it could be argued that in the cases of interjections (in general), onomatopoeic words (of the kind involving sudden and unrepeated sounds), and the *kesshéy* greeting, inversion has become embedded in the very phonology of these words *as words* and cannot be relegated to some separate realm that lies outside the "ordinary" usage that serves as the foundation for writing a grammar. But if we accept this argument and expand our list of Zuni phonological rules to accommodate inversion in lexical items, we are then faced with a further problem: The usage we have thereby accommodated is continuous, in both form and meaning, with larger-scale usages that affect whole groups of words of widely varying syntactic composition and may even stay in force, line after line, for hours on end. In other words, Zuni stress and pitch inversions, in their full range, refuse to correspond to a single, well-defined level in a hierarchy of Zuni grammatical forms.

There is another way in which the present discussion breaches the boundaries of linguistic business as usual, and that begins with my choosing to center it around a way of speaking for which there is a descriptive phrase in Zuni—*ana k'éyato'u*, "raise it right up." Note that this is not merely a species or genre label within a taxonomy of speech events, but refers to a way of speaking that cuts across generic boundaries just as it cuts across syntactic ones—in fact, it even reaches beyond speech in general (*pénanne*) into song (*ténanne*), though I have not pursued it beyond the threshold of Long Horn's songlike "Long Talk" in the present treatment. In following out the phenomena labeled by this phrase, and in weaving a Zuni speaker's interpretive comments into the summary statements made above, I have crossed from "language structure" in general, which is supposed to be largely if not entirely unconscious in the native speaker but discoverable by linguistic science, to what Michael Silverstein calls "linguistic ideology," or "sets of beliefs about language articulated by the users as a rationalization or justification of perceived language structure and use." Linguists of the Boasian tradition have handed down a teaching that warns us to set aside native linguistic ideology, or what Boas called "secondary explanations." But as Silverstein points out, "to ra-

18. Newman does discuss one unusual type of Zuni intonation (*Zuni Grammar*, p. 15), involving the ideophonic lengthening of the final vowel of a verb, but this device, though it does involve a final (3), is not to be confused with the combination of stress and pitch inversion discussed here. Bunzel, for her part, treats line-final stress as a matter of literary style ("Zuni Ritual Poetry," p. 620).

tionalize, to 'understand' one's own linguistic usage is potentially to change it," which makes linguistic ideology a potential key to the understanding of the historical dialectic between language (as structure) and speech (as action).[19]

I do not wish to speculate here as to whether the larger applications of raised-up Zuni delivery developed historically on a base of final-stress words or whether final-stress words might have penetrated downward from the larger applications—perhaps even from song. Nor do I wish to speculate on the question as to whether the Zuni ideology of raised-up speech is at present the bare beginning of a Zuni recognition of a scheme "immanent in practice," or an established norm "produced by reflection on practice,"[20] though I suspect the latter. But I do hope it is sufficiently clear that exceeding the boundaries of formal elicitation—and of an approach that sees native texts as auxiliary sources for sentences—does not merely lead to an orderly expansion of the rule of hierarchical grammar into previously unoccupied territory, but may move grammar itself all the way down to the phonological level. Zunis know the word for "hello" in their language, and they even have a way of describing how that word is pronounced when it is actually used. Fortunately, if we are misguided by our Zuni dictionary and stress that word on the wrong syllable, any child will be able to correct us.

19. Michael Silverstein, "Language Structure and Linguistic Ideology," pp. 193, 233–34. Dell Hymes does not allow linguistic ideologies an independent role in his "schema of the components of speech acts" (*Foundations in Sociolinguistics*, pp. 53–62), though they could be partially accommodated under what he calls "conventionally recognized and expected outcomes." Potentially, explicit ideologies could have an impact on any or all of the components.

20. See Pierre Bourdieu, *Outline of a Theory of Practice*, p. 20. Bourdieu provides a useful discussion of the dialectic between practices and norms, but his ultimately scientific or objectifying aims lead him to a warning against native theories that sounds much like the warnings of Boas (in linguistics) and Radcliffe-Brown (in social structure).

-- 7̄7̄ --

Phonography and the Problem of Time
in Oral Narrative Events

Phonography has been with us for just over a century now. Phonography: the mechanical inscription of the voice, coupled with a mechanical reading aloud of that inscription, all without the intervention of alphabetic writing. The machines that first hit the market were like contemporary tape-recorders in one very important respect: They not only played recordings, but also made them. They hadn't been on the market very long when Jesse Walter Fewkes decided to take one into the field; in 1890 he recorded verbal arts, both spoken and sung, among the Passamaquoddy in Maine and at Zuni.[1] Since then phonography (I here apply the term to all sound recording) has had an enormous effect on ethnomusicology, but those who deal with the *spoken* word—whether they be linguists, folklorists, cultural anthropologists, or (more recently) social anthropologists—still seem to re-

First delivered at the conference, "Oralità: cultura, letteratura, discorso," held at the Università di Urbino in 1980; first published in the *Documenti di Lavoro* of the Centro Internazionale di Semiotica e di Linguistica, no. 107 (Urbino, Italy: Università di Urbino, 1981). The first paragraph and the notes have been amplified.
    1. Jesse Walter Fewkes, "A Few Summer Ceremonials at Zuni Pueblo," pp. 55–56.

gard phonography as little more than a device for moving the scene of alphabetic notation from the field interview to the solitude of an office with playback facilities. The real analysis begins only after a document of altogether pre-phonographic characteristics has been produced. The situation is rather like that of early photography, when the camera was often seen as little more than a device for moving the scene of drawing and painting from the field to the privacy of a studio.[2] But photography has long since enabled us to see in ways we had never seen before, whereas phonography, at least for those who study the spoken arts, is only just beginning to have a like effect on hearing.

One reason for this lag in hearing is that the alphabet continues to be seen as an utterly neutral, passive, and contentless vehicle for the notation of the individually contentless particles of sound from which all languages are said to be constructed, as if the phonological adjustment of the alphabet to previously unwritten languages, or to languages previously written in a nonalphabetic way, were sufficient to remove all its inherited cultural and historical idiosyncrasies. One of the few modern linguists ever to offer a dissenting view was J. R. Firth, who pointed out that syllabic writing systems—such as Arabic, Devanagari, and Kana—offer an easier accounting of the prosodic features of speech sounds than do alphabetic systems, and who characterized the development of phonology as a "theoretical justification of roman notation" which has led to "the apotheosis of the sound-letter in the phoneme."[3] The phoneme (or letter) has also been called into question by phonetics, that disciplinary alter ego of phonology whose researchers report on the neural organization, physical production, and sensory perception of speech sounds, calling attention to the continuous and overlapping (as opposed to particulate and successive) nature of these sounds, finding no workable unit smaller than the syllable, and describing other irreducible entities much larger than syllables.[4]

The proper phonologist—and here we will let Roman Jakobson play that role—defends himself against the phonetician by drawing an absolute boundary between "the territory of phonetics" and his own, assigning the investigation of "phonic matter" or "raw materials" to phonetics, a discipline which "falls outside linguistics," and re-

2. See Van Deren Coke, *The Painter and the Photograph*.
3. J. R. Firth, *Papers in Linguistics, 1934–51*, p. 123.
4. Ilse Lehiste, *Suprasegmentals*, p. 155. See Dwight Bolinger, "Meaning and Memory," for extensive evidence that what the memory actually stores and transmits to the vocal organs is quite different from the analytical entities posited by linguists.

serving the question of how this material is "put to use by language" for phonology, which is "an integral part of linguistics."[5] Once we have passed safely into the empyrean of linguistics, a realm from which all materiality has been exiled, the question of the phoneme's mode of existence becomes a matter about which "there has been too much discussion," and Jakobson, as if to leave phonetics even further behind, assigns this question not to the laboratory but to philosophy.[6]

Clearly the voice (or *phonē*) of phon-etics, whose continuities give it gross physicality, is quite different from the "voice" of phonology, whose constituents are, as Jakobson insists, outside of "measurable time."[7] When Jacques Derrida attempts the "deconstruction" of what he variously calls "logocentrism," "phonocentrism," "logo-phonocentrism," "phono-logocentrism," "the Western metaphysic," or "the metaphysics of the voice,"[8] it is the voice of phonology that is (or should be) in question, not the voice of phonetics. But so strong is the commonsensical identification of the phoneme (or the letter) with the physical voice that Derrida ultimately blames the ills of alphabetic writing, with its "linearity" and its "repression of pluri-dimensional symbolic thought," on "the irreversible temporality of sound."[9] Having thus encumbered his version of the voice with what he views as an unfavorable physical property, he seeks escape from speech and from alphabetic writing by proclaiming a higher and more general

5. Roman Jakobson, *Six Lectures on Sound and Meaning*, pp. 20, 45, 109. The *Lectures* date from 1942; in *The Sound Shape of Language* (published in 1979), Roman Jakobson and Linda Waugh announce a different view, ridiculing the "narrow isolationism and futile abstractionism" of *both* phonetics and phonology (p. 48), but in practice they give space in their book only to such phonetic research as marches to the beat of such phonological units as the phoneme, the distinctive feature (chap. 3), and a still more abstract entity called the "ultimate constituent" (chap. 2).

6. Jakobson, *Six Lectures*, p. 69. In Jakobson's and Waugh's *The Sound Shape of Language*, this question is given back to phonetics in the person of the late Pierre Delattre, a collaborator of Jakobson's who claimed to have found (after an effort he himself compared to the quest for the Holy Grail) acoustical evidence for phonological distinctive features (pp. 80–82); Jakobson and Waugh summarily dismiss "the widespread reluctance" to accept Delattre's analysis, leaving the details of the controversy to the reader's imagination (p. 83).

7. Jakobson, *Six Lectures*, p. 106. In Jakobson's and Waugh's *The Sound Shape of Language*, laboratory measurements are cited to support the physical existence of phonological entities (chap. 2), but once these entities take on their proper phonological roles, neither they nor the distances between them retain measurable dimensionality. Jakobson and Waugh complain that objections to such reduction are usually based on "a crude metrical attitude" rather than a "sane" approach (p. 83).

8. Jacques Derrida, *Of Grammatology*, pp. 3, 11–12, 43, 71, 78–79, 99; "Limited Inc," pp. 220, 224, 236, 249. These writings are ten years apart, but the position with regard to the voice has not changed. For a further critique of Derrida, see Dennis Tedlock, "The Science of Signs and the Science of Letters."

9. Derrida, *Of Grammatology*, pp. 72, 81–87.

"arche-writing" which is *prior* to speech—indeed, prior even to mankind, since it can be discerned, for example, in genetic codes.[10] This arche-writing is a writing of pure differences, and as such it looks suspiciously like a higher phonology, existing in an empyrean where even the memory of the voice has been banished.

Our specific concern here is that Derrida's reversal of priority between writing and speaking, which like all magician's tricks confuses our sense of what is metaphysical and what is not, has given critics such as Pietro Pucci license to consider "oral" literature to be literature indeed, ultimately raising no problems apart from those with which literary criticism (or phonologically modeled semiotics) is accustomed to deal, and to accuse those who long for the full presence of orality of trafficking in metaphysics.[11] In one sense Pucci is perfectly right. On the graphic face of its published pages, oral literature has nothing to distinguish it from literary literature, and if we could make English as transparent in this matter as Italian, we would pronounce it to be "letterature." Once the actual reading of the letters begins, what most strikes the eye is various kinds of repetition, and it is repetition, more than anything else, that becomes the identifying problem—and for the cultivated reader, an uninteresting problem—raised by "oral" literature.

But if we wish to transcend the intricate alphabetic and literary blockage of what we might call the *lettered* ear, what is required is not a metaphysics, as Pucci seems to fear, but a technology. Instead of adopting the Homeric posture, which means beginning from a literary document whose original orality can only be longed for, let us begin from a phonographic document, postponing its phonological (or "letterary") description as long as possible. Let us also postpone any properly semiotic consideration, since that would make it difficult to keep free of the web of metaphorical phonology, and instead adopt an approach more apropriate to the natural or physical sciences. Let us try to ignore, for the moment, what our story *says*, and consider it purely as an *acoustic signal*, a signal to be measured rather than a code to be deciphered. We have a tape-recording, half an hour long, of a narrative that happens to have been told in the language of the Zuni Indians of New Mexico.[12] It is a *telapnanne*, as they call it, or a tale, a *racconto*, not a sung or chanted narrative but a plainspoken one.

10. Ibid., pp. 8, 14, 56, 84.
11. Pucci repeatedly made such arguments at the conference at which this paper was delivered.
12. For a full English translation of this narrative, annotated for acoustical features such as those discussed here, see Dennis Tedlock, *Finding the Center*, pp. 1–32.

In order to achieve some measure of scientific objectivity, we will let a machine listen to our tape-recorded story—and, what is more, we will allow this machine, not our own ear and hand, to make a visible transcription for us. The machine will write on a moving scroll of graph paper, using three different pens at the same time (see pp. 200–201). One pen will indicate, by vertical oscillations from what would otherwise be a straight line, the amplitude of the acoustic signal from the tape. The second pen, writing immediately below the first, will inscribe the rises and falls of the fundamental pitch of the signal. The third pen will provide us with an absolute time scale, making a mark with the passing of each second in the thirty minutes of the playing of the tape and the rolling of the scroll.[13]

So there is our score for the acoustic signal of the Zuni story, with amplitude, pitch, and time scale, laid out along a scroll that turns out to be nearly fifty meters long. The most striking, most graphic feature of this scroll comes from the contrast between the jagged vertical marks made by the amplitude and pitch pens when the voice of the narrator was sounding and the straight horizontal line the pens drew when the voice was silent. By actual measurement, these two pens, and the voice they graphed, were at rest 34 percent of the elapsed time of the narrative, or about ten out of thirty minutes. Our narrator paused a total of 580 times, dividing the sound of his voice into 581 cleanly separate utterances, not counting the tiny rests of the pens caused by unvoiced consonants or word junctures.

It should be noted here that a 34 percent proportion of silence falls below the 40 to 50 percent range measured by Frieda Goldman-Eisler in the extended discourse of speakers of English and some other languages;[14] apparently her sample did not include performances of formal genres but was of a conversational nature, which would account for the more rapid (less hesitant) pace of our Zuni storyteller. I know of at least one Zuni performer who can lower his pauses to about 30 percent; that may not seem to put him very far below the narrator of the scroll, but speakers of Zuni who have heard him remark that he goes too fast.

Returning to our fifty-meter scroll, we may note that the utterances (or what I elsewhere call lines) vary greatly in length, ranging from less than one-half second, with the single peak of amplitude and pitch that indicates a single, isolated syllable, up to about eight seconds. The intervening silences range from just under a half second up

13. I wish to thank the phonetician Peter MacNeilage for suggesting and arranging the making of this scroll.
14. Frieda Goldman-Eisler, "Continuity of Speech Utterance" and "The Distribution of Pause Durations in Speech."

to about four seconds. From the shortness of many of the utterances, we may guess that they do not always correspond to what linguists call "breath groups"—indeed, if we return to the tape itself, listening only for its clear evidences of the breathing of the narrator, we will find that more often than not he takes no breath at all during his pauses, and worse yet, he may even continue exhaling. Clearly, we cannot attribute the pauses, or even a majority of them, to the simple economics of physical respiratory needs.

To explore the alternation of utterances and pauses any further, we will have to set foot on the threshold that separates the natural or physical science of language from the semiotics of language, but we may still keep some distance from the full semiotic complexity of the spoken word by limiting ourselves to the question of gross clause and sentence boundaries and staying away from the finer details of morphology and phonemics. For the purpose of reading our scroll the question of clauses and sentences is an intonational one. Generally, the boundary between two different sentences will be marked by a brief and steep fall in pitch and amplitude, followed by a rise to a higher level than that which immediately preceded the fall; clause boundaries involve lesser fluctuations. These greater and lesser boundaries occur some 776 times in the present narrative. Since there are only 581 utterances, this means that at least 195 intonational boundaries, or 25 percent of them, will have to fall in the *midst* of utterances rather than corresponding with their *edges*, but the actual figure is 40 percent. Even when we narrow the field to the greater boundaries, those occurring between the 381 complete sentences of the narrative, it turns out that 24 percent of all these sentences end in the midst of an utterance. And as for the utterance edges themselves, 20 percent are accompanied neither by a clause nor a sentence marker, but rather leave us hanging on the narrator's next word. Just as the silences that separate utterances could not be reduced to a question of physical needs, so they cannot be reduced to a question of grammar.

These last findings point up the dangers of using the epic as the sole model for the description of the general characteristics and limitations of oral transmission in general, as classicists and other literary scholars who depend on the work of Milman Parry and Albert Lord tend to do. The extreme form of enjambment in which a clause is left partially constructed is almost nonexistent in the Yugoslav epic, and Lord holds this absence to be "one of the easiest touchstones" in measuring the orality of a text.[15] But this measure, if we were to apply it

---

15. Albert Lord, *The Singer of Tales*, pp. 54, 284n.; see esp. the text on pp. 272–75 for an idea of how closely Yugoslav epic lines conform to major grammatical boundaries.

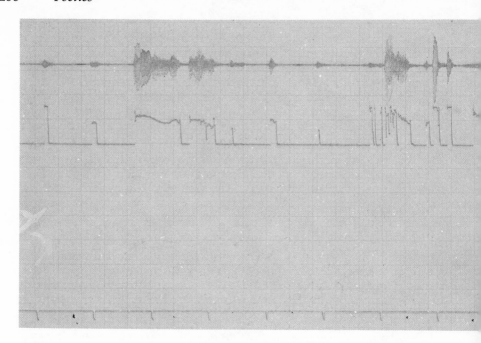

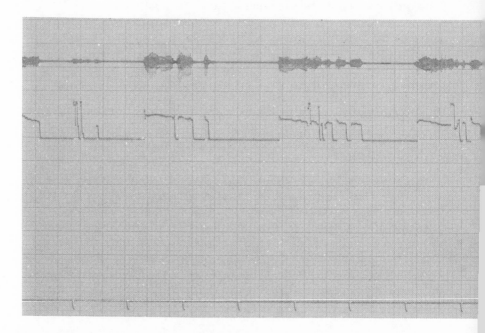

We will allow this machine to make a visible transcription for us: a section of a Zuni story, showing amplitude (*top*), pitch (*middle*), and seconds (*bottom*).

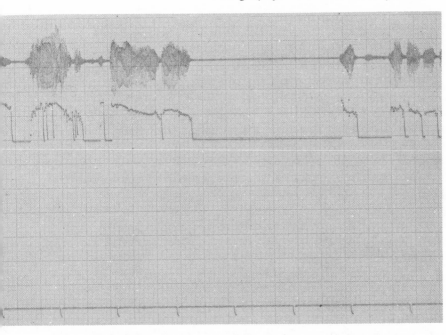

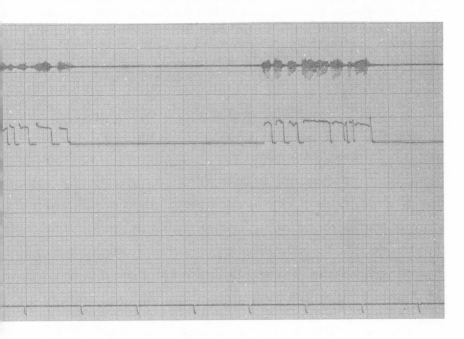

outside the epic genre, could lead us to the absurd conclusion that the Zuni narrative on our scroll is unmistakably of *written* origin!

Returning to the scroll, an inspection of the smallest pulses in the amplitude marks reveals variations, most of them minor, in the rate at which syllables are delivered within the utterances. As Goldman-Eisler has found, that rate normally stays within a range of four to six syllables per second, whatever the language; the major factor in the overall speed of an extended discourse is not the rate of syllable articulation within utterances but rather the rate of pausing.[16] But in the present narrative there are nine different places at which the amplitude and pitch notations indicate that a single syllable is held, at a relatively high monotone, for as much as one to two seconds, or five to ten times longer than a normal syllable. For an explanation of this phenomenon we will have to venture farther across the threshold between physics and semiotics than we have so far; the only point we can make at the moment is that these long syllables occupy a clearly distinguishable place among the gross physical features of our narrative.

Aspects of the speaking voice such as the ones our mechanical transcription graphs so clearly—including vast amounts of silence, utterances that vary greatly in length and often correspond neither with breath-groups nor with intonational contours, hypertrophied syllables, and other features we will leave aside for now—go under the heading of "*para*linguistic" features, a designation that immediately tells us we are in some kind of trouble, disciplinarily speaking. Such features may be dealt with by phonetics, a discipline whose practitioners use instruments like the one that made our scroll for us, but they have no proper place in phonology, a discipline with a strong aesthetic and moral preference for the principles of alphabetic writing. The difficulty is that the semiotics of the spoken word takes its texts (and its models) from these alphabetical linguists, not from the acoustical ones—and no wonder, since phoneticians themselves are reluctant to give any but broad psychological interpretations (when they offer interpretations at all) to phenomena whose importance has not already been attested by authorities (phonologists and grammarians) whose medium is the alphabet.[17]

Phonology does give a small place to silence, or so it might seem,

16. Frieda Goldman-Eisler, "The Significance of Changes in the Rate of Articulation."

17. Lehiste (*Suprasegmentals*), e.g., concentrates on small-scale suprasegmentals that are closely correlated with segmentals, such as vowel quantity, tones (in tone languages), and stress at the syllabic level; she explicitly ties her work to "language" and keeps "paralanguage," by which she means features like the ones under discussion here (together with voice quality), at a considerable distance (p. 3).

by allowing for the "pause juncture," a tiny pause between two words that makes a difference at precisely the lexical level. We spoke of differences in length in the pauses on the scroll, but junctures, as phonologically conceived, are all the same. For that matter, a pause juncture need not be thought of as having any length at all, as that is usually conceived; rather, the notion of a moment passing without any sound, this moment that signifies, if it signifies at all, by means of being nothing but naked time, time passing by, is reduced to the same temporal status as that of any other item in a phonemic or suprasegmental inventory. Within the inventory it is, paradoxically, a timeless segment of time, part of the synchronicity of language; within a text, it has *location* with respect to a succession of other dimensionless units, but it does not *occupy* space or time in a continuous way. It has no *duration*, whether a *relative* duration in comparison with other, neighboring phenomena, or an *absolute* duration as measured by some external standard. For phonological purposes, it is instantaneous. Similarly, intonational features such as the ones we noted on the scroll may be treated as instantaneous. Sometimes there is talk of broad contours, implying duration, but when proper phonological tidiness is demanded the discussion narrows to the phenomena that mark the boundaries of the contours, falling on particular syllables and taking their places as units that may be either present or absent in a succession of durationless units.[18]

The lengthening of syllables finds phonological status under the names "stress" and "vowel quantity." In the case of stress, the problem of duration can be (and usually is) neatly subordinated to questions of pitch and amplitude; but vowel quantity operates independently of pitch and amplitude, so that it raises the problem of duration in a purer form than does stress. Zuni (the language of the narrative under discussion) has vowel quantity, operating at a much smaller scale than the syllabic hypertrophy we noticed on the scroll. As in the case of juncture and intonation, the phonological solution is to render duration durationless, converting the extra vowel length into a "point-like, irreducible unit" called a "mora," succeeding another mora (the single mora of what would have been a "short" vowel) but not continuous with it.[19] Vowel lengthening (if we may still call it that) would seem likely to tempt an orthographer to adopt an iconic sign, but the icon-

18. See ibid., pp. 96–97, for a discussion of these two views. One major linguist who does give a great deal of play to continuous features is Dwight Bolinger, who states that the "digital island" of discrete units "floats on an analog sea" (*Aspects of Language*, p. 17).

19. Jakobson, *Six Lectures*, p. 106.

icity that is indeed chosen by linguists goes against the long vowel's acoustical continuity and instead expresses the abstraction of the mora: After the affected vowel, one need only place a single raised dot.

It should be noted that all the phonological features we have just discussed—pause junctures, intonational markers, stresses, and vowel quantities—lie at the borders of proper phonology. Each one can be and often is treated as suprasegmental rather than segmental, prosodic rather than phonemic, which is another way of saying that each one poses problems for alphabetic writing in its purest or most reduced form, calling for the addition of accents, punctuation marks, raised dots, plus signs, and the like. The one problem all these features pose in common is that of temporality, and a given feature will be accepted phonologically to precisely the degree that a way may be found to reduce its temporality to instantaneity. It is amusing to note that even among proper segments or phonemes, the vowels cause more analytical problems than consonants. The consonants, the "articulations," have less duration than vowels, and of course the quintessential consonants—the ones that come closer than any other phonemes to possessing *acoustical* instantaneity, if such a thing existed—are the stops. It is no wonder that such gross acoustical features as those we discovered on our scroll barely enter into discussions of suprasegmentals, to say nothing of segmentals; such features seem to be at the borders of the borders, or even beyond.

At this point a musical analogy may help us grasp what is left out when the acoustical signal of the speaking voice is transformed into a text by means of phonological reduction. Imagine a musical score with no indication of total performance time, no time signature, no marks of sustained tempo (such as *adagio* or *allegro*), no marks of changing tempo (such as *ritardando* or *accelerando*), no indication of differential time values among the notes, no rests, and no ties—in other words, an imaginary music that made no use of time. It may be a measure of the influence of phonological or textual models on semiotics that we find just such a music in the pages of *A Theory of Semiotics* by Umberto Eco. When he sketches the specific semiotic problems presented by music (as opposed to other codes), Eco makes no mention of temporality.[20] His discussion of musical notation centers around a short staff that bears only a clef and a single note in the C position; he never even mentions that he has chosen a whole note (or semibreve) rather than a note of some smaller relative duration.[21] If musi-

20. Umberto Eco, *A Theory of Semiotics*, p. 11.
21. Ibid., pp. 88–89.

cologists have been slow to adopt the methods and vocabulary of semiotics, as Eco notes, the reason may be that when it comes to temporally complex phenomena, musicology, as Jean-Jacques Nattiez seems to suggest,[22] has more to offer semiotics than semiotics has to offer musicology.

But even in the barest musical score or the barest alphabetic transcription there is one aspect of time that remains, and that is directionality, which orders the notes or letters in a succession. Even directionality is largely implicit: If we may feign illiteracy for a moment, there is nothing on the transcript itself to indicate that it consists of anything more than simultaneous, stationary marks that might be inspected in any order. Even when we recover our literacy, there is still nothing in the individual signs themselves to indicate directionality, except that some of them are asymmetrical. When we begin reading in the proper direction, time is restored, only now it is the time of the reader, with an overall duration and internal changes of tempo that may differ enormously from those of the original speaker or singer.

In the case of a musical score, now fitted out with all the devices we earlier removed, the time of the reader and that of the original singer may be brought into close correspondence, though at this point the reader is likely to vocalize rather than to proceed silently. But in the case of an alphabetic transcription, unless it happens to represent a form of verse with well-known conventions of recitation, the only thing that coincides in the comparison of speaker's time and reader's time is succession, and that only if the reader refrains from jumping ahead or looking back. In fact, of course, the reader does violate textual succession, and when the phonologist moves to the advanced stages of his particular form of reading, the only thing left of succession is a set of rules as to which letters of the alphabet may be placed next to which other letters, and even this disappears when the letters are arranged in a chart, with their positions determined not by succession but by a matrix of distinctive features.

Phonology is very much a reader's and writer's game, and the graphic devices it makes use of in its own written discourse, including the rearrangement of letters in orders (such as matrices) other than those which spell out words, go back to the very dawn of alphabetic writing, as Jack Goody would point out.[23] In Derrida's view, the phonologist's insistence that the object of his investigation is not the written word but the spoken word is nothing but a cover for his disci-

22. Jean-Jacques Nattiez, "The Contribution of Musical Semiotics to the Semiotic Discussion in General," p. 132.
23. Jack Goody, *The Domestication of the Savage Mind*, chap. 4.

pline's originary dependence on alphabetic writing.[24] It might truly be said that phonology, and all the rest of linguistics with it, starts *after* the voice has been set aside. A fresh alphabetic transcription of something spoken in a previously unwritten language is still, in some of its details, a phonetic rather than a phonological document, but it is from the already atomized and collapsed temporality of the document, and not from the intricately proportioned temporality of the voice, that the linguist begins the work that is especially his own, starting with a reduction of the phonetic residue in the text itself and then proceeding with the text's further disintegration into isolated phonemes and its reconstitution in timeless matrices.

Generativism, despite the apparent liveliness of its chosen metaphor, has offered us no restoration of physical temporality: The generativist analyzes alphabetically written sentences and generates alphabetically written sentences, with all their temporal defects. Only now, when the language in question is a European one, the linguist need no longer bother with the phonemic refinement of the spellings given by literate tradition. The phonological mask, the mask that used to disguise alphabetic writing as something new and scientific, has been discarded. Derrida's grammatology, or "science of writing," is not a prospect but a retrospect, the secret name of an all-too-familiar linguistics. At this point we may be ready to remember that it was Aristotle, and not de Saussure, who first argued that meaningful language was constructed from indivisible particles with no meaning of their own, but Aristotle called these particles *grammata*, "letters" (*Poetics* 1456b).

Phonology, whether applied literally or used as a model for larger-scale investigations, does not conceive of time as a dialectic between instantaneity and continuity, of stillness and motion, but rather sets itself firmly on the side of stillness, ever seeking new ways of bringing motion to rest. When Claude Lévi-Strauss states that myth is an instrument for "the obliteration of time,"[25] this is not an insight into the nature of narrative but an artifact of his choice of a method of analysis based on phonology. He applies this method, at the level of an instantaneous unit called the "mytheme," to once-oral narratives whose acoustical time has long since been obliterated at the level of the phoneme. Like de Saussure before him, he uses the terms "diachrony" and "synchrony" as if they offered a complete and balanced description of time, but in practice diachrony refers not to the flow or

---

24. Derrida, *Of Grammatology*, pp. 52–53.
25. Claude Lévi-Strauss, *The Raw and the Cooked*, p. 16.

continuity of time but to a succession of instants. This is a version of time's directionality that makes diachrony subservient to the demands of synchrony.[26] Duration is entirely absent except when we read what Lévi-Strauss has written and supply our own durations at our own shifting tempo. It has been said that structuralism and the linguistics it is based upon are unable to deal with historical time except as a succession of frozen moments, but we may add here that they are also unable to deal with the time it takes to tell a story. When Lévi-Strauss imports a musical model into the discussion of myths, it is not to restore the lost "music" of storytelling itself but to construct a new "music" out of the relationships between differing successions of mythemes. The score has now become an orchestral one, with several staves running along synchronously, but the time signature, tempo marks, note values, rests, and ties are still missing.

Lévi-Strauss, in his review of a book of Zuni narratives which I scored for pauses, changes of amplitude, and other gross acoustical features, calls for the integration of these features in structuralist accounts, though he makes no suggestion as to how this might be done.[27] Eco seems optimistic about the semiotic incorporation of such features, which he calls "extra-grammatical elements," suggesting that they "obey rules which have not yet been isolated."[28] On the other hand, these elements might belong to what Eco calls a "lower threshold," encountered at "the point where semiotic phenomena arise from something non-semiotic, . . . a sort of 'missing link' between the universe of signals and the universe of signs."[29] This notion of a "missing link" is of course the necessary result of a theoretical view which treats the relationship between signal and sign analytically, that is, as a dual opposition with an excluded middle; if the same relationship were viewed dialectically there would be no need for two separate "universes," with the physical universe beginning at the "lower threshold" of the rarified semiotic universe, just as phonetics begins at the lower threshold of phonology. But at least the requirements for the ascent into Eco's version of the semiotic universe are not quite as stringent as those for gaining literal or metaphorical phonological status, or so he claims. His basis for this claim is that phonology requires "absolute discretedness," whereas semiotics al-

26. Paul Ricoeur makes a similar point in his critique of Lévi-Strauss (*The Conflict of Interpretations*, p. 33); Johannes Fabian notes the "hegemony" of synchrony over "real time and history" in grammar and in structuralism ("Rule and Process," p. 19).

27. Lévi-Strauss, review of *Finding the Center*.

28. Eco, *A Theory of Semiotics*, p. 268.

29. Ibid., p. 21.

lows for "gradated continua" so long as "the array of these units has precise boundaries."[30] His main example of such units is the array of color terms, in which "portions of the continuum have been cut out."[31] It is difficult to see how the discontinuous gradation of color terms is any different from that of such phonologically distinctive features as occur along the continuum running from the "labial" back through the "dental," "velar," and "palatal" consonantal positions, or on the two-dimensional continuum of tongue positions for vowels. If a phonology that has always made these accommodations to continua has nevertheless had chronic difficulties with the acoustical phenomena Eco calls "extra-grammatical," it is difficult to see how a semiotics whose continua must likewise have "precise boundaries" or sections that are "cut out" will do much better.

All the acoustical features noted for our scroll occupy continua. In order to establish their status with respect to semiotics, we will have to look for gaps in these continua and establish correlations between the units thus defined, which lie on what Eco (following Hjelmslev) calls the "expression plane," and features which lie on the "content plane."[32]

First let us look at the narrator's tempo, which will be a function of the combination of utterance length and pause length. Passages with many short lines, and therefore with many pauses, will sound slow, even if the pauses themselves are not particularly long; passages with many long lines, and therefore with few pauses, will sound fast. The longer pauses, those of two to four seconds, usually occur amid stretches of short or medium utterances, producing a slowing effect; occasionally they immediately precede or follow a fast passage, but they never fall directly between two long utterances. These are very rough characterizations; slower passages dissolve into faster ones, and vice versa. Within a relatively slow passage there may be utterances of a length falling well within the range of a moderate passage, and within a moderate passage there may be a few utterances falling well within the range of a slow passage; there is a similar overlapping between moderate and fast passages.

We seem to be dealing with a continuum with no obvious gaps in it; our attempts at finding correlations between tempo and content will have to proceed on the basis of an experimental discontinuity imposed by ourselves, that between the very fastest and very slowest passages. When we examine the content of these passages, we find

30. Ibid., p. 176.
31. Ibid., p. 77.
32. Ibid., p. 48.

that the narrator proceeds very slowly when delivering the story-opening formula and announcing the names and locations of the two main bodies of characters. Once the action gets under way, his slowest passages are devoted to the openings of formal speeches by the characters, ceremonial occasions with a series of formal actions, suspenseful searches or other circumstances that involve puzzlement for the characters, turning points coming just before emotional or violent action, and capture or punishment or death coming at the end of such action. The fastest passages contain dialogues in which there are frequent changes of speaker (especially in exchanges of greetings), habitual actions of the characters (as opposed to unique actions with direct effects on the direction of the plot), scenes in which large numbers of people are involved in similar actions, and chases (as opposed to searches).[33] As one might expect, it is more difficult to characterize the passages of moderate speed; they include much of the two opening scenes, in which the plot is first set in motion by the abandonment of a miraculously conceived infant, and several long speeches (except for their slow opening lines).

From out of these lists we may construct two three-part sequences of tempo change: a slow search followed by a fast chase and a renewed slowness at the moment of capture or death, and a fast greeting exchange followed by a speech that is slow at the opening and then moderate until its close. It should be remarked that the degree to which the narrator relies on well-known formulas or must find his own phrasing as he goes along has no direct correlation with how rapidly he may proceed. A story opening, though slow, is highly formulaic. Greeting exchanges and speech openings are both highly formulaic, but the former are delivered rapidly and the latter slowly. When I say "formulaic," I mean repetitions of the sheer words as they would be rendered alphabetically by a typewriter; in fact, there is great variation in the placement of the pauses within these formulas, as well as in the way particular words are singled out by increased amplitude.[34] In this sense, there are no formulas, except perhaps for

33. Alessandro Portelli, in "'The Time of my Life': Functions of Time in Oral History" (undated preprint), found that Italian narrators were faster when taking a personal approach or dealing with the "concluded past" than when discussing general issues or dealing with the "still open present" (p. 4).

34. In a story from the same collection as the one under examination here, a passage involving a formal exchange of greetings is repeated in seven different places with very few changes in the wording, but the pauses shift constantly; in the seven passages taken together, the pauses fell in forty-four different places with respect to the wording, but only two of these possibilities occur all seven times (*Finding the Center*, pp. 97–109).

the opening utterance, which identifies our story as belonging to a particular genre. This is not so in Zuni chanted narration, where the relationship between word formulas, pitch contours, amplitude changes, and pauses is stabilized, producing the oral equivalent of a fixed written text, a text which always says the same thing in the same way.[35] From a strict acoustical point of view, however, no utterance performed by a human voice can ever be identical with any other, and in this sense there are no formulas at all—except on paper.

Pause length, looked at without reference to utterance length, begins to take on a definite relationship with content if we artificially separate out all pauses of two full seconds or longer. Such pauses are most likely to fall between a highly general statement (regarding an entire village, for example) and a specific one (regarding a specific person in that village, for example); between the end of an explanatory digression and the resumption of the narrative proper; between third-person narrative and direct quotation (or vice versa) or between quotations from two different speakers (except in exchanges of greetings); between the descriptions of two different events which are understood to be taking place simultaneously (where the long pause serves a function like the word "meanwhile"); between two actions which are separated by a passage of time for which the events, if any, are not described (in some narratives a two-second pause may stand for as much as four years); and in the midst of a suspenseful passage that is already slow even without the addition of long pauses.

Some pauses correspond to breaks in the action itself at a 1:1 ratio, as with those occurring within quotations. Beyond the upper durational limit of the pauses in the present narrative (and most others in my collection), which falls at around four seconds, I have found two pauses of six full seconds each.[36] Both of these extreme pauses correspond to actual pauses in the action, at a 1:1 ratio, but their effects are quite different. One of them occurs when a character dozes off while speaking, right in the middle of a greeting that would ordinarily be delivered rapidly. The other represents the profound stillness after a group of enemies has flung a thick barrage of weapons at the hero, after which the uninjured hero calmly asks them if their weapons are all gone. The dozing pause is almost enough to put the audience itself to sleep, while the battle pause is a moment of extreme tension, but the two pauses are the "same" acoustically.

The relationship between pauses and grammatical borders is a

---

35. See the discussion of the talk of Kyaklo in Chapter 9, below.
36. *Finding the Center*, pp. 115, 182.

complex one, but some generalizations can be made about the accompanying content. Here again we must resort to a discontinuity of our own making, comparing passages in which the pauses repeatedly leave us hanging, grammatically speaking, with those in which the pauses repeatedly coincide with complete sentences. Situations of the former type are most likely to involve suspense or puzzlement or turning points, where the tempo is slow, and chases or fights, where the tempo is fast. At the opposite extreme, pauses are most likely to fall in line with sentences when the content can be organized in a list, as with a complete description of a character's clothing, the presentation of a series of characters who occupy a fixed hierarchy, or the description of a series of parallel actions that follows a ritualized rather than a suspenseful pattern. But in highly formal quoted oratory, the tension between sound and grammar reasserts itself, but this time pause and intonation work together against the forward thrust of the grammar: Each and every utterance is intoned as if it were an emphatically complete sentence, followed by a clear and deliberate pause, but no one utterance, by itself, actually constitutes such a complete sentence, grammatically speaking.[37] For example, a noun phrase, and even the noun phrase of a dependent clause, may be treated as if it were complete unto itself.

It remains to account for the hypertrophied syllables we noted on the scroll. They are far longer than the phonemic lengthenings of Zuni vowels, even the extra lengthening of already "long" vowels that happen to take a stress, so they have a clear discontinuity with similar phenomena of a smaller scale. In Zuni narratives the syllable most commonly drawn out is the past-tense suffix of a verb describing a continuous action occupying an unspecified time—especially if that action covers not only time but space, as with a lo——ng walk or the lo——ng glides of a vulture.[38] Other enlarged syllables may occur in words meaning "all," especially if the totality in question is an indefinitely large number. In the story-opening formula, the word meaning "long ago" always carries an enlarged syllable. There are variations in the lengths of drawn-out syllables, but these lie along a continuum, with a lo———ng journey or the wea———ving of a basket likely to be longer than, say, the si——nging of a song.

The lengthened syllables that express temporal continuity in the action have counterparts in the long silences that correspond to the

37. For further details, see Chapter 6, above.
38. Similar devices are used elsewhere in North America; see Dennis Tedlock, "Verbal Art." In the long dashes in this paragraph I indicate analogous usages in English.

passage of nights or days or years, the difference being that the silences are not occupied by continuing story action and the sameness being that both devices express the continuous duration of time itself. With these devices, what Lubomír Doložel would call "sign time" is directly harnessed to the motion of "physical time,"[39] and the continuous, durational aspect of time becomes manifest. It may be that phonology, in the cases of juncture, stress, and vowel quantity, succeeds in incorporating very small segments of time into a code (in the strict sense of code), but when a narrator signifies the passage of time in the story by letting time itself become manifest, time naked in the midst of his performance, we need hardly be surprised if the range of pause lengths or syllable lengths is continuous while at the same time correlating with content. That is all in the nature of time, asserting its continuous physicality in the midst of what are almost, but never quite, instants.

Physical, continuous, and "extra-grammatical" though the lengthened syllables may be, we nevertheless committed an inadvertent trespass upon a semantic domain which lies well within the gates of grammar when we discussed the effect of such lengthening on verbs. The domain in question is that of aspect, which concerns the nature of the action of verbs (aside from tense and mood).[40] When a verb tense affix is lengthened in Zuni, its total effect is not only to mark tense itself, which it does by segmental (and properly grammatical) means, but to give the action a continuative aspect. What makes this case especially interesting is that Zuni does possess a verb affix expressing the continuative aspect in the conventional grammatical sense, a suffix that is not used in the same verb in which a lengthening of the tense suffix occurs. In other words, we may here speak of a single semantic function that may be served either by segmental or by suprasegmental means.

The suspenseful use of pausing, in which utterances are repeatedly cut to shapes different from those marked by intonation (and grammar), also involves a trespass on a semantic domain of grammar, though it is less direct and operates at a scale different from the lengthening of syllables. The domain in question here is that of mood, which concerns (in a broad sense) the factual status of the action of verbs,[41] and the particular mood is the indeterminate, which

---

39. Lubomír Doložel, "A Scheme of Narrative Time," pp. 209, 216n.
40. I wish to thank Paolo Fabbri and Louis Marin for urging me to explore the question of aspect.
41. Tzvetan Todorov discusses large-scale phenomena similar to the moods of verbs in his *Grammaire du Décaméron*, but he reads these moods on the content plane rather than the expression plane.

gives the action the quality of an approximation. As in the case of the continuative aspect, Zuni does have a verb affix for the indeterminate mood, but the extra-grammatical counterpart to this affix need not directly affect the verbs themselves, but may follow connectives or demonstratives (for example); the verbs in the affected passage may or may not carry the indeterminate affix (most frequently they do not). When each individual verb in a passage affected by suspenseful pauses is in the determinate mood (which is unmarked), it is something larger that is made indeterminate by suprasegmental means, namely, the effect of the actions of a whole series of verbs. In the case of an episode involving a search, for example, each action that carries the search forward may have a clear and determinate effect in itself, as when it indicates arrival at a place which affords a new vantage point, but considered from the point of view of the goal of the larger action of the episode, it remains indeterminate, an approximation of whatever action might turn out to be the effective one. In such a passage, this indeterminacy is marked by suspenseful pauses, but when the goal is finally reached the pauses suddenly move back into closer synchrony with major grammatical boundaries.

It should be cautioned that although the aspect marked by syllable-lengthening and the mood marked by suspenseful pauses do have corresponding morphemes within Zuni grammar, one need not expect to find a grammatical counterpart to every extra-grammatical semantic category (or vice versa) within a given language. Infrequent pauses (long utterances) often correlate with fast action, but there is nothing in the Zuni inventory of verb affixes that indicates speed of action—for that, one must consult the lexical inventory. Suspenseful pauses like those in Zuni narrative can be and are used by English-language narrators, but there is no indeterminate mood in the morphology of English verbs. The main point here is that the semantic functions of extra-grammatical features and properly grammatical ones *may* overlap, even in the *same* language.

At this point we have two choices: We may, as a linguistically modeled semiotics always will, subordinate the questions raised during our exploration of signals, in this case acoustical signals, to the ultimate demands of signs, retreating back inside the hermetic safety of codes. In the present case, that will mean leaving Zuni grammar exactly as it is, a presumably integral code, and assigning extra-grammatical features to membership in a separate code whose integrity will continue to be open to question, so long as a way cannot be found to eliminate the last vestiges of temporal continuity (and thus materiality) from its signs. In a semiotics thus constituted, we will continue to hear of "*para*linguistics" and "*supra*segmentals," or of

Eco's "*missing* link" or "*lower* threshold" or "*fuzzy* concepts" or "*imprecise* expressive texture"—or the effects of a "*complex* network of *sub*codes,"[42] a network that never quite seems to get unraveled.

If, on the other hand, we are to free semiotics from its subordination to linguistics—a movement which requires a balanced approach to the relationship between signals and signs, one in which the demands of codification are denied any claim to finality—we may allow ourselves to realize that in exploring the region on and around the "lower threshold" of an established code, we have inadvertently discovered that the code itself does not occupy quite as remote a layer of heaven as we thought it did and may even be suspected of having inescapable connections to the ground, given that even the semantic field of its morphemes (to say nothing of its lexemes) is inhabited by gross acoustical features that resist final reduction to the status of perfect signs.

Even phonology itself appears in a new light once we have made ourselves at home on its threshold rather than in its very midst. Eco, arguing from a position well within that midst, writes of "strong and stable" systems and "weak and transient" ones, giving phonology as his example of a "strong and stable" system and stating that it "lasts for centuries,"[43] a notion that sounds more like a description of academic spelling conventions than of the sound systems of spoken dialects. Clearly, phonology continues to serve as a sort of Rock of Ages for semiotics, the constant measure of success in the description of any sign system. Yet phonological systems are themselves subject to movements in the dialectic of continuity and instantaneity, of sameness and difference. Some phonemes are much closer to being the same than others, some are made up of larger bundles of distinctive features than others, and some carry a much greater semantic load than others. This is at least partly because there are phonemes that are on their way out of a code and phonemes that are on their way in, as well as phonemes that are merging and phonemes that are fissioning. There are even cases—Zuni has two such problems—where a phonemic distinction is important with respect to content in some words and melts into a continuum in others; that is to say, one might construct one set of evidence to support a phonemic discontinuity and another set of evidence to support treating two sounds as an allophonic variation of purely phonetic (as opposed to phonological) interest.[44]

42. Eco, *A Theory of Semiotics*, pp. 21, 125, 216, 296; emphasis mine.
43. Ibid., p. 126; see also pp. 76, 214.
44. See Dennis Tedlock, "The Problem of *k* in Zuni Phonemics," which deals with one of these two problems; the other is a vocalic problem, between *e* and *i*.

We began with a phonological obstacle in our path and (hopefully) we end looking back over our shoulders at it. The problem of time in oral narrative events exists between the *matter* of these events and our *manner* of perceiving them in our roles as confirmed literati (or letterati), ever reluctant to adjust our "vision" to the phonographic "image." The problem will always begin with phonology (and grammatology) as long as visible transcriptions of these narratives remain "literature" in the narrowest typographical sense. The exploration of the problem requires not that we refrain from making transcriptions, but that our transcriptions begin to give visible expression to the durations of the sounds of the voice and the silences between them. From the perspective provided by phonography and its visible counterparts, everything else changes. The reverberations shake everything from the phoneme to the mytheme, provided only that we hold our passion for perfectly codified discontinuities in abeyance and allow for measurable continuities with degrees of correlation with content. This may be just the perspective that is needed to put linguistics in its proper place, a specialized area within semiotics. But that is a story that has not yet taken place.

The Forms of Mayan Verse

What happens when our notions about what a poetics might be are held within the orbit of linguistics is well illustrated by the work of Roman Jakobson. In a statement meant to be a general pronouncement on poetics, he argues that the "poetic function" of language is actualized as a "focus on the message for its own sake," specifically the structure of the message, and "since linguistics is the global science of verbal structure, poetics may be regarded as an integral part of linguistics."[1] And just as his phonology involves a repression of the continuous and material nature of speech sounds in favor of their particulate and formal properties, so in his poetics the "referential function" of language, which ties it to the world of objects, is subjected to "the supremacy of the poetic function."

This essay had its beginning in a paper delivered at the I Congreso sobre el Popol Vuh, sponsored by the Instituto Nacional de Antropología e Historia de Guatemala and the State University of New York at Albany and held at Santa Cruz Quiché, Guatemala, in 1979. A Spanish translation of that paper will appear in *Nuevas perspectivas sobre el Popol Vuh*, ed. Robert M. Carmack (Guatemala City: Piedra Santa, forthcoming).

1. Roman Jakobson, "Closing Statement: Linguistics and Poetics," pp. 356, 350, 371.

216

Jakobson's "focus on the message for its own sake" and his peripheralization of referential meaning sound more like a description of linguistics than an adequate foundation for a comparative poetics. He explicitly exiles questions of "value" from both linguistics and poetics,[2] but just as I have already argued that structural linguistics is ultimately founded upon a moral and aesthetic preference for alphabetic sign systems over all others, so I would suggest here that the poetics Jakobson offers us contains, sui generis, an aesthetic that values "a recurrent 'figure of sound'" (in Jakobson's phrase) over what we might call "a recurrent figure of meaning." Jakobson does pull back slightly from this position, criticizing "phonetic isolationism" and quoting Valéry's view of poetry as "hesitation between the sound and the sense," but he nevertheless gives explicit primacy to such conventions as meter, alliteration, and rhyme, treating parallelism only in passing.[3]

The phenomenological poetics of Gaston Bachelard, instead of curving ever inward upon the forms of language, opens up both sides of the dialectic between what he calls the "formal imagination," which we may take to coincide at least partially with Jakobson's "poetic function," and the "material imagination," which in its purest form deals with "*direct* images of *matter*."[4] Here I am reminded, once again, of the question Joseph Peynetsa once put to me while we were working on a Zuni story: "Do you *see* it, or do you just write it down?" And as another Zuni said, taking the narrator's point of view, "If you are really true to a story you make it like it's right in front of you." In Zuni storytelling, then, the material imagination takes precedence over the formal imagination, and my discussions of the poetics of verisimilitude and of time in storytelling (see the previous two chapters) have been, in effect, explorations of the material side of Zuni poetics.

The poetic balance swings toward the formal side in the vocable refrains of Zuni songs, which go so far into "phonetic isolationism" that they are often devoid of denotative meaning.[5] When a composer allows the referentially meaningful parts of a song to spill over into its refrains, his song may be dismissed as follows: "Nothing but words!" The formal and material imaginations come closer to a union in Zuni raised-up speeches, but they never quite meet up. Here there is a re-

---

2. Ibid., p. 351.
3. Ibid., pp. 367, 369.
4. Gaston Bachelard, *On Poetic Imagination and Reverie*, pp. 10–11.
5. This is the section of a song called the *i'ts'umme*, the "strong part," and it is "where they're really singing" (Barbara Tedlock, "Songs of the Zuni Kachina Society," p. 17).

current "figure of sound," a sort of end-rhyme for every line, but this is a rhyme of stress and pitch rather than of consonants and vowels, and it is imposed on the words rather than taking their own stresses and pitches as givens. Therefore it does not constrain the choice of words and does not produce "figures of meaning," except that the prominence it confers on line-final words seems to call (most of the time) for a noun or verb rather than some lesser word.

As Edmonson has observed, there is no meter—in the strict sense of recurrent quantifications of stresses, vowel lengths, or syllables, all at the segmental level—in the indigenous verbal arts of the New World.[6] Even in song texts there are seldom more than two successive lines with identical rhythmic patterns, and the patterns in question are usually dependent on parallel constructions in which there is only a partial change of the wording from one line to the next. Even in songs whose texts consist entirely of vocables rather than words, where tight metrical patterns would be easy to achieve if they were desired, there are seldom more than two or three successive lines that even have the same number of syllables.[7] Clearly, the relationship between the formal and material imaginations is balanced differently from the way it is balanced in European tradition—or, to put the matter in Valéry's terms, the "hesitation between the sound and the sense" is located in a different place. In New World poetics, even when the "referential function" is entirely abandoned in favor of the abstract art of vocables, it is as if the broad and constantly shifting rhythms suggested by the lines and phrases of the speaking voice were still preferred to small-scale and long-sustained rhythms of the kind that can be brought into play when the formal imagination takes on elements even smaller than words.

It is in combined syntactic and semantic parallelism that the dialectic between the formal and material aspects of poetics comes somewhere near a balance.[8] In tightly parallel verse the overall figure of sound established in one phrase may be sustained (with a slight variation) in the next, but without breaking entirely free of the previously established sense; sense itself moves forward, if slightly (unless two successive parallel units form an antithesis), but without entirely disrupting the previously established sound. Parallel verse may or may not follow sustained patterns of quantification; over most of North America there is a tendency to constant shifts in the number

6. Munro S. Edmonson, *Lore*, p. 99.
7. Dennis Tedlock, "Verbal Art."
8. See Jakobson, "Closing Statement," p. 369.

of syntactic and/or semantic recurrences, as there is in the verbal art of Iroquois, Zuni, and Navajo rituals.[9] Dell Hymes has recently shown a shifting but nevertheless quantifiable parallelism in a number of North American traditions, most convincingly in Chinookan, but this operates on a scale larger than phrases or lines to produce a stanza composed of three or five units he calls "verses."[10] He has also attempted to break each verse into three or five phrases or lines, but these smaller units are often parallel only in the broad sense that each contains a predication of some sort.[11]

On the formal side of Mesoamerican and Andean poetics, there is a strong tendency toward quantified parallelism in the form of the semantic and/or syntactic couplet.[12] The pioneering work on Mesoamerican verse forms was that of Angel María Garibay K., whose particular field was the Nahuatl texts abundantly recorded in colonial documents. He has called particular attention to what he calls *difrasismo* in Nahuatl verse, by which he means a parallel couplet containing a pair of metaphors that together express a single thought.[13] The parallelism in Nahuatl verse certainly favors the couplet, but there are frequent exceptions, the most common being a triplet. One of Garibay's own illustrations of *difrasismo* is in fact a triplet, though he does not comment on the fact:

Aun el jade se rompe,
aun el oro se quiebra,
aun el plumaje del quetzal se rasga.[14]

Miguel León-Portilla, a student of Garibay, was the first scholar to arrange passages from Quiché and Yucatec Mayan documents as verse.[15] In the Quiché case, he has presented two oratorical and two narrative passages from the Popol Vuh as verse. On the other hand, he gives a third narrative passage in a prose format, recognizing,

9. For a general discussion of North America and an Iroquois example, see Edmonson, *Lore*, p. 98; for the Zuni, see "On Praying, Exclaiming, and Saying Hello in Zuni," in this book. For an early discussion of form in Navajo chants see Eda Lou Walton, "Navaho Verse Rhythms"; Edmonson's own comments on Navajo chants are in *Lore* (p. 92).
10. Dell Hymes, *"In Vain I Tried to Tell You,"* chaps. 4–6.
11. Hymes, "Particle, Pause and Pattern," p. 7.
12. Edmonson, *Lore*, pp. 98–99.
13. Angel María Garibay K., *Historia de la literatura Nahuatl*, pp. 19, 65–67.
14. Ibid., p. 67.
15. For the Popol Vuh passages in question, see Miguel León-Portilla, *Pre-Columbian Literatures of Mexico*, pp. 51–55, 75, 92–93; Yucatec passages are given on pp. 49–51, 89–91, and 120–21. The Spanish version of this book was first published in 1964.

quite accurately, that the tendency to formal verse in the Popol Vuh does not everywhere assert itself with equal regularity.[16]

Only Munro S. Edmonson has attempted to treat entire Mayan books as verse, asserting that both the Popol Vuh and the Book of Chilam Balam of Tizimín are entirely composed in parallel couplets.[17] He divides the texts of these books and his English translations into clearly marked pairs of lines, from their opening words right through to their closings. In his Tizimín work, if not in his earlier work on the Popol Vuh, he has come to admit that there are passages in which "the structure may become quite loose," that he remains "uncertain . . . whether direct discourse falls inside or outside of the couplet structure," and that he has "sometimes made two lines in one context of an expression which appears as one line elsewhere."[18] He "remains persuaded that Mayan formal discourse tends strongly to couplets," a statement with which few Mayanists (including myself) would disagree at this point, but when he accounts for his problems by saying that "there are good and bad couplets," he reifies a Mayan tendency into a narrow literary canon that blinds us to the possibility that the formal side of Mayan poetics might make its own provisions for variability rather than merely being subject to breakdowns.

Even a reading of the first folio of the Popol Vuh text, which includes one of its most densely formal passages, discloses frequent departures from the form of the couplet. One of the commonest variations is a single line, often beginning with a demonstrative and serving as an introduction to a longer passage containing parallelism, and sometimes signaling the end of such a passage. The other common variation is a triplet, in which the end of a parallel series of three may be signaled by an internal variation in the construction of the final part. Such variation most often involves the addition or deletion of a single modifier or affix, or else the addition of a conjunction. Both the singular line and the triplet are present in the following passage (from folio 1r.7–10), but first I will give it in Edmonson's fully coupleted arrangement:

are cut xchicacam ui
ucutunizaxic,

ucalahobizaxic,
utzihoxic puch

16. Ibid., pp. 121–22.
17. Edmonson, *The Book of Counsel*, p. xi; *The Ancient Future of the Itza*, p. xiv.
18. Edmonson, *The Ancient Future of the Itza*, p. xiv.

euaxibal
zaquiribal[19]

But it seems obvious enough, on both syntactic and semantic grounds, that the form of this passage would be better analyzed as a single introductory phrase followed by a triplet and then a couplet:[20]

are cut xchicacam ui

ucutunizaxic,
ucalahobizaxic,
utzihoxic puch

euaxibal
zaquiribal

which might be translated as follows:

And here we shall take it up:

the demonstration,
the revelation,
and account

of the hiding place,
the dawning place.

This next passage (from 1v.2–6) illustrates both single lines and triplets once again, but Edmonson arranges it as follows:

ARE UTZIHOXIC
UAE

ca catzininoc,
ca cachamamoc

catzinonic
ca cazilanic,

ca calolinic,
catolona puch upa cah.[21]

---

19. Edmonson, *The Book of Counsel*, lines 9–14; I have replaced his orthography and punctuation with those of the Popol Vuh manuscript.

20. These are purely typographical lines meant to highlight the formal features under discussion; they are not to be confused with the pause-marked lines of oral delivery, which are reconstructed for the opening of the Popol Vuh at the end of Chapter 4, above.

21. Edmonson, *The Book of Counsel*, lines 95–102. Capital letters are as given in the manuscript.

Edmonson suggests that an initial *ca* is "missing" in the fifth and last lines here,[22] which would certainly make the text conform better to his rigid notions of Quiché verse form, but the fact is that his insistence on the couplets has obscured rather than revealed the form of this passage, which offers a particularly beautiful illustration of the working of singular phrases and triplets. Both the syntax and meaning point to the following structure: an introductory phrase with a demonstrative; two successive triplets, each dropping the word *ca* in the third line; and a single final phrase, which has the effect of calling a halt to the rhythm of the two triplets and in fact finishes the sentence:

ARE UTZIHOXIC UAE

ca catzininoc,
ca cachamamoc
  catzinonic

ca cazilanic,
ca calolinic,
  catolona puch

upa cah.

Here is the translation:

THIS IS THE ACCOUNT:

it still ripples,
it still murmurs,
    ripples,

still whispers,
still hums,
    and it is empty

under the sky.

At times Edmonson is forced, in his efforts to explain away deviations from the march of his couplets, to supply an entire line that is not present in the manuscript. In this next passage (from 1v.8–9), he inserts the item enclosed in parentheses, explaining in a note that "there appears to be a line missing here":[23]

mahabi o3 hun uinac,
hun chicop

22. Ibid., p. 9n.
23. Ibid., p. 9n.; lines 105–10.

(quieh,)
tziquin,

car,
tap,

che
abah,

[etc.]

Here I read an introductory phrase followed by a triplet—with a variation, as usual, in the third part—and a series of couplets; there is no need to supply a "missing" line:

mahabi o3

hun uinac,
hun chicop
        tziquin,

car,
tap,

che
abah,

[etc.]

The translation:

There is not yet

one person,
one animal,
        bird,

fish,
crab,

tree,
rock,

[etc.]

Edmonson's suggestion that the missing line is *quieh*, "deer," is based on the fact that "deer" is paired with "bird" in a separate passage (2v.4–5):

ri quieh,
tziquin

> *4oh,*
> *balam,*
>
> [etc.]

But it should be noted that "deer" occupies the first position in this later list, whereas it would have occupied the third position had it occurred in the earlier list. We need not suppose it was omitted from the earlier list through some error; rather, it may have been a casualty of the general tendency to vary couplets with triplets, in this case a triplet that takes its third part from what would have been a couplet. For the Popol Vuh as a whole, I would estimate that the ratio of couplets to triplets is in the neighborhood of 10:1, which is too many triplets to attribute all of them to error.

In a few cases, the third parallel phrase in a series, with its expected variation from the pattern established by the first two phrases, is followed by a fourth phrase that returns to the original pattern. This sequence can be treated formally only as a quatrain, because the fourth part has its strongest parallel with the first two lines rather than with anything that might follow it. Edmonson presents this first example (from 1r.35–37) as two separate couplets,[24] but such a reading ignores the bridge that arches over the third part to connect the second and fourth parts, as follows:

> *ucah tzucuxic,*
> *ucah xucutaxic*
> > *retaxic,*
> *ucah cheexic*

which may be translated as follows:

> its fourfold siding,
> its fourfold cornering,
> > measuring,
> its fourfold staking.

A similar structure is exhibited in the passage that gives the Popol Vuh its various titles or epithets (1r.27–30). Here the second and fourth phrases have the closest affinity of any two phrases, providing a strong bridge over a third phrase that is more out of step than it was in the previous example. Edmonson has two couplets here, with *chu4haxic* tacked on to his last line,[25] but I read a quatrain and count

24. Ibid., lines 63–66.
25. Ibid., lines 49–52.

the last word, which refers to the passage as a whole, as standing outside the quatrain proper:

> *ilbal re popol uuh*
> *ilbal zac petenah chaca palo.*
> *utzihoxic camuhibal*
> *ilbal zac 4azlem*
>
> *chu4haxic.*

Here is the translation, with the epithets in quotes:

> a way to see the Council Book,
> a way to see "The Light from Across the sea,"
> "The Account of Our Darkness,"
> a way to see "The Dawn of Life,"
>
> as it is said.

One might also read *utzihoxic*, "the account of," as parallel (semantically) with *ilbal*, "a way to see," with only *camuhibal*, "Our Darkness," remaining as a shortened epithet. In that case, one of the possibilities for variation in the third part of a Quiché quatrain, in addition to the simplification shown in the previous example, is a partial abandonment of strict syntactic parallelism in favor of a more purely semantic link.

It is difficult to find quatrains of the kind just described in contemporary Quiché discourse, but there are abundant examples of couplets, as Edmonson has pointed out,[26] and of the single phrases and triplets discussed here. In the following passage from a narrative, a slight variation (a pluralization of the object noun) is introduced at the end of each of the triplets:

> The town crier called out:
>
> "Come to the *calpul*,
> come to the assembly,
> come before the elders,
>
> we are looking for people.
>
> We have lost the mayor,
> we have lost the alderman,
> we have lost the policemen.[27]

---

26. Ibid., p. xii.
27. Adapted from Barbara Tedlock, *Time and the Highland Maya*, p. 181.

And here is a contemporary example of a triplet with a shortening of the third part:

> They didn't have a match,
> they didn't have anything,
>   nothing.[28]

These next lines are excerpted from a prayer:

> *ixukihelo:*
>
> *3ani su4,,*
> *saki su4,,*
>
> *ri mayul,*
> *ri teu,*
> *ri caki3*[29]

So far we have been placing parallel units one beneath the other, which certainly gives full *visual* display of their syntactic construction, but listening to tape-recordings of actual oral delivery suggests a different approach. Bringing changes of line into consonance with the actual pauses of a speaker, we get the following results:

> *ixukihelo:*
> *3ani su4,, saki su4,,*
> *ri mayul, ri teu, ri caki3*

and in translation:

> and also:
> yellow clouds, white clouds,
> the mist, the cold, the wind

The first of these lines is given a suspended intonation at its end; the next two are each delivered as a single unified phrase or clause, higher at the beginning and dropping somewhat toward the end, but not dropping as decisively as the end of a complete sentence. This pattern of delivery suggests that the division between the internal parts of a couplet or triplet should be treated not as a line break but as a caesura, so long as we understand that this is not an interruption in the *sound* but a transition in the *sense*.

---

28. Ibid.
29. Ibid., p. 190.

If a couplet contains only two to four syllables, even the final stress marking the end of the first word will disappear, producing (in effect) a single compound word. Two such words, common in today's prayers and in the Popol Vuh as well, unite *cho* with *plo* (*palo* in the Popol Vuh), or "lake" with "sea," and *cah* with *uleu*, or "sky" with "earth"; they might be written as *choplo* and *cahuleu*. If a couplet contains more syllables than this, individual words are likely to recover their separate stresses, but even a couplet consisting of two full clauses of several words each is likely to lack a pause between its two halves.[30] In the case of a triplet, the mode of delivery depends on whether the three parts are a frequently used combination, as with the last line of the prayer excerpt quoted above, or whether the third part is an improvised extension of a couplet, a sort of afterthought, as frequently happens in narrative:

> the quail, the rabbits,
> and the jays

and again:

> certificate, identification,
> summons.[31]

Although I have not attempted to do so, the triplets of the Popol Vuh might be differentiated into those which securely belong to general repertory and those which might have been improvised by its writer— or by the performer who recited for its scribe, as the case may be— through a general statistical study of the Popol Vuh text and other Quiché texts of similar vintage.

It remains to demonstrate that departures from the couplet such as those described here are widespread among Mayan languages. Gary Gossen discusses parallelism for Tzotzil; he emphasizes couplets, but his illustrations for Tzotzil, like Garibay's for Nahuatl, include triplets, passed over without comment.[32] The following example illustrates a single introductory line as well:

> San Juan's sheep
>
> most certainly—

30. See Chapter 4, above, for a more detailed discussion of the relationship of Quiché oral delivery to Quiché verse forms.
31. For the full narrative from which these two examples are taken, see "Beyond Logocentrism: Trace and Voice among the Quiché Maya," Chapter 10, below.
32. Gary H. Gossen, *Chamulas in the World of the Sun*, pp. 142–44.

and therefore,
pay attention—

provide white clothing,
provide black clothing.

Gossen does not discuss where the pauses might fall in such a passage.

For contemporary Yucatec, our best evidence comes from the work of Allan Burns. Couplets are abundant, but there are also triplets. Here is an example with a variation in the third part; as Burns's notation makes explicit, this entire triplet is delivered without any pause:

He finds the wood, he finds the stones, hard stones.[33]

And here is a second example, preceded by an introductory line and again lacking pauses within the triplet itself:

"I guess I'll shoot these deer."
BAM! he shoots one there. POW! he shoots one there. BOW! he shoots one.[34]

Staying with Yucatec but moving back in time, we find both couplets and triplets in the Book of Chilam Balam of Chumayel:

On 3 Ben he made all things, as many things as there are,
the things of the heavens, the things of the sea, and the things of the earth.[35]

Here is a triplet from the Chilam Balam of Tizimín, reconstituted from Edmonson's couplets:

Then were cut the throats, the eyes, the ears[36]

And the following Tizimín passage illustrates a quatrain with a variation in the third part, much like the Popol Vuh quatrains given earlier:

mucuc tza
homol tza

33. Allan Burns, "The Deer Secret," p. 136. For a large collection of Yucatec narratives scored for pausing and other oral features, see Burns, *An Epoch of Miracles.*
34. Burns, "The Deer Secret," p. 142.
35. Ralph L. Roys, *The Book of Chilam Balam of Chumayel*, p. 117.
36. Edmonson, *The Ancient Future of the Itza*, p. 19.

tz'on
bacal tza[37]

and the translation:

removal by burial,
removal by dart shooting,
          blowgun,
removal by shot

As for the question of verse forms in hieroglyphic texts, the tendency to arrange glyphs in pairs is well known, but Floyd Lounsbury informs me that there are glyph sequences in which a third glyph extends the semantic or syntactic parallelism established by the previous two glyphs. Whether there are other formal variations is a question I will leave to the epigraphers.

Clearly the variation of couplets with triplets has both wide geographical extent and great time depth in the Mayan languages, and the same is undoubtedly true of single introductory or concluding phrases as well. It remains to establish whether quatrains of the kind described here (with variation in the third part) are to be found outside the Popol Vuh and the Tizimín book, but it seems likely. As for the full patterns of oral delivery for these forms, we cannot yet move beyond the Quiché and Yucatec cases.

If we may speak of rhythm in Mayan poetics, it is a rhythm whose formal dimension stays close to its material (or referential) dimension. A major change of sense on the material side, requiring a new syntactical construction, is likely to establish a fresh sound pattern on the formal side, one that will be repeated only by a further and parallelistic development of the sense. When form and reference pivot around one another without any tilt of their axis, form is held back for the sake of sense in the first part of a fresh coupleted line and reference is held back for the sake of form in the second, and so on. When a sequence of multiple couplets is begun or ended or divided into major sections, this performative act is typically accomplished through the introduction of a singular, unparalleled line. When the rhythm is varied with the introduction of longer parallel units, such as the triplets or quatrains exemplified here, the axis might tilt toward the side of form were it not for the tendency to introduce a variation in the construction of the third part of such a unit, which gives that part at least a partial resemblance to the beginning of a new couplet

37. Ibid., p. 16.

and thus swerves the axis away from form and back toward meaning.

The net effect of variation in Mayan verse forms is probably on the side of the material imagination rather than the formal, causing the attention to hesitate a little over the question of meaning. To demonstrate this would require returning the triplets and quatrains quoted here to their original contexts, to see what kinds of meaning might be thrust forward from among the surrounding couplets, but that is beyond the immediate purpose of this essay. In closing we may recall Alfred North Whitehead's statement that "the essence of rhythm is the fusion of sameness and novelty. . . . A mere recurrence kills rhythm as surely as does a mere confusion of differences."[38] To measure all Mayan texts by the single standard of the couplet is to miss the very essence of Mayan verse rhythms, which move in twos, and sometimes threes, and once in a while arch over to produce a four.

38. Quoted in W. K. Wimsatt, *Versification*, p. vii.

PART THREE

Hermeneutics

The Spoken Word and the Work of Interpretation in American Indian Religion

Our text for this morning comes from the Aashiwi, as they call themselves, or from the Zuni Indians. They live in a town in west-central New Mexico and are now twice as numerous as they were when the Spanish first counted them in 1540. Their language is *shiwi'ma,* one of the 150 languages spoken by the various indigenous peoples of the United States.

The name of the text is *chimiky'ana'kowa.* Literally translated, that means, "that which was the beginning." It *is* the beginning, or "that which *was* the beginning." These words were made by what happened at the beginning, and to tell these words is to happen the beginning again. *Chimiky'ana'kọwa.*

I speak of a *text,* even though the Zunis do not have a *manuscript* of the beginning. But there is a way of fixing *words* without making visible *marks.* As with alphabetic writing, this fixing is done by a *radi-*

First given as an address at the Boston University Institute for Philosophy and Religion in 1978; reprinted from *Traditional Literatures of the American Indian: Texts and Interpretations,* ed. Karl Kroeber, by permission of University of Nebraska Press. Copyright © 1981 by the University of Nebraska Press. The principal revisions here are in the discussion of Dell Hymes and in the notes.

233

cal simplification of ordinary talk. Ordinary talk not only has words in it, in the sense of strings of consonants and vowels, but it has patterns of stress, of emphasis, of pitch, of tone, of pauses or stops that can move somewhat independently of the sheer words and make the "same" words mean quite different things, or even the opposite of what they started out to mean. To *fix a text* without making *visible marks* is to bring *stress* and *pitch* and *pause* into a fixed relationship with the *words*. The Zunis call this *ana k'eyato'u*, "raising it right up," and we would call it chant. In Zuni chant, a strong stress and a high, gliding pitch come into concert on the last syllable of each phrase, or sometimes at the end of a single important word, and are immediately followed by a deliberate silence. All other, weaker stresses occurring between two pauses are equal, and all lower pitches are resolved into a monotone.[1] The number of syllables between two pauses varies from around six or seven to twenty or more. This variation has the effect of giving emphasis to the shortest lines, but this is an emphasis *fixed* in the *text* rather than being left to the voice of an individual speaker on a particular occasion. It all sounds something like this (monotone chant, with strong stress and a quick rise on each line-final syllable):[2]

> *Nomilhte ho'n chimiky'anapkya teya*
> *awiten tehwula*
> *annohsiyan tehwula*
> *ho'na liilha aateyaye. . . .*

> Now in truth our beginning is:
> the fourth inner world
> the soot inner world
> is where we live. . . .

The words, or rather the word, of the *chimiky'ana'kowa*, "that which was the beginning," is fixed in a text called *kyaklo an penanne*, the Word of Kyaklo.[3] Kyaklo is a person, a Zuni, who witnessed some of the events of the beginning. He comes once each four or eight years to give his word. He is a stubborn, cranky cripple who must be carried everywhere he goes by the ten clowns who accompany him,

---

1. See Chapter 6, above.
2. The lines of text and translation quoted here are from my own revisions of the version given by Matilda Coxe Stevenson in "The Zuni Indians," pp. 72–89.
3. Stevenson, "The Zuni Indians," pp. 72–89. This is not a complete version, but it gives a clear enough sense of the texture of the chant. For complete versions of other chants belonging to the same genre, see Ruth L. Bunzel, "Zuni Ritual Poetry," pp. 710–76. My description of Kyaklo himself draws from Bunzel, "Zuni Katcinas" (pp. 980–81) and from my own field notes dating from the period 1964–72.

and he always demands that the smallest one do it. He always comes into town by the same path, the same path he has followed since the beginning. There is a new subdivision whose streets do not follow his path, so he must be carried through people's yards. There is a house that sits in his path, so he must be carried up over the roof and down the other side. When they come to the river, just before entering the old part of town, he insists that the clowns wade through the ice and mud of the river rather than taking the bridge. They always manage to drop him, with all his fine clothes. Kyaklo's face is bordered by the rainbow and the milky way, and rain falls from his eyes and mouth. All he does, besides chanting, is to call out his own name: "Kyaklo Kyaklo Kyaklo Kyaklo." The people who want to hear his word assemble in six different ceremonial chambers, or kivas.[4] He carries a duck in his right hand, and if anyone falls asleep while he talks he hits them with the duck's bill. He goes from one building to the next, still chanting even while being carried through the streets; no one person hears the whole word on one occasion, except for the clowns who carry him. On top of that, he uses a lot of arcane and esoteric vocabulary, so that those who are not well versed in such matters have difficulty following. Worse than that, he chants rather fast and his words are muffled by his mask. To wear Kyaklo's mask, a person must devote his whole life, for one year, to studying for the part.

So there is our text. Like a cleanly alphabetic text, it consists of a sheer string of words. Kyaklo always pronounces the same words in the same way; it is always Kyaklo chanting, not a particular wearer of the mask. There are no shifts of stress or pitch or pause to find a new meaning, to say nothing of a search for different *words*.[5] Such is the nature of what we call "authoritative texts": They go on saying exactly the same thing, over and over, forever. Any way you look at it, Kyaklo is authoritative text personified.

Now, the *interpretation* of the *chimiky'ana'kowa*, "that which was the beginning," is another matter. The story does not end with Kyaklo. There are fourteen priesthoods at Zuni, charged with meditation on

4. For a summary of Zuni religious organization, see Dennis Tedlock, "Zuni Religion and World View."
5. Jack Goody, in *The Domestication of the Savage Mind* (chap. 6), grossly underestimates the human capacity for remembering and transmitting verbatim texts. The night talk of the Council of the Gods at the Zuni Sha'lako ceremony, which lasts four and a half hours, is delivered by five performers speaking in unison, which would seem to preclude any such thing as "oral formulaic composition" of the Parry and Lord sort. Kyaklo's performances, which are solo, may vary slightly, but I doubt whether the variations are any more important than those between two different editions of a Shakespearean play, for example. Joel Sherzer also disagrees with Goody (personal communication), on the basis of his work with the Kuna of Panamá.

the weather and with divination, and each of them has an interpretation of the beginning.[6] There are thirteen medicine societies, charged with curing, and each of them has an interpretation. And in every Zuni household there is at least one parent or grandparent who knows how to interpret the beginning. I say "interpretation" partly because these are not fixed texts.[7] The stresses, pitches, pauses, and also the *sheer words*, are different from one interpreter to the next, and even from one occasion to the next, according to the place and time, according to who is in the audience, according to what they do or do not already know, according to what questions they may have been asked. Even according to what may happen, outside the events of the narrative itself, during this particular telling.[8] Or the interpreter may suddenly realize something or understand something for the first time on this particular occasion. The teller is not merely repeating memorized words, nor is he or she merely giving a dramatic "oral interpretation" or "concert reading" of a fixed script. We are in the presence of a *performing art*, all right, but we are getting the *criticism* at the same time and from the same person. The interpreter does not merely play the parts, but is the narrator and commentator as well. What we are hearing is the *hermeneutics* of the text of Kyaklo. At times we may hear direct quotations from that text, but they are embedded in a hermeneutics.

Now, our own phenomenologists and structuralists also quote their texts, removing words from context and even daring to insert their own *italics*: "Italics mine." But there is a difference here: The interpreter of that which was the beginning must keep the *story* going. And in this process, the storyteller-interpreter does not merely quote or paraphrase the text but may even *improve* upon it, describe a scene which it does not describe, or answer a question which it does not answer.

The Word of Kyaklo, taken by itself, is a sacred object, a relic. It is not a visible or tangible object, but it is an object nevertheless. What we hear from our interpreter is simultaneously something new *and* a comment on that relic, both a restoration and a further possibility. I emphasize this point because ethnologists, down to the present day,

6. The version of the Priest of the East is given in Ruth L. Bunzel, "Zuni Origin Myths," pp. 549–602.

7. Just as the Kyaklo talk is far *more* fixed than the Yugoslav epics discussed by Albert Lord in *The Singer of Tales*, so the "interpretations" referred to here are far *less* so. Extrapolations from Old World metrical epics to "oral culture" in general are ill-founded, to say the least.

8. For an example of the weaving in of chance events, see Dennis Tedlock, *Finding the Center*, pp. 258, 271.

have hankered after the sacred object itself, whenever they could get their hands on it, while devaluing what I am here calling "interpretations." Dell Hymes falls into this pattern when he makes a distinction between what he calls "a *telling about* the story" and "a *doing of* the story."[9] He suggests that we need to gather up the "true performances" from our collections of North American narratives, sorting these out from the mere "tellings," or "reportings," that exist in these same collections. He does allow for "oral *scholia*," but these are given no part in "authentic or authoritative performance."[10] What is stark about this position is that it would seem to leave the "telling about" the story, including commentary and interpretation, up to the ethnologist, while the proper business of the authentic native—digress though he or she may—is the "doing of" the story. This is close to the position of the French structuralists, who limit the native to a narrative or "diachronic" function and leave the analytic or "synchronic" function to themselves.[11] In effect, the collected texts are treated as if they were raw products, to which value is then added by manufacture.

For the Zuni storyteller-interpreter, the relationship between text and interpretation is a dialectical one: He or she both respects the text and revises it. For the ethnologist that relationship is a dualistic opposition. In the end, the text remains the text, still there in the archives and still waiting to be brought to light; the analysis remains the analysis, bearing no resemblance *to* the text and learning nothing *from* the text, and the analyst even takes professional pride in that fact.

The interpretation of the Kyaklo text that concerns us here was given by a man named Andrew Peynetsa, then sixty-two years old, at his farmhouse in the evening.[12] Checking my notes, I find that he gave the first part of this narrative thirteen years ago last Sunday and finished it thirteen years ago today, on March 29, 1965. He was talking to his wife, one of his sons, his clan brother, and myself. I, of course, had a tape-recorder, and my translation from the Zuni follows not only the original words but also the original loudnesses, softnesses, tones, and silences.

Andrew, as a boy, had heard the entire Word of Kyaklo. He and a

9. Dell Hymes, "*In Vain I Tried to Tell You*," p. 321; emphasis mine.
10. Ibid., p. 84. For the Kuna it would be difficult indeed to separate interpretation from performance: A chief's speeches are interpreted for the audience by a spokesman who must himself be a skilled performer, and "all speech . . . involves constant reformulations and explanations of what has just been said" (Joel Sherzer, "The Ethnography of Speaking: A Critical Appraisal," p. 51).
11. See the end of Chapter 6, above, for a discussion that touches on anthropological attitudes toward native self-description and analysis.
12. See Tedlock, *Finding the Center*, pp. 225–98, for a full translation.

cousin had been pestering their grandfather to tell a tale, the kind of story the Zunis tell for entertainment. Their grandfather was a cranky old man who didn't really know any tales, but one night he finally consented to tell them something. It turned out to be the Word of Kyaklo. He kept them awake all night, hitting them with a stick whenever they nodded. At dawn he sent them out to do their chores. The next night he resumed his talk, going on all night again. And so on for another night and another, finishing at dawn on the fourth day.

The Zuni beginning does not begin with a first cause, it does not derive an infinite chain of dualisms from a first dualism that in turn springs from original absolute oneness. When the story opens, the earth is already here, the *awitelin tsitta*, literally the "four-chambered mother." There are four more worlds under this one, darker and darker. In this room we're on the third floor, so the bottommost world beneath this one would be a secret basement below the actual basement of this building.[13] Only the Sun Father is up here in this world. Four stories beneath in the Soot Room, in total darkness, are the people. The problem is not to create human beings, but that they should be up here in this world, making prayers and offerings to the Sun Father and receiving his daylight, his life. The people down in the fourth room beneath are only *moss people*, they have webbed feet, webbed hands, tails of moss, they are slimy. They do not know what fire is, or lightning, or daylight, or even dawn.

In the Word of Kyaklo and in all previously recorded interpretations, the three rooms between this world and the Soot Room are apparently vacant.[14] This is where Andrew's interpretation introduces one of its elaborations or improvements:[15]

> At the beginning
> when the earth was still soft
> the first people came out
> the ones who had been living in the first room beneath.
> When they came out they made their villages
> they made their houses a————ll around the land.

13. This talk was given on the third floor of the School of Theology at Boston University. The Zunis themselves make the analogy between the stories of a building and those of the world. The priesthoods conduct their meditations four rooms beneath the top surface of the main building of the town, in total darkness.

14. See Ruth Benedict, *Zuni Mythology*, vol. 1, pp. 255–61, for a summary of all previous versions.

15. All the passages quoted hereafter are from *Finding the Center*, pp. 225–98.

So the first people out were not ourselves, as in the other versions, but people who were living in the first room beneath this one. But the Sun Father was displeased because "they did not think of anything," they did not give prayers and offerings. When the people in the second room came out, their sulphurous smell, their ozone smell killed all the first ones. They in turn did not think of anything. The people from the third room beneath came out, and their sulphurous smell killed the second people, and they, too, did not think of anything.

Now, the idea that three unsuccessful approximations of human beings preceded ourselves is a common one among Mesoamerican peoples, far to the south of the Zunis. But it is not our concern here to pretend to "explain" the source, the origin of this part of the present narrative. The point is that Kyaklo leaves three rooms vacant, and our interpreter fills them. This may be something "new," or it may even be a restoration of something that Kyaklo forgot. Whatever the case, these first three peoples live and die in a storyteller's *interpretation* and not in the chanter's *text*. They are *not* in the "book."

As we heard before, these previous people "made their villages a—ll around the land." Our interpreter stops for a moment to comment on this:

> Their ruins are all around the land as you can see.
> Around the mountains where there is no water today, you could get
>   water just by pulling up a clump of grass
> because the earth was soft.
> This is the way they lived, there at the beginning.

Not only is this a departure from the official text: it is a departure from the "doing of" the story, and it changes over from third-person narrative to direct address: "as *you* can see." Interpretation, here in the form of a small lecture, in the very *midst* of the *text*. It happens again just a few lines later, as the narrator leads us toward the moment when the twin sons of the Sun Father come into existence. It had been raining all night:

> Where there were waterfalls
> the water made foam.
> Well, you know how water can make foam
> certainly
> it can make foam
> •
> certainly
> that water

made suds.
It was there
where the suds were made
that the two Bow Priests
sprouted.
There the two Ahayuuta
received life.
Their father brought them to life:
they came out of the suds.

And in another place, having told an episode in which Nepayatamu, the patron of the Clown Society, brings the Molaawe, or corn deities, back into the town after a famine, our interpreter comments:

When the Molaawe enter today
the same procedure is followed:
Nepayatamu
does not speak
when he enters
and the priests are completely quiet inside, well you
have seen this yourself, at the kiva.

Such passages as these raise questions about the relationship of text to world. I mean "world" in the sense that Paul Ricoeur does when he says that the task of hermeneutics is to reveal the "destination of discourse as projecting a world," or when he says that "for me, the world is the ensemble of references opened up by every kind of text."[16] But when the ruins are all around the land, as *you* can see; when *you* know how water can make foam, can make suds; when *you* have seen Nepayatamu and the Molaawe yourself, at the kiva, I don't know whether the text is opening up the world, or the world is opening up the text. This problem is written larger in the narrative as a whole. The world was *already there*; we human beings, or "daylight people" as the Zunis call us, were already there; and, as the narrative details, there were already priesthoods and even a whole village down there in the Soot Room, and the priesthoods were in possession of the seeds of every kind of plant that would grow up here in this world. Still, it is true, we were in the dark, and the world up here on this layer, even if it already existed, had not yet been revealed to us. The Sun Father gave his twin sons the *word* that we were to come out into the daylight, and they brought that *word* down to the priests. The

16. Paul Ricoeur, *Interpretation Theory*, pp. 36–37.

priests responded by setting themselves the very lengthy project of getting us out into the daylight. It looks as though the discourse of the Sun Father had, to paraphrase Ricoeur, projected a world for us. Or, if we follow Ricoeur's recent abandonment of the phenomenological concern with the author's intentions, the Word itself projects a world for us. But "project": that seems like the disembodied ghost of the author's intention, the will of God working itself out in the creation of the world. There is something too inevitable about it all. The word in the Zuni beginning, the word brought by the twin sons of the Sun Father, is *pewiyulhahna*, a word that is *yulhahna*: *lha-* means important, or even *too* important, *too* much, but the *-hna* on the end makes that negative and the *yu-* on the front puts the word in the indeterminative: *yulhahna*, "sort of not too important," or the word is of "indeterminate importance." It is a word of *some* importance, but perhaps not *too* much.

The Kyaklo text and the available priestly interpretations hint at a general theme of indeterminacy that goes beyond terminological questions, but Andrew's interpretation develops that theme fully. First of all, when the people from the first room emerge into this world, he does not even mention that the Sun Father played any role. When it comes to the second people, the Sun Father simply remarks, "Well, perhaps if the ones who live in the second room come out, it will be good." For the third people, the narrator says, "Those who lived in the third room beneath were summoned"; if it was the Sun Father who summoned them, this is only implicit, but at least we have a glimpse of a will here. Now, we may think, the next stage will be to put the Sun Father and the will together. Here is the way it goes:

> The ones who were living in the fourth room
> were needed
> •
> but
> the Sun was thinking
> •
> he was thinking
> that he did not know what would happen now.

What does happen is the rain, the waterfall, and the sprouting of the twins from the foam. Then we are told, "Their father brought them to life," which points to the operation of will again, but the very next line simply says, "They came out of the suds," and we were previously told that they "sprouted." Whatever is at work here, or *not quite* at work, there is a meeting of the sunlight and the foam of the waterfall, and out come the twins. When the Sun Father tells the twins about the people of the fourth room, ourselves, he says:

> You will bring them out, and PERHAPS THEN
> as I have in mind
> they will offer me prayer-meal.

"Perhaps," he says, perhaps. The twins say this:

> We will TRY.
> This place where they may or may not live is FAR
> There in the room full of SOOT.

When they enter the fourth room and find the village there, they meet up with a person who happens to be out hunting. This is their first meeting with the *moss people*, the people who are living in total darkness but are about to receive the Word of the Sun Father, the word that will project a world for them. This hunter they meet is a modest person, he speaks with a weak voice. But before they have explained their project, he remarks,

> Well, perhaps I
> might know why it is you came.

He takes them to the village, where they meet the Talking Priest, the Spokesman, and give him their "word of indeterminate importance" concerning emergence into the daylight. He responds:

> Indeed.
> •
> But even if that is what you have in mind
> How will it be done?

And he even asks them directly: "DO YOU HAVE THE MEANS FOR GETTING OUT THERE successfully?" To which they respond,

> WELL
> well, no.

The Spokesman then suggests they call in the Priest of the North. But the Priest of the North doesn't know how to get out of the Soot Room and suggests the West Priest. The West Priest doesn't know and suggests the South Priest, and the South Priest suggests the East Priest, and the East Priest says, "I, least of ALL." He suggests the twins, who brought the word in the first place: "Perhaps they know how to do this after all," he says, and they say,

Well
Well I DON'T KNOW.
But I will TRY something.

The twins take all the people along toward the east for a distance, and then go ahead of them a little. When they find themselves alone, one of them says to the other, "What are we going to do?" And the other makes a further suggestion, prefaced with a "perhaps." With just such questions and perhapses, they manage to find a way up through the third, second, and first rooms. In each room they plant a tree, and the branches of that tree form a spiral staircase into the next and lighter room. But the seeds of all plants were already all there in the dark, in the possession of the priests of the moss people.

When they are all in the first room beneath, where everything is the color of dawn, the twins make an announcement to the people:

NOW YOU MUST STEP FROM BRANCH TO BRANCH AGAIN
UNTIL WE COME OUT, OUT INTO OUR SUN FATHER'S DAYLIGHT.
      EVEN THOUGH IT WILL BE HARD
YOU MUST DO YOUR BEST
to look at your father
for you will hardly be able to SEE.
There in the room full of soot, when we entered upon
      your roads, we could hardly SEE.
That is the way it will be with you, CERTAINLY.

So, just as the Ahayuuta could not see in the Soot Room, so the moss people will not be able to see in the daylight. This is the kind of thing that structural analysis is made of. But wait a minute. This is not a trade-off of opposites: "You will *hardly* be able to see," they say to the people, and they say of themselves in the Soot Room, "We could *hardly* see." The hunter they met there was not in total ignorance but said, "Well, perhaps I might know why it is you came," and the twins, the sons of the Sun Father and the bearers of his Word, said they would *try* something, not that they would simply do it. And when the people finally come out of the dawn room, they come out not in the full brightness of midday but at the same moment the sun *rises*. It is hard, but they *look at* their Sun Father. At daybreak.

Now the twins take the people eastward for some distance, the first step of a migration that will lead to the place where the town of Zuni now stands. The twins make an announcement:

"NOW
we will stay here four days," they said. THEY WERE GOING TO STAY
 FOUR YEARS.
FOR FOUR YEARS THEY LIVED where they had stopped.

So the twins say four *days*, but our narrator tells us they mean (or the text means) four *years*. Kyaklo does not tell us this, it is *not* in the *book*, but this particular detail is a part of *all interpretations*. It is like the comment of a scholiast in an ancient written text, but it has not become embedded in the text itself. At the same time, it is not set apart in a treatise on theology. It is not the subject of an argument over whether the Book really means seven days. What the Ahayuuta *say* is four *days*, and what they mean is four *years*. But there is something more here than just an explanation, a sort of translation, of the mysterious language of the Ahayuuta. We can't just say, "All right, they really mean four years," and be done with it. It still remains that they *said* four *days*. And if we look again, we see that our interpreter didn't say they *meant* four years. The Ahayuuta say, "We will stay here four days," and the interpreter says, "They were going to stay four years." But this is not a deviation from *plan*, either. After the four years are up, the Ahayuuta say, "We've been here *four days*." But I don't want to say, therefore, that they *meant* four years, in some kind of code language. When we decode that we've got nothing left. We might as well erase "days" and replace it with "years." But our interpreter puts four days *alongside* four years and in fact he does it two different times, once at the opening of this episode and once at the close, just in case we might miss it.

Now, suppose we've heard an interpretation or two of "that which was the beginning" and we finally have an opportunity to go and listen to Kyaklo. When we hear him saying "four days," then we'll know . . . What will we know? Whatever we *think*, he *says* four days. But we can't stop knowing about the four years. Something is happening with time here, within time, something with its marking and its duration, and it is happening *between* the text and the interpretation. It seems like *ages*. It seems like only *yesterday*.

Who are these Ahayuuta, these twins, who talk like this? Their name is a clue, because they both go by the same name, Ahayuuta, whereas no two living people should ever have the same name. Once in a great while the Ahayuuta reveal, as they do elsewhere in the present narrative, that they also possess separate names of their own, but they are as close as they could possibly be to the rift between being the same person and a different person. The Kyaklo text and all the interpretations tell us that although they are twins, one of them is the elder and the other is the younger. Of course. Twins are born one at a time. But they are as close to the rift of elder and younger as they could possibly be. They are called Ahayuuta *an papa*, "the Ahayuuta's elder brother," and Ahayuuta *an suwe*, "the Ahayuuta's younger brother." They are named by reference to each other. If I refer to the elder brother, I am in effect naming his younger brother "Ahayuuta" and then saying that Ahayuuta has an elder brother. If I refer to the younger brother, I am in effect naming his elder brother "Ahayuuta" and then saying that Ahayuuta has a younger brother. What is called Ahayuuta is between them.

Neither text nor previous interpretations tell us what stage of life these Ahayuuta are in, beyond the fact that they are not fully grown, but now that we can listen to the voice of a narrator as he speaks their lines, rather than merely reading a conventional alphabetic transcription, we hear that the younger one has a high voice that tends to crack.[17] In other words, the two of them are differentiated by the rift of adolescence, even though they were almost born simultaneously.

The twins make everything possible; they are, in Heidegger's terms, "the rift of difference" itself. That rift, he says, "makes the limpid brightness shine,"[18] and this is the time to say that the Ahayuuta carry weapons, and that those weapons are lightning. This is their *brilliance*. The people say they are *ayyuchi'an aaho"i*, "extraordinary, amazing beings." The people say they are *pikwayin aaho"i*, "surpassing, miraculous beings." *Pikwayina* is the Zuni term for miracle, it means something like "pass through to the other side." If the rain comes through our roof, somehow, and a drop forms on the ceiling and falls, then *k'a pikwayi*, the rain has passed through to the other side. But the Ahayuuta say, "Extraordinary beings we are NOT." They're a little small for their age, they are dirty, they have lice in their hair. They sprouted from the alkaline foam of a muddy flash-flood after a heavy rain. But "their Sun Father brought them to life." Is this their point of *origin*? Is the *will* of the Sun Father the first cause of all differences? Did everything begin with his word? But the world was already there, four rooms full of people, already there, these people who might already know something. The Sun Father wants the peo-

17. See *Finding the Center*, pp. 168, 177, 179.
18. Martin Heidegger, *Poetry, Language, Thought*, pp. 202–5.

ple to come out of the fourth room, he has a desire in the matter, but he *does not know*, altogether and in advance, what will happen in the meeting of his will with what already is. And from there the Ahayuuta are "given life." Or: they *sprout*. What does it mean to say this is their origin, their starting-point? The rain was not made, the earth was not made: They always already were. When we go beyond the Kyaklo text and its interpretations to the *tales* about the Ahayuuta, we again find something that's not in the *book*: In all of those tales, the Ahayuuta live with their grandmother.[19] Not with their mother—that would be the waterfall, we may guess—but their mother's mother. They always already have a grandmother. And what is *her* name? She is simply called Ahayuuta *an hotta*, the Ahayuuta's grandmother. Of course. Grandmother of difference. She is the patroness of midwives. And what is her shining? The Sun Father gives daylight and the Ahayuuta travel on lightning. Whenever the Zunis touch a glowing coal or a match to a cigarette, they say they are giving their grandmother a seat in the doorway.

So is *that* the starting of everything? Can we stop here, looking at the face of the Ahayuuta's grandmother? And what is that face? One side of her face is covered with ashes, and the other side is covered with soot. Ashes and fire are already there together. In the live coal, the ashes and soot are not waiting to be projected by the fire. Elder and younger are already there. The Sun and the people are already there. Desire and possibility are already there. The word and the world are already there. The text and the interpretation are already there.

19. See Chapter 2, above, for a lengthy tale involving the Ahayuuta and their grandmother.

10

Beyond Logocentrism:
Trace and Voice Among the Quiché
Maya

. . . . I don't know where to begin this story. Quiché Maya stories occur naturally in conversation. People do not set aside an occasion for
storytelling, where all other kinds of talk come to a stop. It is true that
stories are likely to be heard at wakes, but people don't die just so
someone can tell stories at their wakes.

When an anthropologist asks a Quiché, "Tell me a story," chances
are that he or she will be unable to think of a story, given no reason to
tell a story other than that someone wants to hear a story, any story.
At least one anthropologist decided that there were no stories among
the Quiché Maya.[1]

A Quiché story does not begin with a series of formal opening
announcements that call a halt to conversation and point only into the
story, and it does not end with a series of formal closures that call a
halt.[2] The story may include or refer back to bits of the previous con-

First delivered at "A Symposium on the Problems of Reading in Contemporary American Criticism," held at the State University of New York at Binghamton in 1978; first
published in *Boundary 2* 8 (1979):321–33.
    1. Sol Tax, "Folk Tales in Chichicastenango: An Unsolved Puzzle," p. 125.
    2. For examples of formal openings and closings, see Chapter 5, above.

versation, and when it is over, bits of the story are caught up in the conversation that follows.

The Quiché hearer does not remain silent, or merely affirm from time to time that he is listening. Rather, the listener may ask a question, or else echo the words of the story now and then.[3] The Quiché story of the creation, like Genesis, tells of creation by words, but the words are a dialogue, not a monologue.[4]

A Quiché story does not carry us away into another world or another aeon, a separate reality that has no connection to the world of the conversants. It does not go on for an hour, or even half an hour, but lasts only five or ten minutes, and once in a great while twenty.[5] The story does not move strictly forward along the path of its events, but always gets a little ahead of itself here and looks back on itself there.[6]

I do not know where to begin this story. It has one root that runs backward into the conversation that immediately precedes it, with runners that connect it to conversations of previous days, and it has another root that runs forward into the rest of its own day, with further connections to following days. On what grounds do I introduce such a story into my statement here, to you? If it is to be truly an example of Quiché storytelling, it must be connected, as something more than an isolated object held up for examination, to the rest of the conversation of our conference here. What is there about the present occasion that calls for this story? The story has to do with being in jail. In terms of the world of the body, as the Quiché see it, being in jail is like being caught in someone's armpit. It's not quite as bad as being at the bottom of that canyon behind the folded knee; that is the grave itself. There is some talk that we are all, all of us here, caught in the armpit just now, not knowing quite how to get out. One name we give to our prison is language. Jacques Derrida calls this prison "the Western metaphysic," "God," "logocentrism," "phonocentrism," "logo-phonocentrism," "phono-logocentrism," and he doesn't know how to fight his way out without getting a further sentence for attempted escape.[7] The problem, as he sees it, is that we in the West are trapped by the voice. Trapped by our alphabetic writing, which fol-

---

3. The Zuni audience is limited to saying *eeso* periodically, which has the effect of "yes, indeed" (see Chapter 5, above).

4. See Chapter 11, below.

5. Zuni stories, by contrast, last from half an hour to well over an hour, even in their ordinary hearthside versions.

6. This is true even in the Popol Vuh; see Chapter 4, above. In some Popol Vuh episodes the course and outcome of a story are announced before it even begins.

7. Jacques Derrida, *Of Grammatology*, part 1, and "Limited Inc."

lows the voice. The voice is linear, in his view: There is only one thing happening at a time, a sequence of phonemes. On a larger scale, the unidimensional march of the voice is replicated in our linear view of history, what Derrida calls "the epic model."[8] The bars of the prison, then, are made of speech and of oral poetry, and the way out, in Derrida's thinking, is through a writing and a literature that finally realize their full potential by severing their connections with the voice.

While our hero goes on seeking escape through an examination of the spaces between the bars, the rest of us might do well to take a second look at the prison itself, to see how the bars were set into the wall, and what they are made of, and whether they are substantial. First of all, does alphabetic writing, or the refined alphabetic writing that linguists call phonemic—is this writing in servitude to the voice? Derrida himself, toward the end of the *Grammatology*, touches here and there on the fact that writing slights what he calls, or Rousseau calls, "accent," and to that we could add features like pausing, tone of voice, and amplitude.[9] As Derrida puts it, writing writes only that part of the voice which is already most inscribable, the so-called articulations, the one-at-a-time sequence of items that interrupts vowels with consonants. The entire science of linguistics, and in turn the mythologics (or larger-scale structuralism) that has been built upon linguistics,[10] are founded not upon a multidimensional apprehension of the multidimensional voice, but upon unilinear writing of the smallest-scale articulations within the voice. The *purest* linguistic transcription, in fact (*here, speak in a monotone*), has only lower-case letters of a single style (*here, exaggerate stress accents*), includes only such accents and tones as occur at the level of isolated words (*here, run the words together*), only grudgingly admits spaces between words (*monotone*), and excludes all punctuation. It is sheer (*pause*) alphabet. On this everything else is built. The grammatology, the science of writing Derrida calls for, already exists—for the alphabet, at least— and it is called (*pause*) linguistics. Even glimpsing this, as he does at the end of the *Grammatology*, we find him ten years later still blaming the voice and seeking freedom in writing, still looking at the holes in the enclosure he has described for himself.[11]

And what of that unilinear poetry of the voice, the epic? Just as

8. Derrida, *Of Grammatology*, pp. 72, 85–87.
9. The classic critique of what I like to call "alphabecentrism" in linguistics is that of J. R. Firth, *Papers in Linguistics, 1934–51*, pp. 121–38.
10. "Mythologics" is of course a direct translation of Lévi-Strauss's *mythologiques*, with its deliberate retention of the suffix (surname) of its claimed parent.
11. Derrida, *Of Grammatology*, p. 315; "Limited Inc," pp. 220, 249.

we questioned whether the alphabet is in servitude to the voice, so we may ask this question of the epic, with its long march through events in hexameter time. Is this the voice of the preliterate Greeks we hear? Or is it oral *literature*: written literature meant to be recited aloud, as all literature was up to the time of the Renaissance. When we look at the earliest written literature, that of the Sumerians, we find no such verse epic. When we look at cultures known to have been free of alphabetic or syllabic writing, not only African and Amerindian but also Chinese, we find no epic. Wherever we find epic today, in Islamic Africa, in Central and Southeast Asia, in the Balkans, it always exists within a literate tradition that uses alphabetic or syllabic writing, and the oral versions, though sometimes performed by individuals who are themselves illiterate, always exist in close proximity to written versions.[12] This was in fact the case with the Homeric epics as they existed in classical Athens, where upper-class schoolchildren were taught to recite a written Homer but not to read it.[13] For all we know, this metrical epic, this genre we have enshrined as the quintessence of oral poetry, was born within writing, literature indeed. This question cannot be finally settled. The Greeks, for their part, did much of their writing on perishable surfaces, something most historians of the alphabet would say they were already doing at the time of—let us call it the Homeric—war,[14] and for our part, there is no way we can take a tape-recorder into antiquity. It might still be that the epic came *before* the alphabet, as part of the same tendency of mind that produced the alphabet in Greece, while other minds in other places went their own ways. What matters here is that the epic, far from typifying the oral poetry of nonliterate peoples, in fact typifies the oral poetry of alphabetic and syllabic peoples. I, for one, have no objection to calling the epic oral *literature*, in the strict sense of that word: made of *letters*. Even when sung, the epic tends toward the univocity of alphabetic writing: The varied spacing of spoken accents

12. For a discussion of the metrical epic and its distribution, see Ruth Finnegan, *Oral Poetry*, pp. 9–10. The epic she mentions as occurring in China is Central Asian, not part of indigenous Chinese tradition. Throughout my own discussion here, I use "epic" in the strict sense, meaning a heroic narrative with a metrical, sung text. For the strongest introduction to the African alternative to such epics, see Isidore Okpewho, *The Epic in Africa*.

13. Eric Havelock, "The Preliteracy of the Greeks."

14. Berthold Louis Ullman, *Ancient Writing and Its Influence*, p. 21. Havelock ("The Preliteracy of the Greeks") would disagree with this because he wants to picture preliterate Greece as lasting much longer, teeming with people who are veritable storehouses of memorized hexameter and only waiting for the opportunity to write it down. He ignores the entirety of the ethnographic literature on living nonliterate societies, which discloses no metrical verse at all in the absence of direct influence from alphabetic or syllabic written traditions.

or vowel quantities is reduced to a predictable meter, and the varied contours of spoken pitches are reduced to a single melodic line, repeated over and over, line after line. The epic is a marvel of small-scale sound engineering, and its perfection, and perhaps even its invention, were greatly facilitated by alphabetic writing.[15]

Yet for all this, Derrida is right in saying that writing writes something that was already written in the voice, it writes articulations, traces, differences that are missing when the voice simply cries out without talking. We can extend this and say that the epic writes something that was already written in oral narrative, something that is missing when talk tells no story. We cannot escape our enclosure simply by reversing Derrida and saying that the name of the bars is writing, and that the name of the spaces between them is the voice. We do not wish to choose between writing articulate but endless letters from prison, as David Antin does—it is true that he speaks, but his voice is the voice of the typewriter before the tapes are even transcribed—we do not wish to choose between talking without a shift key and roaring like a tiger in a cage, as Michael McClure did in his beast-language poems.[16]

But here I've gone too far again. The bars, the stripes that Antin wears are at least sawn through. He puts in blank spaces, the breaths as they occur, and the spacing of these blanks is anything but a marvel of engineering. McClure, for his part, articulated his cries with alphabetic transcription, even if he did it all in caps and with his own hand. If we could only navigate the difference, the dif-ference between them,[17] we could speak with articulate passion and write with passionate articulation.

Well then.

Perhaps it's time to begin the story, the Quiché Maya story I promised you. But I still don't know where to begin. But the story does have a jail in it, and writing, and the voice. And animals. We had been talking, in a town in Guatemala, with a person who is a weaver and a diviner by profession. We had been learning about omens. You may wonder what an American Indian diviner will have to teach us

15. David Antin, in "Notes for an Ultimate Prosody," asserts that the Beowulf meter is entirely the creation of nineteenth-century scholarship, having no existence in the text. He also suggests that meter has been largely visual, rather than auditory, in its effects on poetry, but what I am arguing here is that an early purpose of written meter was to create a mechanical (and memorizable) *sound*. See Dennis Tedlock, "Toward an Oral Poetics," p. 507.

16. David Antin, *Talking at the Boundaries*. For examples of Michael McClure's work, see "7 Los Angeles Poems."

17. In matters of dif-ference," I follow Martin Heidegger, *Poetry, Language, Thought*, pp. 202–5.

about "Problems of Reading in Contemporary American Criticism." The answer is already partly there in the word "reading." At its Teutonic root, that word means "to make clear what is obscure," and it still has that meaning when we say things like "What's your *reading* of the situation?" The Romance (and German) words for reading have, at their root, the meaning "to collect, to gather," as when one recognizes words in groups of letters. Now *sortilege*, as a technique of divination, contains the same root and has the same meaning, it is a gathering. What a diviner does, as a profession, is make a gathering that renders clear what is obscure.

Well then, we are conversing with a diviner. For some reason we were talking about quail, and he said that just as people have chickens, so the *Mundo*, the Earth-deity, the Mountain has quail. We had been learning about omens, so we asked whether it was good luck to come across a quail in the woods. He said that it was a question of whether the quail crossed one's path, and in which direction:[18]

> A movement to the right is good
> to the left is evil.

That seems a clear enough way to read the quail, and it even corresponds to our own valuation of the right and left hands. He goes on:

> The Mundo sends it
> as an announcement it is sent.

So omens are sent not by God, but by the World, the Earth, the Mountain, the owner of the quail. The missionaries attempted to teach the Quiché, as they succeeded in teaching our own ancestors, that those who read omens are deceived by the devil, that nothing but ill can come of it.[19] But the Quiché say that it is not the devil who sends an omen:

> The Mundo sends it
> as an announcement it is sent.
> Since animals don't talk

18. Transcribed and translated from field tape Q50, side 1, in the author's possession.
19. I am thinking here of the seventeenth-century Catholic catechism in Ernesto Chinchilla Aguilar, *La Danza del Sacrificio y otros estudios* (pp. 65–76), but its frontal attack on omen-taking, dream interpretation, and divination has been repeated many times around the world. One could not want a purer expression of the "Western metaphysic," including those parts of it which have become implicit for most of its adherents, than is found in missionary catechisms.

they pass by
almost in one's path.

So the Mundo, or the animals it sends, don't *talk*. They articulate by making a *mark* in the path ahead, leaving a *trace*. This is what Derrida would call writing,[20] but it is not delivered in words. The Word, we may guess, belongs to God, that voice from the sky. God speaks only the Good, but the Mundo writes of both good and evil. The Mundo writes *boustrophedon*, like the preimperial Greeks,[21] moving back and forth across our field of vision rather than always one way.

At this point our diviner thinks of a story, but the first sentence of his story in no way interrupts the conversation: It half belongs to the conversation and half to the story, it's like a title for the story. He says, about these announcements of the Mundo:

It's like the squirrel
it happened to a guy from just above here
he's almost a neighbor of ours.

So we're not in for any excursion into some far-off fantasy land, some "other world" to be projected for us by the text, a world that exists only because of this text: The hero is *almost* our neighbor.[22] All the more reason for us to be afraid.

Now this guy
in the time of Ubico
in '36 or
'37
when all kinds of papers were asked for—
certificate, identification
summons, I don't know
how many papers—

We're under a Central American dictator, everywhere we go we have to show our papers to the authorities.

20. Derrida, *Of Grammatology*, pp. 9, 55, 62, 65, 70; "Limited Inc," p. 190.
21. See Ullman, *Ancient Writing* (pp. 27–28), on the direction of ancient writing.
22. Paul Ricoeur's notion of a "world" created by texts, lying "beyond" or "in front of" texts which are "freed" from a "dialogical situation" to pursue the true "destination" of discourse (*Interpretation Theory*, pp. 36–37), seems foreign to the present text in its violence of directionality. Ricoeur is at pains to free himself from what Derrida calls the metaphysical "enterprise of returning to an origin" ("Limited Inc," p. 236), but in the process he seems to have simply moved the "other world" from behind the text to a position in front of it.

> now this guy
> didn't take his papers with him
> he didn't remember
> when he took the road to San Francisco, he went to sell
> his blankets
> but when he left his house, he was now about a
> league and a half, or two leagues
> from his house—

The distance is a league and a half, or two leagues. The time is '36 or '37. We need a certificate, or an identification, or a summons, or all of these, we don't know. Diviners stay close to "the rift of difference," as Heidegger calls it, even a small difference. They leave us between two points, or *at* both of them, and sometimes three.

> but when he left his house, he was now about a
> league and a half, or two leagues
> from his house—
> then a squirrel came out
> it crossed the road
> to the left
> it went inside a
> tree—
> because there are trunks of massive trees
> that have holes—

So our diviner stops the flow of the story here to remind us that massive trees have hollows in them, the trees we all know, not just the tree occurring in this story, he strikes a chord here rather than just playing the melody. Having done this, he goes on:

> and the squirrel went inside there

We've already heard that a few lines ago, but he has to get the story back on the track again after his lecture about trees.

> and the squirrel went inside there
> llloooooooking at this guy as he came along

This llloooooooking makes the voice do more than one thing at a time. It has no place in phonology or grammar or a structuralist analysis except as just plain "looking," but llloooooooking tells us that the squirrel is looking continuously at our hero, looking from a distance and through a time, looking in a way that should've gotten his atten-

tion, that gave him every chance to think, to read what had already
been written there,

> but the guy didn't think about what it announced, this
> this animal
> then
> he went down to San Francisco el Alto
> he just handed himself over.

Our diviner doesn't keep us from what's obviously going to happen in
the next moment. He announces it in advance. We already knew that
our hero didn't have his papers, and we already knew that a movement to the left is evil. Now we're told he handed himself over. But it
hasn't quite happened yet:

> They were looking at the
> tickets

Tickets? They were looking at the—(*pause*)—*tickets*, our diviner has
carefully chosen this word. We've already heard about papers, certificate, identification, summons—*summons? That* sounds ominous—
and now it's *tickets*. Where is our oral repetition of formulas? Of one
thing we can be sure, this story is no epic. But let's get on with it:

> They were looking at the
> tickets
> the poor guy went for a stay in jail.

Because he didn't have the tickets, he énded up in jail. People who
have tickets get somewhere, they move on; people without tickets
have tickets for jail, they move nowhere. I've just made a classic structuralist move here, or was it me? Could it have been our diviner,
about to put the hero in jail, while he hesitated long enough to choose
the word "tickets"? Do I have the right to say, with Lévi-Strauss, that
our storyteller is an unconscious structuralist, while I am the literate
discoverer of the workings of his mind? Could it be that our diviner
spéaks with the wíles of a wríter? But there's more:

> Now he didn't sell
> his wares
> he just handed himself over.

This doesn't move the story forward, but dwells on what we already know. The pauses here have no place in writing and therefore no place in linguistics or mythologics, but they do describe a form. In their relationship to the words, they echo the structure of the previous sentence. Here are both sentences in juxtaposition:

they were looking at the / Now he didn't sell
tickets / his wares
the poor guy went for a stay in jail / he just handed himself over

We've heard that last line before: "he just handed himself over." It's the only exactly repeated line in the whole story. But it doesn't have the weight of those epic formulas, it's not clunky. It's something one might say in conversation. *Is being said* in conversation. In the present context, it takes on a fuller meaning:

Now he didn't sell
his wares
he just handed himself over.

He didn't "sell," but instead "just handed over," and it wasn't his wares he left there in San Francisco, but himself. "He just handed *himself* over." Now, if there is any remaining thought that the "civilization" of our Mayan diviner is merely lying dormant in a "savage" mind, waiting to be excavated, the next sentence should take care of that. He now looks back over the story:

This was the announcement the animal gave
looking at him here as if he were already in jail there.

So the hero failed to see himself, there in the hollow of the tree; he did not meet the gaze of the squirrel's lllooooooooking. To paraphrase Heidegger: If we could only see, for once, just where we are already.[23] And who's "we"? What is said here is not only between the hollow in the tree and the jail, but between the story and the rest of our conversation. "Where we are *already*": We can wait for more, but our diviner never *will* tell us that this story is the *origin* story of omens, the starting point even of this particular *kind* of omen. *That* would have to take place long before '36 or '37, and it certainly couldn't have happened to our next-door neighbor. If the omen *has* an origin in any other way than just being *seen*. Already.

But now that I've managed to get us into the story, I don't know

23. *Poetry, Language, Thought*, p. 190.

how to get us out of it. Our diviner already seems to be done with it, to have summed it up, but now he will go right on. It is not only squirrels who make announcements, but—

Such are all the animals
the quail, rabbits
and the jays—
the JAYS: when
one
goes on the road

And we're on the road again, but this time it's not a story about some neighbor, it's when *oneself* goes on the road, there's no hero unless it's us.

Now, our diviner got through quail and the rabbits, but he lit up when he got to the jays. He told us before that animals don't talk, but now he comes again to the rift of difference with these jays:

they suddenly whistle:
"SHAOwwww (*whistling*) shiiiieww"
then, there is
evil
in the road
since the jays are whistling.
And when they just sing:
"SHAOww SHAOww SHAOww"
it doesn't mean anything
but when it's, "SHAOwwww (*whistling*) shiiiieww"
there's
a problem in the road
yes.

So when the jay merely sings, repeating itself, its voice has no meaning, but when it cuts from its song to a whistle, then something is written in its voice, something which asks to be read. It moves sharply from full voice to a closing down of the voice, to something like a sigh or a gasp. I don't know whether the Mundo here has a voice after all, or whether jays are sent by God. Or whether this is an intelligent question.

At this point our diviner pauses for several seconds, expecting us to speak. He has now held the floor for some fiiiive minutes. Now we will ask him about the coyote that ran across the road in front of our car, yesterday. The coyote is the dog of the Mundo, and this one went *left*. But did he go up the mountain after that, or down in the canyon?

He went up, so this is good, even though he went to the left. And so we go on talking about omens, today and again on some other day, and I do not know where to end this story.

But there is a loose end from back at the beginning, and that concerns Derrida. We have left him in jail, a prisoner of logocentrism, of God. God, the First Cause, that would-be monologue artist of creation whose Name, let us remember, is written only in consonants, only in articulations, and must never be pronounced out loud. God, whose own words have been written down once and for all. But are we sure he's in there? Derrida, I mean. Is Derrida inside the enclosure, scratching away at the mortar? We can say this much: He engages in dialogues with his texts, quoting them in their entirety in the process;[24] no monologue artist he. Stanley Cavell resents having read the *Grammatology* and says he would have to give Derrida a B− in undergraduate philosophy at Harvard. I think that's because Derrida uses too many rhetorical questions, too many exclamation points, too much underlining, too many parenthetical remarks—those things our grammar school teachers beat out of us. The same teachers who earlier made us stop moving our lips (and our bodies) when we read. What I'm saying is, Derrida has put a lot of *voice* into his writing. He hypostatizes writing with the voice. I have never *heard* his voice, but he signed his name in public,[25] and we can just as well divine through graphology what we could have divined from his voice. If the voice has writing in it, then handwriting has voice.

According to the Quiché, God and the Mundo, Heart of Sky and Heart of Earth, Only One and Plumed Serpent, created "everything, whatever there is."[26] There were always already two of them, there was no beginning from one. No beginning at all, as we understand that. They talked,

> then they thought, then they wondered, they agreed with each other,
> they joined their words, their thoughts,
> then it was clear, then they reached accord in the light,
> and then humanity was clear.

So they are described as speaking with one another rather than sending their papers to one another in advance. They speak with the voice, but their breath is full of the writing of difference:

24. In "Limited Inc," which is Derrida's reply to criticisms of John R. Searle, he quotes every (copyrighted) word Searle wrote.
25. Derrida, "Signature Event Context," p. 196.
26. See Chapter 4, above, for the larger context of the Popol Vuh lines quoted here.

There were always already two of them, there was no beginning from one: Andrés Xiloj, narrator of the story of the omen of the squirrel, with his son Anselmo and daughter-in-law Manuela, in their patio.

> it was just like a cloud, like a mist
> now arising, unfolding

Their act of creation is done "by their cutting edge alone." The Quiché word here is *puz*, which means to butcher, or to cut a sacrifice open. That is all that is needed, because the creation is already all there, but

> it is at rest, each thing is motionless.

Through their dialogue they find the rift of difference, they cut open the enclosure:

> Then let it be sown, then let it dawn:
> the sky/earth,

and all of this takes place *pari 3ekum, pari a3ab,*

> in the blackness, in the early dawn.

We have to translate with two words, "early dawn," because English has no monolexemic way of referring to the time that is called in Quiché *a3ab*, when it is still night but there is just a trace of light in the east, very very early, or else when the morning star has already risen. In this creation it is already early dawn, then, always already dawn. "We would like only, for once, to get just where we are already." . . .

Creation and the Popol Vuh: A Hermeneutical Approach

Generations of Americanists, including such figures as Brinton and Morley, have held the Popol Vuh to be the most important single native-language text in all the New World, and much emphasis has been laid on the pre-Columbian character of its contents. But the Popol Vuh also has contents that reflect the fact that it was written after the Conquest, contents that have long been a source of embarrassment for Americanists. Bandelier wrote a century ago that the Popol Vuh "appears to be, for the first chapters, an evident fabrication, or at least an accommodation of Indian mythology to Christian notions—a pious fraud. But the bulk is an equally evident collection of original traditions of the Indians of Guatemala."[1] More recently, Edmonson called the Popol Vuh's opening creation story a "syncretistic paraphrase of Genesis,"[2] again leaving the bulk of the book with a clean bill of health. Both these scholars make an issue of aboriginality,

First delivered at the XLIII Congress of Americanists, held in Vancouver, B.C., in 1979; considerably revised here.
    1. Adolf F. Bandelier, "On the Distribution and Tenure of Lands," p. 391.
    2. Munro S. Edmonson, "Narrative Folklore," p. 359.

one of them recognizing that positive quality in all but the opening section and the other calling the opening a "paraphrase" of a nonindigenous book. What Bandelier called a "pious fraud" is given by Edmonson the more subtle term "syncretism," but even syncretism carries negative connotations that go all the way back into Old World antiquity and were very much alive when anthropologists borrowed the term from modern historians of religion.

But when it comes to the negative valuation of indigenous American cultural products that bear the marks of European missionization, there is no need to single out Bandelier and Edmonson for special attention. Just as the cultural anthropologist is pleased to see the natives burning copal, but at least secretly disappointed when they cross themselves before doing it, so he is pleased at the pre-Columbian promise of the Popol Vuh (or of an idealized Popol Vuh that has never come to light), but disappointed when he has to read his way past post-Conquest obstacles in the opening section. Implicitly, the aboriginal traditions of the New World are viewed as part and parcel of the ever-shrinking *natural* world of the Americas, a passive world that is continuously eroded and pushed back by the *cultural* invasion of Europe. If the missionary who enters this American wilderness is a pastoralist, the anthropologist is a naturalist, and for him the landscape of the Popol Vuh, although it should have been an unquestionable candidate for national park status, is marred by the presence of a sheep ranch within its very gates.

For Francisco Ximénez, the Dominican friar who discovered the manuscript of the Popol Vuh, it was the very aspects of the text that "naturalists" object to that seemed pristine, and what they would call aboriginal was for him exactly what spoiled the text. In his prologue he warns the reader that although the manuscript "starts off dealing with God, . . . alluding to what we know through the revelation of the Holy Spirit in the Holy Scriptures," what truths it contains are "wrapped in a thousand lies and tales" authored by none other than "the father of lies, Satan . . . in order to deceive and mislead these wretches."[3] In his commentaries on the Popol Vuh, Ximénez gives Satan particular credit for the metaphors encountered in the manuscript;[4] as we shall see, metaphors are indeed an excellent guide in identifying the indigenous aspects of the passage under discussion.

René Acuña has recently argued a position complementary with that of Ximénez. He asserts that it is the scriptural rather than the he-

3. Francisco Ximénez, *Popol Vuh*, p. 10.
4. Francisco Ximénez, *Escolios a las historias del origen de los indios*, p. 10.

retical aspects of the passage that raise questions of authorship, and he accordingly shifts the authorship from Satan to the sixteenth-century Dominican friar Domingo de Vico, who wished to prove "that the Indians . . . originally had the knowledge of a creator god, . . . and that, furthermore, even if in an adulterated way, they preserved the memory of certain universal experiences, [for example] the creation."[5] The search for a hidden author with a hidden purpose (whether good or evil) may unite Ximénez and Acuña, but otherwise Acuña's position is an extreme form of the "naturalist" one, leaving the natives (or *naturales*) with what he calls their "varied and, at times, incoherent indigenous traditions,"[6] in such a passive position that even syncretism itself must be invented by Europeans.

The fundamental fact that the opening of the Popol Vuh describes a watery, primordial world, moved and shaped by uncreated beings who make a platform of earth and populate it with living creatures, has no bearing one way or another on how aboriginal or how biblical the opening may be. The mythic ideas in question are widely distributed among the native peoples of the Americas; in North America, for example, they occur in nearly every culture area, from California across to the Eastern Woodlands and from the Mackenzie Basin down to Mexico.[7] The problem, as Brotherston has realized, is that as members of European culture we cannot read an American version of these ideas without having our own biblical version come to mind in a sort of involuntary comparative reflex,[8] and therein lies a great danger to the accurate perception of the Popol Vuh. What may sometimes seem like flashes of recognition may turn out to be false leads when we remind ourselves what Scripture actually says, as when Acuña finds the primordial calm of the Popol Vuh to resemble that of Genesis when in fact Genesis describes the primordial state as a maelstrom.[9]

The problem of interpreting the Popol Vuh might be easier were it not for the fact that the author deliberately calls missionary teachings to mind on several occasions. He first arouses our anxieties as naturalists by stating, "We shall write this now amid the preaching of God, in Christendom now" (1r.23–25),[10] though we may be reassured when he goes on to indicate his intention to preserve the account con-

5. René Acuña, "El *Popol Vuh*, Vico y la *Theologia Indorum*."
6. Ibid.
7. Stith Thompson, *Tales of the North American Indians*, pp. 279–84.
8. Gordon Brotherston, *Image of the New World*, pp. 152–53.
9. Acuña, "Problemas del *Popol Vuh*," p. 127.
10. References are to the Popol Vuh manuscript; translations are mine.

tained in "the *original* book and *ancient* writing" (1r. 30–31). We might be content if he let the problem of his own historical context as a writer and thinker drop right here and proceeded to behave as if he knew nothing about "the preaching of God," but instead of performing a stage role as the passive conduit of ancient traditions, he will make all sorts of interpretive asides, not only in the opening but here and there throughout the book, and some of these asides will be allusions to what he has heard in "the preaching of God." The curious thing is that although we may presume to think our way across the horizon of his world and comment on his thought, and to do so without corrupting ourselves, his ventures across the horizon of our world will elicit such words as "fabrication," "fraud," "paraphrase," and "adulteration," and will even result in gossip to the effect that he is a friar disguised as an Indian.

The first allusion to Christian teachings comes when the introduction of the divine epithet "Heart of Sky" is followed by the remark "This is the name of the *cabauil*, so to speak" (1v.31–32). *Cabauil* was once a generic Quiché term for images of deities, but the early Dominicans attempted to use it as a translation for Dios,[11] as if this new and purer meaning could bleach out the word's accumulated pagan stains. But even if the author did have the Dominican usage in mind here, he elsewhere uses *cabauil* to refer to wood-and-stone images of the titular deities of the ruling Quiché lineages (35v.14–23). Further, the passage at hand, read literally rather than as an allusion to Dios, in no way departs from Quiché religion as otherwise known to us. Later in the Popol Vuh, Heart of Sky, paired with Heart of Earth, is among the names or epithets uttered before three *cabauil* of the wood-and-stone variety (54r.45–54v.23).

Returning to the opening of the Popol Vuh, our next problem comes shortly after the mention of *cabauil*, when we are told that the name Heart of Sky actually covers three different personages: Caculha Huracan (literally "Lightning One-Leg"), Chipa Caculha ("Youngest" or "Smallest Lightning"), and Raxa Caculha ("Sudden" or "Violent Lightning") (1v.46–2r.4). If the previous mention of Heart of Sky contained an allusion to Dios, then surely this passage alludes to the Holy Trinity. But once again, if it is read literally rather than as an allusion, it is not necessarily in conflict with Quiché religion. The aboriginal Quiché trinity consisting of the three linage deities Tohil, Auilix, and Hacauitz is memorialized not only in the Popol Vuh but also in

---

11. Robert M. Carmack, *The Quiché Mayas of Utatlán*, p. 318.

the very architecture of the Quiché capital, which had three central pyramids,[12] and in fact it is the images of these three deities that are addressed in the previously mentioned *cabauil* prayer, complete with the epithet "Heart of Sky." But whether the three lightnings of the opening are equivalent to the three *cabauil* or not, they bear little resemblance to the Christian trinity, which in the very names of its members links heaven and earth through the metaphors of procreation (Father and Son) and wind (Spirit) rather than through lightning. Indeed, this lightning trinity might even be interpreted as a counterproposal rather than as "an accommodation to Christian notions."

On the third page of the Popol Vuh we encounter the lines that are perhaps the greatest single stumbling block for the seeker after aboriginal purity: "Then the earth was separated by them, it was simply their word that brought it forth: for the separation of the earth they said, 'earth'" (2r.16–20). Here, our attention as purists is distracted from the aboriginality of the insistent third-person plural by the magical power of the word "earth," which strongly recalls the creation by word in Genesis. But once again, even if the author intended such an allusion, a literal reading produces no necessary conflict with Quiché conceptions. Just a few lines later, the phrase *xa quitzih*, "only their words" (2r.17–18), is elaborated with *xa quinaual*, *xa quipuz*, "only their *naual*, only their *puz*" (2r.24–25), which reduces "only their words" to the status of one of a series of figures of speech for a larger ritual that involves much more than *tzih*, "words." In Quiché, *naual* refers to the spiritual essence or character of a person, animal, plant, stone, or geographical place; when it is used as a metonym for shamanic power, as it is here, it refers to the ability to make these essences visible or audible by means of ritual. *Puz*, all the way from its Mixe-Zoque (and possibly Olmec) sources[13] down to modern Quiché, refers literally to the cutting of flesh with a knife, and it is the primary term for sacrifice. If it is read as a synecdoche in the present passage, it means that the creation was accomplished (in part) through sacrifice; if it is read as a metaphor, it means that the creation was something *like* a sacrifice.

Through their *tzih*, their *naual*, and their *puz*, the Quiché creators "carried out the craftsmanship of the *huyub tacah*" (2r.25–27), literally "mountain(s)-plain(s)." *Huyub tacah* is what might be called a pair of antonymic synecdoches for the earth as a whole; at the same time, the two nouns together are the principal Quiché metaphor for the human

12. Ibid., pp. 264–81.
13. Lyle Campbell, "Préstamos lingüísticos en el Popol Vuh."

body, sometimes phrased in modern prayers as "my mountains, my plains."[14] Indeed, the Popol Vuh itself, elsewhere in the passage under consideration, makes it clear that the creators conceive both the earthly and human forms at the same time (2r.6–16). Confronted with a world apparently containing only a sky and a featureless sea, they make manifest an essence concealed in the sea, namely the *huyub tacah*. They do so by words and, as it were, by making a sacrifice.[15] It will take them four tries, stretching over more than half the Popol Vuh, to realize a being that will not only have human form but be capable of human speech, but their intentions are clear even at the time of the featureless sea. In all of this the Popol Vuh takes us far from the events described in Genesis. That text gives no indication that God thought of Adam before the sixth day, when everything else was complete, and once Adam is created, in just one try, his ability to speak is taken for granted.

In this commentary that started with *xa quitzih*, "only their words," I have considered a larger stretch of Popol Vuh text than in the cases of the *cabauil* and Heart of Sky commentaries. In so doing, I have already started to shift away from an atomizing approach, in which the text is treated as a collection of artifacts whose provenience must be identified, and in which a stratum containing even a few European artifacts must be sharply segregated from those which do not. The approach I am shifting toward is the hermeneutical one, in which questions of culture history are held in abeyance long enough to get the drift, to hear the tenor, to follow the path, to see the world of the text before us. Comparison is still open to us here, but it is a comparison of tenor and of paths and worlds rather than of artifacts.

When we open the book of Genesis to the first chapter, we find the "confusion and chaos" of a "maelstrom," a primeval whirlpool of air and water in which the presence of God is a rushing *ruah*, literally "wind."[16] There is no light, which must wait for the first act of creation, and there is no distinction between sky and sea, which must wait for the second act. In the opening scene of the Popol Vuh, the sky and sea are already there, already distinct. There is no maelstrom, but rather, "It is at rest, each thing is motionless, it is kept solitary, it is kept at rest under the sky" (1v.15–17). There is, nevertheless, a faint suggestion of motion in the existence of primordial sounds; these are indicated by the repeated use of such verb stems as *tzinin-*

---

14. Barbara Tedlock, *Time and the Highland Maya*, pp. 190, 224n.
15. It may be recalled that for the Aztec the first true humans were created through the agency of a blood sacrifice.
16. Everett Fox, "In the Beginning," pp. 9, 148, 157.

(1v.3, 22), *chamam-* (1v.3, 21), and *lolin-* (1v.5), which are onomatopoeic for very soft sounds, such as ripples, murmurs, whispers, and hums— the kinds of sounds one hears when there are no other sounds, but which are here the background (or "white") noise of the creation itself. As I have already mentioned, one of the major problems of the Popol Vuh is that the sound of articulate human speech should be heard; between the meaningless sounds here and the realization of that speech, the text will let us hear, as the markers of intervening ages, the chirps and calls of speechless animals and the false speech of macaws and monkeys. In Genesis, the only specified sound, other than that of fully formed speech, is the rushing of God's wind through the Garden.[17]

Returning to the primordial scene in the Popol Vuh, it remains to say who is present there. There are, first of all, *tzacol*, "mason, builder, constructor," referring to work in stone, bricks, or earth; and *bitol*, "former, shaper, modeler," referring to work in such plastic media as clay and (metaphorically) to the work of raising children (1r.10, 1v.23). Neither of these epithets would seem an ideal one for a deity who creates from nothing, but both Ximénez and Acuña take them to refer to God as Creator. Ximénez is not altogether satisfied with *tzacol* and *bitol*, but he does find these epithets preferable to others which occur in the same lists with them. There are, for example, *alom* and *4aholom* (1r.11), "bearer of children" and "begetter of sons," or *e alom* and *e 4aholom* (1v.24, the same but in the plural), names with which Satan meant to make God seem a "breeder" (*criador*) rather than a "creator" (*creador*).[18] To make matters worse, Satan, "taking metaphors from animals," added such epithets as *uuch* and *utiu*, "possum" and "coyote" (1r.12). Finally, apropos of the fact that the divine names on these lists are paired, Ximénez notes that Satan has made God into a "Duodeidad."[19]

As Ximénez recognized, there is a general principle of bitheism running through Quiché theology. At one point even the aforementioned Tohil—Auilix—Hacauitz trinity is evened out by the insertion, ahead of Tohil, of *pizom 3a3al*, "fiery bundle," a sacred relic left by the first Quiché ancestors as a memorial (54v.19–20). As with the triplets that vary the couplets of Quiché prosody,[20] evenness can be restored through the addition of an anomalous fourth element to a series of three, in this case "fiery bundle," which addresses not an image, as

17. Ibid., p. 15.
18. Ximénez, *Escolios*, p. 9.
19. Ibid., p. 10.
20. See Chapter 8, above.

do the three names with which it is grouped, but a sort of cloth-wrapped ark with mysterious contents.

Where Ximénez found a demonic bitheism, Acuña finds a Dominican monotheism. For the author of the Popol Vuh, he says, "the existence of one creator god, of one supreme *tzakol* and *bitol*, was incontestable."[21] Yet the lists of divine epithets which include *tzacol* and *bitol* are never treated grammatically as if the names referred to a single subject. Further, as Ximénez pointed out, *tzacol* and *bitol* are made into a "bearer" and "begetter" by the epithets *alom* and *4aholom*, and he could have added that they are also called *chuch* and *cahau*, "mother" and "father" (1r.41). These references to parenthood appear to be metaphorical in the Popol Vuh, but Genesis avoids even the metaphor.[22] The monotheistic transcendence of sexual difference in Genesis is achieved not through the medium of an androgynous creator, but through the suppression of the female principle. Genesis makes no secret of God's gender, nor of the fact that he is without a female counterpart. Adam, at least, turns out to contain a feminine potential, but this amounts to no more than a single (and expendable) rib in him. In the Popol Vuh, the first human females—four of them—are made after the first four males, just as Eve is made after Adam, but divine women exist from the beginning, while human women, rather than being derived from men, are created separately, and they are never made to carry the stigmas that God inflicts upon Eve.

As if sexual dimorphism were not enough to set the Popol Vuh creators apart from the God of Genesis, the primordial scene finds them not in a rushing wind, as with God, but in the waters of a calm sea (1v.19–25).[23] They are not in the company of Heart of Sky, but are rather with Tepeu, whose Nahua name declares that he (or she) has dominion, and *4ucumatz*, or "Quetzal Serpent." Together, these gods in the sea are a "glittering light" (1v.25). The problem is not that light needs to be created, as in Genesis, but that it is hidden, enclosed in blue-green quetzal feathers (1v.26). In the Popol Vuh, the movement from hidden light to a false dawn to the rising of the morning star and of the sun itself is a lengthy allegorical counterpoint to the movement from incomplete or false approximations of human beings and their speech to a fully articulate and religious humankind. In Genesis, the

21. Acuña, "El *Popol Vuh*, Vico y la *Theologia Indorum*."
22. Fox, "In the Beginning," p. 157.
23. Acuña translates *pa ha* (1v.19) as "above the waters" ("Problemas del *Popol Vuh*, p. 127), thereby making the creators seem purely celestial. But *pa* means "in" or "inside"; "above the waters" would be *chuui ha*. Further, the text makes it absolutely clear that Heart of Sky, on the one hand, and *tzacol* and *bitol* and company, on the other, are in two separate places until the former come down to the latter for the discussions that result in the creation.

story of light (first day) and of the heavenly bodies (fourth day) is all over before Adam is even created (sixth day), and the nearness of the divine is signaled not by light but by wind.

We still have one more step to go before the primeval scene of the Popol Vuh is fully set, ready for the first movement—the first movement, that is, other than the pulsing of those soft noises and the glittering of that hidden light. Having named the deities that are in the water, and having praised them as "great knowers" and "great thinkers" (1v.28–29), the text goes on to name Heart of Sky, who will later turn out to be the lightning deities already discussed. Here again in lightning is primordial, pre-creation light, missing from Genesis. In fact, Genesis never does mention light in the particular form of lightning, not even when the rains come upon Noah.

Now that our description of the primeval scenes is complete, we are ready for the first acts of creation. In the one scene we have a maelstrom, and in the other a calm disturbed only by slight pulsations; in the one case a whirl of wind and water, and in the other a sky over a flat sea; in the one case total darkness, and in the other a covered light in the sea and at least a potential for lightning from the sky. As for the gods, they are, in the one case, a solitary bachelor, and in the other a moiety whose members are, or who include, both "bearers" and "begetters," at least in the seaward half. What now happens in Genesis is that God begins his monologue, a monologue whose imperative, unidirectional insistence is elsewhere distilled as the single Word that opens the Gospel of John. In Genesis, no other voice is heard until Adam, in a monologue of his own, names first the animals and then Woman, all of this in the third person: "She shall be called woman."[24]

The first quoted *dialogue* in Genesis—and here we come to the bottom of the hole, the canyon that separates the Judeo-Christian and Toltec-Quichean cosmogonies—is the disastrous dialogue between Woman and Serpent, and in the second dialogue God vents his wrath upon Adam. In the Popol Vuh, dialogue is a positive force, necessary before the creation can even be conceived, and it is the first step beyond the meaningless murmurs and flickerings of the primeval scene. The Heart of Sky—or "they" who are the Heart of Sky—come to the deities of the sea (1v.36–41):

> They spoke now, then they thought, then they wondered
> they agreed with each other, they joined
> their words, their thoughts:

24. Fox, "In the Beginning," p. 14.

then it was clear, then they reached accord in the light,
and then humanity was clear. . . .

Here we have the description of a dialogue, and the first direct quotation in the Popol Vuh comes from the same dialogue. The first sentences of this first quotation are not commands but questions: "How should the sowing and dawning be? Who will be the provider, nurturer?" (2r.6–8), and the discussion goes on from there. It is only after this first dialogue, when the creators begin to carry out their plan, that they use the compulsive power of words (along with *naual* and *puz*), and when their initial work is finished they resume their discussion before going on, asking one another questions and suggesting possible answers at each stage. Before they solve the problem of creating humankind, they will have called still other gods into their deliberations, including Xpiyacoc and Xmucane, a husband-and-wife divining team (3v.–4r.), and they will not discover the proper substance with which to create human flesh until the fox and coyote, parrot and crow bring them the news of a previously unknown mountain made of yellow corn and white corn (32v.45–33r.1). In sum, the continuing growth of creation requires not a series of commands from a single source but an ever-widening discussion.

At the broadest level, the dialogue in the Popol Vuh is a particular manifestation, in the domain of discourse, of a more general tendency to treat duality as belonging to the very nature of the primordial world and of anything that might be created in that world. But the gods of the Popol Vuh do make one experiment with singularity, and it just happens to be an attempt to make a person out of mud. All their other attempts to make humankind proceed by twos and fours, but in the case of mud they make a solitary shape. The result is the only created being in all the Popol Vuh to utter sounds that cannot even be quoted through onomatopoeia, and the only being fated to have no descendants among the living creatures of the present world. What does happen is that "it immediately dissolves in the water" (3v.14). If we were to step outside our hermeneutics at this point and read this passage, as we earlier read others, as an allusion to Christian teachings, we would have to read it not as an "accommodation to" or a "paraphrase" of the idea of Adam, but as a *negation* of Adam.

It would begin to seem that for the writer of the Popol Vuh, as for the Aztecs described by Klor de Alva, not only "accommodation" but "conflict and resistance . . . were indeed significant reactions to the superimposition of Christianity."[25] But with or without an intentional

25. J. Jorge Klor de Alva, "Christianity and the Aztecs," p. 7.

negation of Adam, the failure of the solitary and inarticulate mud person points once again to the rift that separates the Popol Vuh from Genesis. Genesis has its own dualism, but the difference is that in Quichean (and Mesoamerican) thought, dualities are complementary rather than oppositional,[26] contemporaneous rather than sequential. In Genesis, God precedes World, darkness precedes light, male precedes female, monologue precedes dialogue, and declaration and command precede question and speculation. In the Popol Vuh, creation proceeds not through the violation of original onenesses or unities or solitudes, but from dualities—and occasional trinities and quaternities—that already exist. Here are primordial world *and* divinity, light *and* darkness, sky *and* sea, female *and* male, and the creation moves not according to the gusty wind of God's will and the clandestine questioning of a miserable serpent, but according to the increasing light of a widening dialogue. When, on just one occasion, the gods attempt an experiment with singularity, a monad of mud, it disintegrates without even having uttered something so quotable as an animal cry.

26. Tedlock, *Time and the Highland Maya*, p. 42.

12

Word, Name, Epithet, Sign, and Book in Quiché Epistemology

For an exploration of Quiché epistemological boundaries, the Popol Vuh is without rival as a starting place. Its writer takes a good deal of trouble to indicate his epistemic grounds, which until he reaches the sixteenth century at the end of the book lie beyond the limits of anything he himself experienced—or, to put that into Quiché, beyond anything *xuuachih*, "he faced," which is the Quiché way of saying "saw with his own eyes." In the middle of the book, as we shall see, he even sets forth an explicit epistemological theory.

It is in the opening sentence that the writer of the Popol Vuh makes his first epistemic claims: "This is the beginning of the Ancient Word, here in this place called Quiché" (1ro.).[1] By using the words *oher tzih*, "Ancient Word," the narrator doubly removes his discourse from the plane of ordinary narrative and doubly requires a suspen-

---

This essay appears here for the first time in English. A German translation is forthcoming in *Unter dem Pflaster liegt der Strand*.

1. Citations are of the Popol Vuh manuscript; translations are mine. In passages from the first two folios, there are slight differences between the translations given here and those in Chapter 4, above.

sion of disbelief on the part of his audience. First, the time of the narrative will be *oher*, when the very quality of events was different from what is possible in the present time. Second, this will not merely be *4hauem*, "talk"; rather, it will be a *tzih*, a "Word" that was spoken with the intention that it be preserved and that its provisions be carried out (this is a special sense of *tzih* made clear on 11ro., 16ro., 18vo., and elsewhere). What is more, at least for the earlier part of the Popol Vuh, this will be *uxe oher tzih*, literally "the *underneath* of the Ancient Word"—that is, the root, foot, base, foundation, or origin of the Ancient Word, which removes it as far as anything can be removed from the present. But for all this temporal distance, the Word is "*here* in this place called Quiché," it has the concrete authenticity of place (repeated in the final sentence of the Popol Vuh, 56vo.), and it belongs to the same place in which the author is about to write it down in his book.

A few lines later, the author tersely mentions the coming of Christianity, which of course posed (and still poses) the greatest single threat to the truth claims of the *oher tzih* of the Quiché. Speaking of the Quiché gods, whom he has just listed, he says (1ro.):

> They already said everything, and did it,
> with a clear position and in clear words.
> We shall write this now amid the language of God,
> in Christendom now.

He thus makes a much stronger statement than did Snorri Sturluson, who wrote his *Edda* in order to preserve Icelandic traditions in the face of recent Christian domination. Snorri, who made no secret of his authorship, covered his position by writing a preface that affirmed the Christian faith and apologized for a lack of "spiritual understanding" on the part of the ancients;[2] further, he put a framing story around the ancient narratives in which the Christian who elicits them from their tellers constantly disbelieves them and even attempts to refute them. The writer of the Popol Vuh, who chose anonymity, needed no such intratextual cover and made no apology—indeed, he made a claim for the "clarity" of the Ancient Word.

The Popol Vuh author does not go so far as to attack Christianity—to this day, the Quiché traditionalist sees religious change not as a matter of replacement but of accumulation—but he does choose his words in a way that places Christian doctrine on an unequal footing

2. Snorri Sturluson, *The Prose Edda*, p. 24 (the surname here is Snorri, given first in Icelandic).

with the contents of his own book. His book is the *oher tzih*, but Christian doctrine is *u4habal Dios* (1ro.), literally "the means [or way] of talking to Dios" or "the language of Dios." The doctrine, unlike the *oher tzih*, is of European origin (note the use of the word *Dios*) and is a "way of talking" rather than being an alternative Ancient Word. Apparently "ancient" in Quiché means *authentically ancient in this place*; the "Word," it may be recalled, is something that was said *in order to be remembered*. By withholding the term *oher tzih* from what Christians have to say and applying the word *4habal*, the speaker of Quiché, now and in the past, implies that although Christianity may have a language one can learn to speak, there is still some question as to whether what Christians say was *meant to be remembered in this place*. As Quiché traditionalists put it today, when faced with renewed attempts to disconnect them from their roots, "The customs of the *chuchkahau* are older than those of the Church," by which they mean "older in this place."[3] *Chuchkahau*, literally "mother-father," is a title properly belonging to the priest-shamans who head patrilineages; they schedule their rituals according to the Prehispanic calendar rather than the Gregorian one, and they preserve narratives they consider to be *oher tzih*.[4]

Here and there throughout the Popol Vuh, the writer appeals to an authority of language that is vested not in *oher tzih*, in the broad sense of a connected account of ancient things, but in the concreteness of names that are drawn from the Quiché lexicon. Whenever he gives the proper names of deities, persons, places, or buildings, and especially if the names are not etymologically transparent, he is likely to follow them with *ubi* or *quibi*, literally "its name" or "their names." The great trouble he takes to set down these names and point them out *as names* has ample parallels, by the way, in Snorri's *Edda*. At bottom, he is merely claiming an existence, beyond his personal say-so, for the names *as such*, but of course the authority of the names seeps over into the events that are constructed around them as the narrative proceeds.

On a slightly less concrete level than that of names, the author of the Popol Vuh claims the authority of established figures of speech, such as "the four sides, the four corners" (a composite metonym for the entire world, 1ro.), or "heart of sky, heart of earth" (a composite epithet for the god whose name is Huracan, 2ro.). He often points

3. Barbara Tedlock, *Time and the Highland Maya*, p. 45.
4. Ibid., pp. 180–87.

these figures out by following them with *chuchaxic* (often incorrectly written *chu4haxic* in the manuscript), literally, "as it is said." Once again, there are many parallels in the *Edda*.

Neither *ubi* (*quibi*) nor *chuchaxic* is to be confused with the ordinary Quiché quotative, though the quotative does make use of the same verb stem as *chuchaxic*, taking the form *cacha*, "it says." Contemporary speakers of Quiché use the quotative, periodically entering it at the ends of clauses, during narrations that describe events that were not actually witnessed by the speaker in waking life (thus dream narratives are marked by the quotative) but that do belong to the present era rather than to *oher tiempo* or *el tiempo de Tecún*, as the indigenous ancient time is now called, or to *el tiempo de Jehová*, as biblical time is called. The effect of the quotative, at its simplest, is to say that whether what is being narrated was actually experienced by someone or not, it is something that is talked about by persons other than the present narrator. It is not claimed that the exact wording is drawn from this third-person source, as in the case of *ubi* or *chuchaxic*, but rather the content, the story.

In the Popol Vuh, the ordinary quotative (*cacha*) is never used except, once in a great while, within the quoted statements of the characters. In the example that comes to mind, Xquic, daughter of a lord of Xibalba, is musing about the tree that bore fruit for the first time when One Hunahpu's head was placed in it, a tree she has not yet seen. She says, "Its fruit is truly sweet, it says (*cacha*)" (15vo.). She thus cites general hearsay, but as it turns out, the fruit of this tree is not even edible. Given the rarity of the quotative in the Popol Vuh, this episode stands out as a comment on the value of general hearsay, as contrasted with the text of the Popol Vuh itself.

Very occasionally the author of the Popol Vuh does say something, in his role as narrator, that he himself thinks might be a matter of hearsay, but instead of signaling his doubts by the simple insertion of *cacha* at the ends of clauses, he makes an explicit statement. Further, while the ordinary quotative can be used repeatedly to place entire stories within hearsay, the writer of the Popol Vuh cites hearsay only on some specific detail. At the end of the story of the *omu4h 4aholab*, "four hundred youths," he comments, "And it was said (*x4ha*) that this was how there came to be the stars that are called Motz because of them" (9vo.). He calls attention to his quotative use of the stem *cha* (written *4ha* in the manuscript and prefixed for the complete aspect) by placing it at the beginning of a clause rather than at the end, and he then adds a further clause that specifies the nature of his doubt in the matter under discussion: "though perhaps this is just a play on words" (9vo.), that is, a play between -*mu4h* in the word meaning "four hundred" and Motz, the Quiché name for the Pleiades.

In addition to claiming the authority of the Ancient Word, of names, and of epithets, while at the same time showing his intention to keep his distance from mere hearsay, our anonymous author founds his epistemic claims on instances of the nonverbal "mark" or "sign" called *etal* in Quiché, a sign that can be present to the senses while at the same time giving evidence of past or future events. For example, when he describes the overthrow of the wooden people who once populated the earth, he points out that their demise *x4ohe ui retal*, "left its sign," the sign being "that monkeys are in the forest today" (5vo.). It is not monkeys themselves, as flesh-and-blood creatures, that are signs, but the fact "that" monkeys are now there. In insisting on this abstractness for the Quiché concept *etal*, I am not merely reading our own concept of the sign into the text. The immateriality of the *etal* is made clear when One Hunahpu, in his form as a skull in a gourd-tree, spits into the hand of Xquic; when she sees that the saliva she expected to find in her hand is not there, the head in the tree says, "It's just a sign (*retal*) I've given you, that saliva, my spittle," and goes on to explain to her that even though a man's own flesh is lost after death, his "face" (*uuach*) survives, not only in the sense that his children look like him, but in the sense of their identity as lords, warriors, craftsmen, or speakers (15vo.–16ro.). From this point on, Xquic is pregnant, but she continues to insist, quite rightly, that she is a maiden.

Among the contemporary Quiché, as in the Popol Vuh, a sign (*etal*), whether of the past or the future, always has an intention behind it, whether that of a living human, an ancestor, or a divinity. Animals may be the instruments for signs by crossing a person's path, but the intention that these crossings be signs does not originate among animals. In a similar way, the images in a dream, the number of seeds contained in the hand of a diviner who has just performed an act of sortilege, and the movements a diviner feels within the blood of his or her own body are all motivated signs, specifically ancestral or divine.[5] Each sign is nonverbal, but each is meaningless unless and until *ubixic*, "its announcement," can be at least tentatively determined, an announcement that will be put into words. In all of these examples, the announcement may reveal something either about the past or the future, whereas the author of the Popol Vuh attempts no

5. Ibid., chap. 6.

prophecy from signs, rather citing them to support his account of past events. From this, and from the fact that he mentions or alludes to the Quiché divinatory calendar only in passing, even when describing a calendrical divination (3vo.–4ro.), we may guess that he was not himself a diviner.

Beyond citing the Ancient Word, names, epithets, and signs in his support, our writer takes considerable trouble to make the point that his work was preceded by another book. In order that we understand the gravity of this claim, it must be pointed out that the prestige of books was and is enormous in Quiché culture. Today, the narrator who places a story within the Ancient Word or in the times of Tecún or Jehová will often claim that "this is all written in a book I have, there in my house." Often this book turns out to be a Bible, or perhaps an old catechism written in Quiché; sometimes it turns out to be a Quiché document of colonial vintage. In any case, it is seldom a book whose contents are precisely known by the owner; the point is that now, as in the past, important statements about events not directly experienced by the living should be backed up by a book, and there is a general feeling today that no home is complete whose treasures do not include at least one book.

Even in the case of the Popol Vuh, there seems to be a distance between the narrator and the reading knowledge of the book he cites. He introduces the subject of this book by saying, "We shall bring it [the Ancient Word] out now because there is no longer [the book]" (1ro.). A few lines later he raises the possibility of the book's continued existence by saying, "There is the original book (*nabe uuhil*) and ancient writing (*oher tzibam*)," but then he adds, "but he who reads and interprets it hides his face" (1ro.). The total effect is thoroughly ambiguous, perhaps by design; possibly our anonymous writer is himself the "hidden" reader and interpreter, or perhaps he is covering his collaboration with such a reader, who in those times would have occupied an even more dangerous position than his own. But whatever the exact nature of the connection between the alphabetic writing now before us and the ancient writing now lost (or unreadable), our writer does invoke the authority of a prior book, and that authority reflects on all he does.

The writer strengthens his use of the ancient book's authority by giving its name (*ubi*) and by repeating its epithets (identified by the use of *chuchaxic*). The name is written as *popo uuh* (1ro.) or *popol uuh* (54ro., marked in this latter case as *ubi*), literally, "Of-the-Mat Book (or Paper)," *popol* being a metonymically derived term for a council that sits on a mat; thus the book is the Council Book (the council being that of the highest-ranking Quiché nobility). The epithets are *zac pe-tenac chaca palo*, "the light that came from across the sea"; *utzihoxic camuhibal*, "the account of our darkness"; and *zac 4azlem*, "life in the light" (1ro.). The second and third epithets refer to the eras before and after the first true sunrise and thus correspond to the two largest divisions of the text produced by our writer. The first epithet is clarified when, at the end of his description of a pilgrimage made by the Quiché ancestors to receive the paraphernalia of kingship, he says, "Then they brought the writing of Tulán from across the sea" (48vo.). Tulán, in one sense, was a divine city not of this earth, but it was also a title claimed by any town where the investiture of kings could be performed. The specific Tulán referred to here may well have been Chichen Itzá,[6] and the "sea" (called "lake" in another Quiché document), which was crossed on something that sounds very much like a causeway (38vo.), may have been one of the lakes near Cobá.

However that may be, the point here is that the original book invoked by our writer (or part of it) came from what was, from his point of view, the ultimate City. Therefore his claim to an authenticity of place for his work is double: There is the place where he writes, Quiché, at the center of the former Quiché kingdom, but there is also the fact that the sources for part of what he writes lie not in secular Quiché but in sacred Tulán. What he includes in his work documents both the legitimacy of the Quiché nobility in their own place in Guatemala, established over a long period of time and with heroic hardships and successes, and two separate pilgrimages by these same nobles to obtain or renew a higher kind of legitimacy at the ultimate royal court of Tulán. The Quiché know their place, but they have also been to the center of everything.

The nature of the original book cited by our writer can be pieced together from what he says about it in scattered places. It contains *tzibam* or *tzibal* (1ro., 48vo.); I have been translating this as "writing," but the stem *tzib-* (it should have been written *4,ib-*), in both Quiché and in its Yucatec equivalent, applies to both writing and painting, indivisible arts that were practiced by the same individuals. That the *tzibal* in question may have been of the Mayan rather than the Mixteca-Pueblan kind is indicated by the fact that one of the two monkey-god patrons of *tzibal* in the Popol Vuh bears the non-Quiché name Chouen, familiar in Yucatec as a day name (generally glossed as "monkey") and as a term for "artisan." But whatever the *tzibal* was, it was *uztibal tulan* (48vo.), "the writing/painting of Tulán."

6. Robert M. Carmack, *The Quiché Mayas of Utatlán*, pp. 46, 48.

The contents of the original book, whether or not they covered the full variety of things set down by our present writer, are said by him to have included (1ro.):

> the marking of all the sky-earth:
> the fourfold siding, fourfold cornering,
> measuring, fourfold staking,
> the folding of the cord, the stretching of the cord
> within the sky, within the earth,
> the four sides, the four corners, as it is said.

Both the act of bringing the four-cornered sky-earth into existence through measurements and the presence of a stretched cord in the sky are also described in the Chilam Balam of Chumayel,[7] but in this version (unlike that of the Popol Vuh) the episode is put in the framework of the divinatory calendar. Both accounts could have a common source in a book of a type that has not survived in hieroglyphic form.

In addition to an account of the beginning of the world, the book cited by our Quiché writer included an account of at least one of the two pilgrimages to Tulán: "They spoke about their entrance [into Tulán] in it [the book]" (48vo.), which makes it clear that the book was not limited to whatever ready-made writings were available in Tulán itself, though it could still be that it was the writers of Tulán, rather than anyone among the pilgrims themselves, who set down this "entrance" in a book.

The uses to which the original book was put begin to be revealed in the fact that it is referred to in two passages as an *ilbal* (1ro. and 54ro., written *ibal* in the latter case), literally, "place (or instrument) for seeing." Today, *ilbal* (or *ilobal*) is the common term for crystals (for gazing), mirrors, eyeglasses, telescopes, etc. What was seen by means of the book is revealed in the second of the two passages (54ro.):

> They knew whether war would occur;
> everything they saw was clear to them.
> Whether death, hunger, or conflict would occur,
> they simply knew it.
> And there was a place to see it, there was a book:
> "Council Book" was their name for it.

So the original book was a book of prophecy, which again makes it sound like the Chilam Balam books of Yucatán.

---

7. Ralph L. Roys, *The Book of Chilam Balam of Chumayel*, pp. 155, 166.

The ultimate epistemological importance of a book in which "everything they saw was clear" is revealed in the middle of the Popol Vuh, in a passage that sets forth the ultimate epistemic problem of humankind. The first humans created by the gods are described as follows (33vo.):

> They saw all and knew all;
> everything under the sky was in view;
> every time they turned around and looked around
> within the sky and earth,
> everything was seen without any obstacle.
> At first they didn't walk around
> to see what was under the sky;
> they stayed there in the same place when they looked.
> Their knowledge became detailed;
> their vision penetrated trees, rocks,
> lakes, seas, mountains, plains. . . .
> They saw the four sides, the four corners.

Under such conditions, epistemology is not even at issue. Apparently their original knowledge does not go *beyond* the world—that is, outside the four corners—but that is not a specifically human problem, given that the gods themselves are described as being in or of the world. The only epistemological gap would be in that moment just before the all-seeing gaze is turned in a particular direction. But the gods have second thoughts about these all-seeing humans and decide to shrink their epistemic grounds (34ro.):

> They were blinded as the face of a mirror is breathed upon,
> their eyes were weakened,
> now they could only look close by,
> just as far as what was obvious.

What is left for those whose own eyes, unaided, can see only close by, is the testimony of the Ancient Word, and of names and epithets and signs. But still more important, there is (or once was) the Book, the means or place to see not only the vanished past, but also the designs of things yet to come, "new" events but events with precedents. The Book contains not only the doings of gods and of humankind, but the measurements of the world itself. Today the ghost of this Book occupies a place near the center of every Quiché home, and its Ancient Word is breathed every time the ancient calendar is reckoned and every time the four corners of the sky-earth are invoked in prayers.

There remains an important difference between this Mayan Book and the Book handed down within the Judeo-Christian tradition. Judging by the cases of the Chilam Balam books in Yucatán, those who possessed such books and remained able to interpret them went right on adding new chapters. The more they added to the account of known events, the more they might have foresight.

PART FOUR

Toward Dialogue

13

Ethnography as Interaction: The Storyteller, the Audience, the Fieldworker, and the Machine

One November evening at Zuni, New Mexico, for the first time in a year's devotion to the ethnography of Zuni storytelling, I suddenly found myself in near-perfect conditions for the witnessing of Zuni storytelling as it really should be, rather than in near-perfect conditions for the making of a studio-like recording. I had gone with Andrew Peynetsa, an accomplished raconteur, to the house of his eldest son.[1] Andrew's daughter-in-law, Jane, her twenty-year-old brother, and several grandchildren were there, but his son, with whom he desired a conversation, had not yet returned from his job at a gas station. A couple of the grandchildren, aged around seven to ten, saw an opening here: *nana, telaapi,* they said, "Grandpa, tell a story!" They were asking for a particular kind of narrative called a *telapnanne,* a story about the *inoote,* "long ago" but not so long ago as the beginning of the world.

Delivered at the conference "Native American Interaction Patterns," held at the University of Alberta in 1982; published here for the first time.

1. For examples of Andrew Peynetsa's narrative performances, see Dennis Tedlock, *Finding the Center,* in which all but a third of the narratives are his; "When the Old Timers Went Deer Hunting"; and Chapter 14, below.

So there it was. Spontaneous storytelling was about to take place. Not a storytelling session scheduled in advance by a mythographer, not a session with an audience invited to be present so as to simulate a spontaneous session, and not in a place arranged so as to be apart from radio, television, clattering dishes, unexpected intruders, and all the other random auditory disasters of a household conducting business as usual, but a session initiated by the natives, for the natives, at the proper time of the native day and year, and in the very center of the native household.

From my point of view, there were only two imperfections in this unexpected gift. The first, of course, was that *I* was there—there in the room *with* the natives. That problem would be solved, I hoped, if I simply kept my mouth shut and sat on the sidelines while the natives focused their attention on the business of storytelling. The second problem was a much larger one, from my point of view: I had left my tape-recorder at home. Even so, I thought, this evening certainly won't be a total loss. As for the story itself, I could now understand the Zuni language well enough to follow the plot, and if the story turned out to be one I had already heard, I could easily spot any thematic additions, subtractions, or rearrangements that would differentiate it from a previously recorded version. From the beginning I had made it my practice never to whip out a notebook when the situation was not that of an interview, even when I was familiar with all the participants, but by now I had developed my mnemonic skills and would easily be able to organize and retain a large amount of information long enough to jot down a few key words soon after leaving the present scene and then type out a detailed account within the next day or so. Of course such a procedure still amounts to carrying around a *mental* notebook; such a notebook may not be visible to others, but it does make one more distant from the situation at hand.

In at least one concrete way my lack of a tape-recorder promised a direct benefit. I had long since discovered that although Zuni listeners are supposed to respond to a story by periodically saying *ee——so*, or "Ye——s indeed," it is almost impossible to get them to do so in a recording session. In effect, they see themselves as being witnesses at a speech event whose dialogical ground lies principally between a storyteller and an ethnographer with a recording device, rather than between a storyteller and themselves. So now, I thought, I would discover when and how often an audience responds, rather than relying on Zuni descriptions of the proper reponses.

It further occurred to me that if the story did indeed turn out to be a familiar one, I could find out whether a live performance would be shorter or longer than one that was not only arranged but involved the payment of fees. I had sometimes wondered whether my performers dragged out their stories to fill up more recording time, though this thought was balanced out by the secure knowledge that Zunis value verbosity, whether in stories, speeches, or prayers.

My disappointment at not having my tape-recorder along had passed within a couple of minutes of reflection; I was comforted by the thought that I at least had my pocket-watch. I settled back to await the unfolding of a drama that could have come before me only by luck; I concentrated all of my aural attention on trying to follow what was about to be said. But here another problem arose. Andrew, who had come here for a conversation with his son, was taken off guard by the request for a story; he would have expected to find his grandchildren gathered around the television set rather than demanding a story. It wasn't that he didn't want to tell them a story; rather, he couldn't decide which story to tell. When they didn't come up with any specific request—and he didn't give them very much time—he threw that decision directly to me, and although I could have understood him had he asked me in Zuni, he sharpened his focus on me by asking in English. After all, no one present could surpass me in having an active interest in the stories, and by this time no one present had nearly as many stories freshly in mind as I did. One might generalize the problem this way: The more a fieldworker knows and is known, the less that fieldworker can avoid joining the action. The other side of this is that the less a fieldworker knows and is known, the greater will be that fieldworker's inability to interpret the actions of others, whether those actions take him into account or not.

Within an instant everyone present had fallen silent to await my decision. I realized that my failure to name a story would not only put the progress of the storytelling event itself in jeopardy, but would also make me look just plain stupid. Remembering that the distorting effects of recording sessions had seemed to reach their maximum in the case of bawdy stories—Andrew had scarcely been willing to tell these at all and had intimated that he might have to cut out some of the juicier details—I made my choice, calling for a story he had recorded the previous winter. I called for *ahayuut okya*, the story of the "Female Ahayuuta," in which a desirable but misguided and reclusive young man puts his suitors to a test and rejects them, one after the other. What he does to each suitor is measure "that which gives a woman her being" (to preserve the Zuni circumlocution) with a notched stick. After he has gone through suitors who have come from four other villages to his own, the Ahayuuta, the twin war gods, decide to teach him respect for the bodies of women. The younger brother Ahayuuta, not only in drag but with an appropriate prosthetic device mounted in place, measures up to the young man's standard (actually going over the mark) and marries him, later to shame him and give him a lecture on proper courtship and marriage.

Andrew accepted my choice without hesitation and started the story with a very loud SO'NAHCHI! This has the effect of "Now we're taking it up." Like many other native North American framing or keying devices placed at the beginnings or ends of stories, this one directly acknowledges the larger dialogical grounds upon which a sustained third-person narrative must be introduced: "Now *we* are taking it up"—you, the hearers, and I, the storyteller.[2] And this is also one of the only two places in a Zuni story where the entire audience always gives the *eeso* response, in unison. After a brief pause, but even before the last response has died out, comes the second half of the opening: *sonti inoo——te*, which has the effect of "Now it begins to be made lo——ng ago."[3] Here the narrator has left the first and second persons behind; he will use them again only when the characters in the story talk to each other. Now the audience gives the second of its two obligatory responses. In so doing, its members have consented to being transported away from the time of the room where they sit and into a past whose indefinite distance is indicated by the lengthening of "lo——ng ago."[4] So far this could have been the beginning of any story about the long ago, but now the narrator will begin to narrow down the possibilities.

A particular story of the long ago is first differentiated by statements that list the places where the characters live and may also name

2. As Paul Ricoeur had observed in *Interpretation Theory* (p. 35), "the absolute here and now" of the dialogical "we" is "shattered by writing." Those who make written documents from tape-recorded discourse have a strong tendency to get swept away in the monological currents of writing; Edward Ives, in *The Tape Recorded Interview* (pp. 95–100), makes it an explicit rule of transcription that an English-language narrator's "you know" and "you see," along with an interviewer's "sure" and "I see," should all be edited out.

3. For an etymological discussion of the opening and closing formulas in Zuni, see Chapter 5, above. The use of the first person is most likely to occur in the closing (unlike the Zuni case), as it does in Penobscot, Menomini, Iowa, Quileute, White Mountain Apache, and Hopi; see Dennis Tedlock, "Verbal Art."

4. Thus it is not only writing that shatters Ricoeur's here-and-now, but third-person narrative in general. To understand an oral narrative's departure from the dialogical grounds of speech, it is not necessary to argue that this departure is made possible through techniques for the "fixing" of oral "texts" (through formulas, etc.), as Ricoeur does (*Interpretation Theory*, p. 33), but only to remember that any language has the capacity to describe events and objects not present to its speakers, a capacity that speakers utilize daily.

one or more of those characters. In the case of the present story, Andrew stated that the Ahayuuta were living at Corn Mountain, then listed five different places where villagers were living, starting with Katiikya, which would turn out to be the village of the young man with the measuring device, and then naming the four villages from which his suitors would come. One of the latter villages was *Itiwan'a* "Middle Place," the location of the house in which we were all presently sitting, but all the others were some miles away, each of them a place that had been abandoned for centuries. Having taken us away to these ruins and having restored villagers to all of them, he still had not set us firmly on the course of this one particular story, but when he next told us that at Katiikya "many proposals were being made to the Sun Priest's son," the story had to be one about a proud and reclusive young man who would submit his suitors to some sort of unreasonable test and in which the Ahayuuta would teach him a lesson.

Now Andrew continued, after a pause, with a sentence that must have been much like the one he had delivered on tape. If so, it partially reiterated the previous sentence and then moved forward: "Proposals were being made (*pause*), and he had some sort of measuring device." The importance of the latter of these two pause-divided lines, at least on the tape, was signaled not only by the reiteration of "proposals were being made," by a pause that interrupted the intonation contour of a complete sentence, by a slowing down of syllable articulation on "measuring device," by giving the final few syllables the steepest and lowest-reaching terminal intonation yet attempted in this story, by the fact that the narrator leaned forward while saying it, and by the deliberate pause that followed it, but by a voice quality that unsuccessfully concealed a chuckle. Whether the corresponding sentence in the spontaneous version carried every single one of these features or not, it was widely followed by the *eeso* response.

From here on we had nowhere to go but into a unique story, provided we had never before heard of a suitor's test quite like this one, which most of us—myself excepted—had not. From now on the *eeso* response was more scattered, coming from one or more audience members every six to a dozen lines; I, too, was expected to respond, but of course I tried to follow the cues of the others, even though there was no microphone to pick up the participation of an observer. The response seldom occurred except where the completion of a sentence (both grammatical and intonational) was followed by a definite pause, but it did not automatically come at such a juncture. The next time Andrew got a widespread response he was back on the measuring device, back on a steep and low-reaching terminal pitch contour, and back on a slowing of the syllables of a key word, all followed, as before, by a deliberate pause. If all the other details were the same as they had been on the tape, what he said was, "He measured her (*pause without terminal intonation*), well, he measured that which gave her being, and he wasn't satisfied," with a slowing down on "he wasn't satisfied" and a steep drop that took him all the way down into what is technically called "pulse," the gravelly lower end of a person's vocal range, a zone that Zunis find to be suggestively sensual. At least one humorous Zuni story, that of "Pelt Kid and his Grandmother," centers on an innocent adolescent boy whose breaking voice reaches down toward pulse but who is totally baffled when the girls he meets think his voice is cute.[5]

It is not difficult to see why an audience response is likely to come when reiteration, a strong terminal contour, and perhaps other features such as the prominence given by the slowing of syllables all converge on a point that is followed by a deliberate pause. If someone were to end a sentence this way in conversation, it would be a definite signal that the other party might be able to take a turn—unless the meaning of the larger discourse were clearly incomplete, as is the case here. In a continuing story of the long ago, all the audience should say is *eeso*, answering but not interrupting.

Once a narrative is well under way, the possible openings actually chosen for the *eeso* response are most likely to be those in which the performer departs from the story proper to offer an interpretive aside.[6] An aside is often reiterative, but not so much in its actual wording as in calling attention to an irony or turn of the plot, as already narrated, whose importance the audience might have missed. I say "aside" not only in the sense that the ongoing narrative chain is momentarily left to one side, but in the sense that the narrator, who most of the time looks not into the eyes of his hearers but off into space (or even at the backs of his own eyelids), moves his head in order to establish direct eye contact with one or more members of the audience. In the present narrative such an aside came with these words, after the young man had measured the Ahayuuta and found "her" acceptable: "When real girls came he had refused them, but when it came to the Ahayuuta (*pause with suspended intonation*)—that girl, he married."

So it turned out that the *eeso* response, at least some of the time,

5. Tedlock, *Finding the Center*, pp. 191–213.
6. For further examples of Zuni interpretive asides, in some of which the narrator even makes use of the second person (but in a genre other than the one under discussion here), see Chapter 9, above.

was not, as I had once thought, merely a generalized acknowledgment of attention, dimly perceived by a performer who was otherwise fully occupied with his vision of the action and his performance, but a momentary acknowledgment, however restrained, of the dialogical ground that underlies speech in general, even including so-called monologues. When the narrator either delivered his lines as if he were about to turn over a conversation, or else addressed asides directly to his hearers, both audibly and visibly, he was likely to get direct answers.

Some minutes into the story, while the young man was still dealing with suitors who were "real" girls, Andrew's daughter-in-law slipped into the next room to make us some coffee; she could still hear him clearly through the doorway of the kitchen. When Andrew came to a passage in which the boy in the story takes one of these girls "into the next room," he suddenly chuckled and then broke out of the frame of the story—so far as I had previously understood that frame —in several different ways at once.[7] It wasn't just that he said, "It was about this time of year" or "It was a night like this one," which are common Zuni ways of breaking out of the long ago of stories, though he did indeed move to merge the story with the then and there of its telling, latching on to the fact that Jane had gone to "the next room." He accomplished this merger by switching into English, though stories are supposed to be devoid of even a single word from such profane non-Indian tongues, and saying directly to me (with eye contact), "Wouldn't it be funny if Jane were that girl and my son had that measuring thing?" The audience found this very funny (all but the preschoolers understood some English) and there came a giggle from the kitchen. With one stroke, Andrew had erased not only the temporal and spatial distance of the story, but the personal distance as well, at the same time acknowledging that the usable codes present in these two rooms (if not in the two rooms of the story) included English.

Having never really lost the momentum of the story action, Andrew immediately withdrew back into ancient times as if nothing had happened. As he continued, Jane served coffee to him, to her brother, and to me, and took some for herself. About this time another suitor had arrived in the young man's house and had been asked to sit down. Then, where Andrew would have said that the young man's mother served dinner, he said instead that she served *nochapiiwe*, "coffee." Again he got a good laugh. He had broken frame again, but

7. For a general discussion of Zuni frame-breaking, see Chapter 5, above.

without switching codes, not only matching up story action with present action, but intruding coffee, which is regarded as relatively recent, into the long ago. At the same time he had shifted his daughter-in-law back into a more dignified role, that of a matron rather than that of a hapless suitor.[8]

When Andrew got to the part of the story where the younger brother Ahayuuta is outfitted as a woman, he included a description of how he was equipped with "that which gives a woman her being." In the recorded version he had saved the anatomical problem for the scene in which the young man who marries the Ahayuuta discovers the truth, making some of the action hard to follow; it was as if he had been debating, until that moment, whether to include this information at all. But now he not only explained that the Ahayuuta wore a *shoppa*, or bottle-necked gourd, which forced him to take small steps and keep his legs somewhat apart, but added a detail which he later confessed he had deliberately censored in the recorded version: In order to give the gourd the proper smell, the Ahayuuta twins rubbed it on the womanhood of their own grandmother!

Here we were, with a Zuni audience that included the narrator's daughter-in-law and children of both sexes, and the narrator was telling all. The audience at the recording session had been a strictly adult male one, so there was no doubt that the crucial factor in Andrew's earlier censorship had been neither his own nor his immediate audience's prudishness. Rather, Andrew had been mindful of the larger audience that might lie somewhere on the other side of that tape-recorder, an audience that might include the kinds of Anglo-Americans he had met up with in government boarding schools, back in the days when Indian students were treated to mandatory Sunday-school attendance, corporal punishment, and even confinement in on-campus jail cells. Here, then, was a reminder that however much the mythographer may try to normalize a performance by gathering a native audience and by building rapport at the level of personal interaction, the presence of a tape-recorder and the eventual goal of publication raise larger questions of what might be called interethnic rapport. The problem of the mythographer is not merely to present and interpret Zuni myths as if they were objects from a distant place and time and the mythographer were a sort of narrow, one-way conduit, but as events taking place among contemporaries along a frontier that has a long history of crossings.[9]

8. Andrew's movement of his daughter-in-law's social roles by verbal means recalls the language play described by James W. Fernandez in "Poetry in Motion: Being Moved by Amusement, by Mockery, and by Mortality in the Asturian Countryside."
9. As I argue in Chapter 16, below, even the doing of ethnohistorical research

But even with the matter of the gourd's smell out in the open, there was still a sense in which Andrew did not "tell all," and this was one of the subtlest dimensions of the present occasion. Never once did he use the common Zuni name for "that which gives a woman her being," not even here. When I consulted my field notes on the recorded version of this story, I found that I had gone to some lengths to pin down the exact details of the use of the measuring device and of the bottle-necked gourd. When I discussed the story with Joseph Peynetsa, who helped me with the transcription and translation of my tape-recordings, he avoided explicit anatomical details, even in English, but made it plain enough (through circumlocution) what he thought was going on. When I asked him whether Andrew would have been more explicit with an exclusively Zuni audience, he firmly said, "No, I think the Zunis would get the grip of it." When I persisted in this line of questioning, he finally gave me a lecture, in an irritated tone of voice, not unlike the lectures that are given the young man in the story. Didn't I know that the bodies of women are *tehya*— precious, valuable, guarded? No, it wasn't just a matter of sex: "That's secondary. It's their *bodies* that are *tehya*." Finally, in one last effort to make me understand, he crossed the horizon of my own mythic world and said, "It's like Eve. She found she wanted to be *tehya* at that spot, so she put a big leaf to it." And so there she was, Eve as a Zuni saw her, not discovering evil and shame, but choosing to make a part of herself precious, valued, and guarded.

My notes revealed that I had also pursued the matter of the anatomical details of the story with Andrew. When I asked him to elaborate on the bottle-necked gourd, he did no more than to have me take a look at the bottle-necked gourd hanging on the wall behind him. Asked to clarify the act of measurement, he explained, with neither a smirk nor any visible sign of indignation, that the young man had measured his suitors across the hips! During this entire conversation one of his sons, then in his late teens, first developed a case of the giggles and finally burst into a fit of uncontrollable laughter. Andrew meanwhile remained the perfect straight man. Only now does it occur to me that his notion of hip measurement, like Joseph's citation of Eve and her big leaf, was in part a last-ditch effort to reinterpret the story in terms I might finally understand: He was thinking of beauty contest measurements, themselves a form of abuse of women's bodies in Zuni eyes. For weeks after this discussion Andrew's son chided me, everytime I showed up, for not knowing what a woman has, and

---

can be reconstructed along the lines of an intercultural dialogue, rather than taking the form of an attempt to objectify the other.

he never tired of pointing out the bottle-necked gourd on the wall. But never once did he strip womanhood naked by using either the Zuni or English words that specify what a woman has, and now, months later and with a chance to retell the story without a tape-recorder, neither did Andrew. To be sure, he now brought the gourd into play right away and even gave it the proper aroma, but the thing itself was not named. It was up to the audience "to get the grip of it," just as Joseph had said it would be. As for me, it would be some time before I got the hang of how to talk about, or rather around, matters that are precious, valued, and guarded.

Once the young man and the younger brother Ahayuuta get married, the recorded version has an episode in which the young man goes out hunting for the first time and makes some technical errors in killing and butchering a deer; the elder brother Ahayuuta intercepts him and teaches him the correct procedures in handling the flesh of deer, just as the younger brother will later instruct him concerning the proper respect for the flesh of women. But in the present version, Andrew moved the hunting episode to a position following the revelation of the bottle-necked gourd and the instructions concerning women. The revelation scene, in which the young man is shown the gourd and breaks it, is certainly the climax of the story action; by shifting the hunting episode to a later position, Andrew made it anticlimactic. His present audience now grew visibly restless, whereas his original audience, even including a man who had a reputation for dozing off during stories, had maintained undivided attention throughout. So here was yet another surprise: At least in the one matter of the arrangement of the episodes, the recorded version, for all its other problems, was a better performance.

In both versions the most important words of the story are the lectures given to the young man by the Ahayuuta and their grandmother after the revelation of the gourd. The grandmother's speech, in which she not only summarizes the events of the story but looks beyond them, is the only passage in the entire performance where Andrew goes into the mode of delivery called *ana k'eyato'u*, "raising it right up," a mode used for formal oratory, public prayers, exclamations, and other kinds of statements that carry authority or otherwise demand complete attention.[10] Each line (as marked off by pauses) is delivered as if it were an emphatically complete sentence, though the grammatical units treated in this way are frequently shorter than sentences; an exaggerated stress—what might be called a superstress—is

10. See Chapter 6, above.

placed on the final syllable of each unit, precisely at the point where stress would trail away to its weakest point in ordinary speech. In effect, each line so delivered demands the same attention that otherwise would be given to a single, sudden, and indisputable command. To quote an actual text for the grandmother, I must resort to the recorded version of the story. Note that the fourth line-final stress in the quote is deflected from the grandmother's speech to the quotative phrase that interrupts it. After that her speech is less formal in its delivery and more narrative in its content, but she returns to the line-final stress at the end. In effect, the entire speech is to be understood as carrying the same authority that is most forcefully conveyed in its opening and closing lines:

"Indeed.
You have been a FOOL.
With many of our children of the LIGHT.
With the women's very precious FLESH.
Our flesh is precious," their grandmother SAID.
To the young man.
"You have done many wrongs, and so this grandson of mine
spoke of playing a trick on you, I told him not to, but since that's the
     way you were living your life,
we have played a trick on you.
But when you return to your village,
you must find someone,
you must put your mind to it, and this
measuring device must not be used, and you must not live that way.
And if you should try it again,
something else will have to be done,
and think of it we SHALL."
That's what their grandmother told him.
"Indeed." "Yes, that's the way it is."

In the context of a major religious speech delivered in this style, which would go on much longer, the proper audience response would be *hacchi*, which affirms the absolute truth of what is being said and carries much more force than the storytelling *eeso*. Within the story itself the young man's own response to the speech is instead a more conversational *hayi*, "indeed," delivered with a low and soft voice of embarrassed submission, immediately followed (without a pause) by the grandmother's reaffirmation of what she has just said.

The story audience did not answer the grandmother's speech. For one thing, the speech does not constitute an actual sacred text of the kind that calls for *hacchi*; such texts are never directly quoted (except for a commonly known line or two) in the decidedly secular context of storytelling. On the other hand, the *eeso* response would also have been inappropriate; it indicates an understanding of the *sense* of what has been said, but that is not the same thing as affirming a *truth*. Indeed, *eeso* is so closely associated with storytelling—and stories of the kind under discussion here are not taken to be accounts of real events—that it carries connotations of fictionality; its only use in conversation is to imply that one is being told a story rather than the literal truth. And finally, there is the fact that the grandmother's speech, strictly speaking, was addressed not to the audience but to the young man in the story, and it was *his* to respond.

If we back off and view the acoustical topography of the entire story, the grandmother's speech stands out like a steep-sided prominence among rolling hills. Very strictly speaking, its mode of delivery makes it the only important thing that gets said in the entire narrative. Returning from the question of sound to that of meaning, it is also the location of the most concentrated moral content of the story. Zuni narrators are quite conscious of the didactic function of storytelling, but the subtlety of Zuni moral instruction is such that what one might call its full acoustical force is deflected from the audience by having it addressed not by the narrator to them, but by one story character to another.

Andrew ended both versions of the story with a short episode in which the Ahayuuta grandmother, who disapproves of her grandsons' entire escapade despite its happy outcome, tells them that she and they must no longer live together at Corn Mountain but must separate. The twins go to two separate places that are farther away from Zuni than Corn Mountain, but she goes to a place right on the northern edge of the present town of Zuni. This episode can be used to end nearly any story of the outrageous adventures of the Ahayuuta; it is consequently very widely known. The present audience, already restless because of the anticlimactic placement of the hunting episode, now grew even more so, not only because of the final episode's familiarity but because of the sure knowledge that the story would soon be over and yet at the same time must be put through a few last paces. I had seen this restlessness before, in recording sessions. The addition of a seemingly anticlimactic episode had been a frequent occurrence, and the present experience now made it clear that a narrator would make such an addition even when the filling up of tape was not at issue. During one recording session, Andrew's clan brother had almost brought on a revolt by tacking a short animal tale onto the end of a very long story about humans that had already made the audience restless, the only connecting thread being "and meanwhile Coyote was out hunting nearby." Even with the tape-recorder there, an older woman in this audience had groaned audibly, made as if to stretch her arms the way people do when a story is over, and spoke the story-ending formula in a low but distinct voice: "Enough, the word is short." But the narrator, though he may have speeded up his delivery a little, pressed his gratuitous animal tale through to its conclusion. He ignored the comments that were made afterward—chiefly, "That story was too long"—and offered no apologies.

To understand the story-ending tension between narrator and audience, we must take note of the fact that making an audience restless is not quite the same thing as losing it. By the time a climax is past, a narrator's dominance has a certain momentum, and it is protected by the well-established Zuni notion that a story must be seen through to the end. No one gets up to leave, and no one makes a serious attempt to reestablish the long-suspended and by now forgotten conversations that may have preceded the story. In the case of the tacked-on animal tale, the woman's usurpation of the story-ending formula was in jest. During these final stages the hearers are truly a captive audience. They may be restless, but that at least makes them unable to drop off to sleep. Dozing, as I have observed it, takes place during long and repeated developmental episodes, not during climaxes and conclusions. If there had been any dozing during either version of the story of the "Female Ahayuuta," which there was not, it would have taken place while the opening scene, in which a suitor fails to measure up to the young man's expectations, is repeated for three additional suitors before the Ahayuuta make their entry into the field. In the tape-recorded version, Andrew had run through these scenes without providing much detail; he developed them at greater length in the present version, but it was precisely during these scenes that he resorted to the frame-breaking antics already described.

In the present story, then, the narrator went through a developmental stage in which it was necessary for him to go out of his way to make sure the audience was engaged; a further stage in which the content fully carried its own interest, running from the outfitting of the Ahayuuta as a woman to the breaking of the bottle-necked gourd; a didactic stage, in which the mode of delivery demanded full attention; and a final stage in which the hearers' patience could be stretched without causing them to make an actual exit from the scene of the performance. Andrew knew this end-game better than the storyteller who tacked on the animal tale; I never once saw or heard anyone in his audiences threaten insubordination, not even in hour-long stories.

When Andrew had dispersed the Ahayuuta twins and their grandmother to their respective shrines, he went into the mode of an aside, establishing eye contact with his audience and moving all the way from the long ago to the time of his performance by saying, in what everyone knew would have to be his third-to-last sentence, "This is where their ancient places are today." The etiological statements at the ends of Zuni stories seldom contain any reiteration of their moral content—except in the grand sense, as exemplified here, in which the arrangement of people and the gods in their present-day places in the physical world constitutes the establishment of a moral order.

And now, with his listeners moving to the edges of their seats, looking at each other, and chuckling or making sounds such as "ah," Andrew delivered what is the penultimate sentence of all stories of the long ago: "This happened long ago." As he went on into the final sentence (without any pause), his hearers began to stretch their arms above their heads, laughing and making the kinds of sounds one makes when standing up and stretching. The final sentence always seems to have an ironic tinge after a display of Zuni verbosity: "Enou———gh, the word is short." The narrator himself is the last to stretch, chuckling as he thinks back over some detail of the story. I don't remember whether it actually happened on this occasion, but at this point someone should have offered Andrew a cigarette. Zuni narrators fall silent for at least a few minutes after a story, during which they like to surround themselves with a cloud of smoke. It even takes the audience a few minutes to return to the full chaos of a crowded household; a story not only cuts through that chaos but leaves a wake behind it. Andrew's only comment about the story, after his silence, was to point out to me that he had omitted the detail of the gourd's smell in his recorded version. That performance had taken place nearly nine months ago, but the omission was still on his mind.

I myself got caught up in the wake of Andrew's story. Several minutes had gone by when I suddenly remembered to look at my watch. Adjusting for my lapse, the story had lasted about fifty minutes. It wasn't shorter than the tape-recorded version, but eleven minutes longer, a difference not accountable solely to the restoration of the censored detail. It would seem as though having a responsive audience and the opportunity for unorthodox grandstand plays might have more effect on the lengthening of a story than the temptation to fill up more tape. The recording sessions, then, had been dampening the storytelling event in two ways: Not only did the audience members avoid speaking to the narrators, even within the confines of the *eeso* response, but the narrators avoided speaking directly to the audience in the grandstand manner—though they did establish eye contact during the interpretive asides of recording sessions, sometimes eliciting a muffled "mm" where there should have been an *eeso*.

There remained a question as to whether frame-breaking such as had taken place when Andrew dragged his own son and daughter-in-law into a measuring scene might be limited to humorous stories. That question was answered four years later, when I happened to hear Andrew retell the deadly serious story of "The Boy, the Turtle, and the Deer" without benefit of tape-recorder. On that occasion he incorporated his eldest son and youngest daughter in the story by naming two of the characters after them; he cast them in a way that made the entire story something of an allegory of recent family events. Once again there were remonstrances, and once again they were addressed by one story character to another, but this time they came close enough to home to make people squirm in their chairs.

From the point of view of a mythography whose end was to collect "traditional" or "authentic" or "authoritative" examples of oral literature, and given a story whose content raised no problems of out-and-out censorship, it would seem that studio conditions might be better for the production of the desired texts than a spontaneous situation with, say, a bugging device. To put the matter in the terms of the ethnic arts market, the kinds of objects the natives produced while no one was looking might prove disappointing and even seem corrupted from the point of view of established connoisseurship.[11] On the other hand, given a mythography that takes performances and interactions, rather than textual end-products, as its objects, it would seem that in the case of the "Female Ahayuuta," the unrecorded session produced—or would have produced, had I not forgotten my tape-recorder—the more authentic text, the grounds for authenticity having shifted from its exact wording and ordering to its status as a unique occurrence in an unarranged place and time. The only major

11. Dell Hymes, in *"In Vain I Tried to Tell You,"* issues a warning against the tendency to "expropriate the traditions [of others] as *objets d'art"* (p. 132), but he repeatedly uses a language that belongs to antiquarian connoisseurship in the plastic (as opposed to performing) arts, wanting to single out performances (actually dictated texts) that are "authentic" or "authoritative" or "genuine" (pp. 84, 86, 131, 132, 237, 251). Such works, once one identifies such flaws as a "mismatch between narrative sentences and verses" (p. 233) and restores them "to something like their true form" (p. 382) through the "uncovering of poetic sculpture" (p. 341), can be regarded "as works of literary art" (p. 332) and as "authentic monuments" (p. 384).

flaw in the version favored by a traditionalist or normative mythography is the censored detail, while the flaws in the version favored by a performative or practical mythography lie in the fact that the choice of story was mine, in the brief switch into English, and more generally in the fact that I was there at all.

The natural tendency (or inertia) of ethnomethodology, of conversational studies, and of interactionism—so long as they still insist on retaining goals inherited from text-oriented approaches in pursuit of an illusory objectivity—is demonstrably toward the short and self-sufficient interchange, the bugging device, and the hidden camera.[12] Performance-oriented folklorists and ethnographers of speaking, on the other hand, sometimes seem to think they can escape the effects of tape-recorders and their own presence without resorting to spying, simply by concentrating on genres whose formality is supposed to insulate their performances from the effects of outsiders. And just for good measure, they may ask the natives to make tapes in their absence. But the more insulated an event is from the kind of conversational process that might reach out and encompass the would-be observer, the more that observer will be in need of help when it comes to interpreting the meaning that event held for the participants, as I was when I sought Joseph Peynetsa's help in the transcription, translation, and interpretation of Andrew Peynetsa's stories. Sociological interpretations of interactional events are riddled with statements that rest upon linguistic and cultural grounds supposedly shared by the observed, the observer, and the reader, but ethnographers of speaking, who cannot ignore the fact that they are crossing linguistic and cultural frontiers, must construct a common ground through interaction itself.

From the point of view of a mythography that is rooted in events and abandons an objectivity borrowed from the natural sciences in favor of the intersubjectivity that is the special condition of the social sciences,[13] Regna Darnell's "Correlates of Cree Narrative Performance," in which she gives a full accounting of her own and Anthony Vanek's roles in the shaping of an event, is not merely a circumstantial record of fieldwork, but is far and away the most radical and forward-

12. Erving Goffman, in *Forms of Talk* (p. 31), takes interactionists to task for depending on "self-sufficient interchanges" in the same way that grammarians lean on "self-sufficient sample sentences."
13. To date, the most thorough and penetrating effort to work out the consequences of a phenomenological, intersubjective approach in anthropology is that of Johannes Fabian in "Rule and Process: Thoughts on Ethnography as Communication." The radical nature of this enterprise is hinted in the very title of his article, which is a transformation of the phrase, "Ethnography *of* Communication."

looking chapter in *Explorations in the Ethnography of Speaking*.[14] In the case of the "Female Ahayuuta," my own role both in the storytelling events and in eliciting Joseph Peynetsa's interpretation is not something to be hidden or explained away but a normal part of mythographic discourse. Joseph's remarks are no more to be finally reduced to the form "The Zuni people interpret this story in thus-and-such a way" than Andrew Peynetsa's two performances are to be finally reduced to the form "When the Zuni people tell stories in an authentic manner, they do so according to the following rules." Everything that has been reported here, concerning the events of a certain November evening at Zuni, New Mexico, rests finally on conversational and more broadly interactional grounds, and it was there, just there, that it was even possible for me—and now, I hope, for us—to understand at least a part of what was going on.

Here I say, *leewi*, "all," which means it's someone else's turn.

14. Regna Darnell, "Correlates of Cree Narrative Performance."

14

The Story of How a Story Was Made

What happens when a mythographer is present on the dialogical grounds where oral performances take place might be described, in the case of a tape-recorded tale like "The Girl and the Protector" (see Chapter 2), as a general decontextualizing effect that anticipates the decontextualization involved in playback, transcription, translation, and publication. The response of the native audience is dampened and the performer may be prevented from entangling members of that audience in the story, though in this particular case Walter Sanchez did make an unsuccessful attempt to have Andrew Peynetsa take the part of the heroine's grandfather at prayer. Less subtle is the case of the "Female Ahayuuta" (in Chapter 14), where the absence of a tape-recorder bared the conversational ground not only between the performer and the audience but also between the performer and the fieldworker, complete with a brief code-switch into English. In the

First published in *Alcheringa*, o.s. 5 (1973):120–25, where it was accompanied by a disk recording of the story. The present discussion of the story has been revised and expanded.

Tell me when you get to some empty tape: Andrew Peynetsa with a granddaughter, outside his farmhouse near Zuni. He requested that this photograph be made and chose the location and pose himself.

first case the fieldworker asked for a story; in the second the field-worker happened to be present when natives asked another native for a story. But there remains a third possibility in which a mythographer's presence on the conversational ground of a narrative performance would be still less subtle in its effects. What if the native, in the midst of an informal conversation, *demanded* to record a performance for the mythographer? Considered in terms of the full continuum of possibilities, it should come as no surprise if the story so produced involved a bold departure from native-to-native practice. But I must confess that I make this observation in hindsight.

On June 17, 1972, Barbara Tedlock and I went to the rural farmhouse near Zuni, New Mexico, where Andrew Peynetsa and his family were spending the summer. The Zunis had recently celebrated the summer solstice (it fell before June 21 because they adjust it to the lunar cycle). On this visit I gave Andrew his share of the advance Dial Press had paid for *Finding the Center*; the book was destined not to appear until December of that year, but the manuscript had been turned in months ago. We had brought along a recorder and were playing some tapes of Indian music when, at about nine o'clock in the evening, Andrew suddenly said, "Tell me when you get to some empty tape. I'm going to tell a story." His suggestion could not have been more out of season: *telapnaawe* or "tales" are forbidden between the spring and autumn equinoxes, lest the narrator be bitten by a rattlesnake, who has a special fondness for people who have not been telling the plain truth. Andrew had never before broken this rule, but afterward he explained his behavior by saying that he had in fact told a "true" story and had "just pretended" that it was a tale! His story had indeed been composed from episodes in the recent life of his own family rather than from episodes given by tale-telling tradition, but he felt that these recent events were *like* a tale. Theoretically it is impossible to make up a "new" tale, fiction though tales may be, but Andrew wanted his new story to sound like a tale—that is, he wanted the truth to sound like good fiction.

Given his self-assigned task, Andrew had the most difficult possible audience. Most of the members were familiar with the real events behind the story, and at the same time they knew very well what a "real" tale should sound like. Even with these difficulties, the story received only one concrete criticism: Andrew should have portrayed the grandmother as crying in her distress over whether the two boys would cut their deer correctly. This detail would have worked in two ways: The real grandmother really did cry, and even in tales grandmothers cry over the risks their grandsons take.

Andrew made several departures from ordinary good form which were more obvious than the matter of the grandmother, but these passed without comment. Perhaps because he was still worried about the season, he left off the first half of the introductory formula, *So'nah-chi*, retaining only the second half, *sonti inoote*; for their part, his hearers refrained from saying *eeso*, the traditional response to a *telapnanne*. After the opening, Andrew should have mentioned the names of the places where the story events were to take place, but that would have been redundant in this case, since we were sitting in the very house where the events were centered. Since tales take place in the "long ago," there are normally no sheep in them, but sheep are mentioned in tales borrowed from Mexicans, and here Andrew even uses a borrowed word (the only one in the story) for them, *kaneelu* (from Spanish *carnero*). He mentions his wagon and its tongue and bolts, but avoids mention of the fact that he pulled the wagon not with a team of horses but with a tractor. The knife in the story is no problem because it could have been a stone knife; the guns, on the other hand, should have been bows and arrows.

Normally the characters in tales are not given names, at least not when they are human; Andrew does mention one name here, Sayku, but only by way of identifying another person (Sayku's mother) whose own name he does not mention. He avoids any other naming in the story, though all of the people in it are real. The grandparents are Andrew and his wife, the two boys are their grandsons, and the father of the boy who killed the deer is their eldest son. All of these were present for the telling except the eldest son.

At the end of a tale, just before the closing line, there is often an etiological statement, such as "That's why the coyote has yellow eyes." Andrew here turns this convention upside down by describing the making of the story itself: Instead of a story which accounts for the way things are at present, he gives us present events which account for a story.

The translation that follows was made with the help of Joseph Peynetsa.

NOW IT BEGINS TO BE MADE LO——NG A GO.
•
It seems
•
the children—
when the hunting opened—

it seems their fathers left them and went out hunting in different
    directions
while these two (*indicates his two grandsons*)
let their sheep out, they let their sheep out and
the two of them
went out herding.
And their fathers had gone out elsewhere.
They went around, all day they went around.
And their grandfather
was working in the fields until late afternoon and
he came up and
their grandmother told him
"Our grandsons
killed a deer." "Where?"
"Over there someplace around back."
"I see.
What happened?" "ONE of them came after a KNIFE.
He got the knife and I
told him to castrate it, maybe they castrated it."
"I see."
"Oh dear, my poor grandsons
maybe you'll do it right."
That's what their grandmother had told them.
And now their grandfather had come and, "It looks like I'll have to
    go and get it,"
he said, and he
went to his wagon
and got it READY.
He headed out and went around to Tree Crescent, he got there and
that's where the sheep were spread out, he got there. "Where?
    Where is it?"
"At the far side of that clearing, by a grove of trees, that's where."
•
"Why don't you get in and we'll go."
Those two boys
just left their sheep. (*softly*) Both of them were all covered with
    blood.
Their grandfather took them along, they went on over there.
"Where?" "Right over there by that grove of trees."
They went over to the trees. "Right over there.
On the north side."
(*softly*) They got to the far end of the trees, (*louder*) to a clearing,
    "HOW did this HAPPEN?"

"Oh— there were three of them.
One of them
was crippled, and there was a doe, and her—
we just let her be.
When they came up
the other two stopped
with this one in front—
pow!
I dropped him.
(*softly*) I dropped him
but then I didn't have a knife.
So, 'Well
well now—'"
he said to the other boy, "Listen:
you go get a knife and I'll look after the sheep."
So then this
other boy
went to get the knife
he went to their grandmother's.
(*softly*) He went to their grandmother's and
(*louder*) ran all the way.
"Oh dear, grandson
why is it you're
running like this?"
"Well we've killed a deer," he said. "WHERE?" she said. "Over
     there.
It's a great big buck." "Oh dear, my grandsons, so you've
ended someone's ROAD.
Perhaps
one of your fathers might end someone's road too."
That's what their grandmother said.
"When your grandfather comes I'll tell him."
Sure enough, when their grandfather came she told him, so now all
     of them were going along together, together
the two boys with their grandfather, and when they got to where
     the deer was, it was s o b i g.
"What are we going to DO?"
"LISTEN:
why don't we put him in the wagon antlers first
then we'll all lift up on the other end."
So then
they put him in the wagon antlers first and they all got together and
     lifted him up

and finally they managed to get him in. "Now that he's in, let's go
    back."
"Where are the lungs and the heart?"
(*sheepishly*) "Well, lying over there."
"Hey—— they're big ones, a lot of fat around the lungs."
"Yes indeed there's a lot of fat, but it got sand on it, let's go."
Then their grandfather turned around and they came along
  •

came along until they got to where the road was too rough for the
    wagon
and the BOLTS got LOOSE on the tongue.
Then the two boys
got left behind there and their grandfather went on
and when he looked back his
wagon was way back there.
"Why didn't you SPEAK UP when that happened?"
They laughed and
he backed up, their grandfather fixed it for them.
They came along, came along until
  •

they
got to their yard. "How're we going to get it down?"
There were two old ladies, their grandmother and
and
Sayku's mother. "With those two women, we can probably get it
    down."
They laid a plank from the wagon to the door and pulled it down.
They put it down inside.
Now the sun was about to go down
it was halfway behind the horizon when their fathers came home.
When their fathers came home their deer was lying inside.
It had thirteen points.
"Oh— who killed it?"
"Well these two killed it."
"Thanks be."
After a while
others came in.
Everyone breathed life from their deer and went back outside.
They went outside, went outside, and their
grandfather
said a prayer, (*softly*) he said a prayer and they all came back in
to sprinkle cornmeal, and in this way they completed it.

Then the father of the boy who killed the deer said, "NOW
this was a day
when something terrible happened to me." "What?"
"Well now
I thought there was a bear in the canyon, that's what I thought.
It was growling-n-growling, 'Where could it be?'"
This was the father of the little boy who killed the deer.
"Where was it?" "Well right there by that gap in the canyon."
"Where? Where was it?" "It was right there by that gap, he was
    growling-n-growling.
I thought it was a BEAR, so I went up very quietly.
I went up very quietly and when I got CLOSE to it
right up close
it kept on growling-n-growling.
So I got my gun in a good position.
(*softly*) 'Well, when I see him I'll blast him.'"
When he looked over the hill
he wasn't GROWLing-n-GROWLing, he was SNORing-n-SNORing,
    ASLEEP.
It was a HUNTER.
"Aw——— it sounded just like a bear."
Then he went on down there.
"HOW COME you're sleeping so hard, you're growling-n-growling
    like a bear," he told him.
This was the father
of the little boy who killed the deer
that's who was talking.
"Well I just lay down here and I must've slept for a long time, I was
    so tired."
That's what he said. "I see.
But that shouldn't happen."
That's what he told him.
"Anyway let's go now, the sun's going down."
Both of them went on down.
When their father got home he told them about it.
"How could this happen? A person out hunting isn't supposed to go
    to sleep,"
he told their grandfather.
•
"Well then
•
well then, what can I DO about it?"

"Why not make up a story?"
"Why not?" he asked the boys' grandmother.
"It's up to you." "Let's go ahead and make one up.
We'll tell it as if it happened long ago."
So their grandfather talked about what had happened.
A STORY was MADE.
He talked about what had happened
and when it was all straightened out
it was about the father whose boy had killed a deer, and that
hunter who had gone to sleep
and was snoring-n-snoring and wasn't a bear growling-n-growling,
     it wasn't a bear but a sleeping hunter.
This happened long ago, enou————gh, the word is short.

After finishing the story, Andrew explained that the canyon walls amplified the snoring. His son (a younger brother of the son who found the sleeping hunter in the story) then added a further comment about this place: "It looks like it's two canyons, but it's only one." He thus added one further paradox to the story. It seems safe to say that what made these real events from recent family history seem like a tale to Andrew and his family was more their interconnected paradoxes and other surprises than any specific resemblance to some tale in his repertoire, though there are tales with hunting scenes and tales in which animals reveal an underlying human form. In real tales a girl may go out hunting rabbits instead of a boy, a mere boy may kill a huge ogress, girls may come courting a boy instead of the other way around, or a boy may pass himself off as a girl. In Andrew's made-up tale, the main paradoxes are summarized in his next-to-last sentence, which constitutes his own analysis of the story: The father goes out hunting and the boys go out sheepherding, but they bring back a deer while he comes home empty-handed—since the growling of a wide-awake bear turned out to be the snoring of a sleeping hunter.

In many tales the resolution of paradox involves the institution or reassertion of a custom, or else a death or an apotheosis; either way, fiction purports to have a lasting real-life result. But in this case, when real life seemed like fiction, the only solution was to institute a new tale. But the process did not stop there. Once the tale was told, it called into existence its own concrete claim to lasting results. Right away, while we were hearing about the two canyons that were really one, the two grandsons had gone outside to get the antlers of the deer they had shot in the story. We heard their footsteps on the roof (that is where antlers are kept), and now here they were with the evidence, and of course we counted the points, all thirteen of them.

Nor did the process stop even there. The boys went outside again to put the antlers back and were gone a bit longer than we would have expected. Suddenly they came back running, saying to everybody, "Come outside and you'll see something amazing!" We all went outside, and there in the north, coming out from behind the horizon, were pink and white rays of light. No one there except Barbara and myself had even seen the Northern Lights before—they are almost never visible as far south as Zuni—so I gave them their English name and offered a sort of popular-science explanation that failed to impress anyone. On the way back into the house Andrew said, nasalizing his vowels and changing his "g" to a "ch" so as to imitate a Navajo accent, "It's strange." After all, the very cosmos had moved in concert with his act of creation.

13

Reading the Popol Vuh over the shoulder of a diviner and finding out what's so funny

One day several years ago—it was Uucub Ahmac or "Seven Sinner" on the Mayan calendar—I found myself looking at the Quiché text of the Popol Vuh, a text written some centuries ago, over the shoulder of a Quiché who was not only very much alive, but who was laughing about something he had just read there. This was a man named Andrés Xiloj, reading the story of the encounter between Zipacna, self-styled as "the maker of mountains," and the hero twins, Hunahpu and Xbalanque. Aside from the broad humor contained in the fact that the twins defeat Zipacna by decoying him with an artificial crab, I had never seen anything downright laughable in this passage—and neither, apparently, had previous translators of the Popol Vuh. What made don Andrés laugh required acts of interpretation that gave the entire episode a second meaning at the symbolic level, as will be seen. In making this reading, he provided us with one of our finest days in what I might've called a project in "ethnopaleography," or what he, as a practitioner of *4hobonic*, "understanding" or "divination," saw as an

First published in *Conjunctions* 3 (1982):176–85.

effort to bring a means of understanding that was practiced in *oher tiempo*, "ancient time," into *sak 3alah*, "clear light."

By this time, the Popol Vuh has been translated over thirty times and into seven languages, but only a third of the translators have troubled themselves to work directly from the Quiché text, the others relying on various Spanish versions. Half a dozen translators have drawn on firsthand knowledge of Quiché language and culture, as I myself have done, but what makes my effort new is that I have given the text to a literate traditionalist for reading and interpretation—not to a longtime Protestant convert or an urban secular romantic, as in the cases of a couple of Spanish translations, but to a practicing diviner who is the head priest-shaman of his patrilineage and is explicitly barred from the Eucharist by those who still carry on the Roman version of the war against the *oher tzih* or Prior Word.

What follows answers the question as to why don Andrés laughed on the day Seven Sinner, while I looked on at what he was reading. It results from our joint reading of the fourteenth (thirteenth in Edmonson's version) of the Popol Vuh's ninety-seven sections. Rather than give a literal transcript of every word we said, I have cast my account of our proceedings as a dialogue between my English translation of the Quiché text of the Popol Vuh (set in roman) and my translation of his comments and asides in Spanish and Quiché as he read his way—aloud—through that same text (set in italics). If this account is read aloud, it should be spoken by two voices; each change of line represents a pause. In the case of the Popol Vuh narrative, the pauses have been reconstructed by following some of the patterns indicated in the modern narrative (in Quiché) that don Andrés introduced into the discussion. This latter narrative, and most of don Andrés's other statements, were recorded on tape. The direct transcription and playback of speech sounds is a long step beyond alphabetic transcription, but it remains in the same lineage. It is through the agency of both these devices that we may now open not only our eyes but our ears to the Prior Word.

Now this
is the defeat and death of Zipacna,
no, I don't know what Zipacna means,
it sounds like a name to me,
but maybe it's the Nahua name for alligator, as you say—
when he, in his turn, was defeated by the two youths,
they're going to terrify Zipacna, these two youths,
Hunahpu, Xbalanque.

And those are names also,
Hunahpu is the name of one of the twenty days,
the day of the grandparents, the ancestors,
and I don't know this Xbalanque,
but it seems to have balam in it, "jaguar,"
and yes, if que is queh, that's "deer,"
and you say that an x in front of words used to mean "small,"
so Xbalanque could be "Little Jaguar Deer."
Now this
is the outrage the two youths felt
over the killing of the Four Hundred Youths by Zipacna.
Their thoughts were stirred up—
yo3 qui4ux, it says,
"their hearts were kneaded," like dough,
they felt mistreated.
He just looks for fish and crabs in the water,
this Zipacna is on the shore of a river, or the sea,
but he's eating every day,
going around looking for his food by day
and backpacking mountains by night.
And then
comes the counterfeiting of a big crab
by Hunahpu, Xbalanque.
They're the ones
who used bromelia flowers,
it says the "face" of the bromelia, meaning the "fruit,"
but for a bromelia that would be the stalk with its flowers,
the ornamental bromelias that are in the forests,
the ones that are used to decorate arches, for fiestas.
These
became the forearms of the crab,
where its scissors are,
and where they opened was the claws.
They used a flagstone for the back of the crab, which clattered.
A crab is just like a wristwatch:
it has the meat inside and it's pure bone outside.
And then
they put its shell beneath an overhang,
beneath a waterfall,
beneath a great mountain.
Meawan is the name of the mountain,
no, I don't know where that is,

he was defeated there,
he was terrified there.
And then
when the youths came along
they found Zipacna by the water.
"Where are you going, boy?"
Zipacna was asked.
"I'm not going anywhere,
I'm just looking for my food, boys,"
said Zipacna.
"What's your food?"
"Just fish and crabs,
but there aren't any I can find.
It's been two days since I stopped getting my meals.
By now I can't stand the hunger,"
Zipacna said to them,
to Hunahpu, Xbalanque.
"There is a crab, it's down in the canyon,
a really big crab!
May this be the day, sir:
you'll eat it, maybe."
It's a matter of the day, the right time,
his luck, his destiny.
"We were just getting bitten.
It wouldn't let us get ahold of it, and we got scared.
If it hasn't gone you could catch it,"
said Hunahpu, Xbalanque.
"Take pity on me,
please go along, point it out, boys,"
said Zipacna.
This Zipacna is abusing the youths here,
he's saying they shouldn't be afraid.
It says here, quibe ta iuaba,
which could be, quibe ta iuabaa,
"If only you would go along to iuabaa —to point it out,"
but it could also be, quebe ta iuabah,
"If only iuabah—your stones, your balls—would go along."
Today, when someone runs from a fight, the saying is,
queeme ta iuabah,
"Don't hide your balls."
So Zipacna is saying,
"Don't you have any balls, boys?"

They're still young.
"We don't want to, so just go on.
You can't miss it, so just follow the river,
and you go straight on over there below a great mountain,
it's clattering there at the bottom of the canyon,
beneath the waterfall.
"Just head on over there,"
said Hunahpu, Xbalanque.
"But won't you please take pity on me?
What if it can't be found, boys?
Go anyway, I'll show you something."
There it is again, now it's nuuaba,
"I show you something,"
or else nuabah,
"my balls"—he's got balls.
"There are lots of birds,"
and you know what else "bird" means,
it's there at the center of the body, with the "stones."
"Please go along, do some shooting—
I know where they are,"
Zipacna replied.
Even though *he* had begged *them*, he went ahead of the youths.
"What if you can't catch it?
Just as we had to turn back, so will you.
Not only didn't we eat it, but—
all at once it was eating us.
We were entering face down there,
but when it got scared we were entering on our back.
We just barely missed reaching it then,
so you'd better enter on your back," he was told.
"Very well,"
Zipacna replied, and they left.
Now Zipacna had company as he went;
they came to the bottom of the canyon,
beneath the waterfall.
The crab is there on its side,
its shell is gleaming red there.
Yes, I know that crabs aren't red unless they're cooked,
but it clearly says, "red, gleaming red."
At the bottom of the canyon,
at the bottom of the waterfall,
is their sham.

"That's good!"
Zipacna is pleased now.
He wishes it were already in his mouth,
so it would really cure his hunger.
He wanted to eat it,
he just wanted it face down, he wanted to enter,
but since the crab backed away he came back out.
"You didn't reach it?" he was asked.
"No indeed—
it was just backing away.
I've just barely missed reaching it on the first try,
so perhaps I'd better enter on my back," he replied.
Clearly,
the crab is a woman.
As you already know, a woman does it on her back,
but here it's in reverse:
the man is on the bottom and the crab will go on top.
These are trial runs.
In ancient times, I think,
they didn't know what sin was, they were looking
for a way to understand everything.
And then
he entered again, on his back.
He entered all the way—
only his kneecaps were showing now.
My God! All the way to the knees!
He gave a last sigh and was calm.
Nothing will bother him now.
The great mountain came to rest on his chest,
now he couldn't turn over.
And Zipacna turned to stone,
he remained as a stony place.
Such, in its turn, was the defeat of Zipacna by the two youths,
Hunahpu, Xbalanque,
this "maker of mountains,"
as his previous pronouncements had it,
the first son of Seven Macaw.
Now
this Zipacna,
who was "backpacking mountains":
he's just like Yewaachi.
Who knows what year it was then,

when
the patron—
yes, the saint—
went out on his horse,
then he met up with a lord named
Yewaachi,
then he said to him,
"Join up with me.
I'll give you as much of—
my land, as much of my livelihood as there is."
Then
the patron said,
"No.
I don't need work,
I've got coins," he said.
He put his hand in his pocket:
"Look here, I've got coins"—
but it wasn't coins, it was paper—
"just as I said."
Then
this Yewaachi thought,
"So this man, this captain
isn't afraid of me,"
thought Yewaachi.
Then
he said, "If this is what you really want,
that I should join up with you,
then go down and get me one
backpack load of bananas from the coast.
Then, when you come back,
I'll give you that girl, Isabel,"
since
the patron had this woman, 'tis said, in ancient times,
who was named Isabel,
over there where we live now.
Yes, Santa Isabel.
Now
the patron, well, he knows very well that he's going to win,
to win against Yewaachi.
Then
that Yewaachi went down to the coast,
he went to get a backpack of bananas,

weighing about three hundredweights,
that one crate of bananas.
Then
he came back as far as the pass—
Diligence Pass,
as we say—
up above Woodpile,
in the pass,
near the volcano now, at the foot of the volcano.
Yes, the Volcán Santa María.
Then
he got tired, 'tis said,
then
he put down his load there,
he drank
a gourd of atole—
that's why it's called Diligence Pass.
Well.
Then
he went to get his load,
to lift it up again,
but now he couldn't lift it.
Now
it was planted there, a volcano.
Because of this
the volcano faces the coast
and here,
behind it, is where we are.
The patron wouldn't allow it here—
the patron is a
captain.
Yes indeed, he's rigid,
he doesn't just let things happen.
Such is the story of the—
the patron.
Because of this
the patron is fierce
and we are fierce.
Rare are those who have anything of—
patience.
The rest—ouch!—
are the fiercest,

even the girls, when they're wooed,
"Humph!"—
they just turn their backs.
Yes.
Well.
And as for Zipacna,
what are the last words here?
He was defeated,
he was deceived,
beneath the great mountain named Meawan,
he was defeated by genius alone,
by the nagual, by the spirit familiar
of Hunahpu and Xbalanque.
He was the second to magnify himself,
and now we shall speak what is spoken of another,
so that it will never be forgotten.
So here's another word, another story.
Shall I come again tomorrow, on the day "Eight Thought"?

The Analogical Tradition
and the Emergence
of a Dialogical Anthropology

Right now,
suppose we had a mirror.
We could go out in the street,
and if the sun were out
we could position this mirror:
then,
the reflection could reach anywhere.

—Andrés Xiloj

Prologue

The words that follow were composed for a Harvey Lecture in Anthropology at the University of New Mexico, delivered on the eve of
the first day of spring, 1979. I mention this here (rather than in a foot-
note) because it is consistent with the theme of the lecture itself that
the circumstances of anthropological discourse, whether that discourse comes from the field, the armchair, or the podium, should be
kept in open discussion rather than being hidden away in footnotes,
appendixes, and unpublished manuscripts.

First published in *Journal of Anthropological Research* 35 (1979):387–400. An Italian translation will appear in *I giorni cantati*. The only additions here are the mentions of works
of Vincent Crapanzano and of Kevin Dwyer; Dwyer's work was called to my attention
by Crapanzano.

321

Having been introduced to the audience, but before beginning the lecture proper, I said, "I'm always in search of an epigraph," and as I said this I pulled out a weapon, loaded with live ammunition. The weapon was a Sony TC-55, loaded with a cassette recording of human voices. With the speaker pointed at the audience and my finger poised over the button marked "FWD," I explained that "as with any proper epigraph, the relationship of this one to the talk itself will be somewhat cryptic." I then pressed the button, but I finally had to hit the machine with the flat of my hand to get it running. Such are the wonders of technology.

What the audience heard, once the tape came on, was a man speaking accented Spanish, though only I could have known, in that context, that his accent was that of the Quiché Maya. In the course of his Spanish he quoted several Quiché words and one complete Quiché sentence. A second voice gave periodic assent, repeated one of the Quiché words, and asked a question in Spanish, all of this with the accent of a speaker of English. After about two minutes, when I noticed that some members of the audience were growing restless, I cut the tape short, even though it was almost over anyway. My plan had been to let the tape stand as a foreign-language epigraph, but having cut it off I offered an English translation of what would have been the last two sentences, sentences spoken by the voice with the Quiché accent. That translation comes to rest here as the epigraph printed above.

Lecture

Behind that peculiar genre of fiction we call "the ethnography" lies a great deal of the kind of talk you just heard, a dialogue, a "speaking alternately"—or, to translate the Greek *dia-logos* literally, a "speaking across." Just at the point where the tape was cut off—or rather, where I had planned to cut it off—the parties to this particular dialogue decided they had reached a sufficient understanding, for the moment, about the particular matter under discussion.

Now it is true that in the field we anthropologists do much more than engage in dialogues. We may watch when the people under study hunt, or gather, or herd sheep, or hoe their gardens, or shuck corn, and we are very likely to be present, all eyes and ears, when a ritual takes place, and to enter an elaborate description in our notebook afterward, even if we didn't really understand a single word of the speeches, prayers, and songs that ran all through the ceremony. If

sociocultural anthropology were founded upon nothing but silent observations, there would be nothing to distinguish it from the natural
sciences. But the moment we talk about this hunting or singing with
the people who participated in it, we have entered the realm that is
the special province of the social sciences. Alfred Schutz calls this
realm "human intersubjectivity,"[1] but we could equally well call it
"human interobjectivity." Bennetta Jules-Rosette calls it "a repertoire
of knowledge and expectations, or a common culture, that was shared
with participants and created in interaction with them."[2] The anthropological dialogue creates a world, or an understanding of the *differences between* two worlds, that exists between persons who were inde-
terminately far apart, in all sorts of different ways, when they started
out on their conversation. This *betweenness* of the world of the dialogue is something I want to keep before us, or between us, all the
way through this talk.

It is elusive, this betweenness of the field situation in the social
sciences, because the situation of the armchair, where the "preparation for publication" takes place, tempts us to *simulate* the natural sciences. When we take the natural sciences as our model and speak of
"objectivity," or of the overcoming of "subjectivity," then the intersubjective, interobjective world of the original dialogue, the very situation that marks off the social sciences from the natural sciences,
shrinks toward the vanishing point, hidden behind the fictions of,
say, the 101st Holt, Rinehart & Winston Case Study. As Schutz has it,
the "objectivity" normally claimed in the social sciences is really nothing more than the "subjectivity" of the observer,[3] making his own
claims over and above those of the observed. Here we leave behind
the possibility of an anthropology that remains true to the dialogical
situation and enter the realm of what I call analogical anthropology.
A dialogical anthropology would be a talking across, or alternately,
which is something we all do in the field if we are not purely natural
scientists. There is no reason this dialogue must stop when we leave
the field. I say this even aside from the possibility of correspondence

1. Alfred Schutz, *The Phenomenology of the Social World*, chap. 3. See also Johannes
Fabian, "Language, History, and Anthropology."
2. Bennetta Jules-Rosette, *African Apostles: Ritual and Conversion in the Church of
John Maranke*, p. 21. Jean Rouch, who takes a similar view of ethnographic film-making,
calls for an *anthropologie partageé* ("On the Vicissitudes of Self," pp. 8, 2). George
Quasha, under the influence of phenomenological anthropology, proposes a reconstruction of postmodern poetics along the lines of conversation and "shared transmis-
sions" ("The Age of the Open Secret," p. 71).
3. Schutz, *The Phenomenology of the Social World*, pp. 31–32. Vincent Crapanzano
would add that the writing of an objectifying ethnography is a psychiatric "symptom of
extreme confrontation with otherness" ("On the Writing of Ethnography," p. 72).

through the mails, such as Robert Lowie carried on with James Carpenter, his Crow interpreter.[4] The armchair dialogue I have in mind here involves the interpretation of the discourse recorded while in the field. Again, this armchair dialogue is something we all do, listening, puzzling, questioning, and, as it were, talking back. It still partakes of the specific nature of the social sciences; it is still dialogical anthropology. But so far, we do it mainly *prior* to publication, rather than *in* publication.

Analogical anthropology, on the other hand, involves the replacement of one discourse with another. It is claimed that this new discourse, however far removed it may seem to be, is equivalent or proportionate, in a quasi-mathematical sense, to the previous discourse. *Ana-logos*, in Greek, literally means "talking above," "talking beyond," or "talking later," as contrasted with the talking back and forth of dialogue. The dialogue is a continuing process and itself illustrates process and change; the analogue, on the other hand, is a product, a result.

Judging from the empirical evidence, as we run through the ethnographies on our bookshelves, it is a law of analogical anthropology that the ethnographer and the native must never be articulate between the same two covers. In the classic ethnography, other anthropologists may be quoted at length, but no native ever utters a complete sentence, whether in text or in translation. In the exceptional cases where the natives do speak at some length, they speak only as a group, through excerpts from myths or prayers. There are, of course, those ubiquitous "native terms," but they do not constitute articulate speech, to say nothing of eloquence.

Longer segments of speech, such as myths, are sometimes thought of as the verbal equivalents of the masks, implements, and drums displayed in museum cases, but I think the proper analogy is to be found not in myths, which carry a great deal of self-explanation with them, but in the "native terms" sprinkled through an ethnography, each one accompanied, as it were, by an explanatory placard. One of the functions of these terms, in an otherwise purely analogical discourse, is to give evidence, in just the way that souvenirs do, that the person who now occupies the armchair was once in the field, talking to actual people in an actual far-off place, no matter how much the published findings may sound like a story we have heard somewhere before.

Around the fringes of the analogical discourse, a discourse that

4. Robert Lowie, "My Crow Interpreter."

holds the dead center position in anthropology, is a secondary discourse of a different sort. Here are personal confessions of "what *really* happened in the field" (lately supplemented by essays on ethical issues), native texts with interlinear translations, and native life histories. Sometimes there are fragments of this secondary discourse in the prefaces, footnotes, and appendixes of ethnographies, but its proper place seems to be in separate volumes, as if to leave the progress of the analogical enterprise unimpeded. What these three types of separate volumes have in common with the ethnography itself is that their dominant mode is that of the monologue. It is true that native texts and life histories are direct quotations rather than analogical replacements of native discourse, but they are not shown to us in the full light of primary dialogue. Rather, they are presented as if the anthropologist who collected them had had a tracheotomy prior to entering the field. Again, as in the case of the ethnographies, there may be compensatory marginalia, but otherwise it is now the native who is talking endlessly, in the one case as the supposedly passive conduit of collective tradition and in the other as if he or she were one of those insufferable personalities who can talk only about themselves.

What, then, about that other type of separate volume, the confessions of the anthropologist? Again, there is precious little dialogue to be found, and that is true even of most of the essays in Joseph Casagrande's *In the Company of Man*, each of which is supposed to present the relationship between the fieldworker and a favorite interpreter, informant, or houseboy. W. E. H. Stanner offers only a handful of the utterances of his chosen Nangiomeri, a man known in English as Smiler, and one of those utterances is what Smiler said to a third party rather than to Stanner. What he said was (pardon my Nangiomeri), "Well, fuck you!"[5] Incidentally, rereading my own venture into the reflective genre, I find the following sentence: "This made Daniel mad, and he swore in English."[6] In Paul Rabinow's recent book, *Reflections on Fieldwork in Morocco*, the natives manage very few complete utterances, and the only two quoted in Arabic, the language of Rabinow's chosen village, come not from villagers but from a Berber. One of them (pardon my Arabic) is *moul-taxi la-bas*, which he translates as "How's the driver?" and the other is *numero wahed*, which he translates as "first class."[7] Turning to Clifford Geertz's first-person account of a Balinese cockfight, we find once again that the natives have very little to say, and on the one occasion when they speak their own

5. W. E. H. Stanner, "Durmugan, a Nangiomeri," p. 86.
6. Dennis Tedlock, "An American Indian View of Death," p. 252.
7. Paul Rabinow, *Reflections on Fieldwork in Morocco*, pp. 68–69.

tongue, they do so collectively. That is when the authorities arrive and everybody shouts (pardon my Balinese), *pulisi, pulisi!*[8]

I'm not quite sure what to make of these examples, but a partial formulation would be this: In the classic ethnography, the informants, collectively, speak occasional isolated words in a totally exotic language; in confessions or reflections, on the other hand, where contact between individuals and between cultures is an undeniable reality, informants are allowed occasional complete utterances, but these are likely to contain or even to consist entirely of words from contact languages. In any case, the dominant mode, even of the confession, is the monologue. The confession bears the same relation to the ethnography, on the anthropological side of the picture, that the life history bears to a collection of myths, on the native side of the picture. All four genres are monologues, each with marginalia (and occasionally even snippets) that overlap with one or more of the other three.

But it needs to be added here that the published native discourses are monologues only in the primary sense that each of them was delivered by one particular voice. Within this monologue, in the life history but even more so in the myth, there are quoted dialogues in great number. So much is this so in the case of Zuni narrative, for example, that one might almost say that the straight narrative passages are there simply to provide the contexts and interpretations for a series of dialogues. The same cannot be said, on the anthropological side, for the ethnography and the confession. Dell Hymes, commenting on the confessional genre, remarked that "what is considered known and how it came to be known are still compartmentalized,"[9] but what I am calling into question here is how much even the confessions tell us how things "came to be known." Instead of letting us *hear* things in the process of coming to be known, they tell us *about* that process, and in that sense they are already analogical products or results, differing from the ethnography only in the degree to which the monologue is overtly personalized.

Beyond the ethnography and its three auxiliary volumes lie "synthetic" or "theoretical" works that "rise above" or "go beyond" previous discourses to the point where even isolated native terms disappear, except for a few that have become common anthropological currency. These are the anthropologist's equivalents of *pulisi, numero, taxi,* and "Fuck you!" I am thinking of words like totem, tabu, mana, and shaman—though no doubt Lévi-Strauss's exorcism of totemism[10]

8. Clifford Geertz, *The Interpretation of Cultures,* p. 414.
9. Dell Hymes, *Reinventing Anthropology,* p. 380.
10. Claude Lévi-Strauss, *Totemism.*

could be repeated for mana, tabu, and shamanism. A synthesizing Americanist, whether archaeologist or ethnologist, might wish to purge his discourse not only of the totem, but of atlatl, berdache, hogan, kachina, kiva, metate, milpa, peyote, potlatch, wampum, wickiup, and windigo as well.[11]

As the original dialogue, and even the accompanying souvenirs, recede ever farther from view, the analogical discourse, this created object that rises *above* or comes *after*, increasingly claims to describe rules or laws that lie *under* or come *before* what the natives do and say. As Pierre Bourdieu has it, "the objects constructed by science" tend to become endowed with ontological priority.[12] Robert Murphy states the ontological claim of the analogical faith this way: "*Underneath* the *veneer* of cultural differences there is a *primordial* humanity." He goes on to say that this primordial humanity "must be *accounted for* as well as *respected*,"[13] thus touching on the perpetual moral dilemma of the analogical anthropologist, who reaches toward an "account" that will resemble those of the natural sciences, on the one hand, and experiences a twinge of humanistic guilt and sentimentality on the other. It is difficult to "respect" this primordial man, once we get a look at him. Judging by the accounts I have been able to piece together, he has a Stage I Color Terminology (but it no longer matters how the actual terms are pronounced and the only referential meaning is the Munsell color chips), he possesses a "deep" or "universal" grammar (a scientific version of Esperanto), and his myths (here I follow Lévi-Strauss) have only letters of the alphabet as their characters, while the relationships and actions of these characters are limited to "transformation," "contrast," "congruence," "non-congruence," "identity," "difference," "conjunction," "disjunction," "presence," and "absence."[14] Note that one thing the characters don't do is *speak* to each other. If we should ever meet up with an example of this primordial man—and be prepared, Lévi-Strauss styles him as *L'Homme nu*, he hasn't got a stitch on, except maybe one of those Amazonian penis sheaths—he would certainly be, for analogical anthropology at least, the ideal informant. In fact, we wouldn't even have to learn the native language.

Now, lest you think that here we are merely dealing with the foibles of "idealists," "mentalists," and the like, the "materialist" is

11. See the glossary in E. Adamson Hoebel, *Anthropology: The Study of Man*, for other borrowed terms.

12. Pierre Bourdieu, *Outline of a Theory of Practice*, p. 27.

13. Robert F. Murphy, *The Dialectics of Social Life*, p. v (italics added).

14. Claude Lévi-Strauss, *From Honey to Ashes*, p. 9.

equally far to the hither side of the dialogical frontier. Marvin Harris reaches after "a culture-free description of cultural things."[15] The description itself, of course, transcends materiality and takes the form of universal laws that claim to govern all phenomena.[16] The only difference is that, while the idealist or mentalist ultimately locates these laws in the cerebral cortex (or else in the interstices of a collectivity of cerebral cortices), the materialist locates them within or among external objects, exclusive of the human body itself.

Among analogical discourses, the ones that lay the most concrete claim to abstract transcendence are those in which even the sentences of the hand writing from the armchair recede from view, themselves succeeded by the charts and tables Jack Goody has been writing about lately,[17] together with Arabic numerals, isolated letters of the Roman alphabet (and sometimes Greek), and algebraic signs—though these objects, like masks, implements, drums (and native terms), seem to require explanatory placards. The appearance of these devices within the anthropological discourse, judging from the anthropological articles that are sometimes allowed inside the clean white covers of *Science*, is taken as evidence that anthropology is at last gaining its proper place among the other sciences—meaning, in this case, the natural sciences, the sciences in which no dialogical ground was possible in the first place. Not far beyond these charts and tables and formulas might lie the realization of the ultimate analogical dream, a dream that Murphy, although not himself a contributor to *Science*, describes as "a theoretical synthesis that will, I hope, find pertinence to all societies and not just our own."[18] To me, at least, such hopes look like the intellectual after-image of a collapsed empire, an empire transformed into a theory upon which the sun never sets.

This is a good point, I think, at which to try out some of our own medicine, considering the fate we have meted out, and mete out here, to those people we dialogued with back there in the field, now subject, all unknowing, to the retrospective laws we imagine ourselves to be passing. If we stop our *participation* in the analogical progression just for a moment and take up the role of *observer* with respect to our own works, we may be able to see our charts, tables, and algebra for the highly culture-specific artifacts they are, now purged of the last traces of other voices in other places. Suddenly, and precisely at this point, all those warnings about the dangers of going native come to

15. Marvin Harris, *The Nature of Cultural Things*, p. 7.
16. See Robert Paul and Paul Rabinow, "Bourgeois Rationalism Revived," p. 122n.
17. Jack Goody, *The Domestication of the Savage Mind*.
18. Murphy, *The Dialectics of Social Life*, p. vi.

mind, all those stories about Frank Hamilton Cushing and the Zunis. Could it be that there are *two* kinds of "going native," one far to the "other" side of the dialogical frontier and the other far to "this" side, "our" side?

Cushing has long been cited, especially in oral tradition, as the classic case of the anthropologist gone native. Lévi-Strauss attempts to snatch him far back into the fold by awarding him "a seat at Morgan's right" and naming him a "great forerunner" of structuralism,[19] a classic Lévi-Straussian reversal. But what is more interesting is that the Zunis themselves draw quite a different lesson from the example of Cushing, one that should give us pause. One day at Zuni, Andrew Peynetsa asked me what I knew about *kuushi* and *tims okya*, Cushing and Stevenson (how's that for a pair of native terms?), and I told him that Cushing claimed to have been made a Bow Priest. He then recalled the following story, which he thought might well be about Cushing:

> Once they made a white man into a Priest of the Bow,
> he was out there with the other Bow Priests—
> he had black stripes
> on his white body.
> The others said their prayers from their hearts,
> but he read his from a piece of paper.

The subtle part of the joke has to do with the black stripes on Cushing's body. In Zuni, the written page is *ts'ina* (there I go with a native term), literally, "that which is striped." Further, on Cushing's skin, the stripes of the Bow Priesthood made him look a little like a black-and-white striped *neweekwe* (native term again), or clown. To translate all this, what *kuushi* was all about was not revealed solely by the piece of paper he held in his hand. It was written all over him.

Now, in an analogical approach to this narrative we might look strictly for what it may tell us about Zunis, not for what it may tell us about ourselves, to say nothing of the relationship between ourselves and the Zunis. In fact, the story is not a fit document for analogical anthropology in the first place, since one of the characters (the main one) happens not to be a Zuni—or even an Indian, for that matter. Worse yet, the dialogue in which this story occurred began when the informant asked the anthropologist a question.

If we read this story not as a possible background document for a projected analogical description of Zuni, or the Zuni mind, but as an

19. Claude Lévi-Strauss, *Structural Anthropology*, p. 282.

example of the way, or one way, that Zunis explore the problem of ethnicity, then the most striking thing about it is that it tells us simultaneously who the "Zunis" are and who "we" are, all the more so by bringing us together in the same short narrative—between the same two covers, so to speak. The Zunis said their prayers from their hearts, but Cushing read his from a piece of paper; they said theirs from the inside, and the anthropologist said his from the outside. But at the very same time, Cushing *is* a Bow Priest, and he *is* out there in the plaza with the other Bow Priests, and he *does* have the stripes on. Coming back the other way, striped piece of paper though Cushing's prayer may be, it *is* the prayer, and it reflects back upon the stripes that everyone there is wearing, making *all* the stripes a visible counterpart of the spoken prayers. Yet, at the same time, to touch on the *difference* again, Cushing is *more* striped than the others, in the double sense of his striped paper and the fact that his body stripes stand out so clearly.

When I said earlier that this sharp black-and-whiteness made Cushing a clown, I was already extending the dialogical process beyond what was actually said on a particular day in conversation with Andrew Peynetsa. Now, if we take this story a step further into the armchair, but still keeping it before us rather than letting it disappear before the analogical demand that we get down to the business of describing the object called Zuni, it may call to mind, our mind as anthropologists, the debate between Robbins Burling and the ethnoscience establishment in the pages of the *American Anthropologist*, back in 1964. Burling called the ethnoscience enterprise into question by wondering aloud whether it might be wise to "admit that we are just fiddling with a set of rules which allow us to use terms [and otherwise behave] the way others do,"[20] and to forget the idea of "discovering the cognitive system of the people."[21] Dell Hymes and Charles O. Frake tried to win him back into the fold, but in his reply he said, "I am entirely skeptical about getting 'inside people' via their behavior,"[22] thus rejecting the mentalist version of the analogical project.

When we juxtapose this story of Burling and the ethnoscientists to the one about Cushing and the Zuni priests, what jumps out is that piece of paper in Cushing's hand. "The others said their prayers from

20. Quoted in Charles O. Frake, "Further Discussion of Burling," p. 119.
21. Robbins Burling, "Cognition and Componential Analysis: God's Truth or Hocus-Pocus?" p. 27.
22. Dell Hymes, "Discussion of Burling's Paper." Frake, "Further Discussion of Burling." Robbins Burling, "Burling's Rejoinder," p. 121.

their hearts, but he read his from a piece of paper," that is, he used a device that allowed him to say the same words the others did, but we are left in doubt as to whether, or to what extent, the Bow Priests got inside his head—or, in the Zuni phrase, inside his heart. They did apply their paint to his very body, but the stripes really stood out.

We could keep on going back and forth over this story, following its alternating black-and-white stripes, and that is just the point: As long as we have a document like this right out on the table, we cannot make it go away except by postponing it, saving it for our memoirs, or for a collection of texts in which it must occupy the back pages, the front ones being properly reserved for a pristine creation myth. Then we could get on with business as usual. If we could just wash off the last traces of that black paint we might even be allowed, one day, to don a clean white lab coat. But even as I say this—or rather, even as I wrote it—I kept thinking of another story.

One summer at Zuni we offered to take Andrew Peynetsa over to Walpi for the Hopi Snake Dance, which he had never seen before. When the day came and we found ourselves walking out on that precarious neck of sandstone that connects Walpi to the rest of First Mesa, Andrew turned to me and said,

> Straight down!
> Both sides!
> You jump one way, and
> I'll jump the other.

But of course what we really did was walk straight ahead, staying within earshot of each other.

When we examine our works as anthropologists from the footing of this dialogical path rather than taking a leap to one side, a host of problems can be seen in a new way, all at once. Take, for example, the perpetual quest for methods that will make it possible for us to extract data without leaving the telltale marks of our own tools. This quest is fundamentally contradictory to begin with, as we all know, but the analogical tradition leads us to regard tool marks as unfortunate side effects rather than as a symptom of a deeper problem. Just as the ultimate analogical interpretation of data should be free of all traces of the native hand, so the ultimate data would be free of all traces of the anthropological hand. Efforts to reduce the anthropological traces toward their vanishing point involve the tactical avoidance of full and open dialogue, either through a flanking action or by means of direct aggression. In the case of the flanking action the anthropologist actually makes an exit from the field, having turned the work of ethnography into a cottage industry whose products will be collected at a later date. That is what happened, for example, when Franz Boas instructed George Hunt in the alphabetical writing of the Kwakiutl language and then set him to work on the production of a gigantic volume on the ethnology of the Kwakiutl.[23] Similar projects continue to this day, with the difference that the instructions of the departing anthropologist increasingly concern the proper production of magnetic tapes.

From the analogical point of view, the problem with these attempts at hands-off eavesdropping is that writing and recording, together with the act of instruction and the fact of future collection, all leave their own marks on the data, though there is a curious sense of relief in knowing that it is now the native who wields the mark-making tools. But when we trace the products of this cottage industry to the point of preparation for publication, there arises a more fundamental problem: In the end, eavesdropping merely postpones the dialogue between anthropologist and native to another occasion, that of the translation and interpretation of the recorded discourse.

At the opposite extreme from the installation of a cottage industry that will carry on production in the absence of the anthropologist lies the establishment of a closely supervised assembly line. In place of the flanking action comes a direct confrontation in which the anthropologist sustains the initiative. Whereas the cottage industry was prolific but wasteful and unmanageable, direct control over production through such devices as the eliciting frame permits the rapid manufacture of precisely the items desired. Now the relationship between data and interpretation is reversed: In the case of the cottage production of data, interpretation was postponed, but with the change to the assembly line the interpretation exists *prior* to the data, in the form of systematically loaded questions.

But it is not that the dialogical path requires the general abandonment of existing methodology, or even of the eliciting frame in particular—after all, even the natives have methods, as the ethnomethodologists have it. And it is not the case that the dialogue is itself a method, in the sense that it might supplant "other" or "previous" methods. A method is a "means to an end" and tends to be seen as a "necessary but temporary evil." The dialogue is not a method but a *mode*, a mode of discourse within which there may be methodical moments, on either side, and within which methods number among the possible subjects under discussion, both in field and armchair. In the

23. Franz Boas, "Ethnology of the Kwakiutl."

writings of a dialogical anthropology, methods will be seen in their full range from happy accident to utter disaster. We will see for ourselves that some conversants absolutely refuse to play an ethnoscience or similar game, while at the other extreme there are conversants who, for the moment, cannot remember a single story, even though we were hoping to settle back and enjoy a monologue.

Two generations ago Margaret Mead wrote that "the fieldworker is not in the field to talk but to listen, not there to express complicated ideas of his own that will muddle and distort the natives' accounts."[24] She was a student of Boas, who himself had warned us, all the way back in 1911, against the dangers of working with "intelligent Indians" who "may have formed a theory" about what we are doing.[25] Between these two injunctions, we can see that our job as analogical fieldworkers, facing dangerous conversations but with the safety of the armchair awaiting us, was to play dumb with smart informants and play smart with dumb ones. But within the dialogical path, conversations will stand or fall on their own merits as the meeting ground of two worlds, not on the basis of whether the investigator got what he claims he had been looking for (and at whatever cost). The danger lies to either *side* of the dialogue, and it is just as near in the armchair as it is in the field.

Nothing would seem safer, from the analogical viewpoint, than the doing of ethnohistory, but that too is open to a dialogical questioning. When it comes to the colonial documents of Mesoamerica, for example, we have tended to use them as clues to the reconstruction of Prehispanic culture and society. We clip out what we judge to be truly aboriginal and cast aside anything that appears to us to be contaminated by the presence of Spanish missionaries—who are, culturally speaking, our own cousins, and worse yet, they got there first. So it is that Sahagún's record of the sixteenth-century debate between the so-called Twelve Apostles (a group of Franciscans) and a group of Aztec priests is only now being fully translated into both Spanish and English.[26] From all over Mesoamerica there are catechisms, written in the native languages and in the knowledge of native customs,[27] but they are read, when they are read at all, only with an eye to ethnographic tidbits (or else they are read by historians for tidbits of church history). In the case of that most famous of Mesoamerican ethno-

---

24. Margaret Mead, "Native Languages as Fieldwork Tools," p. 196.
25. Franz Boas, "Linguistics and Ethnology," p. 15.
26. See J. Jorge Klor de Alva, "The Aztec-Spanish Dialogues of 1524."
27. See, e.g., Ernesto Chinchilla Aguilar, *La Danza del Sacrificio y otros estudios*, pp. 65–76.

historical documents, the Popol Vuh, the opening creation story, which contains allusions to the Bible, has been dismissed by a hundred years of scholarship as "an accommodation to Christian notions" or "a syncretistic paraphrase of Genesis"[28] not to be compared with the rest of what is otherwise a perfect document—never mind that it was all written in the Roman alphabet.

From a dialogical point of view, such documents as these are interesting not in spite of the fact that some European got there first but precisely because of it. They show, from both sides and with moments of thunderbolt clarity, the dialogical frontier between European and Mesoamerican cultures during the colonial period. In some ways, the opening of the Popol Vuh tells us more about the sixteenth-century Quiché Maya than anything else in that document, precisely because it simultaneously shows us, with respect to the question of cosmogony, who those Quichés were and who our Spanish cousins were, how they met up and how they did not meet up.

Now that I have raised the specter of missionaries, and even of the Twelve Apostles themselves, we might as well look more closely at these particular cousins of ours, or rather, at why we anthropologists become nervous when we talk about them, why we seem to have a store of antimissionary jokes—and, too, at why we keep up the pretense that we ourselves are free of all metaphysical notions, unlike both missionaries and natives. Bronislaw Malinowski, I think, put this problem on the proper footing when he made missionary and anthropologist into a pair of inverted twins. He saw the missionary as "translating the white man's point of view to the native" and said that the task of the anthropologist is "to translate the native point of view to the European."[29] We can carry this twinning of missionary and anthropologist a step further by taking a harder look at their respective senses of ultimate purpose. The missionary starts from a single story, supposed to apply to all mankind, and tries to persuade all mankind to tell that one single story to the exclusion of all other, competing stories. The anthropologist, on the other hand, gathers the stories of all mankind and, if he is true to the very *end* of the analogical discourse, shows that *all* these stories were really only *one* story all along—it's just that the natives were unaware of this fact. When we read our way into this one single myth, we are led to the strange male

28. Adolf F. Bandelier, "On the Distribution and Tenure of Lands and the Customs with Regard to Inheritance Among the Ancient Indians," p. 391. Munro S. Edmonson, "Narrative Folklore," p. 359. For a further discussion of this matter, see Chapter 11, above.
29. Bronislaw Malinowski, *Coral Gardens and Their Magic*, vol. 2, p. xxi.

nude I spoke of earlier. When we go up inside his head, or even higher up than that, what we find there, as described by Lévi-Strauss, strangely resembles our old friend the Logos (with a capital L), that ultimate monologue artist, the main character of Aristotle's *Metaphysics*, the Logos who turns up again in the Gospel According to John—which is, by the way, the first book of the Bible that an S.I.L.-trained missionary translates into a native tongue.

To put this another way, Lévi-Strauss has gone native, only it's the *hither*, rather than the *yonder*, kind of native. Oh, but all those hundreds of South American myths, you may say. Doesn't he engage in dialogue with them? But if we take a second look, not a single South American Indian is ever allowed to be eloquent in all those pages. The myths are given only in brief synopses, clearing the way for further transformations that will finally leave them unrecognizable. Lévi-Strauss describes his own mode of operation this way: "Like a brush-fire, my mind burns its way into territory which may sometimes prove unexplored; . . . I snatch a harvest or two, leaving devastation behind me." [30] To paraphrase Gregory Bateson, how's that for an ecology of mind? But as I suggested earlier, a text, once it is put right out on the table, is a resource not so easily exhausted, and when we approach it dialogically there is no overwhelming metaphysical purpose that demands its complete and final replacement with our own words.

Now, in some moment of resistance to all this, you may have formulated the retort that I am myself proposing the replacement of "earlier" anthropological discourse with a "later" kind of discourse, the replacement of the monologue with the dialogue. But the dialogue, even in the armchair, has no need of replacing anything; previous discourse is quoted rather than replaced. Further, the dialogue is not wholly new in anthropological publication, but is rather a constant possibility that has already had its moments of realization in print. Close at hand, in the armchair-to-armchair setting, are the "discussion and debate" sections of professional journals, and of course there are all those recent essays and books with words like "rethinking" in their titles. Insofar as such works do not seek an imaginary victory over previous thought, they are true to the spirit of dialogue. One step closer to the field situation is the armchair meeting of "our" myths with "their" myths, as in Miguel León-Portilla's *Aztec Thought and Culture*, where Aztec discourses, right there for us to read without consulting one of those separate volumes, are brought into direct

30. Claude Lévi-Strauss, *Tristes Tropiques*, p. 56.

comparison with the discourses of our own ancient Athenian cousins. Another example is Stanley Diamond's comparison of a Dahomean trickster tale with the Book of Job;[31] he quotes both narratives within his own discourse, giving us room in which to modify or disagree with his interpretation.

In the search for published dialogues that occurred face-to-face or side-by-side in the meeting grounds of cultures, we have been preceded by Paul Radin, in the introduction he wrote for the 1957 edition of his 1927 book, *Primitive Man as Philosopher*. When it comes to matters of philosophy, he criticizes unilateral "formulations by outsiders" and prefers the establishment, however difficult, of "a true philosophical dialogue."[32] He quotes one example of such a dialogue in full, an exchange that took place around the turn of the century between the physician J. R. Walker and an Oglala shaman named Finger.[33] Radin also mentions the original French version of Marcel Griaule's *Conversations with Ogotemêlli*. Griaule's book remains the reigning classic of anthropological field dialogue, despite his straining after the abstract object called Dogon; at times he struggles to keep himself dumb in the presence of the intelligent Ogotemêlli,[34] but the point here is that his struggles are there for us to read, as part of the record of the dialogue.

Shorter examples of the direct reporting of field dialogue may be found in the works of Monica Wilson, Kevin Dwyer, and Billie Jean Isbell.[35] Dwyer presents a dialogue in which he elicits a Moroccan Arab's view of his own field research enterprise; in the process he lays bare the political and ideological asymmetries of the relationship between fieldworker and informant. Isbell's dialogue, between herself and an Andean village elder, is given in both Quechua and English; this may be the first published text to show an anthropologist speaking the native language in complete sentences and getting complete sentences in return. Isbell informs me that the published version is only a part of a much longer dialogue, shortened in a necessary compromise with an editor who had argued, with all the authority of that genre called "the ethnography" behind him, that a dialogue would be an imposition on the reader.

In theory, at least, Clifford Geertz comes close to advocating a

31. Stanley Diamond, *In Search of the Primitive*, pp. 281–91.
32. Paul Radin, *Primitive Man as Philosopher*, pp. xxx–xxxi.
33. J. R. Walker, "The Sun Dance and Other Ceremonies of the Oglala Division of the Teton Dakota," pp. 154–56.
34. Marcel Griaule, *Conversations with Ogotemêlli*, pp. 145–46.
35. Monica Wilson, *Good Company*, pp. 194–95. Kevin Dwyer, "On the Dialogic of Field Work." Billie Jean Isbell, *To Defend Ourselves*, p. 170.

turn to dialogue, but when he urges us "to converse with them," he apparently means a purely metaphorical conversation with a collective "them," and judging from the extreme paucity of quotations in his own work, the practice of what he calls "thick description" amounts to a gag rule on native discourse.[36] But if Geertz preaches conversation and practices the monologue, Victor Turner comes close to doing just the opposite. In the first chapter of *The Forest of Symbols*, he makes the classic argument that it is he, and not the Ndembu, who is possessed of objectivity,[37] as if giving himself permission to enter upon a monologue. But in practice he makes no secret of his dialogues with Muchona, or of Muchona's intelligence, even when the conversation exceeds the bounds of strictly Ndembu matters to touch upon the Old Testament and the British flag.[38] Turner's work is a dialogue, or enough of a dialogue, to invite reinterpretation, even from paragraph to paragraph; it is not an attempt to construct an exhaustive argument while hiding the previous discourses on which that argument is based.

Johannes Fabian, in his own search for signs of a "language-oriented anthropology" that might effectively rest on "the foundation . . . of human intersubjectivity," finds "the ethnography of speaking" advocated by Dell Hymes to be more promising than any other recent development.[39] But if this "ethnography of speaking" were to explore the dialogical path I have spoken of here, its practitioners would have to see it as something more than a mere methodological means to the theoretical ends of an analogically conceived sociolinguistics, a sociolinguistics that would systematically transform native discourse into lists of what are aptly called "rewrite rules."[40]

Hymes sees the relatively untouched domain of sociolinguistics as the result of an historical oversight, or as "holes in a scientific pattern," and he urges us to "pass over and occupy the land."[41] But what I want to venture here is that the "holes" are not there because of some accident of scientific history, but because the sciences of society and of language, insofar as they have both followed the model of the natural sciences, have *necessarily* left precisely the holes that sociolinguists now desire to fill. To take notice of these holes, through the invocation of the social dimension of language (or the linguistic di-

---

36. Geertz, *The Interpretation of Cultures*, pp. 13, 24, 6.
37. Victor Turner, *The Forest of Symbols*, pp. 25–26.
38. Ibid., pp. 21–33, 135.
39. Fabian, "Language, History, and Anthropology," pp. 23–27.
40. See, e.g., Dell Hymes, "Models of the Interaction of Language and Social Life," pp. 66–70.
41. Dell Hymes, *Foundations in Sociolinguistics*, p. 208.

mension of society), is to raise the question of dialogue, and the question of dialogue necessarily reaches out to encompass the would-be observer. The ultimate implications of dialogue can be postponed by eavesdropping on the discourse of others, but if such discourse is to be translated and interpreted, then the ethnographer of speaking must sooner or later become a speaking ethnographer. The grounds where language and society overlap are far from being unoccupied, and the only way for anthropologists to explore them is to walk their frontiers in the company of people like Andrés Xiloj, James Carpenter, Smiler, Andrew Peynetsa, George Hunt, Finger, Ogotemêlli, or Muchona.

Epilogue

Franz Boas and Stith Thompson observed long ago that there seemed to be almost no "true creation myths" in North America,[42] by which they apparently meant origin myths on the metaphysical model of Genesis 1, John 1, and, for that matter, Aristotle's *Metaphysics*. But Boas did note that there are, in northern California, myths in which "creation by will" takes place.[43] When we reread the Maidu and Kato versions of these myths, it turns out that there are two creators, male and female, and that they are present in a world that already has physical existence at the very beginning of the story.[44] The changes that then take place in the world come about when this man and woman engage in a dialogue—there is no solitary male nude saying, "Let there be this and that." A similar dialogue is at work in the Popol Vuh, and it constitutes the Popol Vuh's profound rejection of Genesis. To argue that "underneath the veneer" of myths such as these lie the workings of a single universal Logos is to cast a vote for the Western metaphysic and against dialogue. But the Popol Vuh asks to be approached dialogically, and the way to write about the Popol Vuh might be to set down the opening words, *Are uxe oher tzih uaral Quiche ubi*, and then go on from there, quoting and questioning all along the way.

42. Franz Boas, *Race, Language, and Culture*, p. 468. Stith Thompson, *Tales of the North American Indians*, p. xvii.
43. Boas, *Race, Language, and Culture*, p. 468.
44. Thompson, *Tales of the North American Indians*, pp. 24–37.

Epilogue:
When Mountains Shine

On October 13, 1976, Barbara Tedlock and I were in Chuua 4,ak, a
Quiché Maya town in Guatemala, talking with Andrés Xiloj. We were
undergoing training in Quiché divination and dream interpretation
during this period.[1] The day before, I had told don Andrés of dream-
ing that a shining white mountain had spoken to me with the voice of
an old woman, saying, "Come with me." He had commented that
"worlds" do indeed shine, "worlds" (*mundos*, from Spanish) being a
favorite Quiché metaphor for mountains. In the singular, "World" refers to the earth deity at his/her full planetary scale, sometimes called
pachulum Mundo, "round World."

The notion that worlds (or mountains) shine had haunted me
since the previous day, and now I brought the conversation back to
that topic with the question that opens the transcription (from tape)
given below. The ensuing discussion led don Andrés to tell a story,
but like the story about the blanket merchant and the squirrel,[2] the
fabric of the narrative is closely woven into the rest of the conversa-

1. See Barbara Tedlock, *Time and the Highland Maya*, chap. 1.
2. See Chapter 10, above, for a full translation of this story.

tion. I have chosen not to attempt to snip it out and present it as if it were an independent piece of weaving, but rather to show how the threads run for some distance before and after don Andrés introduced its design.

It is not as though the story has no boundaries at all. Its beginning is signaled by a standard framing device for historical narratives, but this device is part of a larger sentence that is thoroughly entangled with the previous conversation. The sentence begins this way (I have put the formula in italics): "Only Nima Sabal, that one, yes, because *I do———n't remember what year it was. . . .*" If we were to make a cut right after "because," we would in effect be saying that a story can perfectly well begin in mid-sentence, and that the formula itself is the important thing. But by making the cut there we would be leaving out the place name Nima Sabal, which is not given again until near the end of the story.

Don Andrés repeats the opening formula during the beginning of the second episode of the story, but once again he makes it part of a sentence that is dependent for its sense on previous discourse: "And within a short time, well—it seems that then there came a downpour, *I do———n't remember. . . .*" The framing device that first signals the coming end of the story is "For this reason they say . . . ," and the final sentence, in which it is pointed out that the protagonist (and "we" people in general) failed to see the events of the first episode as auguries of the events of the second, is typical of the closing sections of stories of this kind. Nevertheless, don Andrés might well have gone on from here, thoroughly entangling the story with the rest of the conversation, had not his first pause after this sentence been filled with my next question. As it was, I myself wove the story into the rest of the conversation, in which I was in perfectly good Quiché form.

A few details of the transcript require comment. Four Cauuk, Nine Can, and Nine Tihax are all dates on the Quiché divinatory calendar. The man from San Vicente Buenabaj (a canton of Chuua 4,ak) visited Nima Sabal on a day numbered nine because such days are the proper ones for visiting the shrine there. The particular days named for his visit, Can and Tihax, are likely to send dream auguries of literal or figurative enemies or quarrels, respectively. Don Andrés specifies that the visit was in the summer because the divinatory dates he gives, belonging as they do to a 260-day cycle rather than a solar one, tell us nothing about the season.

Nima Sabal, Paclom, and Tamancu are all mountains in or near Chuua 4,ak, all with shrines. Pajaa ("at the water") is at the bottom of a canyon, but for ritual purposes it can still be considered a "world" or "mountain," referring to the mounds of ashes from burnt offerings that mark the place. Pajaa is visited on days numbered one; the shrines on Paclom, Tamancu, and volcanoes are for the numbers six, eleven, and thirteen, respectively. These numbers, and the nine of Nima Sabal, correspond to the relative physical elevations of the various places. In both the numerical and elevational senses, then, Nima Sabal is outranked by Tamancu and the volcanoes, but only Nima Sabal—the name means "great place of declaration"—has shown itself to be a *shining* world.

After the story, don Andrés answered my attempt to establish *cahulhutic* ("it shines") as a general metaphor for anything that gives a sign or omen by thinking of a case in which a sign may be sent by something that literally shines. Whatever the meaning of his example, its glare and glitter forced the conversation to change course slightly, returning to the topic of dreams, which is where the passage quoted here had started. But we still held onto a "shining" thread, like the metallic threads that cross through the dark areas of Guatemalan textiles. Beyond the discussion quoted here we would learn, for example, that a world can appear in a dream as a "shining" person.

If I were to present the following passage in an auditory rather than a visual channel, I would want it to fade in at the beginning and fade out at the end, to the accompaniment of electrical pops and cracks.

. . . .

Q: About that dream of Four Cauuk:
   you said that worlds shine?
A: These mountains are brilliant,
   like Nima Sabal, it's a brilliant mountain,
   the greatest of all the mountains.
Q: Does Pajaa shine?
A: No,
   it has lesser rank.
   The larger mountain shines more,
   it's like a president:
   his clothes aren't the same as his aides' or his soldiers',
   and so it is with the World.
   The clothes, the decorations of a president shine.
Q: Does Paclom shine?
A: No, because it has lesser rank.
   It's a mayor.
Q: Tamancu?

A: The same as Paclom.
Q: Do volcanoes shine?
A: No——or they shine,
    but we haven't studied this, we haven't visited those places.
Q: Can one see how a mountain shines?
A: Perhaps so, but we don't know about this.
    Only Nima Sabal,
    that one, yes, because
    I do——n't remember what year it was, well,
    it was on Nine Can or Nine Tihax,
    when a man came from San Vicente Buenabaj,
    he slept beneath the trees.
    There, in that place.
    In the summer—
    yes, in the summer.
    Then,
    he was sleeping, 'tis said,
    when he heard it SHOUT,
    this mountain, like a woman, 'tis said,
    she cried out.
    And he felt something like a tremor;
    when she was crying, the earth moved.
    Then he told about it,
    saying,
    "Who knows what's going to happen?
    This mountain has NEVER cried
    and NEVER moved."
    And within a short time, well—
    it seems
    that then
    there came a DOWNPOUR,
    I do——n't remember, '53——or it was '54,
    when it came down,
    the mountain of Totonicapán, 4oxtun, as it's called.
    There was a landslide:
    it carried people away,
    and it happened to us, too,
    above here,
    and over this way near Pani4 Ta3ah,
    there are some fairly large little hills,
    and when it rained—
    I don't know,
    perhaps 48 hours or MORE, or 60 hours,

on the last day,
when this rain was about to end,
that was when these mountains slid down.
Houses moved.
They went down until they came to rest at the bottom of the
    canyon.
Now, this is the SIGN that was given
by Nima Sabal.
For this reason they say,
"This mountain
shines, it glitters,"
because it gave notice.
It gave notice, but we didn't succeed
in understanding the announcement it made.
Q: Then,
    one can use the word "shine"
    for a notice—
A: yes indeed—
Q: —it's not just
    like a light, simply.
A: No. So,
    it's like a notice.

    •

    For example, right now
    suppose we had a mirror.
    We could go out in the street,
    and if the sun were out,
    we could position this mirror:
    then,
    the reflection could reach anywhere.
    So it is.
    This gives notice, then.
Q: Can one say that a clear DREAM shines?
A: Yes indeed, it's very brilliant.
    One can say,
    "This dream is clear white, it shines,"
    or "it glitters.
    The dream gives its white clarity."
    When a dream clearly gives notice,
    "it shines, it glitters,
    in the blackness, in the early dawn."

    . . . .

Bibliography

Acuña, René. "Problemas del *Popol Vuh*." *Mester* 5 (1975): 123–32.

———. "El *Popol Vuh*, Vico y la *Theologia Indorum*." In *Nuevas perspectivas sobre el Popol Vuh*, edited by Robert Carmack. Guatemala City: Piedra Santa, forthcoming.

Adams, John W. *The Gitksan Potlatch*. Toronto: Holt, Rinehart & Winston, 1973.

Antin, David. "Notes for an Ultimate Prosody." *Stony Brook* 1–2 (1968): 173–78.

———. *Talking at the Boundaries*. New York: New Directions, 1976.

Aristotle. *Rhetoric and Poetics*. Translated by W. Rhys Roberts and Ingram Bywater. New York: Modern Library, 1954.

Astrov, Margot. *The Winged Serpent*. New York: John Day, 1946. Reprinted as *American Indian Prose and Poetry*. New York: Capricorn, 1962.

Bachelard, Gaston. *On Poetic Imagination and Reverie*. Translated by Colette Gaudin. Indianapolis: Bobbs-Merrill, 1971.

Baldwin, Charles Sears. *Renaissance Literary Theory and Practice*. New York: Columbia University Press, 1939.

Bandelier, Adolf F. "On the Distribution and Tenure of Lands and the Customs with Respect to Inheritance Among the Ancient Indians." Peabody Museum *Annual Report* 11 (1878): 385–448.

Bascom, William. "The Forms of Folklore: Prose Narratives." *Journal of American Folklore* 78 (1965): 3–20.

Bauman, Richard. *Verbal Art as Performance.* Rowley, Mass.: Newbury House, 1977.

Benedict, Ruth. *Zuni Mythology.* Columbia University Contributions to Anthropology 21. New York: Columbia University Press, 1935.

Black, Robert A. "The Hopi Grievance Chants: A Mechanism of Social Control." In *Studies in Southwestern Ethnolinguistics*, edited by Dell H. Hymes and William E. Bittle, pp. 54–67. The Hague: Mouton, 1967.

Boas, Franz. "Ethnology of the Kwakiutl." Based on data collected by George Hunt. *Annual Report of the Bureau of American Ethnology* 35 (1921): 43–1481.

———. "Linguistics and Ethnology." In *Language in Culture and Society*, edited by Dell Hymes, pp. 15–26. New York: Harper & Row, 1964.

———. *Race, Language, and Culture.* New York: Free Press, 1940.

———. "Tales of Spanish Provenience from Zuni." *Journal of American Folklore* 35 (1922): 62–98.

———. "Tsimshian Mythology." *Annual Report of the Bureau of American Ethnology* 31 (1916): 29–1037.

Bolinger, Dwight. *Aspects of Language.* New York: Harcourt, Brace & World, 1968.

———. "Meaning and Memory." *Forum Linguisticum* 1 (1976): 1–14.

Bourdieu, Pierre. *Outline of a Theory of Practice.* Translated by Richard Nice. Cambridge: Cambridge University Press, 1977.

Brasseur de Bourbourg, Charles Etienne. *Popol Vuh: Le livre sacré et les mythes de l'antiquité américaine.* Paris: Arthus Bertrand, 1861.

Bright, William. "A Karok Myth in 'Measured Verse': The Translation of a Performance." *Journal of California and Great Basin Anthropology* 1 (1979): 117–23.

Brinton, Daniel G. *Aboriginal American Authors and Their Productions; Especially those in the native languages. A chapter in the history of Literature.* Philadelphia, 1883.

Brotherston, Gordon. *Image of the New World: The American Continent Portrayed in Native Texts.* London: Thames & Hudson, 1979.

Buber, Martin, and Rosenzweig, Franz. *Die Fuenf Buecher der Weisung.* Berlin, 1934.

Bunzel, Ruth L. "Introduction to Zuni Ceremonialism." *Annual Report of the Bureau of American Ethnology* 47 (1932): 467–544.

———. "Zuni Katcinas: An Analytical Study." *Annual Report of the Bureau of American Ethnology* 47 (1932): 837–1108.

———. "Zuni Origin Myths." *Annual Report of the Bureau of American Ethnology* 47 (1932): 545–609.

———. "Zuni Ritual Poetry." *Annual Report of the Bureau of American Ethnology* 47 (1932): 611–835.

———. *Zuni Texts.* Publications of the American Ethnological Society 15. New York: G. E. Stechert, 1933.

Burgess, Dora M. de, and Xec, Patricio. *Popol Wuj.* Quezaltenango, Guatemala: El Noticiero Evangélico, 1955.

Burling, Robbins. "Burling's Rejoinder." *American Anthropologist* 66 (1964): 120–22.

———. "Cognition and Componential Analysis: God's Truth or Hocus-Pocus?" *American Anthropologist* 66 (1964): 20–28.

Burns, Allan. "The Deer Secret." *Alcheringa,* n.s. 3, no. 1 (1977): 134–46.

———. *An Epoch of Miracles: Oral Literature of the Yucatec Maya.* Austin: University of Texas Press, 1983.

Campbell, Lyle. "Préstamos lingüísticos en el Popol Vuh." In *Nuevas perspectivas sobre el Popol Vuh,* edited by Robert Carmack. Guatemala City: Piedra Santa, forthcoming.

Carmack, Robert M. *Quichean Civilization: The Ethnohistoric, Ethnographic, and Archaeological Sources.* Berkeley: University of California Press, 1973.

———. *The Quiché Mayas of Utatlán.* Norman: University of Oklahoma Press, 1981.

———. Review of Munro S. Edmonson, *The Book of Counsel. American Antiquity* 40 (1975): 506–7.

Casagrande, Joseph B., ed. *In the Company of Man.* New York: Harper & Row, 1960.

Chávez, Adrián I. *Pop Wuj.* Mexico City: Ediciones de La Casa Chata, 1979.

Chinchilla Aguilar, Ernesto. *La Danza del Sacrificio y otros estudios.* Guatemala City: José de Pineda Ibarra, 1963.

Coke, Van Deren. *The Painter and the Photograph: From Delacroix to Warhol.* Albuquerque: University of New Mexico Press, 1972.

Corrigan, Robert W. "Translating for Actors." In *The Craft and Context of Translation,* edited by William Arrowsmith and Roger Shattuck, pp. 127–46. Garden City, N.Y.: Anchor Books, 1964.

Crapanzano, Vincent. "On the Writing of Ethnography." *Dialectical Anthropology* 2 (1977): 69–73.

Crosby, Ruth. "Oral Delivery in the Middle Ages." *Speculum* 11 (1936): 88–110.

Crowley, Daniel. "The Singing Pepper Tree." Told by Luzilla Jones. *Alcheringa,* o.s. 5 (1973): 107–9.

Curtin, Jeremiah. *Myths of the Modocs.* Boston: Little, Brown, 1912.

Cushing, Frank Hamilton. "Outlines of Zuni Creation Myths." *Annual Report of the Bureau of American Ethnology* 13 (1896): 321–447.

———. *Zuni Breadstuff.* Indian Notes and Monographs 8. New York: Museum of the American Indian, Heye Foundation, 1920.

———. "Zuni Fetiches." *Annual Report of the Bureau of American Ethnology* 2 (1883): 9–43.

———. *Zuni Folk Tales.* New York: G. P. Putnam's Sons, 1901. Reprinted in 1931, New York: Alfred A. Knopf.

Darnell, Regna. "Correlates of Cree Narrative Performance." In *Explorations in the Ethnography of Speaking,* edited by Richard Bauman and Joel Sherzer, pp. 315–36. London: Cambridge University Press, 1974.

Demetracapoulou, Dorothy, and DuBois, Cora. "A Study of Wintu Mythology." *Journal of American Folklore* 45 (1932): 373–500.

Derrida, Jacques. *Of Grammatology*. Translated by Gayatri Chakravorty Spivak. Baltimore: Johns Hopkins University Press, 1976.

———. "Limited Inc" *Glyph* 2 (1977): 162–254.

———. "Signature Event Context." *Glyph* 1 (1977): 172–97.

Diamond, Stanley. *In Search of the Primitive*. New Brunswick, N.J.: Transaction, 1974.

Doložel, Lubomír. "A Scheme of Narrative Time." In *Semiotics of Art*, edited by Ladislav Matejka and Irwin R. Titunik, pp. 209–17. Cambridge, Mass.: MIT Press, 1976.

Dorsey, George A. *The Pawnee: Mythology*, Part I. Carnegie Institution Publication 59. Washington, D.C.: Carnegie Institution, 1906.

Dundes, Alan. *The Study of Folklore*. Englewood Cliffs, N.J.: Prentice-Hall, 1965.

Dwyer, Kevin. "On the Dialogic of Field Work." *Dialectical Anthropology* 2 (1977): 143–51.

Eco, Umberto. *A Theory of Semiotics*. Bloomington: Indiana University Press, 1976.

Edmonson, Munro S. *The Ancient Future of the Itza: The Book of Chilam Balam of Tizimin*. Austin: University of Texas Press, 1982.

———. *The Book of Counsel: The Popol Vuh of the Quiché Maya of Guatemala*. Tulane University, Middle American Research Institute Publication 35 (1971).

———. *Lore: An Introduction to the Science of Folklore and Literature*. New York: Holt, Rinehart & Winston, 1971.

———. "Narrative Folklore." In *Handbook of Middle American Indians*, vol. 6, edited by Manning Nash, pp. 357–68. Austin: University of Texas Press, 1967.

Else, Gerald F. *Aristotle's Poetics*. Cambridge, Mass.: Harvard University Press, 1957.

Fabian, Johannes. "Language, History, and Anthropology." *Philosophy of the Social Sciences* 1 (1971): 19–47.

———. "Rule and Process: Thoughts on Ethnography as Communication." *Philosophy of the Social Sciences* 9 (1979): 1–26.

Fernandez, James W. "Poetry in Motion: Being Moved by Amusement, by Mockery, and by Mortality in the Asturian Countryside." *New Literary History* 8 (1977): 459–83.

Fewkes, Jesse Walter. "A Few Summer Ceremonials at Zuni Pueblo." *A Journal of American Ethnology and Archaeology* 1 (1891): 1–61.

Finnegan, Ruth. *Oral Poetry*. Cambridge: Cambridge University Press, 1977.

Firth, J. R. *Papers in Linguistics, 1934–51*. London: Oxford University Press, 1957.

Fischer, John L. "The Sociopsychological Analysis of Folktales." *Current Anthropology* 4 (1963): 235–95.

Foster, Michael K. *From the Earth to Beyond the Sky: An Ethnographic Approach to*

Four Longhouse Iroquois Speech Events. Canadian Ethnology Service Paper 20 (1974). Ottawa: National Museum of Man.

Fox, Everett. "In the Beginning." *Response* 14 (1972): 9–159.

Frake, Charles O. "Further Discussion of Burling." *American Anthropologist* 66 (1964): 119.

Garibay K., Angel María. *Historia de la literatura nahuatl*. 2 vols. Mexico City: Porrua, 1953.

Geertz, Clifford. *The Interpretation of Cultures*. New York: Harper & Row, 1973.

Goddard, Ives. "Philological Approaches to the Study of North American Indian Languages: Documents and Documentation." In *Native Languages of the Americas*, vol. 1, edited by Thomas A. Sebeok, pp. 73–91. New York and London: Plenum, 1976.

Goffman, Erving. *Forms of Talk*. Philadelphia: University of Pennsylvania Press, 1981.

———. *Frame Analysis: An Essay on the Organization of Experience*. New York: Harper Colophon, 1974.

Gold, Peter. "From 'Easter Sunrise Sermon.'" Performed by the Rev. W. T. Goodwin. *Alcheringa*, o.s. 4 (1972): 1–14.

Goldman-Eisler, Frieda. "Continuity of Speech Utterance: Its Determinants and Its Significance." *Language and Speech* 4 (1961): 220–31.

———. "Discussion and Further Comments." In *New Directions in the Study of Language*, edited by Eric H. Lenneberg, pp. 109–30. Cambridge, Mass.: M.I.T. Press, 1964.

———. "The Distribution of Pause Durations in Speech." *Language and Speech* 4 (1961): 232–37.

———. "The Significance of Changes in the Rate of Articulation." *Language and Speech* 4 (1961): 171–74.

Goody, Jack. *The Domestication of the Savage Mind*. Cambridge: Cambridge University Press, 1977.

Gossen, Gary H. *Chamulas in the World of the Sun*. Cambridge, Mass.: Harvard University Press, 1974.

Greenway, John. *Literature Among the Primitives*. Hatboro, Pa.: Folklore Associates, 1964.

Grele, Ronald J., ed. *Envelopes of Sound: Six Practitioners Discuss the Method, Theory, and Practice of Oral History and Oral Testimony*. Chicago: Precedent, 1975.

Griaule, Marcel. *Conversations with Ogotemêlli*. London: Oxford University Press, 1965.

Handy, Edward L. "Zuni Tales." *Journal of American Folklore* 31 (1918): 451–71.

Harris, Marvin. *The Nature of Cultural Things*. New York: Random House, 1964.

Havelock, Eric. "The Preliteracy of the Greeks." *New Literary History* 8 (1977): 369–91.

Heidegger, Martin. *Poetry, Language, Thought*. Translated by Albert Hofstadter. New York: Harper Torchbook, 1975.

Hendricks, William O. "On the Notion 'Beyond the Sentence.'" *Linguistics* 37 (1967): 12–51.

Henry of Huslia, Chief. *The Stories That Chief Henry Told.* Transcribed and translated by Eliza Jones, edited by Ron Scollon. Fairbanks: Alaska Native Language Center, 1979.

Hoebel, E. Adamson. *Anthropology: The Study of Man.* New York: McGraw-Hill, 1972.

Hymes, Dell. "Discovering Oral Performance and Measured Verse in American Indian Narrative." *New Literary History* 8 (1977): 431–57.

———. "Discussion of Burling's Paper." *American Anthropologist* 66 (1964): 116–19.

———. *Foundations in Sociolinguistics: An Ethnographic Approach.* Philadelphia: University of Pennsylvania Press, 1974.

———. *"In Vain I Tried to Tell You": Essays in Native American Ethnopoetics.* Philadelphia: University of Pennsylvania Press, 1981.

———. "Models of the Interaction of Language and Social Life." In *Directions in Sociolinguistics,* edited by John J. Gumperz and Dell Hymes, pp. 35–71. New York: Holt, Rinehart & Winston, 1972.

———. "Particle, Pause and Pattern in American Indian Narrative Verse." *American Indian Culture and Research Journal* 4 (1980): 7–51.

———. *Reinventing Anthropology.* New York: Vintage, 1972.

———. "Some North Pacific Coast Poems: A Problem in Anthropological Philology." *American Anthropologist* 67 (1965): 316–41. Reprinted in Dell Hymes, *"In Vain I Tried to Tell You,"* pp. 35–62.

Isbell, Billie Jean. *To Defend Ourselves.* Austin: Institute of Latin American Studies, 1978.

Ives, Edward. *The Tape Recorded Interview.* Knoxville: University of Tennessee Press, 1980.

Jacobs, Melville. *Clackamas Chinook Texts.* Publications of the Indiana University Research Center in Anthropology, Folklore, and Linguistics 8 (1958) and 11 (1959).

———. *The Content and Style of an Oral Literature.* Viking Fund Publications in Anthropology 26. Chicago: University of Chicago Press, 1959.

Jakobson, Roman. "Closing Statement: Linguistics and Poetics." In *Style in Language,* edited by Thomas A. Sebeok, pp. 350–77. Cambridge, Mass.: M.I.T. Press, 1960.

———. *Six Lectures on Sound and Meaning.* Translated by John Mepham. Cambridge, Mass.: M.I.T. Press, 1978.

Jakobson, Roman, and Waugh, Linda. *The Sound Shape of Language.* Bloomington: Indiana University Press, 1979.

James, Susie. *Sít' Kaa Káx̱ kana.áa: Glacier Bay History.* Transcribed by Nora Florendo. Sitka: Tlingit Readers, 1973.

Jules-Rosette, Bennetta. *African Apostles: Ritual and Conversion in the Church of John Maranke.* Ithaca: Cornell University Press, 1975.

Kaplan, Bert. "Psychological Themes in Zuni Mythology and Zuni TAT's." In *The Psychoanalytic Study of Society,* vol. 2, edited by Warner

Meunsterberger and Sidney Axelrod, pp. 255–62. New York: International Universities Press, 1962.

Kate, H. F. C. ten. "A Zuni Folk-Tale." *Journal of American Folklore* 30 (1917): 496–99.

Kelley, David Humiston. *Deciphering the Maya Script*. Austin: University of Texas Press, 1976.

Klor de Alva, J. Jorge. "The Aztec-Spanish Dialogues of 1524." *Alcheringa*, n.s. 4, no. 2 (1980): 52–193.

———. "Christianity and the Aztecs." *San Jose Studies* 5 (1979): 6–21.

Knab, Tim. "Three Tales from the Sierra de Puebla." Performed by Francisco Ortigosa Tello. *Alcheringa*, n.s. 4, no. 2 (1980): 2–36.

Kroeber, Alfred L. "A Mohave Historical Epic." *University of California Anthropological Records* 11 (1951): 71–176.

Lehiste, Ilse. *Suprasegmentals*. Cambridge, Mass.: M.I.T. Press, 1970.

León-Portilla, Miguel. *Aztec Thought and Culture*. Translated by Jack Emory Davis. Norman: University of Oklahoma Press, 1963.

———. *Pre-Columbian Literatures of Mexico*. Norman: University of Oklahoma Press, 1969.

Lévi-Strauss, Claude. *From Honey to Ashes*. Translated by John and Doreen Weightman. New York: Harper & Row, 1973.

———. *The Raw and the Cooked*. Translated by John and Doreen Weightman. New York: Harper & Row, 1969.

———. Review of *Finding the Center* by Dennis Tedlock. *L'Homme* 14 (1974): 162–63.

———. "The Story of Asdiwal." Translated by Nicholas Mann. In *The Structural Study of Myth and Totemism*, edited by Edmund Leach, pp. 1–47. Association of Social Anthropologists Monograph 5. London: Tavistock, 1967.

———. *Structural Anthropology*. Garden City, N.Y.: Doubleday, 1967.

———. "The Structural Study of Myth." *Journal of American Folklore* 68 (1955): 428–44.

———. *Totemism*. Translated by Rodney Needham. Boston: Beacon Press, 1963.

———. *Tristes Tropiques*. Translated by John Russel. New York: Atheneum, 1963.

List, George. "The Boundaries of Speech and Song." *Ethnomusicology* 7 (1963): 1–16.

Lord, Albert. *The Singer of Tales*. New York: Atheneum, 1965.

Lowie, Robert. "My Crow Interpreter." In *In the Company of Man*, edited by Joseph B. Casagrande, pp. 427–37. New York: Harper & Row, 1960.

Mahl, G. F. "Exploring Emotional States by Content Analysis." In *Trends in Content Analysis*, edited by I. Pool, pp. 89–130. Urbana: University of Illinois Press, 1959.

Malinowski, Bronislaw. *Coral Gardens and Their Magic*, vol. 2, *The Language of Magic and Gardening*. London: George Allen & Unwin, 1935.

Matthews, Washington. *Navaho Legends*. American Folklore Society Memoirs 5. Boston: Houghton, Mifflin, 1897.

McClure, Michael. "7 Los Angeles Poems." *Caterpillar* 6 (1969): 40–46 and front cover.

Mead, Margaret. "Native Languages as Fieldwork Tools." *American Anthropologist* 42 (1939): 189–205.

Mooney, James. *The Ghost-Dance Religion*. Chicago: University of Chicago Press, 1965.

———. "Sacred Formulas of the Cherokees." *Annual Report of the Bureau of American Ethnology* 7 (1891): 301–97.

Murphy, Robert F. *The Dialectics of Social Life*. New York: Basic Books, 1971.

Nattiez, Jean-Jacques. "The Contribution of Musical Semiotics to the Semiotic Discussion in General." In *A Perfusion of Signs*, edited by Thomas A. Sebeok, pp. 121–42. Bloomington: Indiana University Press, 1977.

Newman, Stanley. "Vocabulary Levels: Zuni Sacred and Slang Usage." *Southwestern Journal of Anthropology* 11 (1955): 345–54.

———. *Zuni Dictionary*. Indiana University Research Center in Anthropology, Folklore, and Linguistics Publication 6 (1958). Bloomington.

———. *Zuni Grammar*. University of New Mexico Publications in Anthropology 14. Albuquerque, 1965.

Okpewho, Isidore. *The Epic in Africa: Toward a Poetics of the Oral Performance*. New York: Columbia University Press, 1979.

Olson, Charles. *Selected Writings*. Edited by Robert Creeley. New York: New Directions, 1966.

Parsons, Elsie Clews. "Notes on Zuni." *Memoirs of the American Anthropological Association* 4 (1917): 151–327.

———. "The Origin Myth of Zuni." *Journal of American Folklore* 36 (1923): 135–62.

———. "Pueblo-Indian Folk-Tales, Probably of Spanish Provenience." *Journal of American Folklore* 31 (1918): 216–55.

———. "The Scalp Ceremonial of Zuni." *Memoirs of the American Anthropological Association* 31 (1924): 1–42.

———. "Zuni Tales." *Journal of American Folklore* 43 (1930): 1–58.

Parsons, Elsie Clews, and Boas, Franz. "Spanish Tales from Laguna and Zuni, New Mexico." *Journal of American Folklore* 33 (1920): 47–72.

Paul, Gaither. *Stories for My Grandchildren*. Transcribed and edited by Ron Scollon. Fairbanks: Alaska Native Language Center, 1980.

Paul, Robert, and Rabinow, Paul. "Bourgeois Rationalism Revived." *Dialectical Anthropology* 1 (1976): 121–34.

Pittenger, Robert E.; Hockett, Charles F.; and Danehy, John J. *The First Five Minutes*. Ithaca: Martineau, 1960.

Quasha, George. "The Age of the Open Secret." *Alcheringa*, n.s. 2, no. 2 (1976): 65–77.

Rabinow, Paul. *Reflections on Fieldwork in Morocco*. Berkeley: University of California Press, 1977.

Radin, Paul. *The Culture of the Winnebago: As Described by Themselves.* International Journal of American Linguistics Memoir 2, 1949. Baltimore: Waverly Press.

———. *The Method and Theory of Ethnology: An Essay in Criticism.* New York: McGraw-Hill, 1933.

———. *Primitive Man as Philosopher.* New York: Dover, 1957.

———. *The Trickster: A Study in American Indian Mythology.* New York: Schocken, 1972.

Rasmussen, Knud. *Iglulik and Caribou Eskimo Texts.* Report of the Fifth Thule Expedition, vol. 7, no. 3. Copenhagen: Gyldendal, 1930.

Recinos, Adrián. *Popol Vuh: Las antiguas historias del Quiché.* Mexico City: Fondo de Cultura Económica, 1947.

Recinos, Adrián; Chonay, Dionisio José; and Goetz, Delia. *The Annals of The Cakchiquels; Title of the Lords of Totonicapán.* Norman: University of Oklahoma Press, 1953.

Recinos, Adrián; Goetz, Delia; and Morley, Sylvanus G., trans. *Popol Vuh: The Sacred Book of the Ancient Quiché Maya.* Norman: University of Oklahoma Press, 1950.

Reichard, Gladys A. *An Analysis of Coeur d'Alene Myths.* Memoirs of the American Folklore Society 41. Philadelphia: American Folklore Society, 1947.

Ricoeur, Paul. *The Conflict of Interpretations: Essays in Hermeneutics.* Edited by Don Ihde. Evanston: Northwestern University Press, 1974.

———. *Hermeneutics and the Human Sciences.* Edited and translated by John B. Thompson. Cambridge: Cambridge University Press, 1981.

———. *Interpretation Theory: Discourse and the Surplus of Meaning.* Fort Worth: Texas Christian University Press, 1976.

Rios, Ted. "The Egg." Recorded by Kathleen Sands. *Sun Tracks* 6 (1980): 151–54.

Risser, Anna. "Seven Zuni Folk Tales." *El Palacio* 48 (1941): 215–26.

Rothenberg, Jerome. *Technicians of the Sacred.* Garden City, N.Y.: Doubleday, 1968.

Rouch, Jean. "On the Vicissitudes of the Self: The Possessed Dancer, the Magician, the Sorcerer, the Filmmaker, and the Ethnographer." *Studies in the Anthropology of Visual Communication* 5 (1978): 2–8.

Roys, Ralph L. *The Book of Chilam Balam of Chumayel.* Norman: University of Oklahoma Press, 1967.

Schutz, Alfred. *The Phenomenology of the Social World.* Translated by George Walsh and Frederick Lehnert. Evanston: Northwestern University Press, 1967.

Scollon, Ronald, and Scollon, Suzanne B. K. *Linguistic Convergence: An Ethnography of Speaking at Fort Chipewyan, Alberta.* New York: Academic Press, 1979.

Seitel, Peter. *See So That We May See: Performances and Interpretations of Traditional Tales from Tanzania.* Bloomington: Indiana University Press, 1980.

Sherzer, Joel. "The Ethnography of Speaking: A Critical Appraisal." In *Linguistics and Anthropology*, edited by Muriel Saville-Troike, pp. 43–57. Washington: Georgetown Round Table in Linguistics, 1977.

Schultze Jena, Leonhard S. *Popol Vuh: Das heilige Buch der Quiché-Indianer von Guatemala*. Stuttgart and Berlin: W. Kohlhammer, 1944.

Silverstein, Michael. "Language Structure and Linguistic Ideology." In *The Elements: A Parasession on Linguistic Units and Levels*, edited by Paul R. Clyne et al., pp. 193–247. Chicago: Chicago Linguistic Society, 1979.

Snorri Sturluson. *The Prose Edda*. Translated by Jean I. Young. Berkeley: University of California Press, 1954.

Spinden, Herbert Joseph. *Songs of the Tewa, Preceded by an Essay on American Indian Poetry*. New York: The Exposition of Indian Tribal Arts, 1933.

Stanner, W. E. H. "Durmugan, a Nangiomeri." In *In the Company of Man*, edited by Joseph B. Casagrande, pp. 63–100. New York: Harper & Row, 1960.

Stephen, Alexander M. *The Hopi Journals of Alexander M. Stephen*. Edited by Elsie Clews Parsons. Columbia University Contributions to Anthropology 23. New York: Columbia University Press, 1935.

Stevenson, Matilda Coxe. "The Zuni Indians." *Annual Report of the Bureau of American Ethnology* 23 (1904): 3–634.

Stevick, Robert D. "Scribal Notation of Prosodic Features in *The Parker Chronicle*, Anno 894 [893]." *Journal of English Linguistics* 1 (1967): 57–66.

Stravinsky, Igor. Album notes to *Symphony of Psalms*. Columbia Records 6548 (1963).

Tax, Sol. "Folk Tales in Chichicastenango: An Unsolved Puzzle." *Journal of American Folklore* 52 (1949): 125–35.

Tedlock, Barbara. "El c'oxol: un símbolo de la resistencia quiché a la conquista espiritual." In *Nuevas perspectivas sobre el Popol Vuh*, edited by Robert Carmack. Guatemala: Piedra Santa, forthcoming.

———. "Songs of the Zuni Kachina Society: Composition, Rehearsal, and Performance." In *Southwestern Indian Ritual Drama*, edited by Charlotte J. Frisbie, pp. 7–35. Albuquerque: University of New Mexico Press, 1980.

———. "Sound Texture and Metaphor in Quiché Maya Ritual Language." *Current Anthropology* 23 (1982): 269–72.

———. *Time and the Highland Maya*. Albuquerque: University of New Mexico Press, 1982.

Tedlock, Dennis. "An American Indian View of Death." In *Teachings from the American Earth: Indian Religion and Philosophy*, edited by Dennis Tedlock and Barbara Tedlock, pp. 248–71. New York: Liveright, 1975.

———. "Coyote and Junco." In *Coyote Stories*, edited by William Bright, pp.

171–77. International Journal of American Linguistics, Native American Texts Series, Monograph 1. Chicago: University of Chicago Press, 1978.

———. *The Ethnography of Tale-Telling at Zuni*. Ann Arbor: University Microfilms, 1968.

———. *Finding the Center: Narrative Poetry of the Zuni Indians*. Translated from performances in the Zuni by Andrew Peynetsa and Walter Sanchez. New York: Dial, 1972; Lincoln: University of Nebraska Press, 1978.

———. "Finding the Middle of the Earth." *Alcheringa*, o.s. 1 (1970): 67–80.

———. "The Problem of k in Zuni Phonemics." *International Journal of American Linguistics* 35 (1969): 67–71.

———. Review of *The Zunis: Self-Portrayals*, by the Zuni People. Association for Study of American Indian Literatures *Newsletter*, n.s. 1 (1978): 24–28.

———. "The Science of Signs and the Science of Letters." *American Anthropologist* 82 (1980): 821–30.

———. "Toward an Oral Poetics." *New Literary History* 8 (1977): 507–19.

———. "Verbal Art." In *Handbook of North American Indians*, vol. 1, *Introduction*, edited by William C. Sturtevant. Washington: Smithsonian Institution, forthcoming.

———. "When the Old Timers Went Deer Hunting." *Alcheringa*, o.s. 3 (1971): 76–81.

———. "Zuni Religion and World View." In *Handbook of North American Indians*, vol. 9, edited by Alfonso Ortiz, pp. 499–508. Washington, D.C.: Smithsonian Institution, 1979.

Thompson, J. Eric S. *A Commentary on the Dresden Codex*. Philadelphia: American Philosophical Society, 1972.

———. *Maya History and Religion*. Norman: University of Oklahoma Press, 1970.

Thompson, Stith. *Tales of the North American Indians*. Bloomington: Indiana University Press, 1929, 1966.

Titon, Jeff. "Son House: Two Narratives." *Alcheringa*, n.s. 2, no. 1 (1976): 2–9.

Titon, Jeff, and George, Ken. "Dressed in the Armor of God." Performed by the Rev. John Sherfey. *Alcheringa*, n.s. 3, n.2 (1977): 10–31.

———. "Testimonies." Performed by Rachel Franklin, Edith Cubbage, and the Rev. John Sherfey. *Alcheringa*, n.s. 4, no.1 (1978): 69–83.

Todorov, Tzvetan. *Grammaire du Décaméron*. The Hague: Mouton, 1969.

Toelken, Barre, and Scott, Tacheeni. "Poetic Retranslation and the 'Pretty Languages' of Yellowman." In *Traditional Literatures of the American Indian: Texts and Interpretations*, edited by Karl Kroeber, pp. 65–116. Lincoln: University of Nebraska Press, 1981.

Trager, George L. "Paralanguage." *Studies in Linguistics* 13 (1958): 1–12.

Turner, Victor. *The Forest of Symbols*. Ithaca: Cornell University Press, 1967.

Ullman, Berthold Louis. *Ancient Writing and Its Influence*. Cambridge, Mass.: MIT Press, 1969.

Vansina, Jan. *Oral Tradition: A Study in Historical Methodology*. Chicago: Aldine, 1965.

Villacorta Calderón, José Antonio. *Popol Vuh*. Guatemala: José de Pineda Ibarra, 1962.

Voegelin, C. F., and Euler, Robert C. "Introduction to Hopi Chants." *Journal of American Folklore* 70 (1957): 115–36.

Walker, J. R. "The Sun Dance and Other Ceremonies of the Oglala Division of the Teton Dakota." *Anthropological Papers of the American Museum of Natural History* 16 (1917): 51–221.

Walker, Willard. "Toward the Sound Pattern of Zuni." *International Journal of American Linguistics* 38 (1972): 240–59.

Walton, Eda Lou. "Navaho Verse Rhythms." *Poetry* 24 (1924): 40–44.

Wilson, Monica. *Good Company*. Boston: Beacon Press, 1963.

Wimsatt, W. K. *Versification*. New York: New York University Press, 1972.

Ximénez, Francisco. *Escolios a las historias del origen de los indios*. Sociedad de Geografía e Historia de Guatemala, pub. 13 (1967). Guatemala City.

———. *Popol Vuh*. Paleography and Notes by Agustín Estrada Monroy. Guatemala City: José de Pineda Ibarra, 1973.

Zuboff, Robert. *Ḵudatan Kahídee: The Salmon Box*. Transcribed by Henry Davis, Gabriel George, and Crystal McKay. Sitka: Tlingit Readers, 1973.

———. *Táax'aa: Mosquito*. Transcribed by Dick Dauenhauer. Sitka: Tlingit Readers, 1973.

Zuni People, The. *The Zunis: Self-Portrayals*. Albuquerque: University of New Mexico Press, 1972.

Index

357